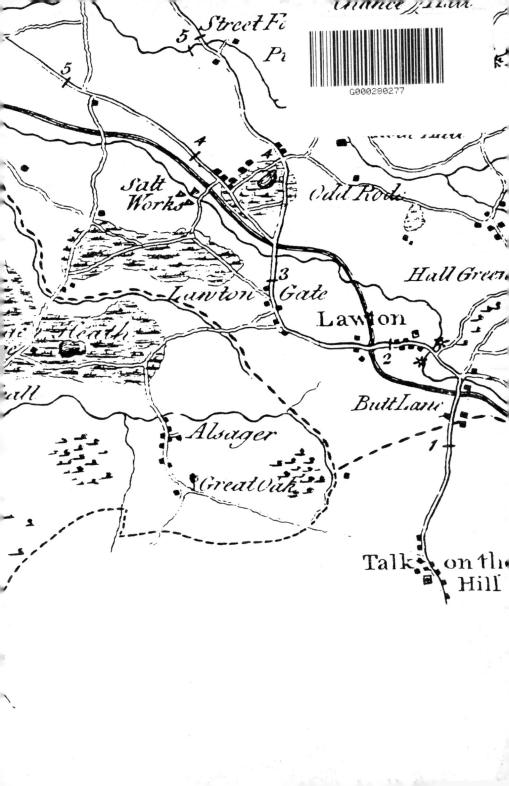

Dedicated to Robert Speake, M.Litt., Adv.Dip.Ed.

Without whose encouragement and example this book would probably never have been written.

ALSAGER

the Place

and its People

Compiled and written by
The Alsager History Research Group

Edited by
James C. Sutton, M.A.

Published by The Alsager History Research Group
1999.

Acknowledgements.

The Group acknowledges with thanks the help, encouragement and support given by all those whose assistance has been sought during the preparation of the book. In particular thanks are due to; Alsager Town Council, The B'hoys of Alsager, Messrs Butters, Freshpack Ltd, Cheshire County Council (Archives and Local Studies), Caradon Plumbing Solutions, National Westminster Bank PLC, all of whom have been generous with financial support. In addition research support has been forthcoming from St. Bertoline's Church Barthomley, Cheshire County Record Office, Keele University Library, The Manchester Metropolitan University, The Royal Ordnance Factory Radway Green, Staffordshire Sentinel Newspapers Ltd, and many Alsager residents who have provided the authors with information and access to their papers and memories. Our thanks are also due to Syd Edwards who assisted with proof reading.

Abbreviations used in the text.

Brit. Lib.	British Library
c.	century
CRO.	Cheshire County Record Office, Chester
M.M.U.	The Manchester Metropolitan University
OE.	Old English
PRO.	Public Record Office
R.O.F.	Royal Ordnance Factory, Radway Green
SECSU.	Southeast Cheshire Studies Unit, Manchester Metropolitan University, Hassall Road, Alsager
SHC.	Staffordshire Historical Collections
SRO.	Staffordshire County Record Office, Stafford
VCH.	Victoria County History

Outside Cover. The Map of Alsager Heath accompanying the Inclosure Award of 1834 *(By kind permission of the Cheshire Record Office)*
Front Inside Cover. Extract from Burdett's Map Of Cheshire 1777. *(By kind permission of the Cheshire Record Office)*
Back Inside Cover. Extract from the 1897 revision 6″ Ordnance Survey, Cheshire Sheet LVII. Geological information added 1900.

Printed by Herald Printers (Whitchurch) Ltd., Whitchurch, Shropshire.
ISBN 0 9536363 0 5

Contents.

The Alsager History Research Group

During the past three or four years members of the Alsager History Research Group have met on a regular basis in the South East Cheshire Studies Unit of The Manchester Metropolitan University on the Alsager Campus. The Group has had the use of the resources and facilities of the Unit as well as carrying out its own independent research. The Group comprises:-

Raymond Anelay - formerly Principal Lecturer and Head of History at Crewe + Alsager College (now MMU). Author of *Christ Church, Alsager 1789-1989* and contributor of the material dealing here with **Christ Church.**

Gilbert Band - retired businessman. His family have lived in Alsager since about 1860, when William Band arrived as an apprentice shoemaker. He has a long interest in the history of the town and gives talks to community groups and organisations. He has made extensive contributions to **Communications** and matters relating to Non-conformism in Alsager.

Margaret Bebbington - a member of the Holland family, which has resided in Alsager since c.18th. She is a retired teacher, a lifelong member of the Guide Movement and a Vice-president of the Cricket Club; a contributor to *Barthomley, an Estate Village*, she gives talks to local groups and is the author of the **Introduction,** the chapter on **Education** and a significant contributor to **Village Miscellany.**

Beryl Fox - also a member of the Holland family. A retired teacher, whose interests are singing and acting, Beryl is the author of **Poor Law and Welfare** and has made contributions to **A Religious Survey** and **Village Miscellany.** She also contributed to the Barthomley book.

Stanley Fox - born at Barthomley into a farming family. Retired Civil Servant, London & St. Annes; Air Crew observer and navigator during War. Contributed to the Barthomley book. He has made extensive contributions to the chapter on **Communications.**

Terence Holland - born in Alsager, retired British Rail manager who started work at **Alsager loco sheds** and has written the section of the book dealing with that subject. Interests - genealogy (the Holland family tree) and Alsager History.

Freda Maxfield - has lived in Alsager for many years. Research Assistant in the South East Cheshire Studies Unit at The MMU. Writes articles about Alsager History. With Mary Morris, produced calendars and a photographic booklet: *Alsager's Village Past.* Her contributions are **From a Sleepy Village to a Thriving Town** and **Catholicism in Alsager.**

Carol Micklewright - worked on the Barthomley book with other members of the group, she lives in Haslington but was delighted to join the A.H.R.G. Though having no personal ties with Alsager, she wished to bring a better understanding and a clearer picture of their heritage to those who have. She researched and wrote **Origins,** and **Land Use and Occupation.**

Tony Morgan - a retired engineer. A native of Wolverhampton, he came to Alsager in 1971 to work for Copestick & Farrell in Fenton, leaving in 1979 to become self-employed. Worked on the Barthomley book and was easily persuaded to join the Alsager Group and compiled the chapter on **The Inclosure of Alsager Heath.**

Mary Morris - has lived in Alsager since 1970. Head of History, Alsager Campus of The Manchester Metropolitan University, Director of the South East Cheshire Studies Unit. Mary is the author of **Alsager in World War Two.**

Alex Shaw - retired teacher. His family has lived in Alsager since his great grand-father, Donald Macbeth, was appointed station master after the coming of the railway. Well known for his collection of pictures showing the development of Alsager. Alex has been Pictures Editor for this publication and is the contributor of the section on **St. Mary's Church.**

Jim Sutton - has lived in Alsager for 30 years, a Chartered Surveyor, he holds a degree in Local History Skills and is an Independent Researcher. He has written the chapter on the **Early Years** and **Warfare** and contributed to the **Village Miscellany** as well as co-ordinating the work of the Group.

It should be noted that the views expressed in this book are those of the authors and must not be taken as in any way representing opinions held by those from whom financial support has been received.

Preface.

This book is not about the affairs of the realm nor about the state of England, that story is told elsewhere. It is about one small part of England, not even England at that, but a small part of the county palatine of Cheshire. Alsager cannot, historically, claim even to have been a parish, it was the smallest and least significant part of early government, that is a township. Nevertheless it has existed and its people have existed for as long as have the great, the good and the famous, and if this book is able to give some account of the people who have tilled its fields and travelled its roads over the past millennium it will prove to be a memorial to those men and women who have lived and died here, some within living memory, whose stories can be fully told; others, from the distant past, of whom we can only catch a fleeting glimpse. Their stories are unlikely to be told elsewhere but they deserve their place in history. The authors hope the book will fulfill its purpose in ensuring that a greater knowledge of the past leads to a better understanding of the present.

The views expressed, particularly in the chapters covering the early development of Alsager, reflect today's interpretation of available knowledge. As more evidence becomes available from presently untapped documentary sources, of which there are so many, that interpretation might change, and opinions currently held will need to be revised. Hopefully, at some future date, this book will not be the repository of all knowledge of early Alsager, and it will require updating. Those chapters dealing with the later history of the town, particularly with those matters for which there are printed and published records, can be assumed to be more definitive in their illustration of events recounted. Notwithstanding these comments the authors hope that they have produced an account of Alsager's past that can be relied upon to inform, constructively, the interested but previously uninformed reader, whilst at the same time proving to be an easily read volume with the capacity to entertain.

Alsager.   23rd May 1999.

Introduction

Today Alsager is a prosperous and busy suburban town set in the south Cheshire countryside, midway between the North Staffordshire conurbation and Crewe. At the 1991 census it is recorded as having a population of about 12,500 and a total of 4683 dwellings. There are seven churches, five primary schools, a large secondary school, a campus of The Manchester Metropolitan University, an impressive sports complex, many sporting amenities and a public library; in short all the requirements of a well balanced modern community. There has been modest industrial development in the town, including railway sheds which have come and gone, the manufacture of armaments, sanitary ware and a variety of other products. The town has its own railway station, on the Crewe-Derby line, and has access onto the M6 motorway within three miles.

Politically it forms part of the Borough of Congleton, though retaining its own Town Council as successor to its former Urban District Council which lapsed in 1974 as part of English local government reorganisation. It has long since thrown off the shackles of being a mere appendage of Barthomley, insofar as parish organisation is concerned, and is well able to manage its own affairs, both spiritual and temporal.

It lies at the edge of the Cheshire Plain, in the Southeast corner of the county, where the land begins to rise into the hilly areas of North Staffordshire and the Pennine foothills. Radway Green is about 275 feet above sea level, and the ground rises to 500 feet on the hilltop overlooking Mere Lake. To the east the skyline is dominated by the mass of Mow Cop, which rises to a height of 1050 feet. The whole area drains to the west by way of two principal watercourses; the first being the brook descending from the direction of Audley, running along Audley Road, passed St. Gabriel's school and the Plough and so down to Crewe, this is known as Valley Brook, becoming the River Waldron, and it joins the River Weaver at Woolstanwood. The second is Alsager Brook which flows down from Linley, passed Twyford's factory and Hoose Hollow, on Lawton Road, continuing passed the Wilbraham Arms at Cresswellshaw, to join the River Wheelock at Wheelock.

It was not always as seen today, during the Triassic period, approximately two hundred million years ago, the area formed part of a low lying region surrounded by a high broken mountainous terrain, which was continually changing. Debris fell into the deep hollows and formed a huge basin full of keuper sandstone. The area would have resembled a red arid desert.

Earthquakes, during the Tertiary period, sixty-five million years ago, caused great cracks to appear in the sandstone, and the upthrows divided the lowlands into ridges, as seen at Mow Cop, Linley Wood, and Talke. This is where the 'Great Cheshire Fault' begins. It follows a line from Barthomley, south to the Bickerton Hills. This fault is clearly visible at Mere Lake, known locally as the Saddle Back. The fall is rapid to the Cheshire side where sandstone is now overlaid by keuper marl. On the Staffordshire side it gives way to the coal measures. It is from this sandstone rock, porous in nature, that Alsager once obtained its water supply from boreholes.

During the Ice Age huge sheets of ice, a thousand and more feet thick, moved from the higher ground to the lowlands. These ice masses scraped away huge chunks of rock, grinding them into pebbles, clay and sand. Striae marks on boulders indicate the direction of the flow. Local sandpits have revealed erratics and seashells from other areas many miles away. During this movement the keuper marl was uncovered, this contained gypsum, which with the salt from the glacier, formed the large salt bearing area of Cheshire.

More importantly, what has determined the character and development of the town, are the glacial and the post-glacial deposits. These have laid down a series of strata masking the basic geological formations; the deposits in this area are largely boulder clays and sand, sometimes laid in series, with the intrusion of pockets of salt.[1] These formations, where bands of clay and sand overlie one another, give rise to the water bearing and water yielding properties found on the stiffer soils of the township, generally to the north of the former heath along the boundary with Betchton and Hassall, and to the south of the heath bordering the boundaries of Barthomley, Audley and Lawton. On page 201 of *"Geology,"* reference is made to the sequence of deposits taken from the borehole at map reference 7884-5678, this is the field adjoining the environmental refuse site at Heath End, through which the footpath passes from Hassall Road to the old mineral line. Anyone accustomed to walking this path will know it is frequently wet and muddy, indicating the presence of ground water. In the Tithe Award of 1840 this field was called 'Far Spa Well Meadow', the adjoining field being 'Near Spa Well Meadow'; this name indicates the presence of a spring utilised as a well or trough. The borehole reveals the presence of stratified sand, clay and peat.

These deposits have also given rise to the formation of Alsager Mere, formed by crater subsidence, where a natural pocket of salt has been eroded by ground water, allowing the surface above to collapse inward, and the cavity

---

[1] *Geology of the country around Macclesfield, Congleton, Crewe, and Middlewich* H.M.S.O. 1968. pp.182 and 185. [*Geology*].

so formed to fill with water.[2] Similarly, with the growth of vegetation, as plant life died in such hollows beds of peat developed and there is documentary evidence of these beds being worked during the medieval and early modern periods as a source of fuel..

The presence of the heath itself results from sandy deposits not overlaid with boulder clay, which accounts for this area remaining out of formal agricultural production until enclosed in the middle of the nineteenth century; and, possibly why the modern urban development has occurred on land that was former heathland, rather than on the better quality agricultural soils which have largely remained in agricultural occupation. The presence of sand in commercial quantities resulted in the excavation of Barker's sand quarry on the former Brund's Farm, to the north of the railway, adjoining the site of Twyford's factory; now developed by housing.

This book traces the transition of Alsager, from its early beginnings, to the modern town which we know today. The authors believe that it will provide a better knowledge of the past which in turn will lead to a greater understanding of the Alsager of the twenty-first century.

[2] *Geology.* page 156.

Chapter 1

Origins.

Prehistoric Alsager.

Peat cutting, at White Moss, has revealed the remains of an extensive prehistoric forest preserved within the peat. The moss was once a peat bog lying over glacial sands, possibly a late glacial lake, formed in the same way as Alsager Mere. In the early post glacial period pine trees were dominant, then deciduous trees arrived after the lake became infilled.[1]

The soils of badly drained glacial clays, thickly covered with oaks and dense undergrowth, impeded early settlement and almost all signs of prehistoric man in the Alsager area occur, not surprisingly, on the sandier soils near to the Church Lawton crossroads. Here there is a group of Bronze Age barrows, north and south of the B5077, close to the former railway line.[2] These monuments may represent a site of special significance within a larger territorial area as opposed to being a permanent residential settlement. The Bronze Age folk who probably constructed them were of south European origin, with Mediterranean features, and first arrived in Cheshire around 1500 BC from Yorkshire and the Peak District. These pioneers were pastoralists, more in control of their lives than the earlier nomadic hunter-gatherers had ever been, obliged to settle to tend their crops and animals on which their livelihood depended.[3] Excavations of these barrows reveal differing burial customs, suggesting use over a prolonged time span, and possibly the presence of different races.

The discovery of cremations with and without cinerary urns, so typical of Celtic tradition, suggests that some of the remains may date from the second half of the first millennium BC, which saw the arrival of the Celts in Cheshire. The combination of a stone circle and a barrow on the southern site is possibly unique in Cheshire, and may have been a cenotaph to someone of

---

[1] *Cheshire Past;-* an annual review of archaeology in Cheshire. Published by Cheshire County Council; Issue 1. 1992.

[2] V.C.H. Cheshire. Vol.I. pp.50-80 for various references.

[3] W.J.Varley; *Prehistoric Cheshire.* Cheshire Rural Community Council 1940. pp. 36-49.

high status.[4]

The farmers of this time may also have used the circle as a calendar which, in conjunction with the stars, would have told them when to plant or harvest crops, and when to hold their rituals of worship. Around 500 BC stony, very coarse pottery, associated with the salt industries for either transport or measure, was reaching the Upper Severn Valley from the present day Nantwich - Middlewich area of Cheshire.[5] It is conceivable that the Church Lawton monuments were on a routeway associated with this trade, and that the circle acted as a landmark.

The discovery in the late 18c. of a wooden anthropomorphic figure in Oakhanger Moss, *"rude and grotesque, but complete with eyes, nose and mouth,"* suggests that our prehistoric forbears may have indulged in ancestor worship; or the cult of the Norse god Odin, who was believed to have fashioned man from two logs he and his two brothers found on the sea-shore. This figure probably belonged to the first half of the first millennium BC.[6]

In 1996 a barbed and tanged flint arrowhead was found in the stream that runs behind St. Gabriel's School in Well Lane, and is likely to date from early Bronze Age.[7] The 2nd half of the 3rd millenium BC witnessed the innovation of this superior design in arrowheads, reasonably attributable to the users of Beaker pottery. Perhaps hunting had become a social activity or sport rather than purely a means of acquiring food.[8]

Celto-Romano Alsager.

The Celts were a tribal people and accomplished metal workers. With their bronze, and later, harder iron tools, they extended the areas cleared of woodland thus permitting an expansion of the population. Both *Crewe* and *Wheelock* are place-names which pre-date the later period of Anglo-Saxon settlement.[9] The region which included Alsager comprised the tribal territory of the Cornovii, a Celtic or Brythonic tribe based in north Shropshire, whose central place was the Wrekin hillfort. They were repositioned by the Romans

[4] Robina McNeil's papers on the barrow on Twyford's land and the Bronze Age burial mound at Church Lawton. *Church Lawton Remembered - A Short History;* 1992.
[5] N.J.Higham, *The Origins of Cheshire;-* Manchester University Press 1993. p.25.
[6] Bryony Coles 1993. *"A Spirit of Enquiry" - Essays for Ted Wright;* No. 4. Roos Carr and Company. Edited by John Coles and Others. Issn. 1350-2832.
[7] County Sites and Monuments Record Extract. Cheshire County Council, Record No, 2710. 1997.
[8] VCH. Cheshire, Vol I p.79.
[9] Dorothy Sylvester. *A History of Cheshire* Phillimore 1980. p.21.

to the nearby town of Wroxeter, the extensive ruins of which remain today. The name *Cornovii*, 'The People of the Horn,' might possibly have been taken from the shape of the tribal territory, if that could have been envisaged before the days of maps![10] There is no recorded evidence of settlement within the area of Alsager at this time, but there may have been some isolated small holdings here, that remained unchanged during the period of the 400 years of Roman colonisation.

The Romans built a network of roads to facilitate the swift movement of troops and supplies. These roads may well have followed older established trading routes, and in this area would undoubtedly have led to the expansion of both iron and salt industries. There were Roman industrial centres at Holditch in Chesterton, and at Middlewich, with the road linking the two almost certainly passing through Lawton Gate before it divided, with one branch going to the Mersey crossing at Warrington by way of Middlewich and Northwich, whilst the other went to Manchester by way of Knutsford. Alsager was so close to this route that it could well have possessed a settled site at that time.

Evidence suggests that the Romans were tolerant of many of the customs and religions they encountered locally across their empire. We know that they allowed the Jewish people to practise Judaism, and by the same token the spa town of Buxton was known to the Romans as *Aquae Arnemetiae* named after the Celtic river goddess Arnemetia.[11]

Anglo-Saxon Alsager.

The Roman withdrawal of AD 410 opened the gates to raiding hordes of fair haired Teutonic peoples from south Denmark and north Germany. They eventually settled and spread northwards and westwards; taking another 200 years or so to reach Cheshire, which was poor and underdeveloped. These pioneers, on the western fringe of Anglo-Saxon penetration belonged to the kingdom of Mercia, a name meaning 'the people of the boundary'; as in Mersey, 'the boundary river,' and Mere Lake, 'the boundary stream'. They came here to share in a good life, and there is unlikely to have been enmity between them and the Celts, or Welsh, which was the Anglo-Saxon word for 'foreigners.' The latter must have outnumbered the new settlers with whom they merged. By 655 AD, when the pagan King Penda of Mercia was killed

---

[10] Higham; pp.35-68.
[11] John Burke, *Roman England;-* The English Tourist Board's *'Discover England'* series. Weidenfeld and Nicholson 1983, p.22.

in battle with the Christian king of Northumbria, the whole of the Cheshire plain had been incorporated into Mercia and Christianity became adopted.[12]

Clearings of the woodland, or *assarts,* were undertaken as the population expanded and new settlements were created; as is evidenced in the *ley* element, from Old English *leah,* a wood or clearing, in so many Cheshire place-names. Examples include, Barthomley, 'the wood of the dwellers at the barley farm;'[13] Audley, 'the leah of Aldgyth (a woman);' Balterley, 'the leah of Bealdthryth' (a woman); Winterley, 'the leah of Wintra's people,' and many more. Woodland evidence also occurs in Oakhanger, 'the oak slope;' and Haslington, 'enclosure or farm amongst the hazels.'[14] The assart of Ælle, or Ælle's æcer, 'the plot of cultivated land belonging to Ælle,' is the origin of the name, Alsager.[15]

The best soils for cultivation in the area are on the boundary zones between sand and clay, where drainage is good and which presented fewer problems to the Anglo-Saxon farmer with his primitive ox-drawn plough.[16] The lack of good workable soil, and the low population, meant that the Celtic tradition of farming, with small square or rectangular fields was followed. The extensive oak woods encouraged pig rearing, acorns being a favourite food of pigs, and pork and bacon was the staple flesh food of the peasant's diet.[17]

The story of the religious life and development of these early communities is far from clear, but a general picture is now agreed amongst most historians. Missionaries from the Northumbrian church, who came to Mercia, found in this part of that kingdom a Celtic church organisation which had survived from the days of the Roman occupation. One of these missionaries, Chad, became the first Bishop of Lichfield. A number of early dedications to St. Chad survive in the area, one of these, at Wybunbury is considered to have been an early minster church at the centre of a very extensive parish. Another such minster was at Sandbach where the Saxon crosses survive.

There is little doubt that during the 7th and 8th centuries Cheshire was hardly more than a social and economic backwater; plagued by struggles for supremacy, between the Anglo-Saxon kingdoms of Mercia and Northumbria, and the Welsh kingdoms of Gwynedd and Powys.

[12] Margaret Gelling. *The West Midlands in the Early Middle Ages;* Leicester University Press 1992. pp.79-91.
[13] J.McN.Dodgson, *The Place-Names of Cheshire;* pt.III, English Place-Name Society [Dodgson]
[14] Eilert Ekwall, *The Concise Oxford Dictionary of English Place-Names.* 4th Ed. 1960. [Ekwall]
[15] Dodgson, Vol. III. p.2. and Ekwall, p.3.
[16] *Historic Society of Lancashire and Cheshire;*- Vol 108; 1956. p.29.
[17] B.M.C.Hussain. *Cheshire under the Norman Earls;* Chesh. Community Council 1973. pp.14-16.

Further disruption occurred to the county's institutions in the 9th century, when marauding Vikings changed their tactics from raiding to settlement. Only Alfred, king of Wessex, held out. He secured a truce with Guthrum, the Danish leader, whereby a boundary was drawn from the Thames, along the river Lea, then to Bedford, and from there to Watling Street, and then up to the southern Pennines. To the northeast of this line was the Danelaw, to the south-west, English territory.[18] Because of its situation it is likely that Cheshire suffered relatively minor inroads from these invaders, and escaped much of the death, destruction and desecration, suffered by most of England. That there was Norse and Danish intrusion into the area is without doubt. This is borne out by the frequency of Norse place-names in the Wirral and in such names as Holmes Chapel and Scholar Green. Norse settlement in the Wirral was responsible for the seige of Chester in about 907, whilst Bromborough is the likely site for the battle of *Brunanburh* in 937. The Anglo-Saxon Chronicle records that in 924 Davenport, lying between Holmes Chapel and Congleton, on the Dane, was destroyed by a Danish war party led by Sihtric, cousin of king Ragnald of York.

In about 907 Chester, once a Roman garrison but since sadly neglected, was fortified against incursions from the sea by Irish Norsemen. Its strategic importance was recognised and it became an administrative centre. King Alfred's daughter Æthelflaed, 'the Lady of the Mercians', took command of the area after her husband's death in 911, and by about 923 the 'shire of Chester' had emerged, as part of newly constituted England. Like the other newly formed shires it was subdivided into administrative divisions known as hundreds.[19]

The story now comes closer to home; and considers the creation of the parish of Barthomley of which Alsager ultimately formed part. Originally forming part of the minster parochia of Wybunbury, the effective lordship of which might have decayed by this time as it was in the hands of the bishop, an absentee landlord, Barthomley was almost certainly created as a parish with its own church and resident priest by an influential Saxon thegn or lord.[20] Fragments of Anglo-Saxon tiles found on the site of the present church are displayed inside. To support his priest the lord would almost certainly endow his new parish with a plot of land known as *Glebe*, which, together with the annual payment of tithes,[21] provided income for the maintenance of the priest

[18] Margaret Gelling. *The West Midlands in the Early Middle Ages;* Leicester University Press 1992. pp.127-128. [Gelling 92.]

[19] For a description of the new shires in Mercia see *Gelling 92*, pp.128 and 142.

[20] Barthomley had a resident priest in 1086, see *Morgan*, Domesday Book of Cheshire, ref 8.30.

[21] *Tithes*, intended to be the tenth part of the product of the land that was paid to the church. For a better understanding see *The Local Historian's Encyclopedia;* Richardson 1986. ref.C134.

and revenue for the church. The dedication of the new church to Bertoline, an obscure Mercian saint having tenuous connections with the former royal house, is of more than local interest. Æthelflaed had imposed Wessex rule on this part of England, and, in an effort to establish political continuity with the former Saxon kingdom of Mercia, a number of new church dedications to Bertoline were established at this time. These were at Runcorn, and possibly at Thurstaston and Wilmslow, with additional possibilities at Woodchurch and the chapel of St. John, Chester. Was Barthomley part of this political propaganda, or does it represent an earlier dedication to the saint upon which the later cult might have been built? In any case, it is clear that by the end of the Anglo-Saxon period Barthomley had developed into a manorial holding and parochial centre, with church hamlet and scattered farms. The parish may or may not have included the neighbouring estate of Alsager, as the next chapter proceeds to show. The distinction between Alsager and Barthomley at this time can best be seen in their Domesday entries. These suggest Alsager to have been an outlying element of a larger estate, incorporating an area of marginal land; whilst Barthomley appears to have been a manorial centre with a priest and almost certainly a church, both of which added to its value.

Chapter 2

The Early Years.

Alsager Pre-conquest.

The origins of the modern community of Alsager, that is the community for which records exist, are obscure in their beginnings. That they go back almost a thousand years, to the Domesday survey of 1086 and beyond, is without question as the township has an entry in Domesday, but is anything known of this pre-conquest, pre-Domesday Alsager and how it fitted into Anglo-Saxon Cheshire? Although few written records exist from this period relating to Cheshire there has in recent years been a great deal of thought given to early estate organisation with some far reaching conclusions. These throw some light on how Alsager might have fitted into the territorial organisation of the county before the Norman conquest.

Cheshire is first referred to as a county in 980, in an entry in the Anglo-Saxon Chronicle; this followed the shiring of this part of England, after the re-imposition of English control during the Danish wars, by Æthelflæd, the Lady of the Mercians, and daughter of king Alfred. It follows, therefore, that the county had been recognised as such for sometime before this date.

It has been suggested[1] that the hundreds[2] into which Cheshire became divided in the tenth century, and the parishes which formed these hundreds, were the remains of much older land divisions, perhaps Roman, or even Iron Age estates. Within these major divisions there were smaller divisions, perhaps individual farms or small settlements which in many cases became the county's townships, the Alsagers and Barthomleys of this world, each having a functional role within the main estate.[3] The reconstruction of these early estates is difficult as the County has almost no pre-Conquest charters and

---

[1] N.J.Higham, *The Origins of Cheshire;*   Manchester University Press, 1993.   Chapter 5. and *The Middle Ages in the North-West.* Oxford 1995.Chap. 1. *Victoria County History of Cheshire (VCH.)* Vol. I. pp. 263-268
[2] A hundred was an administrative division of a county, often used for the purposes of taxation assessment and the organisation of courts. It was superseded in the late nineteenth century by the Rural Districts.
[3] Higham 1993 pp136-137 et seq.

none containing boundary clauses. These later townships, forming small individual sub-lordships, were often responsible for a rent in the form of a render of produce to support the central administration of the larger estate. Their place-names, passed down to us today, may reflect these commodity rents or perhaps be suggestive of woodland and waste near to the perimeter of each larger estate unit with names reflecting other land uses closer to the estate centre. From place-names it is possible sometimes to see what commodity a certain township was responsible for providing by way of rental to the estate centre. This render rent might have consisted of animals, eggs, honey, grain, bread or fuel. Equally the name might indicate the social status of the people living there.

Alsager lay within Mildestrevic (Middlewich) hundred at the time of Domesday and earlier. The hundred had possibly formed part of an important ecclesiastical estate, based on Sandbach, which might have extended as far north as Davenham. Within this large estate there are a number of significant township names, a few of which make a helpful illustration of Dr. Higham's theory. Leftwich, (Leofric's wic) suggests a render of salt; Moulton, (the farm where the mules are bred); Whatcroft, (enclosure where wheat is grown); Shipbrook, (the watercourse where there are sheep); Church Hulme, (church at the water-meadow); Elton, (farm where the eels are got). All these indicate a variety of estate resources. Alsager means 'Ælle's plot of arable land' and suggests that this was an estate farm in the possession of Ælle which had a responsibility for some form of agricultural produce. In addition Ælle would almost certainly keep livestock and have access to grazing and woodland. He would in fact be almost self sufficient, producing a small surplus permitting him to barter for products such as salt and iron which he was unlikely to be able to produce for himself. Although, in the Tithe Award of 1840 for Alsager, ref. No.1 is called 'Part of wich house fields' suggesting that even salt may have been produced on the estate. Immediately adjoining this is Day Green, a name derived from the O.E. 'dæge', a dairy farm; this may have formed part of Ælle's estate or may have been a separate holding. In any event it suggests that the resources of the area were being extensively exploited at a very early date.

Before perhaps 900 AD, when England became a recognisable state, Alsager formed part of the kingdom of Mercia, and for as long as there has been any record the township has formed part of Barthomley parish. From the twelfth or thirteenth century onwards it has been part of the hundred of Nantwich. The boundary between the Nantwich and Northwich (the later name for Middlewich hundred) hundreds passed between the townships of Alsager and Church Lawton. This was not the case however in 1086. At that time Alsager, though possibly forming part of Barthomley parish, lay in the hundred of Middlewich, with the hundred boundary formed by the

Alsager-Barthomley township boundary. Perhaps this indicates that Barthomley was a comparatively new parish at this time, growing in influence, and had only recently absorbed Alsager from an older parish system, or perhaps Alsager was not yet part of Barthomley parish. It is hard to say, but if the hundred boundary is indicative of a former territorial system it would place Alsager within Sandbach or Astbury parishes both of which are considered to be ancient church centres. It has been suggested that Wybunbury was the former parish centre from which Barthomley was created as a separate parish sometime in the late tenth or early eleventh centuries.[4]

An examination of field names along Alsager's boundaries might help to demonstrate this. Along the Alsager-Audley boundary, that is the county boundary, and, since 1541, the boundary between the Provinces of Canterbury and York, there is evidence of old boundary names such as 'Mere Lake', from O.E. (ge)mære, a boundary and læce, a stream; 'Randle', from O.E. rand, an edge or border. The antiquity of these names suggests that the boundary is older than the formation of the county and might well have represented the boundary of an ancient estate or even a tribal territorial division in the late Iron Age.

Barthomley is a woodland place-name, as are Oakhanger and Haslington. They were possibly the outlying townships of an estate based on Wybunbury parish before Barthomley became a manorial parish in its own right. It is unlikely, therefore, that it would have included Alsager within its parish boundary until the hundreds were reorganised after 1086 and Alsager was transferred to Nantwich hundred. Interestingly, the local government reforms of 1974 effectively put Alsager back into the old Middlewich hundred with the new District Council boundary following the line of its Domesday predecessor separating Alsager from Barthomley and what was formerly Nantwich hundred.

This therefore is the possible state of affairs existing at the close of the Anglo-Saxon period. Alsager was by then an identifiable place, occupied by someone who controlled its economic and agricultural resources, and output; who in turn had obligations to a lord superior in the social hierarchy of the day. A tantalising glimpse of this can be obtained from the 1086 Domesday entry for Alsager when read in context with other entries for the county. The case cannot be proved but it can be strongly argued and, if correct, would link boundaries and territories that have relevance today with Saxon, British and perhaps even earlier inhabitants of this part of Cheshire.

---

[4] Higham, 1993. p.143.

Domesday 1086.

Earl Hugh holds
In Mildesvic Hundred
ALSAGER. Wulfric, a free man, held it. ½ hide paying tax.
Land for 1 plough
Waste. Value before 1066, 3s.[5]

So reads Alsager's rather cryptic entry in England's most famous historic document, or at least the translated version published in 1978. Other translations in other publications will be found to vary slightly but the basic facts remain the same. So what does it mean and what does it tell us of Alsager over and above the bare statement made.

To understand the entry it is necessary to know the purpose of Domesday Book. The views of historians differ but there is common ground that the principal purpose of the survey was to assess the value of the kingdom for taxation and its military capability. The impact of taxable liability fell on those who held land, although the incidence might percolate down to the tillers of the soil. It was necessary, therefore, to assess the value of the assets of men in possession of land held from the crown. At the time no one owned land; it all belonged to the crown and was held by an occupier in an hierarchial system from the crown. For example, the King grants 100 units of land to A with certain obligations attached. A retains 50 of these for occupation by himself and his tenantry; he grants to B a sub-lordship of 20 units, (a process known as subinfeudation), of which B occupies 10 and subinfeudates the remainder. A subinfeudates a further 30 units to C, D, and E, who in turn may subinfeudate. The obligations that A owes the crown for these 50 units pass with the land but the sub-lords owe these obligations to their immediate lord, in this case A, and not directly to the crown.

The poor king had no clear record of who held what from whom nor what it was worth. Accordingly he commissioned a survey of the entire kingdom. The result was the Domesday Book, called Domesday by Richard Fitz Neal in his *'Dialogue of the Exchequer'* of 1179 where he says *"the book is called by the English 'Doomsday', that is the day of judgement. For just as the sentence of that strict and terrible Last Judgement cannot be evaded by any act or subterfuge, so, when a dispute arises in this realm concerning facts which are written down, and an appeal is made to the book itself, the evidence it gives cannot be set at nought or evaded with impunity."*[6]

---

[5] Philip Morgan. *Domesday Book, Cheshire:* Phillimore 1978. ref.1.32
[6] Morgan 1988; p.8.

The survey was carried out by teams of commissioners, each team following a circuit of more than two counties. These commissioners heard their evidence at sittings of the county courts and possibly the hundred courts to which were summoned juries to give the testimony of 'the men of the hundred'. In addition to these jury testimonies written returns were also required from those who held directly of the king. In each case the following questions were to be asked;-

a. what was the name of the estate;
b. who held it at the time of king Edward;
c. how many hides are there, (by this time a fiscal unit, originally reckoned as the area of land necessary to support a family unit and considered to be equivalent to about 120 statute acres.);
d. how many ploughs in lordship and how many belonging to the men;
e. how many villagers, cottagers, slaves, free men (liber homines), Freemen (sochemanni);
f. how much woodland, meadow, pasture;
g. how many fisheries;
h. how much has been taken from or added to the estate;
i. what the total value was and is and how much each free man and Freeman has or had;
    i.   at the time of king Edward,
    ii. when the king gave it,
    iii. at the survey date;
j. can more be taken from the estate than is now taken.

The evidence so collected was then drafted in the form seen above for Alsager.

In Cheshire, after 1066, the king held no land. There were two tenants in chief, holding directly from the crown, the bishop and the earl. Largely because of its military status on the border with Wales the earl of Chester was autonomous in the county and those institutions that were royal elsewhere were of the earl in Cheshire. Those who held of him were his tenants in chief or his barons.

The Alsager entry can now be examined, and hopefully be made more clear. Regrettably the draftsmen of Domesday Book did not provide definitions of the terms used. This limits the understanding of Domesday and its contents but it is clear from the text that certain apparently identical expressions can have a variety of meanings attached to them and it is wrong to place a modern interpretation on particular words used.

It is evident from the entry that Alsager lay in the hundred of Middlewich and in 1086 was in the hands of the earl; that is forming part of the earl's own estate rather than having been granted out to one of his barons. Throughout the county as a whole the earl's estates were extensive, extending to some 50 manors[7] which helped to sustain his military capability in warfare against the Welsh; in other words a strategic larder. The remainder of the county was granted by Earl Hugh to his own tenants in chief in the form of military fiefs, each of which was organised to maximise the efficiency of its mobilisation[8] in the event of attack from the Welsh or internal rebellion. Alsager and Sandbach were the only estates retained by the earl in Middlewich hundred, which may help to substantiate Alsager's long time connection with Sandbach.

The entry fails to comply with the royal direction that all the information should be given three times over. There is no mention of the tenant in chief in 1066, a feature usually lacking in Cheshire entries unless the tenant in chief was also the occupier, but it is likely that Alsager was then held of the crown by Earl Edwin as other of Earl Hugh's entries indicate that he was often the successor to Edwin. The occupier or sub-tenant in 1066 was one Wulfric or Ulvric, a Saxon thane and described as a free man. It is unlikely that he was the sole occupier; it was his estate, or one of his estates, on which he would have workers, servants and perhaps tenants, the number cannot be assessed. Who was Wulfric? What is known of him? Was he dispossessed by the Normans or butchered by them? Did he die fighting or did he live to fight another day, perhaps on another side? The question cannot be answered with certainty but a number of hypotheses can be proffered.

Firstly what is implied by the term *"a free man"*, a question much debated and never satisfactorily resolved, it is generally accepted that the term denotes more than personal freedom otherwise *"Freeman"* would have applied. It probably indicates that Wulfric would have been free to place himself under a lord of his choice rather than that from whom he held the land. In the Cheshire volume of Domesday there are nine references to a Wulfric and a further fifteen in the Staffordshire volume. To suggest that all these refer to the same individual is to invite rejection, but some may, indeed are likely to be, one and the same. In Cheshire, in 1066, besides Alsager, a Wulfric held Bredbury, Butley, Ollerton, Peckforton, Puddington, Pulford, Spurstow, and Wistaston. In 1086 a Wulfric continued to hold Bredbury of Richard de Vernon, and Butley and Ollerton, directly of the earl. In Staffordshire, in 1066, Wulfric held Audley and Balterley, both held by Gamel in 1086. It is possible therefore, that a single or composite estate included Alsager, Audley and Balterley in 1066. It is also just possible that this Gamel of 1086 may have been Wulfric's son as the Cheshire entries for Cheadle and Mottram, which are inserted between those for Butley and Ollerton, state that *"that Gamel holds from the Earl. His father held it as a free man"*. In the case of Butley and Ollerton the entry records that Wulfric himself held it as a free

[7] VCH. Cheshire Vol.I pp. 293 et seq.
[8] Philip Morgan, *Domesday Book and the Local Historian;* The Historical Association, 1988.

man; it might just be assumed from this wording that Wulfric previously held all four of these estates. It is highly speculative but possible. If this was the case the family of Wulfric would have retained a fair proportion of its 1066 landholding in 1086.

On the other hand it must be remembered that there is a twenty year span between the two dates being considered and that many of the 1066 landholders would have reached the end of their natural lives by 1086 in any event, conquest or no conquest. In such cases natural wastage would have enabled a former Saxon land holder to have been replaced by a Norman nominee. If Alsager's Wulfric had died in his bed after 1066, but before the date of Domesday Book, the Wulfric seen to survive until 1086 at Butley and Ollerton could not be the same man.

There is a another possibility. Wulfric was probably Earl Edwin's man, the youthful earl of Mercia. In 1066, with the threat of invasion looming, King Harold guarded the south of the kingdom against the Normans but the attack came in the North with an invasion by the Norwegians in Yorkshire. This was resisted by Earl Morcar of Northumbria with help from his brother Edwin of Mercia who led a force raised largely in Cheshire which might easily have included Wulfric. This army was very badly mauled by the Norwegians at Fulford with Edwin and Morcar barely escaping with the remnant of their forces. This was after the time of King Edward, therefore anyone lost on this campaign would be shown as holding land in 1066 in Domesday Book but not in 1086. As a result of their losses at Fulford, Edwin and Morcar were unable to bring their forces into action to participate at the battle of Stamford Bridge, or to accompany Harold to his defeat at Hastings. Later they were unsuccessful in establishing Edgar the Aetheling as Harold's successor and submitted to William at Berkhampstead before being taken by him to Normandy in 1067. In 1069-70 there was a serious rising by the men of Cheshire and the Welsh. William marched against Cheshire in the winter of 1069-70 and ruthlessly suppressed the county, the population being reduced to great wretchedness. Immediately after, too late to be of help, Edwin fled William's court only to be killed by his own supporters. It may well be that our Wulfric took part in one or more of these encounters; he might have perished at Fulford or in the 1069 rebellion. Equally he might have survived Fulford and been wise enough to stay at home in 1069 thus ensuring that he was able to reappear as a man of Earl Hugh in 1086 and might have still occupied Alsager as the earl's servant.

"½ a hide paying tax". The hide, as described above, was originally a measure of land but by the time of Domesday it had become a measure of taxable assessment. Geld, the tax, was levied at so much per hide and all places were reduced to this common denominator in much the same way as a hypothetical value is placed on property today to determine the amount of

council tax payable. Large estates had high assessments; Acton 8 hides, Eastham 22 hides, Malpas 8 hides, Weaverham 13 hides, and so on.

"Land for one plough". Ploughlands may have reflected the measure of land under the plough or the number of ploughteams available to an estate; in other words, Alsager was perhaps possessed of arable land sufficient to require the services of one plough. However, the question of the meaning of *"ploughland"* has still to be resolved and there is a developing view that the figures represent a new form of fiscal assessment, contemporary with Domesday,[9] that would revalue all an estate's assets for taxation purposes substituting ploughlands for the older and debased assessment of the hide.

"Waste". This has long puzzled historians and the word can have a variety of meanings. It can mean totally devastated, as might be implied in current usage, but it can also mean unprofitable, or not in productive use.[10] There is no doubt that it frequently implies that an estate was laid waste during William's punitive raids into Cheshire in 1069-70. This is usually demonstrated by the expression *"found waste"* suggesting that the place in question was waste at the time possession was taken by its new lord. This has to be distinguished from the expression *"is waste"* which clearly implies waste at the time of the survey. Some entries are quite explicit as on Wulfric's estate at Ollerton and state *"it was waste before 1066"*. At Butley his land *"was waste except for seven acres sown"* but a value of 2 shillings was attributed to it: and other assets in the form of woodland, an enclosure, and a meadow are referred to. It would seem, perhaps, that whilst Alsager was described as being *"waste"* it may not have been devastated: there may have been no land under the plough as there is no mention of the presence of ploughs or oxen, but there may have been woodland grazing, pasture, reserves of peat or other estate assets. There is no level of value attributed to the entry but this may imply that the earl is deriving no income from his estate rather than the fact that there was nothing there.

What of omissions? There is no reference to people but that should not be taken to mean that the place was entirely uninhabited. It is quite probable that if there were persons resident in Alsager in 1086 they were merely servants or employees of the earl, and as such would add nothing to the profitability of the estate; they would receive no mention in the survey. Likewise, there is no reference to livestock. Although details of this might have been recorded it was omitted from the final version of the survey.

It might be concluded therefore, that in 1086 Alsager was held by the earl in reserve, a gift he might bestow on a faithful retainer, or a resource to use in times of need.

---

[9] ibid. Philip Morgan, 1988. p.21.
[10] VCH. Cheshire Vol.I pp. 336/7.

The Palatinate County.

During the Middle Ages, roughly from the time of the Norman conquest until 1540, Cheshire was a Palatinate County, that is, a county where royal power was exercised by the earl and which was not subject to the direct jurisdiction of the Crown. Although a part of the kingdom of England it was administered by its earl and not by central government. It had its own courts, its own system of taxation, its own feudal hierarchy and did not send members of parliament to Westminster until 1543. Its status arose largely from the fact that following his conquest in 1066 William I acquired a kingdom that was militarily insecure. In Saxon times there was continual English expansion into North Wales. English control was established as far as Rhuddlan along the coastal strip. Late Anglo-Saxon kings could afford to apply their military strength to this type of activity but William inherited a very different situation. He had the status of a foreign occupying power in England with a population that was generally hostile. His military resources were largely deployed in controlling this population and safeguarding his new interests, particularly in the south, where the wealth of the kingdom lay. This meant that there were few government resources for expeditions against the Welsh, or to protect the Welsh lands under English control and to guard against incursions by the Welsh onto English territory. As a result, a number of Marcher lordships were established along the boundary from the Mersey estuary down to the Severn estuary. These were semi-autonomous fiefdoms responsible for resisting Welsh attacks and for organising punitive expeditions into Wales from their own resources of land and men. Ultimately Cheshire became the principal marcher earldom and a palatinate county. From 1066 until 1254 the earldom lay outside the crown in the hands of an unbroken family line, the last of whom, John the Scot, died in 1235. When, after some legal wrangling, the earldom finally came into possession of the crown, the Lord Edward, later King Edward the first, took the title[11] in 1254. Since this time the title 'Earl of Chester' has been one of the titles of successive heirs to the throne.

---

[11] For further information on the Palatinate see:-

Dorothy J. Clayton, *The Administration of the County Palatine of Chester 1442-85*. Chetham Society, Vol. XXXV - Third Series, Manchester 1990.

B.M.C.Husain. *Cheshire under the Norman Earls*. Cheshire Community Council 1973. Ch. III.

H.J.Hewit. *Cheshire under the Three Edwards*. Cheshire Community Council 1967.

The Alsagers.

After Domesday the story of Alsager resembles the passage of a train through a tunnel. It can be seen to enter the tunnel in 1086 as a manor in the hands of the earl, situated in Middlewich hundred, apparently unprofitable and without record of value or inhabitants. A hundred and fifty years later it emerges into thick mist which thins only gradually. In the meantime it has moved into Nantwich hundred and has been included in the barony or honour of Malbank, the centre or caput of the barony being at Nantwich or Wich-Malbank. The male line of the Malbanks expired on the death of William, the third baron, sometime during the early part of the reign of Henry the second, 1154-1189. The barony then passed to coheiresses, his daughters Philippa, Eleanor and Auda, between whom it was divided. Alsager formed part of Auda's share, which was known as the Third Division. Greater detail of these divisions is given in Hall's History of Nantwich.[12] The Third Division was further divided into two moieties or sixths the subsequent descent of which is complex. Hall states;-

> *"The descent of this share is, however, confusing and unsatisfactory: and to trace in detail and clear up the difficulties and ramifications of these lands through many families of County gentry, is a task sufficient to discourage the most assiduous antiquary, even "Old Mortality" himself."*

We do not know by what route that portion of Auda's inheritance that contained Alsager came to be granted to the family that took its name from the place, nor of whose lordship they held it.

A 17c. document in the British Library,[13] of uncertain authenticity, asserts that William, son of a Michael de Minshull, was given an interest in two thirds of Alsager for thirty years by Sir Ralph Vernon in 1245-6, but this name does not occur again and the individuals concerned in the document have not been identified.

> *"Robert de Bertrudun gave to Ralph Vernon all his Tenements in Alsacher for 15 marks in hand and 2ˢ a year. And Sʳ Ralph Vernon gave to William son of Machael (sic) de Muneshull 2 pts of the Lordship of Alsacher for 30 years paying 10ˢ a year, 30 H.3. . . . ."*[14]

Care has to be taken to distinguish between lordship and occupation of land when considering all these early documents.

---

[12] James Hall. ' *A History of the Town and Parish of Nantwich'* 1883. Reprinted by Mortons of Manchester 1970.
[13] Brit. Lib. Orme Add. MS . 6031 'Collections of Cheshire History'; folios 126/127
[14] 28 October 1245 - 27 October 1246.

The earliest bearers of the name 'Alsager' were perhaps more of a clan than a family; their relationships and descent are difficult to trace accurately but many of them are recorded in a long series of deeds and land related documents running from the middle of the 13c. to the middle of the 17c. Summaries or calendars of some of these documents are set out below; these show how the Alsager family developed its interest in the township over many years. It is possible that initially all the land included within the boundaries was theirs but they held from a superior lord, who seems to have retained the manorial rights; other families intruded as land was granted by way of dower and life interests to such as the Lawtons, the Bulkeleghs of Eyton, the Savages, the Cholmondeleys and the Breretons, all of whom had interests here at one time or another.

The earliest known record of the family name 'Alsager' occurs in a charter forming part of the collection of the deeds of Dieulacres Abbey at Leek. The original, of uncertain date,[15] is lost but two versions remain.[16] The two copies vary somewhat in the form of places named and doubt has been expressed as to whether the land in question was in fact in Alsager. No one has ever been able to give an explanation as to why it so suddenly disappears from the Dieulacres deeds, nor is there trace of any abbey land here at a later date.

> "... *I Randle de Allesacher have given etc. to God and the blessed Mary and to the lord of Deulacres and for the salvation of my soul etc. the entire land of Bircheley with the assarts therein, that is these boundaries.. ...*"

This land may have been in close proximity to the abbey, somewhere around Merebrook to the north of Leek where the earl of Chester had territorial interests. It may be that Alsager had been granted to some deserving servant of the earl, or of the barony, who already held land elsewhere and the servant subsequently took the name 'Alsager'. Perhaps he was known by other names elsewhere. He may not even have regarded the township as his principal manor or estate and, it may have subsequently devolved on other members of his family who in turn took the name and became 'the Alsagers'.

The earliest evidence of the Alsager family available today, which can be relied upon, comes from an undated deed of around 1250;[17]

> "*Grants by Randle lord of Alzacher, to Nicholas his son, for his homage and service, of all the land formerly held of him by Adam Faber (the Smith) and his son Adam and William de le broc. To include his wood and all the land bounded by le dedemonnesbruche to unachethorn, to Narewesicheheued to Carterslake and then by the boundaries of Bertumleg*

---

[15] It cannot be earlier than 1214 when earl Ranulph III moved the monks of Poulton to Dieulacres. Ormerod, vol.III. p.321 appears to suggest a date of 1210, this is doubtful and lacks supporting evidence.

[16] One, a C.17th copy in the British Library, ref B.L.Harley Ms.2060; the second, a published transcription in Staffordshire Historical Collection, New Series vol.ix. p.318.

[17] Ref. Brit Lib. Add.Ch.53530.

> *and Auditheleg to the brook near le bothumforde and so back to dedemonnesbruche. The second grant is of Randle's mill, mill pool and overflow or inflow with the moltura and toll-vat for the whole of Alzacher. Rendering annually a pair of white gloves or one penny."*

The next,[18] which clearly appears to be related to the first, is dated 1262 and records the following;

> *"Grant by Randle, son of Alan, lord of Allesacher, to "Nicholas son of my uncle Nicholas", of all his lands etc in Allesacher, with the site of the mill and the water and the toll and the suit of the whole town of Allesacher at an annual rent of a pair of white gloves or a penny.*

These documents when read together say quite a bit about the very early township. Firstly they indicate the boundaries of the land granted, secondly they say something of family and personal relationships, and thirdly they tell of economic development in the township at an early date. The boundaries described in the first charter can be followed in part today: the whereabouts of *'dedemonnesbruche'*, deadman's intake or assart is lost, as is *'unachethorn'*, the meaning of which remains a mystery but, from the reading of many of these deeds it becomes clear that *'Narewesicheheud'*, 'the head of the narrow stream,' is almost certainly the stream that passes from Audley to Radway Green, past Brookhouse Farm and the mill. At Radway Green it is joined by another stream marking the boundary with Barthomley; at this junction there were two fields, refs. T.A. 451 and T.A. 452,[19] called Cart House Meadow and Cart House Field in 1840; this second stream is almost certainly *'Cartereslake,'* muddy or boggy stream'. The boundary is then described as running along the boundary between Alsager and Barthomley and Alsager and Audley as far as *'le Bothumforde,'* attributed by Dodgson[20] to be at map reference 798540, where a footbridge today crosses the stream. Clearly, all this land lay in lordship of this Randle Alsager who may have been the same Randle as the one referred to above in the Dieulacres charter.

The relationships given in the document may help to reconstruct early relationships of the Alsager family though care must be taken to regard conclusions made here as possibilities only. There is reference in the first deed to Nicholas, son of Randle, whilst in the second, Randle is described as son of Alan and as having an uncle and a cousin each named Nicholas. The only workable relationship is that there were two Randles, grandfather and grandson, whilst Alan and Nicholas were sons of the elder Randle and Nicholas had a son Nicholas, cousin of the younger Randle. In the witness list three men are named who might be members of the family in that they are identified only by their christian names and the christian names of their

---

[18] Ref., Brit. Lib. Add. Ch. 53529.
[19] T.A. indicates Tithe Award reference.
[20] J.McN.Dodgson. *The Place-Names of Cheshire.* Vol. III. p.5. English Place-Name Society 1981.

fathers. Adam son of Julian, Nicholas son of Adam son of Julian and Randle son of Walter. From references found elsewhere it seems possible that the Gillian or Julian referred to here was a further son of the elder Randle.[21] Additionally a further name is introduced, that of Adam Faber; if this name is descriptive of a trade it can be translated as 'the smith', as it has been in this case. From reading this document it would appear that this is a grant by the head of the Alsager clan to another member of the same, of land previously occupied by some one else who has been dispossessed or whose line has run out. If this interpretation is correct it provides some knowledge of the occupiers of this land for two generations earlier, taking us back to perhaps about 1200. If Adam was a smith there must have been a smithy; the 1840 Tithe Award shows there to have been one adjoining Brookhouse Farm where Brookhouse Road meets Fannys Croft, in T.A. ref. 391, but this is a very tenuous connection.

Economic development of the township can be detected by references to a mill, a mill pond and to *moltura or multure,* a payment made for grinding corn at a lord's mill; and toll-vat, a measure of grain, perhaps half a bushel, paid as multure. It seems very likely that the mill referred to here is on the site of the mill adjacent to Alsager Hall Farm today, ref. T.A. 437; further references are made to it in other deeds. The mill toll or 'moltura' was a valuable form of revenue to the person with the right to collect it and it was maintained for centuries. In a marriage settlement dated 15th August 1571,[22] between Raffe Aulsager, son of Robert Aulsager, and Margaret Tenche it is stated;-

> "And that the said Margaret duringe her naturall lieffe aforseid shalle have all her corne and malte grownden Tolle ffree at the milne of the said Robert aulsager in Aulsager..."

Woodland is also mentioned which at that time constituted a valuable commodity and would almost certainly be managed as a coppice or sprink rather than being wild; a probable location is Alsager Sprink, ref. T.A. 486, a portion of which remains today. Reference to a possible smithy has already been made.

That the early Alsager estate extended further than the area of land referred to above is indicated by a number of different sources. The first relates to Cresswellshawe,[23] the farm centred on what today is the Wilbraham Arms. A document in the British Library[24] compiled from earlier records in the 17c., reads when translated;-

---

[21] See also CRO.DVE. 1. B/1/8, for further reference to Adam son of Julian of Allesacher.
[22] Brit. Lib. Add.Ch. 53548.
[23] There is a sequence of documents in the Baker Wilbraham papers in the Cheshire Record Office, refs DBW/A/A/H1-13; which relate to this estate.
[24] Brit. Lib. Add.M.S. 6032.

"Randle lord of Allescher gave a holding called Cresswallshawe
to Henry son of Thomas of Rode. The same Henry had one son issue
Henry de Mole[25] and the said Henry had one son called
William de Mole[26] and the said William had one son issue lawfully called Henry
de Mole, and the said Henry had legal issue John de Mole.[27]
And the aforesaid Henry had a sister called Petronilla Walle
lawfully begotten and she had lawfull issue by her husband
Thomas walle and the said John had a daughter called Elena[28]
and lawfull issue and no more sons nor daughters since the said Elina
> *The Original of this document remains in the possession of Robert Poole*
> *of Cresswallshawe in the town of Alsacher and is attached to*
> *a certain deed of Henry son of Henry de Mole dated 1325*
> *by which charter it is clear that the aforesaid Henry had*
> *a sister called Margery then married to Adam son of Richard de Welinhall*
> *1325.*

Further evidence is forthcoming from the Tithe Award of 1840, and other
documents of the c.19, from which it is plain that the Alsager family interest
included Heath End Farm, and the estate had formerly extended along the
northern boundary of Alsager as far as Day Green.

Other evidence, again from the collection of ancient deeds, relates to a
number of grants to take peat from the turbaries in Alsager which almost
certainly lay in that area of the town which was the heath, enclosed in 1834.
This suggests very strongly that the Alsager lordship extended over the whole
of that area also at an early date.

> *Grant of turbary with warranty by William lord of Alsacher to Richard Le*
> *King of Alsacher, extending to all Williams turbaries in his lordship,*
> *allowing Richard turves for one hearth. Annual payment one half-penny*
> *with payment entry fine of five shillings beforehand."*
> Date c.1303.
> *"Grant by William lord de Alsach' to Sir John called la Deakene, chaplain,*
> *of turfs sufficient for one hearth, under the supervision of his bailiffs in all*
> *his turbaries in Alsach' beginning at Nareuseceheud at a rent of ½d, with*
> *the right to assign except to men of religion and right of cartage."*
> *Dated at Alsacher, 20th June 1311..[29]*

Finally there is evidence that some land was granted away, some to the
de Praers family at Barthomley, some to the Lawtons of Church Lawton and
some within the family. By a grant of 1356:-[30]

---

[25] Henry de Mowhulle was a witness to a number of Alsager charters between 1299 and 1329.
[26] Grant by Alice widow of William de Mowehul to her son Henry, of lands at Cresswallshagh,
25th April 1374. Ref. CRO/DBW/A/A/H1.
[27] John son of Henry de Mowle is referred to in ref. CRO./DBW/A/A/H2. 13th June 1400.
[28] Daughter and heiress of John Moole late of Alsager and Cherchelauton, Ref.
CRO/DBW/A/A/H5.
[29] Brit.Lib. Add.Ch. 53531
[30] Brit.Lib. Add.Ch. 53534

Grant by John son of Nicholas de Alsager to Henry de Hawode, chaplain
of a messuage and two fields and all the land lying in Alsager between the
lane leading to Alsager on the one side and the park at Audley on the other.

It is difficult to identify this land with certainty but it is possible that it relates to the area known later as Bankhouse Farm, which at the time of the Tithe Award in 1840 extended to approximately 53 acres. The two lanes described in the deed might today be footpaths leading from Alsager Hall farm past Bankhouse, which becomes Fanny's Croft, leading from the Hall to Alsager; the second might be the footpath running through Alsager Sprink to Lower Foxley, Higher Foxley and ultimately to Park End in Audley.

The grant appears to be to a cleric which was not unusual at this time. These early forms of settlement in which the priest was appointed trustee enabled feudal dues payable to a superior lord on the death of the land holder to be avoided. This device was used quite frequently as can be seen in a sequence of deeds relating to land at Swallowmoor, Alsager, where John, son of Benedict de Alsacher, received land from Thomas de Budenhall, parson of the church at Rostherne.[31] The Pole, or Poole, family made similar arrangements in respect of their land at Cresswellshawe in 1475.[32]

Other family names emerge from these documents from time to time, some are the names of participants in the agreements to which the documents relate, others are names of witnesses. All the early documents conclude with lists of witnesses which help to tell of the social groups with whom the Alsager family tended to form alliances and look to for support.

Law and Order.

Lawlessness was rife in medieval Cheshire.[33] Mr. Hewitt, in his book, quotes as follows;-

> *"Moreover its people gradually gained a reputation for violence, turbulence*
> *and martial powers. The city and county formed a place of asylum and*
> *sanctuary where debtors and offenders against the law of the land might*
> *remain under the Earl's protection on payment of a fine called an advowry.*
> *.... The infiltration of lawless elements among a people already hardened*
> *by war, produced the men who in the reign of Richard II were both feared*
> *and hated in other parts of England."*

How did the people of Alsager fit into this unedifying description. The township was on the border of England and the Palatinate, which enabled malefactors to cross and recross to avoid and evade the forces of law and

---

[31] Refs. Brit. Lib. Add.Ch's. 53538(Feb.1399), 53539(Aug. 1384), 53540(Aug.1384).
[32] CRO.DBW.A/A/H5 to H8.(19th. 22nd. 22nd. and 23rd. 1475)
[33] H.J.Hewitt, *Cheshire Under The Three Edwards;* Ches. Community Council 1967. pp. 105-7

order which followed their progress. Glimpses of what occurred can be seen from a number of published court rolls relating to of Cheshire and Staffordshire.[34] Examples of these are given below. One of the drawbacks to medieval court records is that the case is rarely reported in full and frequently the judgement is not entered on the roll, so that all we are given is a tantalising glimpse of medieval society. However, a clear impression can be formed of the general nature of this society, and the picture that emerges is one similar to that of the wild west as portrayed by Hollywood.

> Court. ref.130. p.19. County Court 1 June 1260
>
> *"Wich-Malbank.- Honde de Aldeton, bedell, took **Adam de Alisacher**, a fugitive, and his sons and allowed them to go away for 30s. He made a fine. (T)."*

This entry tells us very little other than the fact that Adam and his sons were guilty of some crime. Whether they merely left the precincts of the court or they were expelled from the county is unclear. The *'T'* at the end of the entry stands for *'terminator'* indicating that the case was concluded.

> Court. ref 200. p.27. County Court 13 July 1260.
>
> *"Be it remembered that **Isabil de Alisacher**, found in the company of robbers executed, abjured the country. She took the road to Stafford."*

In his book *"Crime and Punishment in England"*, Dr. Christopher Harrison, speaking of this period states: *"If a felon could reach the sanctuary of a church he came under the protection of the church for forty days. At the end of these forty days, the felon had two choices: either to surrender and submit himself for trial or to accept banishment.. . . . he was then sent by the shortest or most direct route along the king's highway to the nearest port, where he had to embark on the first ship going to a foreign port."* In the case of Isabil de Alsacher it must be remembered that the Palatinate jurisdiction of the earl finished at the county boundary; accordingly, banishment from the 'country' in Cheshire equated with banishment from the kingdom in the remainder of England.

> 1284   SHC. Pleas. Vol. VI. pt.I. p.160.
>
> *"**Adam son of William de Allesacher**, and others sued Roger son of Stephen de Uselwell for half the manor of Swynnerton, claimed as heirs of John de Swynnerton. Sheriff ordered to summon a jury, verdict for the defendants."*
>
> 1285   SHC. Pleas. Vol. VI. pt.I. p.164
>
> *"**Adam son of William de Alsacher**, with others, in mercy for making a false claim against Roger son of Stephen de Uselwell."*

[34] R.Stewart-Brown; *Chester County Court Rolls 1259-1297*. Chetham Soc. Vol.84.1925. [Court].

R.Stewart-Brown; *Chamberlains Accounts*. Record Society of Lancs. and Ches. Vol.90. 1910. [Chamb].

"Plea Rolls." Staffordshire Historical Collections; Vol. vi. pt.I. [SHC. Pleas]

"Stafford Assize Roll 21 Ed.I." Staffordshire Historical Collections; Vol. vi. pt.I. [SHC. Assize]

In this case, the jury determined that the claim of Adam and others was false and subsequently they were brought back to court to be *'in mercy';* to be amerced or fined as a penalty.

> 1286   SHC. Pleas. Vol .VI. pt.I. p.166.
> *"**Adam son of William de Allesager** and others appear in the court of Edmund the King's brother at Newcastle under lyme to answer a writ of the King between them and Roger son of Stephen de Uselwell regarding four messuages and four bovates of land with appurtenances at Great Chell, in which Roger claimed a false judgment had been given".*

> 1286   SHC. Pleas. Vol. VI. pt..I p.168.
> *"Roger son of Stephen de Uselwell who brought a writ of false judgment against **Adam son of William de Allseger** and others did not appear to prosecute it and the suit was dismissed."*

This seems to suggest that there was continuing friction between Adam and Roger. Here it seems that Adam's case has been upheld against Roger who has embarked on an appeal which he subsequently abandoned. This is one of those tantalising cases where there is clearly much more to be told than is included in the court records.

> Court. ref. 24. p.227.   Macclesfield Eyre Roll m.6d. 1286
> *"**Randle lord of Allisacher**, indicted for a trespass as having been found in Muggel' wood with dogs on the Sunday before Saint John the Baptist's day, 12th year(18th June 1284), answered by "Twertnik" according to the custom of the country, denying everything alleged. Richard Starky, the constable's bailiff claimed him for his lord's liberty according to the manner of the country, and it was allowed. Let him bring him to four County Courts. This was done and Randle was quit at the liberty &c. (Ad com'. 1°, sec°.)"*

This is a case from the forest court. A forest was an area reserved for royal hunting, or in Cheshire, reserved to the earl. Normal economic activities were carried out in the forest area but there were punitive game laws. It appears that Randle and Robert had been found either hunting or more likely with dogs capable of hunting, within part of the designated forest, the southern boundary of which was the river Dane; *'the wood of Muggeleg'* can be identified with Midgley which lies just off the Congleton to Buxton road at Allgreave, map ref. SJ 980670. The plea of *'Twertnik'* could be offered for certain offences as a simple denial by the accused; it was abolished by the Black Prince in 1346 as being the *'foster mother of disorder'.*[35]   Reference *'to the law and custom of the county'* is to the so called *'Magna Carta'* of Cheshire, granted to the county by Earl Ranulf III in 1215 or 1216. Having pleaded, twertnik, the accused's lord could claim to hear the case in his own court instead of that of the earl and so retain any profits resulting from the

---

[35] PRO. C53 162 m11.

case.[36] This seems to have been the situation here where the constable's bailiff claimed Randle for his lord's liberty or justice. The condition of this being that Randle first attended four County Court sessions to make his plea of 'twertnik'. The figures in brackets at the end of the entry indicate that he came to the court on a first and second occasion, the clerk evidently failing to note the third and fourth appearances. The reason for a defendant wishing to transfer the case from the earl's court to that of his own lord were twofold. Firstly, the matter might not proceed further in his lord's court and secondly, if it did it would be heard amongst the accused's associates and familiars with there being a better chance of acquittal. In this case Randle and Richard Starky, the bailiff, had both been witnesses to a charter enrolled on the court roll in April 1260 and might therefore have been close associates.

> Court. ref.194 p.97. County Court 15 June. 1288
> *"Henry de Thirlewode v. **Randle de Alsacher and William his son;** taking beasts. William not found and must be arrested if found."*
>
> Court. ref.19. p.118. County Court 19 October. 1288
> ***"Thomas son of Adam de Allesacher v. Randle de Allesacher;** taking cattle. Plaintiff did not prosecute; his pledges were amerced-- Randle son of Adam and Henry de Shavinton. (40d.)"*
>
> Court. ref.51 p.121. County Court 30 November. 1288
> *"Dike de Pull amerced (2s.) for not appearing at an assize between Henry de Berthumlegh and Adam son of Adam de Laughton and **Randle Dunn** (?) [perhaps Dom.(lord)] **of Alisacher.** Robert de Tunlegh and Hugh Wordwall amerced for same. (12d. each.)"*
>
> Court. ref. 316. p.151. County Court 20th September 1289.
> *"Amerced for not attending the assize concerning land in Sidenhal between Geoffrey le Spicer and Isabel his wife v. Richard de Undrewode and others: Richard de Swetenham(2s.), Thomas Smith of Worleston(12d.), **Wilke son of Randle son of Walter of Alsacher(12d.)."***
>
> Court. ref.83. p.126. County Court 18 January 1290.
> *"Adam de Birthumlegh v.**William son of Randle de Aldsacher, Ralph and Randle his brothers;** trespass. Defendants did not come; to be distrained etc."*
>
> Court. refs.85-6. p.126. County Court 18 January 1290
> ***"Randle de Alisacher (40d.)** and Adam son of Adam de Laughton (40d.); disseisin against Henry de Berthumlegh. Each was pledge for the other."*

This group of six cases stand together and usefully illustrate the sort of disputes which arose between neighbours, on a regular basis, at this time. It is, of course, possible that Randle and his son William were professional cattle rustlers and this possibility is reinforced by William's disappearance; but equally the disputes might easily have arisen from the inter grazing of cattle on common pasture. It is perhaps unfortunate for his posthumous record that Randle is the defendant in the second case also. He seems to have been a

---

[36] Eng. Hist. Review, Vol.xl, p.13 (Jan 1925). R.Stewart-Brown.

man well acquainted with the courts! The names which occur and recur are very similar to and can often be identified with those seen in the deeds and charters relating to land. We are seeing here the day to day social structure and working of an agricultural community in the c.13. In the third case potential witnesses who failed to appear to give evidence have been fined by the court. The final case appears to be the rehearing of case number three and concerns the wrongful ejection of someone entitled to the freehold of land; what a pity the intimate details are omitted. The *P* at the end of the fifth case represents a marginal note on the roll *'preceptum est'* indicating that an order has been made for some action to be taken, usually by the sheriff.

1293   SHC. Vol. VI. pt. I. pp.283-4. Stafford Assize Roll 21 Ed.1.

*"Of Indictments they say that Robert le Bykere, **Adam de Allesacher, Nicholas and Richard his brothers**, William de Gresele, and Robert his brother, Adam de Sheynton, and Benedict his brother, had withdrawn themselves for sundry robberies, homicides and larcenies. They are therefore to be outlawed. They had no chattels."*

*"Of Indictments they say that .... and Robert de Bagenholte and John de Bagenholte, brothers of Stephen de Bagenholte, **Adam de Alesacher, Richard brother of Adam**, Roger de Maysham, and thirteen others named, had withdrawn themselves for various robberies committed in company with Stephen de Bagenholte. They are therefore to be outlawed."*

These two examples are clearly more serious criminal cases than those recited earlier. There is no absolute certainty that we are dealing here with residents of the township of Alsager but there is great similarity of names. Nor can we be sure that Adam de Alesacher is one and the same as Adam son of William de Allseger referred to in the earlier records: or as Adam de Alisacher who with his sons went away as a fugitive in 1260 but there is every possibility that either they are one and the same or close family links exist. In any event, they seem to have been bad lots and boast the Alsager name. It should be remembered that as expulsion from Cheshire allowed fugitives to seek refuge elsewhere in England, so did expulsion from other English counties enable fugitives to enter Cheshire in search of asylum, and those mentioned in these cases may have slipped back over the border to escape justice in Staffordshire. When men were outlawed any chattels they had were forfeit to the crown and their lands reverted to their lord.

Chamb. pp.50-54. Fines made at the County Courts of Chester 1303-4

At the second County Court.

Bertreda de Absach(sic) (Alsach) indicted . . . . . . ½ mark.(1 mark=13s.4d.)

Benedict de Sutton, for the same . . . . 1 mark.

At the fourth County Court.

William de Alsacher and others . . . . .1 mark.

At the eighth County Court

Beatrice, daughter of Ranulph de Alsacher . .   5s.

Amercements of the Crown.

Fourth County Court on Tuesday next after the feast of the Purification of the Blessed

> *Mary in the said Year.*
> *William de Alzacher* . . . . .   . *12d.*
>
> Sixth County Court on Tuesday next after the Ascension in the 32nd year.
>
> *Adam son of Thomas de Alzacher, for licence to agree* . .   *12d.*

These fines represent sums paid to the County Court by the Alsager residents during the period November 1303 to November 1304. The Court was held every six weeks, on a Tuesday. In addition to fines as we understand them today payments, might also include sums which we would regard as licence payments. At the first Court, 48 payments were made, the highest being 1 mark and the lowest 2 shillings, (10 pence); at the second, 34 payments ranging from 10 pounds to 1 shilling; at the third, 17 payments, ½ mark to 1 shilling: whilst at the seventh, eighth and ninth Courts there were 6, 7, 3 payments respectively. Those with Alsager connections clearly maintained their averages. We know that Bertrada de Alsacher was the widow of Randle, lord of Alsager, and brought suits of dower against his heirs. She married for a second time, Benedict de Sutton, who held land in Alsager adjoining the boundary with Haslington.[37] Others encountered before include Adam son of Thomas de Alzacher who paid for a licence, for what is not known.

> County Court of Chester, Tuesday, feast of St. Chad (2nd March) 1311.[38]
> *"Henry de Erdelegh and William son of the same summoned at another time concerning the death of Reginald de Kirkebi by fine to have bail until the next Court by the pledge of **William lord of Alsacher, Adam son of Thomas de Alsacher and Richard son of Randle son of Walter de Alsacher** - 24. shillings.*
>
> *The same have gone bail for them to make peace with John, brother of the foresaid Reginald on pain of £40.*
>
> *William Croket of Audley, indicted for the burglary of the house of Henry, son of John de Bechyngton and carrying away goods, fined and released from the King's suit by the pledge of **William de Alsacher** - 6 shillings and 8 pence. "*

It appears that members of the Alsager family were not unduly concerned with whom they kept company. To be released from the King's suit was to be discharged of the offence so far as the Crown was concerned, before trial, but others were still free to prosecute.

> *"County Court of Chester on Tuesday after the feast of the translation of St. Thomas the martyr in the 48th year of the reign of King Edward the third after the conquest.(11th July 1374) m.30.ref.161.3*
>
> *Hugh de Cholmundelgh, Ralph de Crannache, Richard de Vernon of Lostock, Robert Seyntpere, Roger de Moldeworth, Randle de Legh, Robert*

---

[37] In a grant ref CRO.DVE.1/A.1. dated c.1303, Benedict de Sutton is referred to as having land adjoining the waste and close to the boundary with Haslington.

[38] Unpublished Court Rolls ref. PRO. Palatinate of Chester, Plea Rolls 29/24.

de Cholmundelegh, Peter de Wetenhale, William de Wetenhale of Al[. . .], William de Troghford, and Thomas de Merbury say on their oath that **John de Alsacher the younger** <fine> **wearing hauberk (sleeveless coat of mail) and Jack (padded coat worn under chain mail)** *and other men in armour on Thursday, the feast of the apostles Peter and Paul in the 48th year of the reign of king Edward the third from the conquest (29th June 1374),* **with a drawn sword in his hand,** *assaulted Roger de Pulton and John his brother at Haselynton and chased them to their own house in the same township and [. . .] sword struck John the brother of Roger against the peace.*

And that John Fox came **with John de Alsacher** *on the above date and pursued Roger de Pulton with a drawn dagger in his hand, and because he could not catch up with Roger to strike him, because Roger fled, John Fox threw his dagger after him and struck him in the shin with the handle of his dagger by force and arms against the peace".*[39]

Clearly, whatever it was that had provoked the wrath of John Alsacher, he and his friends had gone to Haslington prepared to do business and it appears they were successful in their efforts. It makes present day football hooliganism pale into insignificance! At the next Court, held on the 1st August 1374, John de Alsager was a member of the jury!

> 1406 SHC. Vol. .XV.(1895) p.120
> **John Alsegger the elder and John Alsegger the younger** *charged with others for disseising William Marchall of four messuages and eight acres of land in Bettelegh. Found proved and that they had used force and arms.*

It seems as though the passage of time did very little to mellow John Alsegger the younger; he appears to have been a man of choleric disposition. One wonders just how old John Alsegger the elder might have been at the time of this last incident in Betley bearing in mind that it occurred thirty years after the case relating to Haslington. According to Ormerod, John the younger's sons may have been little better than their father. They were forced to enter into an undertaking with the crown in 1434 or 35 in the sum of £10, that Eva' Vergh Howell ap Bleth, a servant of John de Alsacher, keep the peace towards Thomas Geselyng, and all the tenants of James le Bruyn in Bedulph, Staffordshire.

Whilst the above examples of the records of court proceedings are no more than a modest sample of what occurred over several hundreds of years they do provide an indication of the social turbulence that prevailed in this part of the country during the later part of the middle ages and they substantiate, more or less, the comments of Mr. Hewitt quoted at the beginning of this section.

---

[39] This unpublished transcript from the *"Cheshire Indictment Roll, 1354-1377.* is reproduced with the kind permission of Mrs. Phyllis Hill of Tarvin.

Dower.

Dower was a payment made to, or made for, a widow out of the estate of her deceased husband, as a life interest, for the continued support and sustenance of herself and the children of the marriage. When a man died leaving an estate of land which was his to dispose of, the widow was entitled to hold a third of this land, as tenant in dower, for the term of her life. This right, until 1833, extended to land which her husband had disposed of absolutely in his lifetime or by his will. As a consequence it is not difficult to see why there was much litigation, and why the Court rolls are full of cases of widows suing for their rights.

The case of Bertred, or Beatrice, widow of Randle de Alsacher,[40] must have caused quite some commotion locally when her various pleas were heard in the County Court. Details from the Plea Rolls give remarkable insight into local goings on at the turn of the thirteenth and fourteenth centuries. In all, Beatrice brought 21 separate actions against relatives and neighbours in the area of Alsager between 1298 and 1307.

Randle de Alsacher, Beatrice's probable former husband,has already been met with. It will be recalled that he granted the mill to his uncle Nicholas in 1262; he was caught poaching in the Forest of Macclesfield in 1286 and with William his son took beasts belonging to Henry de Thirlewood in 1288. He is also the man who transferred the Creswellshawe land to the de Mowhull family and was sued with Adam de Lauton in a case of dispossession against Henry de Berthumlegh. After his death his widow sought to recover dower from his heirs and assigns.

She sued Thomas son of Adam son of Julian for dower of four acres in Alsager. From the evidence of surviving deeds and other cases, this would appear to be the same Thomas who brought a case against Randle for taking cattle in 1288: he is also referred to as having an assart, an area of land recovered from the waste or woodland, in a deed dated 19th April 1289.[41] Another deed dated around 1290 refers to a grant of land by Randle son of Adam son of Julian. Accordingly, it is possible that Randle deceased and Thomas were brothers and that Beatrice was seeking dower from land given to her brother-in-law by her late husband. Against this suggestion is reference to a further case brought by Beatrice against Margery, wife of Randle son of Adam. It is barely conceivable that Randle could have been married to both Beatrice and Margery simultaneously, and both appear to have survived him. The Alsager family relationships at this time appear so tangled, with so many

---

[40] Ormerod. Vol. III p.321
[41] Court p.134 ref. 156.

repetitions of the same name, it is quite impossible to establish a reliable family structure.

She claimed against Henry son of William de Badeley for twelve acres. In December 1298 and January 1299 there are four separate court appearances relating to this case. In the first, Randle de Wodenot failed to come to give evidence; in the second Beatrice brought pledges, Patric de Creuwe and Hugh de Calveley, to support her claim; in the third hearing the case was postponed with a further hearing date appointed. Finally, in the last entry, Henry states that Beatrice's husband Randle de Alsager was never in possession of the land claimed and accordingly requests that the plea fails. The ultimate outcome is unknown but it seems as though Henry managed to muster an effective defence.

There is a case against Adam de lauton and Alice his wife, for twenty four acres. Details of this are lacking but it appears that Adam and Randle had been close associates in a number of matters, and Alice may have been the sister or daughter of Randle, and land in Alsager may have been given as her dowry on her marriage.

Henry de Mowhul and Robert his son did not escape Beatrice's attention. They were sued for a messuage, that is a dwelling, eighty acres and 12.s. rent. Almost certainly this refers to the grant of the Cresswellshawe estate to the de Mowhul family as described earlier. Although Ormerod refers to a claim for eighty acres, the actual plea roll refers to twenty acres and tells us that Henry was represented by his attorney and the claim was denied. At a previous court Henry had claimed that Randle, son and heir of the dead Randle, had guaranteed this claim. He had been summoned but failed to appear, accordingly the sheriff was ordered to seize goods to the value of the claim from the young Randle. As a result Randle subsequently appeared and guaranteed Henry's claim, paying the dower to Beatrice. He was fined for unjustly detaining what he should have paid earlier. In a later entry William, the son of Randle, takes the place of young Randle who may be presumed to have died and to have been succeeded by his brother. It seems as though the de Mowells were successful in their resistance to this claim, perhaps because it was guaranteed by Randle's heirs.

A Richard King was sued for ten acres and 5s. rent. Precisely who he was is not known, but a Richard King or le Kinges was granted a right to dig peat in Alsager, by William, lord of Alsager, in 1303,[42] and he witnessed a charter of William in 1311. His grand-daughter Matilda conveyed all his lands and tenements in Alsager to Richard le Tipper in 1330. The name occurs again in connection with the Black Death in 1349.

---

[42] ref. CRO.DCH.J/6A.

Alice de Ormeshalgh was sued for twelve acres. Ormerod reckons the name Ormeshalgh reflects the name of such a place in Alsager but it is not noted elsewhere than in this case. Alice came to court and said she held the land by rent, and requested that the matter should be enquired into, *"and therefore it was done according to the law."* Again the final outcome remains unknown but it is clear that in many cases these pleas of dower could be resisted for various reasons and were possibly unsuccessful.

In the County Court in December 1298 William de Smalle and Amicia his wife, and Richard son of Nicholas, son of Hudde, were sued by Beatrice for twelve acres which was pledged by Walter de Alsager and Patric de Creuwe.

William son of Randle, which William and which Randle we have to guess, was sued for a bovate (about 15 acres), two acres and 5s. rent. Nothing further has been noted in respect of this claim which is possibly against the William who became lord of Alsager on his brother Randle's death.

In February 1299 Beatrice appears to have been fined 2s. for failing to pursue a case for two sessions against Richard, son of Nicholas son of Hugh, and against Alice the mother of Richard; in this case the pledges were Patric de Crewue and William de Alsager.

Of the remaining nine cases listed, specific details are not recorded. One concerns Ralph, son of Randle, who may well have been a third son of the deceased Randle, who with his brothers William and Randle were sued for trespass by Adam de Birthumlegh in 1289. William de Alsager, Randle's ultimate heir, was sued for two messuages, two carucates (approximately 240 acres), eighty acres of waste, four acres of meadow and rent of 4s., a substantial amount in total.

We are not told in every case whether or not the land giving rise to the claim was in Alsager, in some cases it may not have been, but in total the claims rested on over 563 acres. Bearing in mind that these were probably customary Cheshire acres, which contained 10,240 square yards compared with 4840 square yards in a statute acre,[43] the total could come to about 1200 acres, plus the messuages; not an inconsiderable area of land. In addition there was a sum of 62s. in rents.

It is possible, from the evidence of these cases, to draw the conclusion that by this time the Alsager family holding was beginning to fragment. If the township had been granted as a whole to the first lord of Alsager it was no longer held in its entirety. We have seen evidence relating to the grant to the de Mowhull family, and there is evidence in these cases of grants to other

---

[43] There are 2.47 statute acres to the hectare.

persons also, many of them possibly members of the Alsager clan. The family estate was beginning to be replaced by a more open agricultural community, the members of which may well have had many family ties and were not only mutually dependent on one another but also social equals.

Arrangements for dower continued for many years after the date of Beatrice's case. They were frequently made at the time of the marriage in the form of a marriage deed or settlement. Two examples of these relate to Alsager farming families in the sixteenth and seventeenth centuries, and others may be found. By an agreement reached on the marriage of Rauffe aulsager in 1571, between Robert his father and Robert Tenche of Newhalle, the father of Margaret the bride, it was agreed that;-

> *"... And moreover that the said Margaret Doughter of the said Robert Tenche shall .... enioye the said moitye of all the said landes, howsse and howssinge, with all meadowes .... thereunto belongynge for terme of her lieffe in as large and ample manner as the said Robert aulsager nowe or hereafter dothe or shall occupye the same for and in the name of all her wymturs and **dower** .. and that the same landes nowe and hereafter shall so be and continewe ffree of .... wymtures, dowers and all other incumbrannces whatsoever Savinge the **wymtures of Elizabeth aulsager mother of the said Roberte and Katheryn alsager wyeffe of the said Robert aulsager** ....[44]*

The second is a marriage deed between John Brereton the younger, of Brereton's Tenement, or Lane End Farm, now 'The Holly Trees' hotel, and Martha Shaw, dated 17th August 1688.

> *".....from and after the decease of the said John Brereton the Younger permit and suffer the said Martha Shaw and her assignes peacably and quietly to have hold .... as she the said Martha Shaw shall happen to live for her joynture and in **full satisfaction of her Dower**. ....[45]*

These documents can provide much more information than appears on face value. The 1571 agreement sets out a detailed family relationship as well as referring to the mill and the right to tolls from its use together with field names. In this case Margaret Alsager was widowed, possibly in 1597, after which she continued with her father-in-law to take an active management in the running of the estate as is seen by a lease dated 1602.[46] In the Brereton settlement the document gives the division of the farm as between the parents and the son and daughter-in-law.

Pestilence.

One of the most momentous events of the later middle ages was the

[44] Brit. Lib. Add. Ch. 53548.
[45] CRO. DBW./L/20/5
[46] Brit. Lib. Add. Ch. 53550.

visitation of the plague: it arrived in western Europe in the form of the Black Death in 1347 and devastated the population with unremitting ferocity, travelling almost at the speed of the proverbial galloping horse, affecting all classes of society and all types of community. Its main impact was felt in England during 1349, but it lingered on as an endemic problem for a period of about three hundred and fifty years flaring, periodically into epidemic proportions, inclined to affect urban rather than rural communities.

Various estimates have been made concerning the death toll during the initial outbreak of 1349; these vary between a minimum of 20-25% of the population to a maximum of 33-50%. Both may be correct, as the transmission of the disease was more widespread in congested urban areas than it was in the more sparsely populated countryside. One of the difficulties in making an estimation is the lack of effective records or statistics. At the best we can tell from most contemporary records only who survived rather than who succumbed. The best records of the time were kept by the church, and new appointments to livings had to be made when an incumbent died. As the clergy were more likely to be in contact with those in extremis due to infection from the plague, they were more exposed to risk and the resultant perceived level of their deaths might be significantly higher than average. It has been estimated that up to 47.6% of beneficed clergy in the diocese of Bath and Wells died of the Black Death.[47]

So what of Cheshire, what was the impact of the plague here; is there any evidence as to how Alsager might have been affected? In general terms some idea of its impact can be obtained from Ziegler, pages 150-155. He tells us that John le Strange of Whitchurch died on 20th August 1349 leaving an estate and three sons. By the time his Inquisition was held on the 30th August his eldest son was already dead; before his Inquisition could be held the second son had died, and the third inherited a shattered estate. The value of his mills had declined by half because there were none left to grind; an area of his land formerly worth sixty shillings was now worth nothing because the domestic servants and labourers were dead. He tells us that in Cheshire the abbot of St Werburgh's, Chester, the prioress of St Mary's, Chester, and the prior of Norton, all died within a few weeks of each other. Courts couldn't be held, the bridge of Dee remained in disrepair, and there was much evidence of economic decay.

More locally, it seems that Thomas de Praers of Barthomley died on the 26th September 1349 and at his Inquisition held on the 30th September it was said by the jury that;-

> *"...he died seised as of right of .... one carucate of land which was worth 40s. and is now worth 13s.; also, two acres of meadow worth 2s. per ann.*

[47] Philip Ziegler *"The Black Death"* Alan Sutton Publishing 1991 [Ziegler] p.99.

also, from rents of tenants who used to pay £16 per ann., but now only 100s. per ann; also two parts of a water-mill formerly rented at 53s.4d., and now only at 13s.4d. which tenants are dead; also in the manor of Crewe ....two carucates of land formerly worth £4 per ann., now only 26s.8d.; also three acres of meadow valued at 3s. per ann., a water mill formerly worth 40s. per ann., now only 10s., pasture in three places formerly worth 40s. now worth 13s.4d.[48]

The table of the Rectors of Barthomley, reproduced in *'Barthomley, The story of an estate village,'* edited by Robert Speake, indicates that William de Praers continued as rector from 1315 to 1354: he appears to have survived the catastrophe, so also do the incumbents at Acton, Astbury, Haslington, Sandbach and Wybunbury. At Audley, Audlem, Lawton and Middlewich, by contrast, a new incumbent was installed in 1349 *"because of the death of the last rector or vicar".*[49]

At Lawton there was an important custom post where goods entering and leaving the county were charged tolls and other dues; this was farmed, or let, on an annual basis; in 1319 it was let to Adam de Lauton, William de Alsach and Thomas de Crosslegh by the earl for 5 marks (£3-6-8), the same rent that Adam de Lauton paid in 1303 and in 1320. Ziegler tells us that its value fell by half in 1349.

In the published Chamberlain's Accounts for the year 1350-51 there are two interesting entries;[50] the first, under the heading, *"Sheriff's Account, Pleas and Perquisites Before the Justices"*;-

> *"2s. for **Roger le Bolt**, because he did not make his appearance before the justice in his eyre, held in the 23rd year, for his **tenements in Alsacher**, as appears in the same eyre, and in the roll of the debts of moneys remaining to be levied after the sheriff's account for the 23rd and 24th years."*

The second appears under the entry for Drakelowe and is titled, *"Decay through the Pestilence."* This lists the names of 57 persons dead of the plague where rents are not paid because new tenants have not come forward to take up the holdings. One name in particular included in the list is relevant to Alsager, that is the name of Richarde le Kinge, the name of the person granted rights of turbary in Alsager in 1316. He was also involved in a suit of dower of Bertred, widow of Randle de Alsacher, in 1299. We may be dealing with more than one Richard le Kinge, but at least it is possible that the name refers to an individual holding land both in Alsager and Drakelowe who definitely died of the Black Death.

There is a gap in the record of land transactions in Alsager between 1330 and 1356. Some identifiable individuals cross this gap and clearly survived

---

[48] James Hall. *A History of the Town and Parish of Nantwich.* 1883. Reprinted 1970. p.26.
[49] Ormerod. *A History of Cheshire;* Vol III.
[50] Chamb. pp. 175 and 196.

the plague, two such were John, son of Nicholas de Alsager, and his brother Benedict. A second brother William is not recorded after 1329, nor is there mention of William, lord of Alsager, after 1342, when there is an oblique reference to him, but this does not prove him to be alive at that date. There is no doubt from the surviving documentary evidence that the Alsager family appears far less complex and slimmer after 1350 than it does before. Nor after this date is there any reference to anyone bearing the title 'lord of Alsager'.

The evidence is inconclusive but it is inconceivable that Alsager could have fared significantly differently from its neighbours in this crisis, and, even if by some chance, the plague did pass the township by its effects both social and economic must have been felt for many years to come.

Taxation.

Few medieval records remain regarding early taxation in Cheshire. This was a complex hybrid system, neither truly national nor truly palatinate. The best introduction to the subject is contained in P.H.W.Booth's book, *'The financial administration of the lordship and county of Chester 1272-1377'.*[51] Mr. Booth explains how the taxation system of Cheshire evolved separately from that of the kingdom as a whole. Here it is sufficient to note that early records are lost but between 1292 and 1346 there is no evidence of national taxes being imposed on the County, other than on the clergy. Cheshire differed from most of England where lay subsidies, in the form of Poll-Tax, left behind invaluable documentary evidence giving detailed accounts of population and families at a number of different points in the 14c. In sixteen financial years between 1346 and 1376 levies were charged upon Cheshire ranging from £500 to £833. These levies, or charges, became known as a 'Mise', taken from the Latin for payment, or expense, but in this case meaning more 'an imposition'. The earliest surviving assessment list for the mise[52] is dated 1406 and resulted from the imposition of a fine on the County of 3,000 marks for a pardon following the rebellion of Henry Percy, Hotspur, in 1403, which resulted in the battle of Shrewsbury. The County assessment was broken down into hundreds, in respect of each of which a list of townships was produced and Collectors allocated, the assessment for each township being given along with the proportion of that amount for which the lord is responsible. This list of 1406 is considered by Mr. Booth to represent a much older assessment which had become fossilised and which may date back to

[51] Chetham Society 1981; Vol. XXVIII.-Third Series.
[52] John Rylands Library, Manchester. Ref. Tatton 345.

before the date of the Black Death of 1349. If this is the case the disparity in the township assessments reflects their relative economic positions at a date much earlier than the date ascribed to the list.

The list for Nantwich Hundred reads as follows, so far as Alsager and its neighbours are concerned;-

Wich Malbank,	*Collectors at,*	*John de Bromley, John de Kyngesley, John son of John de Wetenhale, John Pygot the younger, John de Wynynton, John de Rope,*
From Leghton, the lord a third,	*xxij.s.*	*the whole paid.*
From Chirchcopenhale, the lord a third,	*xxij.s.viij.d.*	*the whole paid.*
From Munkescopenhale, the lord a third,	*xxij.s.viij.d.*	*paid therefore xv.s.j.d.ob. likewise vij.s.vj.d.ob.[53]*
From Haselyngton, the lord a third,	*lxvj.s.viij.d.*	*the whole paid*
From Hassale, the lord a third,	*xxij.s.viij.d.*	*the whole paid.*
From Betchton, the lord a quarter,	*lxvj.s.viij.d.*	*the whole paid.*
*From **Alsager**, the lord a quarter,*	*xxxiij.s.iiij.d.*	*the whole paid.*
From Bertumlegh, the lord a third,	*lxvj.s.viij.d.*	*the whole paid.*
From Crue, the lord a third,	*xliiij.s.vj.d.*	*the whole paid*
From Weston, the lord a quarter,	*xliiij.s.vj.d.*	*paid therefore xl.s.j.d. and iiij.s.v.d. which is to be paid to the above*

How the lord was identified in the case of Alsager, and whether the amount due from him was collected from more than one person, we are not told. The record as it remains only informs us as to how Alsager compared with its neighbours in economic ranking.

We know from Ormerod that John son of Richard de Alsacher was the first nominated commissioner in Nantwich hundred for the collection of a subsidy of 3000 marks, granted to Henry, prince of Wales, as earl of Chester, in 1403.

---

[53] seven shillings and sixpence ha'penny; or today, thirty-seven and a half pence.

Chapter 3

Warfare and Military Service

The evidence as to military service undertaken by the men of Alsager is scant, but if they were as zealous in undertaking their military obligations as they seem to have been in undertaking those of a legal and civil nature, it may be supposed that most survived to an old age, to die in their beds.

It has already been demonstrated that the men of Cheshire were quick to respond to calls for help to oppose the Norwegian invasion of 1066, and prior to that they had been involved with Earl Harold, later king Harold, in his conquest of North Wales. Independent companies of Cheshire archers accompanied Edward III and the Black Prince on their military expeditions to France during the hundred years war. The Black Prince, also earl of Chester, maintained his horse stud at his manor of Macclesfield; and by the end of the fourteenth century Cheshire companies provided an almost impenetrable personal guard to Richard II. As seen above, the county played an active part, though perhaps an unwitting one, in Hotspur's rebellion of 1403, and suffered severe financial penalties as a result of this transgression.[1]

To find evidence of Alsager involvement in military service it is necessary to go back to the reign of Edward II, and to the year 1322. Here we meet another Randle de Alisachre, his name appears as a witness in a deed dated 2nd May 1322,[2] and in proceedings in the king's court inquiring into the activities of a band of freebooters marauding in Lancashire in that year. At that time England was undergoing one of its periods of unrest, akin to civil war.

Thomas, earl of Lancaster, cousin of the king, uncle of the queen and of three kings of France also, and perhaps the wealthiest man in England, was highly controversial. He was implicated in the murder of Edward's favourite, Piers Gaveston, and had declined to accompany Edward on the Scottish campaign that culminated in Bannockburn. He again emerged in opposition to the king in 1321, sought the aid of the Scots, and was brought to battle and

[1] Details of the military service of the men of Cheshire can be found in Dr. Philip Morgan's book, *War and society in Medieval Cheshire;* Chetham Society, Vol.34; 3rd series. 1987
[2] Brit. Lib. Add. Ch. 53532

defeated at Boroughbridge in Yorkshire on 16th March 1322. Six days later he was executed for treason. It is in these events, of March and April, that Randle de Alisachre appears. The king's army at Coventry included a contingent of Cheshire men under the command of Oliver de Ingham. On the 3rd of March Ingham was appointed to take into the king's hands all the castles, lands and goods, that Lancaster had in Lancashire, and he set out to do this with his Cheshire contingent. Dr. Tupling describes clearly what then happened;-[3]

> "..... He reached Runcorn in time to seize all the available boats and prevent the force collected by Richard del Doustes (Lancaster's men) on the other side of the river from crossing .... The Cheshire men passed into Lancashire on the 15th and for five days ranged the hundred of Salford from Flixton and Stretford to Middleton and Bury. Their activities were not confined to rounding up rebels ...... The widow of Adam de Prestwich complained that while she was at Chester under the protection of the king her manors of Prestwich and Alkrington were so depleted that she had nothing wherewith to maintain her estate; and it was alleged by the jury of Salford and West Derby that horses and other livestock to the value of two thousand marks were taken from men who had never been adherents of the earl of Lancaster."

It was later presented in the king's court, held at Wigan, in October 1323, that six knights accompanied by an armed force had;-

> "... on horse and foot come armed into that County and into the towns of Mamcestre, Chetham, Prestwych, Pilkyngton, Radeclif, Totington, Bury, Middleton, Harewode, Salforde, Wethington, Heton Norreys, Rediche, Pennilton, Pennilbury, Barton, Stretford, Flixton, Cherlton and Ormestom and with force and arms took from certain men (who had never been adherents of Thomas earl of Lancaster or any of the lord king's enemies . . . .) mares, colts and fillies, oxen and cows, sheep, pigs and goats, to the value of two thousand marks . . ."

The writ sets out the names of 96 Cheshire men, including those of Randle de Alsager, Robert and William de Praers and Robert de Bulkeley junior, together with a further list of 30 names of men of Lancashire. Of those named, several escaped punishment on the grounds that they had acted under the king's orders, in a writ issued by the king at Newcastle under Lyme on the 6th November 1323. Randle's name was not included, but he may have been under the protection of someone who could shield him. It is interesting to speculate, whether any of the livestock seized in Lancashire in the king's name was pastured on Alsager heath by the time Randle witnessed the charter of the 2nd of May 1322.

Evidence of some military activity can be found from the account of equipment kept in homes at this time. We saw that in 1374, John de Alsager

---

[3] G.H. Tupling; *South Lancashire in the reign of Edward II.;* Chetham Soc. 1949. Vol.I 3rd Ser.

the younger, wearing a hauberk (sleeveless coat of mail) and a jack (padded coat worn under chain mail); and other men in armour, attacked with a sword, Roger de Pulton and his brother at Haslington. The items mentioned were not items of military equipment drawn from some depot in time of mobilisation for war, they were John's personal possessions, in constant use, and probably regarded by him as necessities of life. Early wills and inventories also give information regarding the possession of military equipment in the home. For example, in 1595 Randle Brereton, yeoman, the tenant of Lane End Farm bequeathed his *"Corselet of Armour"*, to his son John; and in 1631, Thomas Hildich, yeoman of Alsager, left to his eldest son Thomas, *"Armor and harness for warre"*. This may have been the *"costlett and a halberd"*, value £1, referred to in his inventory. In his turn John Brereton of Lane End, in 1636, left *"my Armour or Corslett and pyke thereto belonging"*, to his son Randall. His inventory refers to a corslett and pike valued at £2 and to a 'head peece', a halbeard and a black bill valued at 6s.8d. The inventory of Robert Alsager, dated 1647, includes a musket and furniture to it, £1-13-4, and a musket with a fire lock, 13s.4d.

Yet further information may be gleaned from the services required from the tenants of land. The lease to Elizabeth Galley, widow of Robert Galley, in respect of Galley's Tenement (Manor Farm), dated 1635,[4] from Viscount Cholmondeley, makes no mention of military service; but in a summary of tenancies, granted by the manor court of Wich Malbank, reference is made to another lease of this property, dated 6th October 1683. One of the covenants of this other lease relates to the tenant providing a footman, or the sum of £1 in lieu thereof. On the 6th June 1663 William, Lord Brereton, granted a new lease[5] to Ralph Brereton and his sons, John and William, and to John's wife Mary, of Brereton's Tenement; amongst other things the tenants undertook to provide an able bodied man, suitably furnished, in time of war.

In addition to these family and property documents, the names of Robert Alsager and Randle Poole, of Alsager, appear in the list of those required to provide troops for land defence in 1578.[6]

> *"Septimo October   A booke Conteyninge the Numbre and Names of All the Knights Esquires and Gentlemen with Freeholders Anno Eliz R. XX. within The Countie of Chester, together with Their Horses, Armor and other Furnyture.*
>
> *Namtwiche Hundered.*
>
> *Robt' Awder de Awg'r* }   *Eich one of these particularly*
> *Ranu' Poole of the same* }   *to furnish a plate cote.*

---

[4] CRO. DCH/J/6
[5] CRO. DBW/L/20/2.
[6] Record Society of Lancashire and Cheshire, Vol. 43, 1901.

The Civil Wars

During the civil wars of the seventeenth century, between the King and Parliament, the township found itself in an invidious position. Lord Brereton, of Brereton Hall, Brereton, was a royalist commander of Cheshire levies, and also landlord of a number of farms in Alsager; Lane End, occupied by the Breretons; The Bank or Bank House, occupied by the Hilditch family; Hole House and Heath House, also held by members of the Hilditch family; Brook House, tenanted by Richard Alsager, and at least one further farm, occupied by Thomas Sidway and his family, Lord Brereton's bailiff. Brereton's cousin, Sir William Brereton, M.P., from Cheadle, was the commander of Parliament's forces in Cheshire and the surrounding areas of Shropshire and Staffordshire, and proved to be a successful field commander. He was much involved with the sieges of both Nantwich and Chester, ensuring that the county did not provide free passage to royalist forces. There is some suggestion, as shown below, that Lord Brereton's tenants were more disadvantaged than the inhabitants at large by the Parliamentary forces.

The Barthomley incident,[7] which took place on the 23rd of December 1643, must have had considerable impact on Alsager. The accounts set out in 'Barthomley' indicate that the royalist skirmishers, who were responsible for attacking the church and the deaths that followed, subsequently moved on to Haslington, Sandbach and adjacent places. They engaged and routed a Parliamentary force, under the command of Sir William Brereton, at Middlewich on the 26th December. It is hardly likely that Alsager escaped attention from the pillaging and looting and the search for supplies that accompanied this incident.

In May 1644 a royalist force under the command of prince Rupert moved from Shropshire, through Cheshire, into Lancashire and then Yorkshire, where it ultimately formed part of the royalist army defeated at Marston Moor. On Monday, the 20th May, prince Rupert spent the night at Market Drayton and the following night he slept at Betley;[8] his forces, moving northwards by several routes, must have passed very close to, if not through, Alsager.

After the battle of Marston Moor the Parliamentary forces, in effective command of the county, had to remain here in some strength, to prevent the King from relieving the siege of Chester and reopening the city as a gateway to bring men and munitions into the north. Sir William Brereton was under very great pressure both with regard to men and to money. His letter books[9]

---

[7] Fully recounted in *Barthomley;* pp.133-139.
[8] *Yorkshire Archaeological Journal,* Vol. 59, 1987. pp.95-101
[9] R.N.Dore, *The Letter Books of Sir William Brereton;* The Record Society of Lancashire and Cheshire. Vols. 123 &128.

show that he could not effectively feed the troops under his command, nor could he pay them. In order to carry out his orders he had to make use of significant numbers of Scottish horse and foot and Yorkshire horse; neither of which treated the country in which they were billeted with much respect, particularly when uncertain of their rations and pay. Although the letter books make no reference to Alsager they do indicate that, from time to time, large bodies of men were billeted in close proximity; and indicate further what happened locally when such events occurred. In March 1645 General Lesley was in the area, in command of a force of four regiments of Scottish cavalry and about 2,000 foot. On the 21st of March, Brereton wrote to Lesley, from his headquarters at Middlewich, ordering him to follow in pursuit of the enemy.

> *"Middlewich. Resolved and is the opinion of all the officers at a Council of War that it is the best and most advantageous course to march towards Draighton [Market Drayton] where the enemy quartered yesterday night . . . . Which, if it be thought fit by the Lt.. Gen. of the Scottish army, then we conceive* **Sanbath [Sandbach] and Beetchson [Betchton]** *will be the best quarters for their foot or, if they will march four miles further, then to Betley and Wrinehill . . . ."*

On the 28th March, Lesley wrote to Brereton from Whitchurch;

> *"Ld. Leven has ordered me to return to Yorks. . . . . and intend to lodge our foot at* **Weston and Haslington and the places adjoining** *and our horse at Congleton and rest on Sunday [30th March]. . . ."*

On the 27th March, in a letter written from Nantwich, addressed to William Ashurst, the Parliamentary commander in Lancashire, Brereton intimates that he has recently received 1000 Yorkshire horse, who are now at Newcastle under Lyme. These forces appear to have been difficult to handle. At Wybunbury on the 11th April the Yorkshire Quartermasters issued a warrant to the constables of Stapeley;-

> *"These are to will and command you to bring this day, 11 April, to our quarters at Widdingbury 24 measures of oats and peas, one veal, one mutton and four hens, for the maintenance of Capts. Caunaday and Sharpe. Hereof you are not to fail as you will answer the contrary at your peril. Tho. Rawlinge, John Glendinge."*

And from the Deputy Lieutenants and Gentlemen of Nantwich to Brereton, on the 12th April 1645;-

> *".... The whole townsmen of Wibbenbury are fled from their houses. So that you must expect no money nor provisions from this part of the county while these robbers are suffered to infest them. ..."*

From Richard Smith, the minister at Wybunbury, to Thomas Croxton, Governor of Nantwich, 14th April 1645;-

> *"... Some, such as those that are quartered at my house, carry themselves well, but others are ruder as information will be given. This day my wife and servant boy coming to the market with corn to sell, met two soldiers*

who have robbed her, forced money from her, would have taken a colt unshod that had some corn upon him and spanned their pistols threatening to shoot her the boy and the horses .... What their names are I know not but being told of these things and hearing of outrages committed by robbing and beating in other places, I thought good to acquaint you .... Margaret Beecher said that the Yorks. commanders did upon Saturday last send their warrants to the township of Blackenhall to bring in 14 measures of oats and barley. And the town sent them in 14 measures; notwithstanding the day following they sent for 30s., otherwise this day they do threaten to plunder the same town of all their cattle; ..."

With such reports made concerning troops quartered on the countryside, and with an army commander powerless to make alternative arrangements for the provisioning of his men, it is most unlikely that the people of Alsager escaped attention from one, or both sides, in the conflict. It is possible that during this period the produce of Lord Brereton's farms in Alsager was used to help to feed an army, living off the country, opposing the cause that he espoused.

Although no direct evidence exists to support this supposition, the wills and inventories of Lord Brereton's Alsager tenants make interesting reading. In at least one case it can be demonstrated that tenants of a Brereton farm had horses in their inventories before the conflict started in 1642 but in later inventories, relating to the same families, made during the course of the war, there is no reference to any horses. In April 1636 John Brereton of Lane End had 16 head of cattle, a mare and a nag, produce to the value of £34-6-0 and a woman's riding saddle. His widow Elizabeth's inventory was taken in October 1644, by which time there is no mention of horses but the saddle remains, cattle are reduced to 12 but there are now also 6 sheep and the value of the produce is £22-10-0. It might be expected also that the farm would have been better stocked in October than in April. The evidence to support the argument is slight but no one's wealth appears to have increased as a result of the war.

The case of Thomas Sidway, Lord Brereton's bailiff in Alsager, is rather special and also better documented. He was fined for apparently doing no more than acting as Lord Brereton's servant. A collection of papers relating to his case survives amongst the State Papers in the Public Record Office.[10] These give an account of Thomas's trials and tribulations, in the aftermath of the First Civil War. It appears that Thomas had to travel to London to plead his case and to answer the charges against him before the Commissioners, as it is on record he took the National Covenant in March 1645 when William Barton, minister of John Zacharies in London, certified that;-

[10] Refs. SP. 25/177. fols. 805, 808, 809, 813.

> *"Thomas Sidway of Alsigeir in the County of Chester Husbandman did
> freely and fuly take the Nationall Covenant and subscribe to same upon the
> Fourth day of March 1645".*

He was charged, on the 6th March, that he had assisted Lord Brereton in
raising forces against the Parliament; it was noted that he had taken the
National Covenant two years previously and again two days earlier, also that
he had a holding lying in Alsager, having a clear yearly value, before the war,
of £20 per year over and above the rent he paid. For this a fine of £30 was
levied against him, although the value of the holding was said to have fallen
to £15, on account of the war. Additionally he had a second holding in
Alsager, formerly worth £15 above its rent, now only £10, for which a fine
of £22. 10s. was levied. His personal estate was stated to be worth £160, in
respect of which he compounded a sum of £80. He paid his compounding
charge by borrowing, it being stated;

> *"Which the petitioner redeemed with 80.li. and was forced to borrow 60.li.
> to make up the said 80.li. of one John Hollyday of Congleton in the said
> county of Chester that so he might be inabled to maintain his aged wife and
> 8 children."*

The papers indicate that the matter was concluded by the 23rd September
1645.

The Forty-Five.

There is no tradition of bands of sturdy highlanders marching across Bank
Corner, but the passage of the Young Pretender's army through South
Cheshire and North Staffordshire, together with the concentration of
government troops in other parts of Staffordshire and Cheshire,[11] must have
had its effect on the Alsager community.

In the closing weeks of 1745, the rebel army of Charles Edward Stuart
moved from Lancashire into Cheshire, reaching Macclesfield on December
1st, where its numbers are estimated as variously between 4,000 and 8,000.
The road to London ran through Staffordshire, where government forces,
numbering about 8,000, plus local irregulars raised for the event, had been
concentrating, under the command of the duke of Cumberland, since 16th
November. It was not certain that the Pretender's goal was London when he
reached Macclesfield; it could have been Wales, via Cheshire, north
Staffordshire and north Shropshire; or London via Newcastle, Stafford,
Warwick and Oxford: hoping for a build up of recruits on the way. On the
2nd of December, the government forces formed a screen from Newcastle
under Lyme, where there were three battalions of infantry, two regiments of

---

[11] *"The Staffordshire Campaign of 1745"*; Trans. North Staffs. Field Club. Vol LX 1925-26.

dragoons and a squadron of light horse; through Stone, three battalions of infantry, four troops of dragoons, a squadron of light horse and the artillery; to Stafford, three battalions; Rugeley, one battalion; Gt. Heywood an auxiliary regiment; and Lichfield where there was a further battalion and a regiment of dragoons. In addition to these forces, Lord Gower's auxiliary Staffordshire Regiment and a regular battalion were at Chester. A protective screen of light cavalry was thrown out in front of these forces, with the duke of Kingston having patrols, and possibly, as much as a squadron of light horse at Congleton.

On Monday 2nd December, Lord George Murray led a rebel cavalry force to Congleton, whilst the main force rested at Macclesfield. Kingston's Light Horse withdrew before Murray's force, which advanced as far as Talke where they captured Weir, a government spy, and a number of others, having supper at the 'Red Lion'. Early the following day Murray withdrew and passed over the Cloud to Leek and Ashbourne. The movement of the Prince's main force, disguised by Murray's feint along the expected road to London or to Wales, was to Leek on the 3rd, which was reached in the evening. Following a rest until midnight they then made a forced march to Derby, a distance of 28 miles, which was reached on December 4th. Cumberland then concentrated his forces at Stone, and the subsequent events can be read in the *Trans. North Staffs. Field Club. Vol. LX.*

The threat of a large body of marauding foreign troops in the area caused perturbation to local communities. A good example of this is reflected in papers found in the County Record Office at Stafford,[12] these consist of copy correspondence written by John Craddock, of Betley, in the closing days of 1745. The Craddocks were a well known local family with commercial interests in the Talke, Audley, and Betley areas. John Craddock, the author of the letters, was a lawyer and lived at Betley Court; he ought to be able to present a balanced point of view.[13] From the letters, and notes, it appears that a Mr. Powis, with property at Moreton, Wheelock and Hill Chorlton, removed plate and other valuables from Moreton in advance of the Highlander's approach, and these were carried to Betley by waggon and placed in Mr. Craddock's barn. Craddock, who thought he was sheltering a load of cheese, was upset when the true nature of the waggon's cargo was established. His letter, explaining his subsequent actions, well illustrates the fear and concern in the local community at the events of the time. These fears would be present in Alsager as elsewhere.

[12] Ref. SRO. D.(W)1788. P.61. B.22

[13] For a history of the Craddock family see *"Betley, a Village of Contrasts";* Ed. Robert Speake, 1980. Chap. 7.

"Sir,

It is strange that your neighbour Nathan should forward a report . . . . that I denied Mrs Powis a nights lodging when the Rebels were at Congleton . . . . when the Rebels were near Congleton she came hither about 3 or 4 in the even, I met her at the Coach . . . . about ten a clock as I was going to bed I spoke to one of my servants to let hers lie in their beds . . . . he replyed they must sit up with Mr. Powis's Waggon which was in my barn, I asked Mr. Powis's Waggoner what was in it, he said Cheese, which I apprehended was going to Chorlton Hill, after which one of my servants told me there was plate and other goods of value in it, upon which I desired the Waggoner to take care of the goods himself . . . . About eleven a clock that night that part of our army which lay at Newcastle beat to Arms & soon after retreated to Stone; expecting the enemy, but they having intelligence that we were much superior in numbers & strength diverted their march towards Leek otherwise part must have come through this town. Was this a time to take care of other men's goods? Mrs. Powis did stay that night & till the next Even, (before which time the Waggon was removed) and then she left in great displeasure. I hid the most valuable things I had within the Compass of my own buildings, & Mr. Powis had many more Conveniencys of doing so in his at Moreton, Chorlton Hill or with his tenants at Wheelock, therefore I hope I may (without offence) say it was not using me in a friendly maner to lodge things of such Value in my barn without so much as asking my Consent; I think that was the most dangerous place they cou'd have been put into, it stands near the road, any body might see the waggon go in; Charles Corn that was then with the rebels lived in this town but a few years since, one Wilcockson (a papist & an old tenant of mine) who I have lately displeased by securing my rent, hath oft told a friend of mine that the Leveller was coming (by which I apprehended he threatened me) I expected a battle about Newcastle or Stone, if the rebels had called on Mr. Powis for his plate etc. & presented a pistol to his head, I cannot believe but he would have told them where it was & mine must have gone with it: And I am afraid as the goods of Mr. Powis were in the possession of me & my servant, that I had been lyable to an Action of trover . . . .

> *I am Sr. your friend and humble Servant*

Betley 9 Jan 1745."

It seems clear, that whatever the effect of warfare might have been on combatants during the latter part of the Middle Ages, and into modern times, and no doubt the effects could be very drastic, they were equally as drastic on the civil population if they were sufficiently unfortunate to get caught up in the consequences of military activity. This is clearly demonstrated by what happened to the people of Salford hundred in Lancashire during 1322, to those who suffered at the hands of marauding bands of soldiers from both sides during the civil wars, and those who feared they were in the path of the Highland army in 1745. Even when the fighting seemed to be over, and the danger passed, it was possible to be at risk from an overzealous administration, as poor Thomas Sidway found to his cost.

Chapter 4

Land Use and Occupation

An account has already been given of the Alsager entry in Domesday Book, and of the likely effect the Norman Conquest would have had on a township, such as Alsager, in the county of Cheshire. Once in control the Normans established a social hierarchy, based on the feudal system as developed on the Continent, contrasting with the relatively democratic Anglo-Saxon ways. The earl granted definite rights in the use of land in return for specific services, military and agricultural. As demonstrated above, these terms were passed down the feudal chain to the occupier of the smallest lordship, who then had to ensure he could make a profit out of his tenants on the land.

What has to be appreciated is that the population of the county in 1086 was very sparse by comparison with the later middle ages and early modern period. Domesday Book contains some information on population figures, and these are the best we have to go on, but it was not a census, and the total population and its distribution has taxed the skills of scholars over the years. The Victoria County History of Cheshire states; *"Of the various estimates of the Domesday population of Cheshire no two entirely agree;"* Professor Tait, in his book, 'The Domesday Survey of Cheshire',[1] assesses the recorded population of the county as 1,825, but then goes on to say, *"As at the best only heads of houses were recorded, we need hardly say that the total population, though it must have been scanty indeed judged by modern standards, was much larger than the figure given above"*. Using Tait's figure, Husain[2] gives the total recorded population for the Middlewich hundred as being 149; he adds, however, that this figure requires multiplying by 4 or 5 times to give any realistic total. He considers that the average density might have been around 10 persons per square mile.

Following the conquest, recovery, progress and expansion was at best slow. Ploughed land which had reverted to the wild needed to be reclaimed as the development of Alsager began. New assarts, or clearings from forest

---

[1] Chetham Society 1920.
[2] B.M.C. Husain, *Cheshire under the Norman Earls;* Chesh.Comm. Council 1973. pp.7, 13, 31.

and waste, needed the earl's approval and a licence fee had to be paid. Forest law was maintained by 'Eyres of the forest', that is, circuit courts, from the Latin 'iter' a journey.[3] They imposed heavy fines for breaches of the special forest law which applied in the three designated forest areas of Cheshire, Wirrall, Mara and Mondrum, now Delamere, and Macclesfield. It will be recalled that Randle, lord of Alsager, was brought before the Macclesfield Forest Eyre, in 1286, for having been found with hounds in the forest area.

It is most likely that the first land to be brought into arable cultivation in Alsager was on the southern side of the township, on the rising ground, south of the present railway line, towards Audley and Mere Lake, where some of the better agricultural land lies. The sunken road, leading from Audley Road to Mere Lake, is undoubtedly one of the oldest access routes leading over the moraine up to Talke. It must have joined, or come very close, to the Roman road from Chesterton to Middlewich, and have been convenient for the transportation of farm produce demanded by the earl for rent or render, and for the trade of any surpluses.

The settlements of Ash Bank, Town house, Town End (now the Manor House Hotel), Bank and Oak farms, are all located within a quarter of a mile of each other on a well drained piece of ground, slightly higher than the adjoining land. It is likely they constituted the original township settlement, grouped together as they are, they resemble the compact farmsteads of a traditional open field village with land in common cultivation. Crofts and meadows predominate in the field names here: Barn Meadow, Kiln Croft, Hob Croft, Barn Meadow (again), Over the Lane, Kiln Meadow, Moss Meadow, Well Meadow, Little Croft, Birches Croft, House Croft and two Barley Crofts;[4] all of which tend to suggest that these might have been the crofts and paddocks held in severalty, that is in the possession of an individual occupier, and occupied with the farmsteads, with the township's open fields lying beyond them. However, field names can change significantly over a short period of time, and must not be relied upon exclusively as a reliable guide to land use history; but these enclosures are generally rather small and lie in close proximity to very long established farms.

As the population increased marginal land was brought into cultivation, and because it made economic sense, and because the new land was cleared by the community as a whole, the community developed a co-operative farming practice with shared ploughs and an open 'town field'. The town field

---

[3] ibid. p.69.
[4] Tithe Award Alsager, ref CRO/EDT/12/1. refs. 375, 377, 378, 513, 515, 517, 548, 552, 553, 554, 558, 586 and 587.

was occupied in common. It was sub-divided into units of the same crop production, known as 'furlongs', or 'flats' or 'lunts,' in Cheshire: these in turn were subdivided into 'selions', 'strips', 'butts' or 'lands'. To add to the confusion, in this part of the world 'furlongs' were also referred to as 'fields'. This makes the interpretation of old field names even more difficult! In Cheshire the town field tended to be broken up with its furlongs scattered around the township, and examination of the Alsager Tithe Award and its accompanying plan will show a number of such enclosures, having names that can be associated with open field cultivation, in various places. Each strip was worked by individual tenants and ploughed into ridge and furrow, relicts of which can be seen today, as on Alsager Hall Farm, close to the perimeter fence of Radway Green Ordnance Factory, looking like patches of corduroy on the landscape. The farmer began ploughing in the centre of his allotted strip, up and then back, and so on, moving outwards to its limits. A mould board on the plough turned over the soil, each slice overlapping the previous one, and all were directed towards the centre of the strip. This formed the ridge and the furrows down either side acted as drainage channels. The width of strips varied, according to soil type and availability of land but was gauged roughly on the distance an ox team could plough without rest. In traditional open field districts this was ascertained to be about 16½ feet in width and 660 feet in length, but local variations do apply.[5] Where land was occupied in severalty, a similar system of cultivation was frequently adopted; with a large piece of land sub-divided into flats and ploughed into strips, but the width of the strips were usually narrower than detailed above, and frequently had to be shorter because of the restricted area of the land. Headlands at the ends of strips, where the ox-ploughs turned, became paths and narrow roadways leading into the fields.

Field names taken from the tithe award of 1840 suggest that Alsager may have had two open fields; one close to the farmsteads described above, probably known as the 'Town Field', which is likely to have been an 'infield'; that is one kept in more or less permanent cultivation, on good soil, which could be maintained by manuring and marling. The other would have been an 'outfield', that is land, part of which was cultivated until exhausted, and then left fallow to recover its fertility through natural regeneration. The evidence for this lies in the name 'Fannys Croft', or 'Fallings Croft' reference 350-363 in the tithe award. In 1840 this was still held in strips, or doles. In two medieval deeds of around 1280 and 1315[6] it is referred to as

[5] Andrew Hayes, *Archaeology of the British Isles.;* Batsford 1993. p. 147.
[6] PRO.C146 4929 and CRO.DCH.J6C.

"Falinchecroft". In correspondence Prof. Dodgson has confirmed that this name may well refer to land, newly broken by the plough, which had been left in a fallow condition for a long period.[7] Fallowing was an essential part of the 'open field' system, and the outfield may have been part of the waste, or heath, close enough to the town field to be ploughed and utilised when required. Adjacent enclosures with the names, 'brunts' and 'riddings', are likely to have been asserts from the waste made by way of burning or clearing. These may have formed part of the outfield, or they may have formed new individual holdings; the evidence is not clear.[8] It is likely that the ridge and furrow, noted on Alsager Hall Farm, was created in the medieval period on land held in severalty. A further area of ridge and furrow, visible until recently in the Day Green area, might have been a separate communal field for a small settlement there.

Areas of heath, covered in gorse, fern, and shrub, with poor quality soil, were left uncultivated as open pasture, with specific rights of grazing there. It is interesting to note that all the farms to the south of where the railway runs today had rakeways, tracks leading to common pasture, linking them to the heath land to the north. Between Alsager Hall Farm and Crewe Road, at the rear of the Plough Inn are two fields called, Big Rakes Field and Little Rakes Field, in the tithe award. Brookhouse Road, and the road leading to Home Farm, are other examples of probable grazing tracks leading onto the heath. Common meadow land was also left open, the meadows were frequently formed on wet land, alongside streams, and no doubt difficult to plough. At hay harvest the meadows were pegged out into strips or doles and each man took his allotted share[9] before they were opened to common grazing. In this way the peasant exercised his rights in common. Any animals found straying were rounded up and placed in the 'pinfold', to be released on payment of a fine. Alsager's pinfold was situated where the railway station now is, plot 594 on the tithe map. Tenants were also granted 'turbary rights', i.e. to cut peat for fuel on the mosses, which again could be divided into strips.[10] Evidence of cutting peat in Alsager is provided in a number of early deeds, such as those referred to on pages 23 and 24 above.

In 1215-16, under the terms of the Cheshire equivalent of Magna Carta, Earl Ranulph granted his barons, knights and freeholders, leave to assart

---

[7] The late Prof. John McN. Dodgson is the author of *The Place-Names Of Cheshire*.
[8] See T.A. refs. 392, 393, 500, 615, 619, 620; known as New Broomy Ridding, Far Broomy Ridding, Marl Ridding, First Brund, Big Brun and Little Brun respectively.
[9] Dorothy Sylvester, *"The Open Fields of Cheshire";* Transactions of the Historic Society of Lancashire and Cheshire; vol. 108. 1956. p.2.
[10] ibid p.4.

without payment, in response to their petitions. This resulted in the rapid removal of much woodland, to extend arable areas, in the thirteenth and early fourteenth centuries.[11] About this time there is evidence that tenants and occupiers were exchanging their allocated strips in the common fields, to build up consolidated holdings, which could then be enclosed, thus leading to the gradual demise of the open field system.

> PRO.C146.5252
>
> *"A grant by John de Alsachere to Robert de Bulkilegh and Felicia his wife of half of one land and a tenement within the garden of Robert and Felicia, together with piece of land and a tenement in le brodemeduwe, in exchange for a grant by Robert and Felicia to John for half a land and a tenement lying in broc croft.*
> *Given the Tuesday next after the feast of St. Mark the Evangelist 1322".*

Heath House, in Well Lane; Hole House (Later Home Farm); Brunds, in Lawton Road and Manor Farms, may well have been founded in this manner, becoming islands of croft, assart and enclosure, within the remnants of a common field system.

Woodland that remained uncleared, usually on the periphery of the township, was a valuable and carefully managed asset; as in the case of Alsager Sprink. Coppicing, or the regular periodic cutting back of young trees to the ground to stimulate side shoots, secured a ready supply of poles and staffs to be used in building, making and repair of implements, tools and weapons etc. Larger trees, interspersed in these areas of managed woodland, were allowed to grow into timber before being harvested. Tenants were granted rights, going back to Anglo-Saxon times, to take wood, usually from the waste or their own tenements, rather than from the coppices, to use for 'haybote', 'housebote', and 'ploughbote', that is the repair of fences, houses, and implements, and wood for fuel; despite attempts by feudal overlords to restrict them. The rights granted usually stipulated that timber taken must be used on the tenants' holding, to maintain the crude, timber framed, wattle and daub buildings in satisfactory repair. In a lease made some centuries later, in 1602, between Robert Alger the elder, yeoman, Margaret Alger widow, and Robert Alger the younger, on the one part; and Ralph Alger, tailor, of the other part, all being of Alsager; of a messuage or cottage with buildings and land, the following clause appears:-[12]

> *"as alsoe to have and to take in and upon the same premisses sufficiente and Conveyniente howsboote hedgeboote heyboote fyreboote ploweboote and Carteboote and all other necessarie estovers to be occupyed bestowed and spente*

---

[11] ibid. p. 11.
[12] Brit. Lib. Add.Ch. 53550

in and upon premisses or aboute the necessarie manurinance thereof and not otherwyse".

An intriguing feature of the Alsager landscape, dating from this period, is a moated site in a field called The Moat, T.A. ref. 545. This lies on the left hand side of the lane leading towards Mere Lake, on the lower slope, just after the lane leaves Audley Road. This is noted on the 1947 RAF aerial survey, which revealed the remains of the medieval moat with two appendages, which could have been fishponds. These findings were confirmed by a field survey in 1986.[13] The site has not been excavated or explored in any detail and without this we can do more than guess at its past form, use, and history. But it can be argued that this was the perfect site for the residence of a manorial lord, set apart from the other dwellings of the township, and dominating the scene with its imposing size, defences and position. Fields adjacent to 'The Moat' have irregular shapes, and names suggestive of early enclosure and severalty tenure; these are Near Corn Hay, Far Corn Hay, Cranberry Meadow, Big Heys and Heys Lane. A 'hay' is a piece of land enclosed by a hedge or fence. A less romantic interpretation of the evidence from this site might be that this was no more than a cattle compound, or a stack yard, ditched around as a barrier to stop livestock getting in or out, or to prevent rustling by coveting neighbours. Only further investigation and more detailed evidence will provide greater knowledge.

Notwithstanding the presence of the moat, most evidence from the 13c. and 14c. points to the family which appears to have controlled most of the land in the township, being centred on what is today Alsager Hall Farm. A grant of around 1250 conferring land, including a wood, to his son, names the patriarch Randle as 'lord of Alsager'. The boundary of the land in question follows the brook, from somewhere in the region of the mill, as far as Radway Green, it then follows the boundaries of Barthomley and Audley townships to meet the stream close to Audley Road, which it follows back to its starting point. Details of this deed are set out on page 21 above. Additionally a number of footpaths converge onto the site of Alsager Hall Farm.

The dynasty of the 'Alsager' family in lordship, appears to be, if only briefly, well established, provided it can be accepted that the adjunct 'de Alsager' became the surname Alsager. As seen above, the family also owned the mill, to which the inhabitants of Alsager were obliged to take their corn to be ground, and to pay 'multure' and 'toll-vat' as taxes to the lord for this service. A great vexation to the poor peasant but a valuable source of income to the lord and one which continued for a long time. We see in 1571, in a

---

[13] County Sites and Monuments Record Extract, Cheshire County Council 1997, Record No. 1108, J. Cooper.

marriage settlement, made between Robert Alsager of Alsager and Robert
Tenche of Newhall, in connection with the marriage of Raffe Alsager and
Margaret Tenche, that;-

> Brit. Lib. Add. Ch. 53548.
>
> *"And that the said Margaret duringe her naturall lieffe aforseid shalle have
> all her corne and malte grownden Tolle ffree at the milne of the said Robert
> aulsager in Aulsager ffrom tyme to tyme when and as often as she shall
> have any corne or malte to be grownden".*

It is not recorded how the Alsagers came to acquire their lordship,
although what is known is set out on pages 20-22 above. The usual system
of estate distribution is effectively described by Dorothy Sylvester in, *'A
History of Cheshire'*, published by Phillimore in 1980. Whatever way the
township had been acquired, by the time it came into the hands of the
'Alsager' family, it appears to have been a modest 'lordship;' and by that time
it seems safe to assume that it lay within the parish of Barthomley.

By the late 13c. the rise in population demanded urgent solutions to
preserve the fertility of land under cultivation, as it was used more intensively,
and to enrich the poorer, sandy, soils of the margins, which had been brought
into production as Alsager developed. For lack of winter fodder a large
proportion of stock had to be slaughtered each autumn, resulting in a serious
shortage of farmyard manure. Fallowing large tracts of land for a year, and
leaving them unproductive, was no longer appropriate because of increased
demand and the gradual lowering of the soil's productive capacity. The use
of marl as a fertiliser became widespread; containing clay and lime it added
body to the lighter soils making them more water retentive, improved the yield
of those deteriorated by poor farming practices, and increased the quality of
pasture when used as a top dressing. Marl was excavated, often to a great
depth, from pits which had a sloping side, by which wagons could enter and
be loaded, and a steep opposite side, like a quarry face, where digging
finished.[14] The first reference to a marl-pit in Alsager is made in a deed of
circa 1315, CRO.DCH.J6C., an incomplete and badly damaged document
which refers to *"The flat next to the marl-pit of Richard le Typper."* As time
passed marl-pits became a common feature of the Alsager landscape. The
tithe award makes frequent reference to 'marl-pit' field names, a few examples
being plan refs. 47, 49, 50, 109, 224, 406, and 630. In ref. 236 the pit lay
adjacent to Sandbach Road, opposite the Wilbraham Arms, and has been
landscaped in recent years.

The plague, or Black Death, of the mid 14c. devastated the country killing

---

[14] Geoffrey Scard, *Squire and Tenant, Rural Life in Cheshire 1760-1900;* Cheshire Community
Council Vol. 10. 1981, p.84.

an estimated 30%-40% of the population, and it is unlikely that Alsager was spared. The shortage of manpower and reduction in the population led to a decline in farming, trade, and profits. The tolls at Lawton were reduced to half their previous level. For the survivors the catastrophe had its benefits. They now held strong bargaining positions within the feudal system, because of the scarcity of their craft labour, and they began to assert their independence and increase their wealth. The manorial system began to wane;[15] the many vacant tenancies in the open fields could not be filled by customary tenants, that is, 'holding by the custom of the manor', and they were gradually replaced by enclosed severalty holdings, let for money rents. If the plague did not initiate it certainly hastened the decline of this community cultivation. Cattle raising had become increasingly valuable to Cheshire farmers over the years, because of the unsuitability of the cold damp climate for the cultivation of wheat and other cereal crops. Arable farming was largely confined to fodder growing and meeting the needs of the community; tillage declined in favour of pasture; dairy farming became the way to make a living.[16]

ALSAGER 1590 - 1759

From the available wills and probate inventories of Alsager's previous inhabitants there emerges a vivid picture of life-style, livelihood, and increasing prosperity, and sophistication as time progresses. The will dated 1590, of Rondull Hildyche, a *"husbandman"* or tenant farmer, began with his desire *"to be Burryed in the churche yourde of Bartomley"*. This was typical of all the wills of sixteenth and seventeenth century Alsager, which was still a satellite township of Barthomley parish with its mother church. For his position in the agricultural society of the day Rondull was quite comfortably off, enjoying such basic niceties as brass and pewter ware valued at £3 6s. 8d., and bedding and napery valued at £4. Listed first on his inventory, and without exception on those of his contemporaries in the farming community, so therefore we may assume of most importance, were his 5 oxen, valued at £12 10s. At this date the ox was still used as a draught animal. Horses were not as commonly owned for they required more grazing and had a more selective appetite. He was a mixed animal farmer, owning 8 cows, 6 twinters, (cattle two winters old) 5 stirks, (yearlings) 6 calves, 2 mares, 13 sheep and pigs. His cows were the most valuable of his livestock at £13 13s. 4d. in

[15] Sylvester, *"A History of Cheshire"*; pp. 56-7.
[16] Dorothy Sylvester, *The Open Fields of Cheshire"*; Historic Society of Lancs. and Ches., vol. 108; pp. 12, 15, 26, 31.

total. Corn, an all-encompassing word to include a variety of grains, was used to feed his animals as well as his household, and together with a quantity of hay was valued at £16. Bees at 5s., poultry at 4s. and *"whitte meatte and meatte on the Roofe"*, probably cheese and bacon stored in the loft, valued at only 13s. 4d., so probably for domestic consumption only, complete the rural scene. One can imagine the smells pervading the farmhouse in warm weather!

Rondull and his family evidently had lived above subsistence level for that year at least, for he was owed 3s. 4d. for a bushel of oats, 3s. for rye and 3s. for 3 pigs by Robert Alsager, a yeoman farmer. Since the Reformation the practice of usury, or lending money at interest, which had been condemned by the Roman Catholic Church, was fast becoming an acceptable business procedure. A farmer could rapidly increase his livestock by borrowing money, and in turn lend out money, from the profits made, to further increase his prosperity. Rondull was a debtor of £16 13s. 4d. and a creditor of £1 13s. 7d. Although some details on the inventory are illegible, missing values can be determined by comparisons with the inventories of his contemporaries, and his total wealth, excluding monies owed and owing, be ascertained at close to £80. This helps to put the values of his possessions in context.[17] Through usury and trade he had built a tolerable lifestyle for his family, and the custom of primogeniture, or the right of the eldest son to be heir to the real estate, a legacy of the Norman feudal system, ensured that Rondull Hildyche's holding stayed intact and in the family for future generations to build upon.

Rodger Barnett, who died in 1603, was also a husbandman, but not as wealthy as Rondull Hildyche; his assets amounted to £50 11s. 2d., 32% of which was his team of 6 oxen valued at £16. He had a very small number of livestock; 4 cows at £6 13s. 4d. and 1 horse, 1 stirk, 1 calf, 2 pigs, 2 sheep and 3 hens, altogether worth £4 4s. 3d. From his inventory there is a clear picture of the self-sufficiency of the age. He grew hemp and flax, and had yarn and wool in stock. Most clothing and bedding was home-made, obviously quite simple and coarse. Sacking and rough cloth for winnowing, the process of separating the chaff from the grain, were also produced.

There is a reference to malt, which is grain, probably barley, that has been steeped, germinated and dried for the purpose of brewing. This was an essential household activity when the purity of the drinking water could not be guaranteed. Any residue after the fermentation process was no doubt fed

⁷ CRO Wills Supra (WS.), 1590

to the animals.

Rodger appears to have been a bit of a carpenter as well. He had timber worth 13s. 4d., wheel timber at £4, and a dung cart body. Perhaps he had been assembling a new cart, or repairing an old one, before his death. It is difficult to reconcile his valuable ox-team with the apparently small amount of arable produce: corn upon the ground at 8s., hemp and flax upon the ground at 5s., corn and malt at 16s. Perhaps the farm was on heavier soils, or steeper slopes, than most, making it more difficult to plough. It might have included a marl pit, for Rodger owned two marl carts. More likely the oxen were also used to pull his carts, for he owned a wain, spelt *"weane"* after the local dialect, besides those already mentioned.[18] Was he the village haulage contractor?

The probate inventory of Rondull Brereton dated 1595 describes him as *'yeoman'*, i.e. a superior tenant farmer, and this status is reflected in his wealth and possessions. He was one of the Breretons who occupied Lane End Farm, formerly known as Brereton's Tenement, now the Holly Tree Hotel, under lease from William, Lord Brereton. Just over 40% of the value of his estate of £129 4s. 4d., which was undervalued by 10s at the time, through an error of calculation by the four appraisers, his peers, had been tied up in livestock. Even so, by our modern farming standards, numbers were remarkably small; 6 oxen, 17 cattle - 7 of which were cows; 23 sheep, 4 pigs and 1 mare. The inventory was taken in March, so he had kept them successfully over winter, and even had fodder to spare; hay worth £2 13s. 4d. in the barn, sown corn worth £4, and corn and malt worth £20. Not surprisingly stored in the house, as well as the barn, perhaps for safekeeping.

Rondull and his household enjoyed the creature comforts of good linen and bedding, worth £20, including feather beds and a quilt. Aspirations of gentility are evident; he had a gold ring, a dagger, and a suit of *"best"* clothes including a hat, jerkin, doublet, breeches and stockings. His *"corselet of armour"* may have been an heirloom relict from the feudal system when a tenant was required to give military service to his lord, although in 1663 when William, Lord Brereton, granted a new lease[19] to the Breretons, of Brereton's Tenement, the tenants undertook to provide an able bodied man, suitably furnished, in time of war.

Alongside the trappings of luxury are the reminders that it was a typical, self-contained, working farm of the period. There were wains, ploughs, yokes

---

[18] CRO. WS. 1603.

[19] CRO. DBW/L/20/2.

and *"other implements necessarie to husbandrie"*, yarn and tow, poultry and meat; also a *"heare uppon the kilne"* which was a haircloth, no doubt home-made, on a frame used for drying malt over a fire. The farmhouse itself was probably of quite modest proportions, but a desirable residence for the Alsager of the time. The parlour may have been a dining room cum bedroom, for it contained a table with forms, and bedstocks and a wheelbed. A wheelbed, or trucklebed, was a low bed which was stored out of the way under the main bed during the day, and wheeled out at night. The pattern of sleeping in parlours, as well as bed-chambers, continued through the seventeenth century, perhaps to accommodate children or domestic help. Rondull had his own private bedroom. There was also a buttery, a cool place away from the direct sun where ale and liquids were stored and served, (the word comes from *bott,* a cask;) a storage space above the buttery, containing timber to be fashioned into a chest; and a stable where the garner or 'great chest for corne' stood.[20]

From the 1630's onwards the use of oxen, as draught animals, was phased out, and after the inventory of Richard Merrill in 1669 no further reference to them is made. Until well into the eighteenth century cows become listed first of all their owner's assets. Each cow produced about two hundredweight of cheese a year, the mainstay of the farmer's livelihood. Store bullocks, veal, butter, and bacon, from pigs fed on the whey, were by-products of the business.[21] The extra income brought a rise in the standard of living, and with it, a desire for refinements of comfort and taste.

Thomas Hildiche a farmer who died in 1631 had achieved yeoman status. He lived at the "Hole" or Holehouse Farm. This was the most successful branch of the Hilditch family, (spelt variously at different times) who also occupied the 'Banke' and the 'Heath', possibly Bank House, and Heath House Farms, at this time.[22] A man of piety, *"willinge to settle that estate that god hath lent me,"* Thomas was blessed with a circumspect nature. He had obtained the lease of a farm in Hurleston for his second son, and bequeathed £60 to his youngest son. Thus, he was able to bring financial security, not just to his eldest son and heir. His estate was valued at £132 17s. 6d., miscalculated by the appraisers as £126 4s. 2d. 33% of this was tied up in livestock, while 5% was attributable to money and clothing.[23] The inventory

[20] CRO WS. 1595.

[21] J. Howard Hodgson, *Cheshire 1660 - 1780, Restoration to Industrial Revolution;* Cheshire Community Council 1978. p.71.

[22] *The Parish Registers of St. Bertoline Barthomley;* Vol. I, 1562 - 1788. Audley & District Family History Society 1998. (Barthomley '98)

[23] CRO. W S. 1631.

in 1657, of his son and heir, also Thomas Hildich, shows a substantial increase in the assets of his father's legacy, for the estate is now valued at £300 6s. 3d. The value and numbers of livestock have increased with more emphasis on cattle, and less on sheep; they constitute only 25% of Thomas junior's estate. Conversely, the value of ready cash and clothing has increased to almost 25% at £74 4s. 7d. The farmhouse is of solid proportions with a number of rooms. There is a parlour, a kitchen, the *"house"* (main living room), chambers above each of these, a children's chamber, a little parlour, and the cockloft.

Lodging within the house, at the time of his death in 1640, had been Thomas' cousin, Thomas Cartwright; *"Aboute three score yeares old and very sickly weake and infirme in body."* Of the total value of his inventory, of just over £40, only £5 was attributable to personal possessions; apparel at £3 10s. and bedding at £1 10s. The rest was money owed to him by nine named debtors. As the debility of ill-health and old-age encroached upon his life, Thomas had probably sold his assets, with the exception of one cow, which he hired out at a rent of 5s. per six months. With the cash from the proceeds he appears to have performed the same service as a modern bank, giving loans and making an income from the interest, thereby earning his keep. He left everything to Thomas Hildich, showing concern in an affidavit that a certain Thomas Watson and his wife *"should not have any part thereof."*[24]

Thomas Hildich junior, displaying the same thrifty nature as his father, had retained one of his spinning wheels, and had a quantity of linen cloth, woollen cloth and flax and hemp in store. These were of course implements of *'huswifrie,'* as was his cheese press. At least his wife could console herself with fine *"Burslem wares"* from the Potteries! A sadder reflection of this post civil wars period, and still unsettled time, is that his father's *"certaine Armor and harnes for warre,"* which included a halberd, an evil-looking spear and battle axe combined, has been replaced by two guns.[25] This was a Brereton farm, did the lease include a clause similar to that at Lane End, to supply a furnished man in time of war?

The civil wars particularly, between 1643 and 1645, had had other more far-reaching effects on the local countryside. Cattle and crops were seized to feed the armies, horses were taken for transportation and the cavalry, and often private houses were sequestrated for billets.

---

[24] CRO. WS. 1641
[25] CRO. WS. 1663

William, Lord Brereton, was an ardent Royalist. His tenant, Randull Hildich of the Banke, certainly appears to have had some of his property confiscated for the Parliamentary cause. In his inventory of 1645 there are carts, ploughs, harrows and horse gear, but no horses. His livestock amounts to three cows and one weaning calf only. Little wonder there is no mention of growing corn even though it was the month of May.[26]   In the 1644 inventory of Elizabeth Brereton, a tenant of Lord Brereton at Lane End Farm, a variety of carts are listed together with farming equipment requiring draught animals. She even had a side-saddle but, like Randull, no horse. Both farmers had only modest stocks of grain in house and barn. The estate that Elizabeth had inherited from John, her husband, in 1636 had been reduced to just over half its former value by 1644.[27]

Throughout the 17c. the use of brick for farms and cottages became increasingly popular as the rising standard of living demanded an upgrade of the local architecture. The medieval cruck ends were replaced by rectangular frames and the timber framework was often brick-infilled. Hearths and chimneys were added to outside walls of even the humblest of dwellings.[28] At first bricks were probably hand-made in Alsager, on sites where there were pockets of glacial clays, such as Kiln Croft, T.A. ref. 377, on the south side of Town End Farm (the Manor House Hotel); and Brick Croft, T.A. ref. 606, on the right towards Church Lawton just before the parish boundary. By the late 17c. and early 18c. innovative designs and embellishments appeared, e.g. the semi-detached pair of houses, built wholly of brick with tile roofs, adjoining the Yeoman public house and terrace in Audley Road. These made fine dwellings for a moderately prosperous merchant or craftsman.

Between 1662 and 1689, during the reign of King Charles II, the Hearth Tax was levied, to build up financial reserves depleted by wars. This was immensely unpopular, for his subjects saw it as yet another act by which the king relieved the common man of his hard-earned cash, to line his own pockets. However, to the local historian, records of the tax are a valuable source of information. From the Hearth Tax returns of 1664 we discover that Alsager had only 27 households with an estimated population of 120, that is about half the number of inhabitants of Barthomley at the same period. Alsager Hall and Cresswellshawe, formerly on the site of the Wilbraham Arms, were two of the seven largest farmhouses, all with four hearths. There were four exemptions from payment, probably paupers in receipt of poor

[26] CRO. WS. 1647
[27] CRO. WS. 1636 and 1647.
[28] Sylvester, *A History of Cheshire;* 1980;   p. 63

relief, or persons living in houses worth less than 20s. per year. Some degree of mystery surrounds the Hearth Tax returns; there are family names of people living in Alsager, recorded in the Barthomley parish registers, without any reference to the same names in the tax returns. This may be partly accounted for if some of the larger households contained the families of servants and workpeople.

Randle Lownds paid tax on just one hearth; his probate inventory of 1669 suggests he was craftily avoiding payment on a second. His living room had an iron grate with an array of accessories: *"one payr of Tonges, one payr of Pottracks, one payr of pott hookes, one payr of Golbarts (bars with hooks to hang the spits), two iron spitts, one hanging Brandard (trivet), one false Brandard, one payr of Bellowes, one Iron Bakestone, one bread Iron, one hacking knife, Three Brasse Pannes, Three Brasse Potts, One Iron Kettle."* He had converted his bakehouse, which was also liable to the Hearth Tax, to a workshop and storeroom. From the many planks and boards, some 'oken', some poplar, lying in and around the house, we can safely assume Randle was a carpenter. His collection of tools in the bakehouse corroborate the assumption. There were *"Foure Awgers, one hand saw, three chissells and Gouge (chisel with a concave blade), one spokeshave, one Wimble brace".* Outside he had plough timber, a cart body, and wheel timber, or spokes and *"fellies"* (the curved bits). Yet this household of a manual worker of modest means, his estate was valued at just over £43, also contains items which we would associate with the wealthier classes. His books, wooden butter print and *"Three Earthen Steans with verjuice in them"* (jars of crab apple vinegar), surprisingly suggest that he was also a man of education and some culinary refinement.[29]

The fortunes of the Alsager family had ebbed and flowed since the heady days of the 13c. and 14c. in lordship. When the nave of Barthomley Church was built in the 15c. prominent local families made financial contributions and ostentatiously displayed their coats of arms on the new roof beams. That of the Alsager family does not appear among them; they were merely yeoman farmers. The 17c. was a transition period to gentility for one branch of the family. Robert Alsager was considered a yeoman to his appraisers in 1643, but was described as a 'gentleman' for the registration of the baptisms of three of his children in the records of Barthomley Church. In 1613, alongside Randle Poole and Thomas Knight of Alsager, he had been pronounced a disclaimer at the Heralds' Visitation. This was a public proclamation against

[29]CRO. WS. 1669.

those who had no title to bear a coat of arms, or no right to adopt the rank of esquire or gentleman.[30] Perversely in 1631 he had refused to take a knighthood. After the coronation of Charles I in 1625/6, obligatory knighthoods were offered for a fee of £60 to £70 to raise money. Fines imposed on defaulters were a more attractive, £10 to £25[31]. Robert's priorities lay elsewhere, although by 1664 the Alsagers were bearing arms: at this date the Kents, and the Alsager branch of the Lawtons, were disclaimed. His will of 1642 discloses he was a benefactor of the poor, leaving 20 shillings to Barthomley parish, 20 shillings to Audley parish, and six shillings and eightpence to Lawton parish, for the benefit of the poor. Such munificence and his substantial estate of almost £700 were redolent of minor gentry.

A successful farmer, Robert's livestock numbers were large for the time: 29 cattle, 3 horses and a colt, 26 sheep, 5 pigs, and poultry; together valued at almost £120. Corn and hay in the barn and growing corn amounted to £44., an enormous quantity, required to feed all his stock and household; and his cheese was valued at £18 13s. 4d. While enjoying the little luxuries that his success has earned; silver spoons, pottery, glassware, brass and *"One little Cubbard for hats"*, the thrifty side of the farmer's nature is also demonstrated. Muck and fuel, butter and lard, goose grease and tallow, are itemised and valued. Onions hang with *"esballs"* or ashballs in the local dialect. These, according to Plot,[32] were made from fern burnt when green to preserve its oils, and then fashioned with warm water into balls about 3 inches in diameter. They apparently were used in the boiling and bleaching of clothes, creating an alkaline solution or 'lye'. Apart from £80 cash in the house, half of Robert's wealth was tied up in debts owed to him. With a canny eye, cast on the impending unrest of the civil wars, he had deposited £150 with friends for safe-keeping.[33] This estate refers to the Alsagers of Alsager Hall, who held the freehold of land mentioned in leases granted during the previous 150 years.[34] Robert's only son Raphe married Elizabeth Shaw on the 12th September 1637, the same day that his daughter Anne married William Shaw who was probably Elizabeth's brother. Raphe pre-deceased Elizabeth, for she was head of the household at Alsager Hall when the 1664 Hearth Tax

---

[30] J.P. Rylands, *Disclaimers at the Heralds Visitations;* Transactions of the Historic Society of Lancs. and Ches. 1891/2 Nos. 7 and 8 pp. 78/9 & 86.

[31] J.P. Earwalker, *Compositions for Knighthood;* Record Soc. Lancs. and Ches. Vol 12 1885 pp. 194 & 205.

[32] Robert Plot, *A Natural History of Staffordshire;* 1686. pp. 334-5

[33] CRO. WS. 1647.

[34] Brit. Lib. Add Ch's 53545/50

assessments were made. Records of baptisms were either not kept or went astray for a full 5 years covering the civil war period; if Raphe fathered a son and heir he chose to leave Alsager Hall and move away. In the Wolstanton parish registers the following entries appear;-

Marriages.

1672   *May 27*   *Ralph Alsager of Alsager Chester and Sarah Rowley of Turnhurst.*

Births.

1673   *May 19*   *Ralph son of Ralph and Sarah Alsager of Alsager*

Possibly Ralph took up residence at Turnhurst. It is known that half a century later the family were established in Congleton, for later the burial of a Ralph Alsager of Congleton, gentleman, is recorded in 1729. At Elizabeth's death in 1691 occupation passed to other hands, and by 1739 Ralph Walley, a husbandman, was in residence, possibly having the leasehold.[35]

Another branch of the Alsager family held the leasehold of the 'Brooke' or Brookhouse Farm from Lord Brereton. Described in his inventory of 1688 as a yeoman, John Alsager was a prosperous farmer. He operated the typical mixed farming unit of the day, with the emphasis on dairying. Of his livestock of cattle, two mares, sheep, pigs and poultry valued at £53 2s. 10d., his 12 cows and 3 calves were worth £33. The 22 sheep and 5 lambs he kept were together valued at only £4; cow was queen! His garners and barn, that April day, were sparsely stocked with hay and corn at £5.10s., stocks having depleted over the winter, and growing corn was worth £3. Cheese and bacon amounted to £15 18s. The colourful local dialect reminiscent of the Potteries is evident again in the contents of his living room; *"one table and formes, Cheeres and stowes,"* (chairs and stools). A modest amount of yarn and tow is stacked alongside sieves, baskets, bags, measures and winnow sheets, all together worth only £1 5s. This suggests that any home spinning was for agricultural use; tastes were more sophisticated demanding fine textiles domestically. John's bed, in the parlour, has curtains and a valance and is *"Joynt"* or jointed i.e. made by a craftsman. There is a marked absence of weaving looms from Alsager inventories. The yarns produced at home were probably woven into fabrics by the resident webster, such as Robert Alsager whose death was recorded in 1624; or by itinerant websters.[36] John may have had his children quite late in life, for at his death none of them had come of age. He was particular that his wife used his *"quick and dead goods"* for their maintenance and education. Although books are listed in his inventory John

---

[35] Barthomley '98.

[36] ibid.

was unable to sign his will, just leaving his mark; he may have been too ill and feeble for the task. On the other hand, his will and inventory convey the impression of a shrewd business man; debts owed to him by bills and bonds account for £285 out of the total value of his estate of £401 3s. The overall feeling is of a man who recognised, that, while his illiteracy had not hampered his personal path to prosperity, his children might not be so lucky.[37]

Manor Farm, or Galley's Tenement, as it was called after the family who were tenants from at least the late 16c. to the middle of the 18c., was part of the Cholmondeley estate, until sold to Randle Wilbraham in 1748 for £680. Documentary evidence of estate surveys and leases, combined with the will and inventory of Thomas Galley, yeoman farmer, who died in 1682, give a more composite picture of an Alsager farm at the beginning of the 18c.

Thomas' total wealth was appraised in his probate inventory at a comfortable £290 14s. 8d; an astonishing £110 6s. 8d. of which was tied up in livestock. His herd of 45 cattle, 22 of which were cows, and his flock of 31 sheep are numbers associated more readily with the 19th century, so he no doubt occupied some excellent grazing and growing land; the product of his own industry. The natural accompaniment to such a large number of cows was his valuable stock of cheese at £45, and stored in three different rooms. Corn in the barn at £16, and hay in the barn and in stacks at £19, were stored that November day ready for over-winter feed. No reference is made to horses or oxen, so it must be assumed that his bull, or young bullocks, were used as draught animals. It is likely that Thomas' son, also Thomas, was running the farm before his father died. A small quantity of corn and hay was stored, and appraised, separately, as were thirteen cattle; a means perhaps whereby Thomas senior had provided himself with a superannuation. In the house he appears to have been confined to the kitchen, though not sleeping there. *"In the kitchin where the Testator lived, one Brasse pott, Two Brasse panns, one Brasse Kettle and Two Brasse Skelletts, one Iron pott, one Iron Kettle, one paire of Tongs, one fire shovell and potthookes and Cheires and stooles. Pewter and spining wheeles. One Fouleing Gun."* This room had one of the two hearths listed in the Hearth Tax returns of 1664. The other was in the *'Lower House'*, a room with similar contents which probably served as the living room of Thomas junior and his family. The lower floor of the farmhouse also had a parlour, a buttery and a bakehouse; upstairs were four chambers and a 'little place', all used as bedrooms, three of which contained those ripe cheeses! Outhouses included barns and a cowshed.[38]

[37] CRO. WS. 1688.
[38] CRO. WS. 1685.

The Cholmondeley family commissioned a survey of their entire holdings in Cheshire in 1726, and we are fortunate that it included a detailed plan of Galley's Tenement with its ancient field names.[39]   The farm extended to 82 acres, 2 roods and 13 perches, divided into 19 fields. The farmhouse stood in just over an acre of garden and orchard with an adjacent enclosure of about $^3/_4$ acre called the 'Pingoe' - a corruption of pingle, an old term for a small piece of arable land, which may have served as a vegetable garden, or hemp and flax yard. The largest field was Dunnocks Fold at just over 22 acres. By the 1840 Tithe Award this had been sub-divided into 6 smaller fields. Indeed, the 1726 plan suggests that a pattern of the sub-division of larger units had been in operation for some time. The rectangular shapes and regular sizes of between three and four-acre plots known as 'Flats' suggest they were previously the furlongs of a larger field. A tract of land called Stakeley had been split into Long, Big, Little and Farther fields.   Meadow and Jack (wasteland) were similarly sub-divided. It appears that this outlying farm of the Alsager township had adopted, within itself, an open field system of land management, although occupied in severalty. Other farms developed from the waste, peripheral to the town fields, may have taken the same course; for the open field system was, at the time they were formed, the only method of farming in use. Sadly many of the fields had been renamed by 1840 so we can only speculate on the subject.

Tenant farmers lived under a weight of numerous restrictions and obligations to the landlord, reminiscent of feudal times. In the 1726 survey the occupant of Galley's Tenement had to provide an heriot (a gift by the heir on the decease of a tenant) of the farm's best beast or £5 in lieu; had to find a footman (infantryman) or £4 in lieu; had to attend the lord's manorial court; and had to grind his corn at the lord's mill or pay 5s in lieu.

The terms of a lease of 1635 required an entry fine, or payment, by an incoming tenant, of £140, an annual rent of 19s. and two rent hens and two rent capons, and the maintenance of a hound, greyhound or spaniel on the behalf of Viscount Cholmondeley.[40] It was customary to grant leases for lives, usually the tenant, his wife, children or brothers, rather than a fixed term of years. Of fundamental concern to the landlord was that his tenants practised good husbandry, and maintained its quality, for therein lay the source of his own income. Absentee landlords, such as the Cholmondeleys, who also owned property in Norfolk and London, at least inadvertently allowed their leaseholders certain latitude. In 1748 Lord Carpenter and

[39] CRO/DCH/PP/2.
[40] CRO/DCH/J/6.

William Mellish were appointed trustees for the payment of the amassed debts of £80,000 of George, Lord Cholmondeley, who married Mary, the only daughter of Sir Robert Walpole the Prime Minister.[41] Galley's Tenement passed to Randle Wilbraham, in an attempt to recoup some of the losses, the result in part, perhaps, of the cattle plague that broke out in the 1740's and persisted through the 1750's; or simply of squander and loose living!

At the end of the 17c. and into the 18c. the number of rooms per farmhouse increased, as did the variety of domestic furniture, soft furnishings and culinary utensils. The numbers and values of livestock, and quantities of grain, on the other hand remained static, pointing to improved, more profitable farming standards. The social stratification within the community is more clearly discernible as time passes.

John Lawton and Randle Poole, moderately prosperous yeoman farmers, who died in 1693, had lived their lives in similar circumstances with belongings valued at around £119. Their farmhouses had eight or nine rooms with additional storage space for bacon: John used a *'little clossitt'*; Randle's was *'in the staircase'*. Both men had kept servants: John's manservant was fortunate to have his own room with, "*One chaff bed one wooll boulster one paire of sheets 2 blankitts and one coverlid*". Randle was kindly disposed towards his live-in servants, Thomas Cartwright and Sarah Morris, leaving them one sheep apiece in his will.

John's household effects were more valuable than his livestock and contained some recognizably up-to-date furnishings and furniture. His best chamber had window curtains, upholstered chairs, a folding table, a mirror, cushions, and a trunk storing an assortment of napery and bed linen which included a tablecloth and five dozen napkins. John's baby son had been baptized only four months before John died. His *"Crissoning Suite of Linnen"* and cradle cover were among the contents of the same room; a poignant indication that John had met his death while still a relatively young man. He was buried on the same day as his father, victims perhaps of a tragic accident or contagious disease.[42] The lower parlour functioned as bedroom, dining room and office. A bed with curtains, valance and feather mattress stood alongside a chaff bed, a cupboard, a long table with table runner, two candlesticks and two pewter salt cellars, a form with a set of cushions, and a desk and *"videor"* (perhaps voider or waste basket.)[43] The need for larger

---

[41] CRO/DBW/L/20. Nos. 8, 9, 10.
[42] Barthomley '98.
[43] CRO. WS. 1693.

farmhouses to accommodate large families, extended families, and live-in servants was ever pressing.

Randle Poole lived at Cresswellshawe, or Crappilow, as it was often called. However, the place where 'cress grew beside spring and copse,' was much more appealing to the sensibilities than the place 'by a rubbish mound', and the name of Crappilow was rarely used after the 18th century. In fact the name of Crappilow did the farm a disservice, for Randle was able to grow wheat, a difficult crop in cool damp south Cheshire. A document of the late 13th century held in the British Library refers to the gift of Cresswellshawe to Henry, son of Thomas of Rode, by Randle, lord of Alsager, see page 23 above. This suggests it was already a consolidated holding by this time. Cresswellshawe remained in the Pole family, or Poole as it became, until the end of the 17th century.

Randle's most valuable assets were, his ready cash in silver and gold, and apparel and plate, at almost a third of the total of his estate. Among his possessions were a brass clock and several pieces of woollen cloth - black, yellow, white and thin brown, produced almost certainly from his own sheep. His farmhouse had a *"drink"* buttery with *"Barrells, stoonds, and all Coopery ware, Brasse and pewter, Seaven dozen of trenchars."*[44] This was where casks of home-brewed ale or 'wet' goods were stored, the forerunner of the cellar. Only the largest houses were fortunate to have this separate storage; much brewing, cheese and butter making, was still done in the main living room and the produce stored in any reasonable spare nook or cranny.

A comparison of the inventory of Richard Merrill dated 1669 [45] with that of his son Ralph in 1714[46] presents the unmistakable progress in the evolution of an Alsager farm, in this case Day Green[47]. Richard's livestock was worth £59 6s. 8d. which was just over half his total estate of £110. His son's livestock, valued at £43 12s. was a mere 3% of his total worth, for Ralph had increased the family wealth to a phenomenal £1307 14s., of which £1218 was tied up in money loaned at interest. Ralph was an entrepreneurial businessman; farming had become a sideline. The farmhouse had undergone its own evolution. The cocklofts, containing lumber in 1669, were converted to garret bedrooms, commonly servants' quarters. The store chamber with corn, peck and half-peck measures and a *"Ratts trappe"*, the ground cellar, and the servants' chamber disappeared. The kitchen was extended, retaining

[44] CRO. WS. 1693.
[45] CRO. WS. 1670.
[46] CRO. WS. 1714.
[47] Parish Registers of St. Bertoline Barthomley, Vol. I.

storage space for the barrels from the old cellar, and two new bedrooms were developed over it. A further *"best"* bedroom was added, and the old bedroom, over the living room, was converted to a storeroom for cheese, bacon, corn and malt. Passages between rooms were large enough to accommodate furniture; that from the kitchen contained the cheese press. By 1714 the parlour was no longer used for sleeping in, but the living room still had the cooking range and equipment; the kitchen simply contained brass and coopery ware. Apart from the structural changes to the house, the domestic situation of this shrewd businessman differed only slightly from that of his father. He had, however, permitted himself and his family the frivolity of a pair of virginals (keyboard instrument), the vanity of a looking glass, the modesty of a close stool (commode) in a bedroom, and the benefit of a clock. The most treasured family heirloom was the *"Great Bible"* passed from Richard to Ralph and on to Ralph's son Richard.

From the 1720's onwards appraisals for probate inventories started from within the house, its contents taking precedence over livestock. Peter Somerfield's inventory of 1724 began with the contents of his living room, the *'House place or Hall'*. It was a comfortable sitting room, with armchairs, clock, warming pan and screen, which doubled as a kitchen, with roasting spits and four sides of bacon. His kitchen also had cooking equipment such as a dripping pan, brass kettles and six brass pans, and may have served as brewhouse or even laundry with its brass furnace pan and boiler. But all these accoutrements of his good standard of living only just matched the value of his cheese at £50 and stored in two tuns. The ubiquitous 'corn' is clarified for us in Peter's inventory; he had wheat, barley, winnowed oats, peas and beans. Winter feed was plentiful with two ricks of hay and one rick of oats, valued at £17, and more hay and clover hay at £4 stored over the cowsheds in early February. Grasses and clover were sown in rotation with cereal crops and pulses to 'rest' the soil as fallowing had done. When the soil was well-manured the grass yield was plentiful, the extra hay making unnecessary the annual thinning of livestock late in the year. Successful farmer, with an estate of £487, astute businessman with £229 of it loaned at interest, Peter furthered his ambition. In Sandbach he had sub-let a cottage to Thomas Miler, and a separate plot of land to Elizabeth Baddaley, which were leased to him by Anne Crewe. Sub-letting was a risky undertaking for a landlord, and Peter would have required special permission. If he had proved to be an excellent tenant Anne Crewe would have trusted his judgement that her properties would be well maintained.[48]

[48] CRO. WS. 1725.

Joseph Alsager, a yeoman farmer who died in 1729, had possessed a similar acumen to Peter. Of his total wealth of £493 debts due to him amounted to £241, with a further £71 of 'desperate' debts.[49] His other business accomplishments were property developer and landlord. He had acquired a house with garden and orchard in nearby Newcastle, converted it into three separate dwellings and leased them to Sarah Ford, Peter Sherman, and John Alliby. His farm in Alsager had eleven rooms and a closet; one of the rooms being described as the *"Entry,"* a late architectural innovation and first step towards our modern entrance hall. However, the entry to Joseph's farmhouse was not designed to impress; its contents included a cheese press and a pair of bedsteads. He was one of Alsager's richest men yet the house was in essence a work place, arranged and furnished for industry in precedence over appearances. Consequently, within most rooms there was a hotch-potch of contents. In the living room a clock, six bibles, some other books, a mirror and a *"Viall Inn,"* and the usual fire irons and cooking utensils, jostled for space with a pair of shears and three sickles. The kitchen housed the rest of the cheese-making equipment; a cheese tub, a churn, and a salting turnell (a shallow oval tub), but the 28 cheeses were stored in the corn chamber where, alongside some barley and rye, 55 Brest silver buttons languished. The two butteries were pantries with shelves, trenchers (wooden platters), and earthenware, yet the flitch of bacon was to be found in an upstairs bedroom. Another bedroom contained two beds and a host of agricultural tools; plough irons, scythes, axes, mattocks (pick-axes), crowbar, iron wedges, and a weigh-beam and scales.[50]

In 1696 the death of Daniel Poole was recorded. He was the only son and heir of Randle, of Cresswellshawe, who had passed away three years earlier. There is no record of Daniel having a son, so it is likely that the Wilbrahams of Rode Hall acquired or retained the freehold at this time. The farm became occupied, probably on a leasehold basis, by William Darwall, gentleman, and his wife, who may have been friends of Randle Wilbraham. They were certainly out-of-towners, for the record of the birth of their daughter Elizabeth, in 1697, is the first time the surname appears in the parish registers. William involved himself in parish affairs with a caring and benevolent approach. He was an overseer of the poor for the years 1701, 1711, and 1721, a churchwarden in 1709, and his name appears on a bequest

---

[49] 'Desperate' debts are defined in the *OED* as debts unlikely to be repaid. Having regard to the frequency with which the expression is met in 17c. and 18c. inventories it is possible that the expression is used to distinguish them from 'debts by speciality', i.e. those secured in writing or by a bond.

[50] CRO. WS. 1729.

board, dated 1733, in Barthomley Church, as a benefactor of the school with a donation of £5. His inventory of 1734 is a document of meticulous detail, a treat of a tour round the home of an English country gentleman and a peep into his privacy.

Under William's occupation the structure of Cresswellshawe had been altered and extended, and developments made to its function as a farm by way of additional out-buildings. The family's main living room was the parlour, a large room with fire grate and irons, dining table and chairs, couch, screen, three occasional tables, warming pan, clock, barometer, and four Oxford Almanacks. Other wall adornments included a coppercut of Blenheim House, mirror, five Indian ink drawings by William himself, a hanging plate, six paintings by a Mr Clarke, and confirming Williams's reverence for the church, paintings of Bishop Stratford and Bishop Daws. 'Mr. Clarke' may have been William Clarke, described in the parish registers both as 'gentleman' and 'limner', a painter, particularly of fine detail and minature portraits. He may have been a friend of the Darwalls and resident at Cresswellshawe.

All cooking was done in the kitchen, a room brimming with pewter, brass and iron ware. Furniture included a table, four chairs, four stools, a dresser of drawers, a salt coffer and there was also a wooden knife container. There seems to have been two cooking ranges; one used for boiling, the other for roasting. The first grate had a fender, fire tongs and shovels, bellows, grid iron, pot hooks and racks, and was embellished with a brass ladle, brass skillet (long handled pan with legs), brass boiler, brass skimmers, brass bowls, two saucepans, an iron kettle, a tea kettle, and three smoothing irons for the laundry. The second grate was equipped with fender, fire tongs and shovels, two hanging broaches (spits), a flesh fork and chopping knife, six iron skewers, a slice, and a salamander (metal heating plate possibly used for browning). Twenty six pewter plates, fourteen pewter dishes, twenty four trenchers, four pewter salt cellars, a pewter mustard pot, and four brass candlesticks added further lustre. Three separate cases of knives and forks, one with ivory hafts, one with wooden hafts and one with stag hafts contributed to the gracious lifestyle.

Off the kitchen was a small parlour with an oval table, six chairs and a clothes maid, and decorated with five black and white pictures and a figure. A second small parlour was furnished in similar fashion, minus the clothes maid, but this time the pictures included a black and white plan of London. Is this a clue as to William's origins? The servants had their own dining room. Henry Latham, a labourer, had lived in, with his wife Ann and their family. The birth of their daughter Anna was recorded in 1728 and Cresswellshawe named as the place of their abode. The garret rooms were probably used as their private quarters.

There were six bedrooms listed in William's inventory compared to just three in Randle Poole's. William had named three of them with the pretensions of a stately home, the White Chamber, the Green Chamber, and the Red Chamber. These were sumptuously fitted out with window curtains, mirrors, paintings, chests, tables and joined chairs. The Red Chamber contained ten cane chairs with cushions, and the Green Chamber *"An old Tea Table"*. The beds were four-posters, with testers (canopies), curtains and valances, and feather mattresses and quilts. The bedroom over the closet was more simply appointed with two beds, a table, a cabinet, and a *"spring"* clock worth £4. That over the brewhouse incongruously housed two beds, a corn hopper and a pair of shears, alongside the family silver; a tankard at £8, cup at £2 10s., tumbler at £1 15s., two salt cellars at 12s., a watch at £4, and assorted spoons, amongst which were four teaspoons. Tea had been consumed with some ritual in William's household, reference the special kettle in the kitchen and table in the Green Chamber. In the early 18c. tea was still a scarce, and therefore expensive commodity, and beyond the reach of most Alsager folk. The sixth bedroom, cramped with three beds and two coffers, was above the buttery.

From Randle Poole's inventory of 1693 it is impossible to determine exactly what outbuildings and facilities existed at Cresswellshawe as mention is only made of a barn. Before his death in 1734 William Darwall had made some recent improvements installing a new stable, cowhouse, pigsty, and water pump (this with a trough and "Swine Cistern"). There appears to have been piped water with stop-tap outside for there is another trough *"under the Cock in the Garden,"* in addition to the presence of a well. The old pigsty, old cowhouse, *"little stable,"* and maybe the wain house and mill house, were of Randle's day, but the malt house with its *"Seventeen Loads and halfe of Mansfeild and Loughborough Malt"* valued at £17 10s. was attributable to William. Cheese-making was not of paramount importance at Cresswellshawe; perhaps the cheese was of poor quality for 75 cheeses were valued at only £6. Its equipment and manufacture were relegated to the brewhouse, and it was in brewing that William's main interests lay. His discerning palate had required the importation of best quality malt to the farm, and he had the means to collect it. His long cart with *"Thripples and Savers"* (extensions and removable sides) would have served the purpose nicely, and his three tumbrels (two-wheeled carts) could also have been called into service at the same time, for he owned five horses. At that time the roads had not been turnpiked so the journey was arduous, time-consuming and therefore costly, but to William manifestly worthwhile. His cellar contained seven barrels, 122 bottles, and a further 102 bottles on a rack, and the brewhouse five barrels more.   In a room described as the *"Closet,"* and obviously his den, with its books, writing desk and gun, were another 26 bottles. Did he have a problem? How appropriate that the Wilbraham Arms should be built on this site: William's spirit - please excuse the pun - lives on.

Considering the time of year that the inventory was taken, February, there was a large stock of hay, valued at £13, in the outhouses of Cresswellshawe. Other arable produce comprised peas, beans, vetches, rye, barley, wheat, red and white oats, muncorn (a mixture of grain, usually wheat and rye, and sown together), and more malt, some of which was described as *"not good."* Altogether these were valued at just over £21. Livestock included four horses and a mare valued at £25, eight calving cows at £25, other cattle at £21.10s. and two pigs at £2 3s. No sheep or flax and hemp are recorded, although the bedroom over the brewhouse contains a pair of shears and a spinning wheel. These items were perhaps redundant; a gentleman's needs were above home-spun fabrics. We can however leave William's home with a wry smile on our faces, for what are we, with our modern standards, to make of the presence of *"Three pewter piss pots"* in his milk buttery? [51]

William is buried in Barthomley churchyard alongside his children; Elizabeth aged 28 years, Margaret aged 31 years, Anne, a twin, aged 3 months, and William, aged 3 weeks, who was Margaret's twin brother. His estate of £568 4s. 8d., which included debts due to him of £248 16s. 3d., was left for his wife, his son Randle, who was Anne's twin brother, and any child that may have been born before his arrival in Alsager; but as there is no record of his will this is conjecture. His wife chose to leave Alsager, perhaps returning to the place they had come from. After William's burial the surname Darwall does not appear in the parish records again.

In stark contrast to the opulence of Cresswellshawe was the lifestyle of Joseph Gibson, Alsager's blacksmith, who died in 1759.[52] His house had only three rooms: a living room, which also served as a kitchen and dining room; a parlour which served as a bedroom; and a bedroom, which doubled as storage space for a churn, a barrel, two tubs, and the tools of his trade. Of his estate, which was assessed at just over £26, the contents of his living room with its furniture, cooking equipment, pottery, pewter and glassware, was worth only £2 15s. and £1 15s. of that was the value of his clock. He had

---

[51] CRO. WS. 1734.
[52] CRO WS 1759

owned two sets of tools, valued together at £6: "*I have two Setts of Tools belonging to My Trade. I Do give and Bequeth the Better Sett to my Son Joseph and the worser sett together with all my wareing apparil of what kind Soever I Do give and Bequeth to My Son John*", and both sons plied their trade in Alsager through the 1760's.[53] Smithy Flat, close to Brook House,[54] and Smithy Croft, opposite Cresswellshawe, are the possible sites of their forges.[55] To sustain his family when business was slack, and perhaps to supplement his income, Joseph had kept two cows, which, together with a twinter and a calf were worth £9. Although there is no mention of any arable produce, a harrow is listed in his inventory. Joseph's smithy was likely to have been on a small holding of a few acres, enough to graze his cattle and his mare valued at £4, and perhaps to produce cereals for fodder and domestic consumption. In addition he might have had grazing rights on the heath. It was the middle of the 18c. but the lowly tradesman scarcely lived above subsistence level. When Joseph's son John died in 1768 he left a widow, Ann and surviving six children; his wife gave birth to an illegitimate daughter Sarah in 1770. Alsager town book[56] records, that in 1771 Widow Gibson was in receipt of poor relief of 1s.6d. a week for herself, and 4s.6d., later increased to 5s., in respect of the children. The parish registers record that Sarah died a pauper in 1784. One can readily imagine that the plight of a widow, or those unable to work for whatever reason, would have been appalling.

Alsager mid-18th to mid-19th Centuries

In 1750 the baptism was recorded of the daughter of Evan Jones, a watchman, at Lawton wich.[57] The discovery of salt locally can only have boosted farmhouse cheese making. With herds still small, its manufacture was well within the capabilities of the farmer's wife, assisted by her daughters or dairy maids. The farm dairies of the late 18c. cannot have been hygienic places, as most utensils were made of wood, floors and walls were rough and uneven, and most roofs made of thatch. This assumption of the form of construction of the buildings is borne out by the descriptions of the out-buildings at Town House, as described in John Twiss's insurance policy of

---

[53] Barthomley. Parish Regs. Vol. 1 1562-1788.
[54] A map of the Brook House Estate, dated 1761 shows the position of the smithy and other buildings. Ref CRO.P.278/10/1.
[55] T.A. Award refs 391, 235.
[56] Alsager Town Book 1771-1863 ref. CRO. P278/11
[57] Barthomley. Parish Regs. Vol. 1.

1791.[58] The dairy of Thomas Willock, who lived at Bank House, and died in 1758, also contained unexpected items;

> *"Three Cheese tubs four milking cans seven kimnels* (tubs) *two calves*
> *Nine Cheese fats* (vats) *two stoonds Kneading Trough Basket 8 pan mugs*
> *Two basons three bowls tundish* (funnel) *two piggins* (wooden pail with
> one stave longer to serve as a handle) *three bowks* (bucket) *Churn*
> *Two Cheese presses two Iron furnaces and a boiler two salting turnels".*[59]

The flavour and quality of cheese varied, from farm to farm, for a variety of reasons. Some cows gave a better milk yield than others, the assortment and quality of herbage differed, quantities and milk temperature were measured by experience and guesswork, over-salting hardened the cheese, and over-skimming of the cream for butter impaired its standard. The making of cheese was a seasonal occupation, when the cattle were out on the grasslands; beginning in the spring after the cows had calved, through to late autumn. It was also a daily chore and time consuming. Each morning milk from the previous day was skimmed of cream, then cream and some milk heated, and rennet, or curdled milk, added to produce curd. When the curd set it was cut and the whey, or watery residue, was drained off. Once salt had been added it was milled, weighted, kept warm in an oven overnight, then placed in a press for three days and turned twice daily. After that, it was wrapped in muslin and put into store for anything up to a year and turned each day.[60]

Many farmers in the area suffered severe losses in the mid-18th century cattle plague. Edward Hinchliffe wrote in 1856:

> *"The Cattle Distemper which raged so fearfully about the middle of the last century in England, and called forth the interposition of Parliament to provide measures for preventing its extension, unfortunately attacked the cattle of the farmers in Crewe, Barthomley, and the neighbouring Townships, with great violence, for several successive years, as the following short extracts from a correspondence of that period shews:-*

> *EXTRACTS.*

> 1749.   *The Distemper is very bad in this neighbourhood amongst*
> *January* *cattle. It is at George Alsager's of Radway Green; John*
> *March.*   *Kent's, George Steele's and Samuel Johnson's all in*
> *April.*   *Barthomley; and Widow Latham's, at Elton, likewise.*
>   *The Distemper has been very fatal amongst the cattle at*
>   *Warmingham, almost all having taken it.*
>   *The Distemper amongst cattle still continues very bad.*
> 1751.   *The Distemper is very bad at Latham's, of Barthomley, who*
> *March.*   *has already lost upwards of twenty head, young and old.*

---

[58] See page 249 below.
[59] CRO. WS. 1759
[60] Geoffrey Scard, *Squire and Tenant*, Ches.Comm. Council. Vol. 10 p.63-65. [Scard]

> *The Distemper is very bad amongst the cattle at Haslington*
> *and Blakenhall, and has again broken out at Elton.*
>
> 1752.   *The Distemper is now very bad at Crewe and in Weston, and*
> April.   *at Weston Hall the tenant has lost a great many of his cattle."*[61]

If any of Thomas Willock's herd had succumbed to the cattle plague he made a remarkable recovery. According to his inventory, he was in possession of 17 cows, 3 calves, 2 stirks and a bull, together valued at £60, out of a total wealth of £171. No mention is made of income from sources other than dairying, and its puzzling that no cheese is listed nor ready cash. It is interesting to note that he had owned a tea kettle and a copper coffee pot; articles once considered expensive luxuries, affordable only by the very wealthy, had found their way into the home of a moderately prosperous Alsager farmer.

By the end of the 18c. more roads were turnpiked and properly maintained, further stretches of the River Weaver made navigable, and canals were constructed. Farmers were able to find outlets for their cheeses, beyond carting them to the local markets, using the nearest cheese factors; agents who bought and sold for a commission and distributed to many parts of England particularly London.[62] The early years of the 19c. saw the development of steam locomotion for haulage, and by the middle of the century a good national railway network existed. While this at first facilitated the transport of cheese, local farmers soon realised that the sale of milk was much more viable. Alsager railway station was easily accessible from all the farms, and the expanding large urban areas of the Potteries, Manchester and Liverpool provided ready markets. Dairy farming took on a new aspect; cheese making declined, and pasture became much more important, as the conversion to milk production called for larger herds and better quality grazing.

Limestone was discovered at Astbury in the late 18c., a convenient source of supply for Alsager. Lime, produced from the firing of limestone in a kiln, was recognised to be an alternative fertilizer to marl which had become increasingly expensive to extract. A laborious task, involving teams of men, marling cost about £5 an acre.[63] As improvements were made to drainage, using tiles or broken shells deep within the soil, to replace ditches and ridges, the application of lime as a top dressing increased in popularity. By the middle of the 19c. marling had all but died out. A legacy has been left for us on the landscape from the marlers of old; many of their pits, now filled

---

[61] Edward Hinchliffe, *Barthomley*, 1856 p. 351, 352 [Hinchliffe 1856]
[62] J. Howard Hodson, *Restoration to Industrial Revolution*, Ches. Comm. Council. Vol. 9 p.84.
[63] Scard p.85.

with water, and hosts to a variety of plant and animal life, are to be found in Alsager's fields. Bone meal was another form of calcium used in the 1830's to improve pasture, and many-bone grinding mills were set up in Cheshire.

These new developments proved most beneficial: *"the quantity of stock on some farms has nearly doubled, and the cheese-vat proportionably increased"*.[64] The increase in livestock, farmyard manure, and improved soils, led to the introduction of root crops for winter fodder. Potatoes, turnips, swedes and carrots were grown, and surpluses sold to the urban markets. As the shift to milk production advanced, the importance of this extra winter feed to preserve a level output was emphasised. Root crops grown in rotation with cereals and grass helped to preserve the soil's fertility, and improve the yield of all arable produce.[65] Straw from the cereal crops was much sought after by the pot-banks for packing the wares.

From the 1664 Hearth Tax returns to the first census returns of 1801, Alsager's population grew from about 120 to 275. The figure had increased to 446 by 1831, and then stabilized for the next 20 years, until the railway came to town, when it rapidly increased. On the other hand the population of Barthomley, about double Alsager's in 1664, had increased to 484 in 1801 but then started to decline as the impact of local industries lured the low-paid agricultural workers away, by 1831 it had fallen to 449 and this trend continued following the coming of the railway throughout the 19c.

Between 1720 to 1790 the parish registers of Barthomley church list occupations; of males only of course, females were either housewives or in service. This provides a valuable insight into the structure of society. By 1790 Alsager had its own church, endowed with a licence to conduct burials and baptisms. Essentially an agricultural community, the majority of Alsager's men worked as farm labourers. Farmers, classified as either yeomen, or husbandmen, probably numbered about 20 or so. Tradesmen living in the village served the needs of the rural society; blacksmith, butcher, bricklayer, carrier or waggoner, inn-holder, maltster, miller, nailer, shoemaker or cordwainer, tailor, thatcher, weaver, and wheelwright; there is evidence of an ale-seller as early as 1620.[66] Many of these would have occupied smallholdings and engaged in agricultural activity as a sideline. Because the population was small, only one or two of each trade would be resident at the same time. This pattern had existed, unchanged, for many decades. More

---

[64] Hinchliffe 1856. p.129

[65] Scard p.71.

[66] CRO. DCH.Y/6 Nantwich Hundred Court Estreats 1594-1699.

recent occupations of the time were; a collier, probably living on the north Staffordshire border; a boatsman who may have been employed on the new canals; and professions associated with the new church, such as the clergyman, parish clerk, and stonemason, and possibly the book-keeper. Mention is also made of a pauper and a couple of gentlemen. The nature of their existence is clear from Hinchliffe's description of their dining habits:

> *"Supping, a term for the curds and whey which remain after the cheese is made, is one great ingredient of the meals of a farm-house. I can recollect when buttermilk and potatoes, and a small bit of bacon, formed the dinner of master, mistress, and servants: knives and forks were not used; the piece of bacon was held in one hand, and nibbled at with careful economy, whilst the other hand wielded an iron spoon, which was incessantly dipped in a large brown dish of potatoes, rendered tasty by a sauce of mixed flour, water and bacon grease; and very savoury and good it smelt; a tin can of buttermilk stood by the side of each person".[67]*

An important question in the story of Alsager, is why today it differs so much in character from its neighbour Barthomley? Why should one be so rural in character, whilst the other is so unashamedly urban? It might be said that it was the railway that influenced Alsager's urban expansion, but this is not the whole story. Indeed, before the town developed as we know it today, the railway company had the foresight to build a station, station yard, and station master's house; which they could just as easily have done at Barthomley, either where the line crosses Mill Lane or by Bridge House Farm. The fact that Alsager was the chosen site suggests that the town was already a better commercial proposition before the coming of the railway.

The cause of this lies in the varying pattern of landownership between the two villages. Barthomley was an estate village, almost exclusively in the ownership of a single estate, with an estate owner landlord who was resident, if not in the township then immediately adjoining it at Crewe Hall. This landlord dictated affairs, he determined who should be a tenant, and kept a watchful eye on the way tenants conducted themselves. It was in his interests to ensure the integrity of the estate, and he had no interest in its piecemeal development.

This was not the case in Alsager, where the township had never formed a single territorial landholding, or at least, not for many centuries. The Alsager and Wilbraham families were the principal landowners but the proportion of the land they held was comparatively modest. Reference to the land tax returns of the late 18c. and early 19c. show that landownership was spread amongst approximately twenty landlords, the majority of whom were

---

[67] Hinchliffe 1856, p.134.

not resident in the town, and rarely owned more than one, or perhaps two farms. Accordingly Alsager was an open community, as opposed to Barthomley which was a closed community. This is the principal factor determining the town's later development. Tenants here had a greater freedom of action to exploit the resources of their holdings without being under the constant watch of their landlord; they had alternative landlords if they should get into dispute with one. Freeholders were more inclined to sell small portions of their land, for the development of cottages and dwelling houses for incomers, nonconformists could develop their own places of worship more freely here and amusements, licensed premises, and to a degree disorderly conduct, would perhaps be more tolerated than would be the case in a closed village where the landowner was landlord, patron of the church, magistrate, and had the power to say he didn't want a railway in his village.

It is said elsewhere in this book that the Alsager Inclosure Award was the charter of the modern town, this is true to a large degree, but as this chapter shows, other factors also influenced the development of the town we know today.

Chapter 5

The Poor Law and Welfare.

In England, after the Reformation, the parish church was not only the spiritual centre of the community but also the centre of its civil administration, run by untrained, unpaid officers, although they paid themselves expenses; chosen from the rate paying parishioners. The poor law described in this chapter developed out of this embryonic system of local government. The parish of Barthomley was no exception to this, and detailed records were kept which had to be submitted each year, to Nantwich, for audit and inspection. These records have survived from 1662, and amongst them Alsager's modest early township accounts are found.

In medieval times, the church, as an expression of Christian charity, offered shelter for all travellers, both rich and poor, and provided care for the old and sick in the infirmaries of its monasteries. In Chester, members of the orders of St. Francis and St. Dominic, or black and white friars as they were known, worked tirelessly for the poor. Medieval Nantwich was served by two hospitals, St Nicholas and St. Lawrence, until 1537.

After the dissolution of the monasteries in 1537-40, when the Church's land and property including the hospitals was seized, the infirm poor were left to beg food and shelter where they could. This was at a time when there had been several poor harvests, resulting in numerous unskilled labourers and beggars drifting towards the towns in an effort to find work. If none was to be found they became vagrants and were most unwelcome, particularly the 'sturdy beggars,' who it was thought might have criminal intentions. It has been suggested that the conditions when wandering beggars were becoming a menace to society gave rise to the rhyme:-

> Hark! Hark! The dogs do bark,
> The beggars are coming to town.
> Some in rags and some in jags
> And some in a velvet gown.
> Some gave them white bread
> Some gave them brown
> And some gave them nothing at all
> And whipped them out of town.

The alarmed authorities recognised the potential danger and, from 1563 onward, a stream of regulations was imposed in an attempt to curb this movement of jobless and homeless from parish to parish. To prevent further unskilled workers settling in Chester, the Mayor forbade any cottages to be let to them, and only the 'deserving' poor were given leave to beg. The undeserving poor got 24 hours in the stocks, which every parish was instructed to erect. Parliament finally addressed the problem, and the great Elizabethan Poor Law Act of 1601 was formulated which became the basis of care for the needy for the next 200 years.

The Parish System.

Each parish was made responsible for the financial relief of its own paupers, so a system was devised to identify its own people. By an Act of 1662 every person required a place of settlement, where he belonged and was entitled to poor relief, if he did not rent property worth £10 per annum. Generally this was where he now lived or had been born of a settled father. A woman who married out of her parish took her husband's settlement. Settlement might be gained in another parish on completion of an apprenticeship to a settled master, or by being hired there for a full year. Often indenture papers contained a clause disclaiming parish responsibility, and cannily farmers discharged their men a day short of the year.

At St. Bertoline's church Barthomley, there are charity boards listing bequests which benefited the needy in its parish, for the laity regarded the setting up of charities and providing for the less fortunate as an act of piety. The following can be seen on a board in the church porch;-

> *"Catalogue of the Benefactors of the Parish of Barthomley*
> *begun in the Year of our Lord 1672.*
> *Mr. George Alsager of Alsager gave twelve pounds*
> *to be put out[1] by the Churchwardens for the*
> *benefit of the poor of this Parish.*
> *Matthew Meakin of Crew gave twenty shillings to be*
> *put out likewise for the benefit of the poor.*
> *Other charitable inhabitants of this Parish*
> *whose names are not brought down to the knowledge*
> *of this present generation but are, we hope,*
> *written in the Book of Life, gave twenty-eight pounds*
> *sixteen shillings and eight pence to be put out for*
> *the benefit of the poor of this Parish*

---

[1] To be 'put out,' meant to be offered on loan to some local ratepayers at an interest of 5% which was added to the poor account. A list of borrowers was recorded each year in the Churchwarden's book together with the amount of interest apportioned to each of the five townships.

Churchwardens   *Isaac Lea*

Ralph Hilditch   1752.

It was the above system that was set up in Barthomley. On Easter Monday, in the vestry, the Churchwardens appointed Overseers of the Poor, two for each of the five townships, Alsager, Balterley, Barthomley, Crewe and Haslington, which constituted the parish. These meetings were appropriately named 'Vestry Meetings' and were the centre of local government until 1834.

The Overseers were elected to set, collect and distribute monies, in their respective townships, to the needy for that year. They called for a 'mize'[2] to be gathered (or for two mizes or even half a mize) and the set unit for the entire parish was £6-2-1. The amount yielded by Alsager amounted to 16s.8d. This was the forerunner of our rating system. A typical entry is that for the 15th February 1680:-

> *"It is this day Ordered by the Churchwardens and other parishioners then mett at the church according to publique notice that a lay of two Mizes being twelve pounds foure shillings be allowed and immediately gathered for the use of the Poore of the Parish.*
>
> | *To be gathered in* | *Barthomley* | *£3 - 6 - 8* |
> |---|---|---|
> | | *Haslington* | *£3 - 6 - 8* |
> | | *Crew* | *£2 - 4 - 6* |
> | | *Alsager* | *£1 -13 - 4* |
> | | *Balterley* | *£1 -13 - 0 "* |

Further mizes were called that year in June, September and November. The following February the lay was of three mizes, Alsager's contribution being £2-10-0. The Overseers appeared to work from hand to mouth, setting another levy as funds ran out.

On the whole the system seems to have been a benign one. In 1682-4 Widow Hilditch, of Alsager, was paid a weekly allowance of 6d., later increased to 1s.2d., plus seven loads of coals costing 2s.11d. In her last illness a neighbour was paid to attend her; the final entry concerning her reads:- *"pd Mary Hilditch burial charges"* these amounted to 10s.6d., in 1773.

A hundred at fifty years later at Alsager, in 1828, the pattern was much the same; the weekly pension was between 2s. and 6s., according to the size of family, plus gifts in kind; *"gaive Widow Dale to't Clothing £2,"* these included new clogs, shoe mending, and finally 'care in the community', as is seen by;-

> *"1828 July.*
>
> *15th Gaive Thomas Hancock for sisting Jothan Jackson wen he was ill 5s.*
>
> *16th Gaive John Holland for sisting Jothan Jackson wen he was ill   5s.*
>
>   *paid for Jothan Jackson's coffin.   £1."*

---

[2] Taken from the Latin for payment or expense, but in this case meaning more 'an imposition'.

Bastardy was not regarded so much as a social stigma as a liability to the parish, and every effort was made to 'father' the child. A pregnant woman would be pressed to 'confess her crime', and sometimes, even during labour, a magistrate would be brought in. Court proceedings to avoid being saddled with a bastard could be quite costly as this case in April 1693 illustrates.

> "Atturneys Fees at Sessions at Namptwich about
> defending the Parish from Margery Beckets Bastard Child   3s.4d."
> "Charges and expenses on ourselves and horses 2 days   4s.0d."
> "Pd. John Breretons Bill of Charge for 2 sessions   17s.4d."
> "Pd. for an Order of removal of the same childe   2s.0d."

There is no information which township had to take the child.

In 1828 four men were paying Alsager overseers for the upkeep of a bastard child, two of whom lived in other townships. Richard Simpson was a Chatterley man who was served with a bastardy order by the Alsager overseer:-

> "my joney to Charley to giv Richard Simpson the order.   2s.6d."

The 'lying-in' money was demanded of him and finally a warrant for his arrest was served-

> "my joney to Chatley with the Cunstable to Faich Rucherd
> Simpson   2s.6d."

Following this he was taken before a magistrate at Nantwich, the case was proved, and his annual payment was £2-7-6.

William Barker paid £5-4-0, but perhaps that is because he was a ratepayer and one of the town's leading men. His name appears not only in the bastardy list but at the foot of the 1828 accounts as an auditor. He was the town's constable in 1809.

One particular case, in 1828, concerning Hannah Colclough, or Colkler, gave the overseers not a little trouble and expense. She not only had two children kept by the township, at a cost of £10-8-0 per annum, but there were other expenses for her care and upkeep. When she was found to be pregnant again the overseer visited George Cooper of Rode. A warrant was taken out for his arrest:-

> "my joney with the Cunstable for talk George Cooper".

He was taken before a magistrate:-

> "going with Hannah Colkler to farther her child to Nantwich.
> paid for summons   2s.0d."

At the same time a lunatic form was taken out; "pd for unitick form 6d.," and an order was obtained for Hannah's committal to Knutsford Roundhouse, possibly within the precincts of the prison. Her baby was born in Knutsford in December and the 'lying-in', £1-5-0, was paid. The last charges in the accounts were:-

> "sent to Hannah Colkler to Nutsford to cloth er child   5s.0d."

> *"My joney to Rodee to ask George Cooper for the money* 1s.0d."
> *"recd of George Cooper for Bastard* £3-7-0"

The total cost to the parish was £15-12-3, not a an inconsiderable sum. That year, 1828, the overseers of the poor had the expense of paying John Edwards, 'for constabling', £5-6-0.

Widows and other women were paid to take orphans, bastards and foundling children, into their homes until they were old enough to become apprentices.

> *Oct. 1682. " pd. Anne Boughey for keeping the fundling child. 16s.3d."*

All pauper children were set up with the necessary clothing by the overseers before being bound to a master.

> *1828.* *"paid for binding Haner yardle Ledd prentes* 7s.3d.
> *att the same time gaive Thomas Lowe[3] with im* £5.
> *att the same time gaive Lowe too't Clothing* 12s. "
> *"My joney to Nantwich for the same* 2s.6d.
> *att the same time Expenses with Hanner yardley and*
> *Thomas Holland and Lowe and the lad and myself* 5s.0d."

Overseers preferred to place pauper apprentices out of the township in the hope of getting them settled elsewhere.

> *1828.* *"My joney to Wilock (Wheelock) to let the overser*
> *to no about puting lid (lad) prentees* 2s. "

If the township's able-bodied men became paupers it was up to the overseers to find them work about the parish, such as stone breaking, the digging out and levelling of the causeways and bridge repairs. But should non-settlement men or their families need support, the overseers while helping them on a temporary basis, would go to extraordinary lengths to get rid of them. This entailed a visit, or visits, to a magistrate in Nantwich, as the chief town of the hundred, who would examine the man before deciding whether or not to issue a removal order.

In 1770, Barthomley supported Thomas Booth for 12 weeks at a cost of £1-4-8 plus a load of coals at 1s.8d., when his claim to settlement rights were questioned. The overseers took him to Nantwich where he was examined by a magistrate. There followed a journey to Nuall (Newhall) five miles south of Nantwich in an attempt to settle him there. After further expenses he was rejected by Newhall and, finally, Alsager was charged with being his place of settlement.

> *"Spent at taking Thos. Booth (again) to Nantwich* 4s.4d.
> *Spent at taking Thos. Booth to Alsager* 1s.0d.
> *Spent at taking two notises to Alsager.* 1s.0d.

---

[3] The 1840 Tithe Award records Thomas Lowe Snr. as owning and letting Bankhouse Farm. Thomas Lowe Jnr. was the owner occupier of Lane End Farm

>   *Paid for clearing up Thos. Booth's Goods*   *2s.0d.* "

In all it cost Barthomley £2-18-2 to pass Thomas Booth on to Alsager.

A more complex case concerns the re-settlement of John Lees or Leighs who was resettled in Alsager from Rode in 1680.

> *"It is this day Ordered by the Churchwardens and other parishioners mett at the church according to publike notice that the charges due for the proceedings in the Law by the township of Rode for the removall of John Lees formally inhabitant in Alsager back into Alsager bee discharged by the Churchwardens the summe being fifty three shillings provided that the Town of Alsager take care that the Parish bee put to no further charges about him in the Law.*
>
> >   *Zachary Cawdrey, Robert Bulkley, Joseph Pickering, Ch. Wdns.*
> > *Hugh Kent, Robert Steele, James Beeston, John Hulse, William Kelsall."*

As Alsager had no available cottage in which to house John Lees and family, they were bound to pay his rent in Rode for the time being, the other four townships came to the rescue again in May 1681.

> *"It is this day Agreed by the Parishioners then mett that the present Churchwardens shall erect a Cote in Alsager for John Lees att the Parish Charge and that they likewise pay his house rent in Rode in the meanetime at the Parish Charge alsoe.*
>
> >   *Zachary Cawdrey, Ralph Perceval, John Hulse, Joseph Pickering, Richard Scott, Hugh Barnet, John Noden."*

The local craftsmen now gathered their materials to build him a timber-framed cottage, as shown by the following payments made in 1683.

April 14	*"Charge of John Lees house in Alsager.*	
	Paid for timber	£2-3-0
	To Randle Hilditch for work done	10s.0d.
	To William Stanfield for nailes	2s.10d.
	To John Beckett for filling clay for one day	1s.0d.
	For lugges and springles	1s.0d.
	To Ralph Shaw for Hinges and nailes	1s.6d. "
June 2nd.	*"pd. John Alsager for timber for John Lees house*	2s.6d. "
July 9	*"Spent when wee agreed with Gabriell Smith to build a cote in Alsager*	1s.0d. "
Aug. 29	*"Pd. Walter Whitgrove for halfe an hundred of Rodds and for luggs and springles for the cote in Alsager*	2s.0d. "
Nov.29	*"pd. to Gabriel Smith for building John Lees cote in Alsager*	£2-10-0. "

John Lees was in his cote and living in the parish by Christmas, but in poor health. Or had he been in a fight at Easter? An entry dated 16th April 1683 reads *"given to John Lees when he was wounded 6s.0d. "*

Despite building him a house the parish was united in an attempt to move the family on as the following directive in 1684 makes clear. There is a change in the spelling, Lees to Leighs, possibly because a new parish clerk was appointed in 1683-4; such names in the parish as Buddilee and

Buddileigh were interchangeable.

> *"Sept.2   It is this day ordered by the Churchwardens and parishioners then met according to publick notice that two pounds and ten shillings be allowed out of the poor lays for the removall of John Leighs and his family into Ireland.   And it is ordered that Jerimia Read be allowed reasonable charges for the conducting of them to shipboard.*
> *Zachary Cawdrey, Ralph Merrill, William Steele Churchwardens; Hugh Kent, Mathew Wright, Samuel Wood, Robert Madew, Isaack Wothington, John Smith, Nathaniel Steele."*

There is no way of knowing whether Leighs was Irish, or whether this was an early emigration scheme; however Jerimia Read, who was probably the constable, accompanied them either to Chester or to Parkgate.

> *"Dec.9th.   Pd. to Jerimia Read for going with Leighs when*
> *they went for Ireland.*   *13s.0d.*
> *Given to Leighs when they went fot Ireland.*   *£2-10-0*
> *Spent when we met Leighs and his friends*   *1s.0d.*
> *Spent when we paid Jerimia Read*   *4d."*

But John Leighs was back in the parish two months later.   Perhaps a magistrate revoked an order removing the Leighs to Ireland, he was empowered to do so if the deportee was too ill to be moved.   Later evidence clearly shows Leighs' health to have been poor.

> *"168⁴/₅.*
> *Jan.23.   pd. to John Leighs in his weakness*   *2s.0d.*
> *Mar.28   Given to John Leigh being sick and in great want*   *£1.*
> *June 24.   given to John Leighs*   *1s.9d.*
> *Given him more*   *2s.0d."*

It seems the family were back in their cote and a permanent charge to Alsager.

> *"Sept. 29   pd. for repairs to John Leigh's house*   *£2.*
> *given to John Leighs*   *5s.0d.*
> *Given to John Leighs*   *10s.0d.*
> *168⁵/₆*
> *Given to John Leighs*   *5s.0d."*

This is the last entry concerning him.   After this the township records were not separately listed for a number of years, nor were the poor accounts so detailed.   Possibly the death of Rector Zachary Cawdrey was the reason. He was a former Proctor of Cambridge University, fellow of St. John's College, and an able administrator who had run the parish business most conscientiously for twenty-four years.

A poor person wanting to travel beyond the neighbourhood for any reason had first to be examined by a justice to obtain permission.   This permit was in the form of a letter of request, to be shown to the overseers of townships they passed through, it entitled them to ask for financial and other help.   The Poor Accounts mostly state *"given to a letter of request 6d.,"* but occasionally the items are fuller, as in 1685; *"Given to John Birch and 7 others who had suffered shipwreck;"* and in 1698, *"given to a miller who had his mill and horses burnt 1s.";* and *"given to a clergyman's widow who came from Ireland 1s.6d."* But why Roger Fellows of Smallwood should call with a letter of request is puzzling.   Another intriguing one is in 1690, *"Given to Gentlewoman towards the redemption of some captives taken by the Turks 1s."* In the same year, on March 15th,

> *"Spent on the account of 2 children that were sent on a pass to our parish. Payd for making up a new pass to send them to the place from whence they had come - 6d."*

This was possibly a dispute over settlement rights, and these orphan children were being shuttled too and fro, from one township to another.

Towards the middle of the 18th century items and expenses relating to 'letters of request' no longer appear in the overseers' accounts.

The Unions.

In the early part of the 19c. outdoor relief, a system where payment was made to paupers to provide for themselves in their own homes, increased to such a degree that it caused great concern to ratepayers in general. Although Alsager was not a deprived township; as was Congleton, with its slump in the silk industry; the poor account in 1828 was £367-1-10½, the highest ever. This was in some measure due to high food prices, following a run of bad harvests, and an increase in the cost of living, which rose by an estimated 25% between 1770 and 1830.[4] In some counties, although not in Cheshire, low wages were supplemented by cash payments.

The fear spread among the governing classes, that if poor relief continued to spiral it would make the poor more dependent on charity, and discourage them from honest work. As a solution the Poor Law Amendment Act of 1834 was passed.   This took the distribution of relief, which often appeared haphazard, away from Alsager's local overseers, the farmers, inn keepers and millers, and put it into the hands of Poor Law Commissioners who appointed Assistant Commissioners for local inspection.   It was intended to keep a tighter control over expenditure.   Townships were organised into Unions governed by a Board of Guardians, who were instructed to provide a Union Workhouse.   Barthomley parish was split up; Alsager was included in the Congleton Union, made up of thirty-two townships including Congleton, Sandbach, Brereton and Biddulph; the remainder of Barthomley parish was included in Nantwich Union.

This was the beginning of a harsher and more centralised system.

---

[4] E.C. Midwinter, *Victorian Social Reforms;* 1968.

Outdoor relief for the able-bodied was abolished, and as a discouragement, the workhouse was made as uninviting as possible. This system was known as indoor relief. Congleton Union's first chairman was Randle Wilbraham Sen., of Rode Hall, who served for twenty years and was succeeded by his son Randle, who served for a further twenty-eight years. Alsager and the smaller townships were each represented by one guardian, the larger townships of Congleton and Sandbach by two.

Until a central workhouse could be built, Congleton Poorhouse, capacity 90-100, was used; but what had served one township was woefully inadequate for thirty-two. The Commissioners in London objected to pauper boys being housed in a warehouse to relieve the overcrowding, yet at the same time widows were refused help to keep their families together at home; their children had to be taken 'inside'. When inside families were split up, and the sexes strictly segregated, even in the exercise yards; parents and children were only allowed one hour together in the evening. Mothers with illegitimate children were no longer supported in the community, but were 'offered the house'. At the same time errant fathers were still being diligently pursued.

From the guardians' minute book;-

> *"Feb 1838. . . . that the overseers of Alsager be directed to take proceedings to recover the arrears due from Ralph Boson, the punitive father of Fanny Morris's bastard now chargeable to Alsager."*
> and;
> *". . the bill for £1-1-6 , Constables expenses for apprehending William Ashley for bastardy. Money due to Alsager."*

Thomas Henshall was Alsager's first representative on the Board of Guardians but he had no authority to give relief without the permission of the board. In February 1838 he approached the board for aid and;-

> *"Resolved that Henry Colclough belonging to the town of Alsager be furnished with a new suit of clothes."*

(Henry may have been the son of Hannah Colclough, see above, bound as a pauper apprentice, and listed in the census for 1841 as 'pauper apprentice aged 10,' working for Thomas Timmis at Holehouse Farm.)

Inside the overcrowded Congleton poorhouse the governor was reprimanded, and eventually sacked, for being extravagant; too much lump sugar, candles and coal were being consumed.

Eventually a site for the Union Workhouse was agreed upon and this was built at Arclid, in an isolated situation halfway between Sandbach and Congleton. It opened in 1845 with room for 370 paupers. Alsager's inmates would feel very cut off from their roots, especially as visitors were only allowed twice a week.

On entering the 'house' paupers exchanged their own clothing for workhouse uniform, which was marked like prison garb, so that they would be easily recognisable if they absconded; when caught they were charged with theft of the overalls. Able-bodied men were set to work at stone breaking, two hundred weight per day, chopping logs, picking oakum or looking after pigs. Women were permitted to do household tasks, such as caring for the infants, laundry work, assisting in the infirmary, and so on. Those fit enough were put to carding wool and picking oakum. Some workhouses bought in animal bones to be crushed, but at one house, not in Cheshire, the inmates were so underfed that they ate the decaying flesh from the bones. So a directive went out to all institutions, including Arclid, to discontinue such work. Apart from the pigs and some field work Arclid made very little profit from these projects, if any.

Alsager's initial contribution to running costs was £12-3-0 a quarter, later to be increased to £40-£50; in addition there was a charge for the upkeep of the town's own inmates. Three Alsager paupers spent a total of 179 days inside the workhouse in 1846, probably during the winter months, costing the township £2-7-0 for food and £1-2-0 for clothing. The following year five paupers spent 179 days there, but between 1848 and 1858 never more than one Alsager pauper was taken in, and than for only part of a year. There was a terrible fear of ending up in Arclid. As late as the nineteen-thirties people would say, *"We shall end up in Arclid at this rate"*, or *"I don't want to die in the workhouse"*. Where possible families supported relatives who had fallen on hard times, to spare them the disgrace and discomfort, of the Institution.

In 1855 a farmer absconded to America with a servant girl, leaving his wife, Sarah Lunt, with three children, debts and no home. Rather than go to the workhouse she made her own arrangements; her brother and brother-in-law each took in one of her sons, whilst she hired herself out, as a housekeeper and cheese maker, to a bachelor farmer, taking her infant daughter with her. As soon as she had saved enough money she rented a cottage for the family, in Close Lane, and scraped a living running a dame's school, referred to below in chapter 7.[5]

1847-49 was the time of the great potato famine which, though mainly linked with Ireland, also affected England. Irish vagrants flooded the countryside, and the Guardians were instructed that;-

> *"Irish are to be sent back to Ireland if they cannot give a satisfactory account of themselves."*

Forms were issued to Arclid for the removal of the Scottish and Irish paupers. None are recorded as being removed from Alsager, but there was a large number removed from Congleton and from Sandbach, some of whom had worked as nail-makers or silk workers for up to 35 years. Arclid's Board of Guardians were not happy about these removal orders, and along with other

---

[5] From unpublished autobiographical notes by James Holland Lunt, 1850-1923.

Unions, petitioned Parliament, in May 1847, for the abolition of the 200 year-old settlement laws which were still in place in the 1870's.

Meanwhile, in Arclid, because of the potato famine the number of vagrants was at a peak and 80% of them were Irish. With them came typhus fever, known as the 'Irish fever' and this spread to other inmates; even the Master went down with it, for although tramps were housed overnight in accommodation away from the main wing, the sick vagrants were put into the infirmary of 26 beds along with other patients. Clearly this was unsatisfactory, so a small isolation ward was constructed by putting a roof over the girls' wash-houses. It was later used for local fever cases at a charge of 5.s. per week. Bedding was also fumigated at Arclid.

Following two serious outbreaks of small-pox, a fever feared above any, in 1889 and 93, a special small-pox unit was put up by the Rural Sanitary Authority, in the far corner of the workhouse fields. This wooden building was doubled in size in 1902, and continued to serve the area, including Crewe, as a general isolation hospital until the end of the second world war.

Right up to 1939 vagrants, or tramps and beggars as they were then called, were a common sight trudging through Alsager, calling on households to beg for food and money. They would travel from one workhouse to another, where, with a ticket from the relieving officer, they could get lodging, supper and breakfast the next morning in return for breaking up two hundred weight of stone. Any valuables or cash they might have about them would be buried before presenting themselves to the porter, with the intention of recovering them the next morning. Over the years there have been reports of little hoards being dug up in and around the workhouse. What could not be found in the last century, metal detectors have found in this.

Before 1834 the mentally ill, or lunatics, as they were then known, were mostly kept in the community; although we saw that Hannah Colclough's lunacy certificate landed her in the Roundhouse at Knutsford. Cheshire's first asylum opened at Upton, Chester, in the 1840's, but by 1846 it was already overcrowded and Arclid was required to keep all but the most violent lunatic paupers. In 1855 they had eleven, but clearly had insufficient room as the Master was reprimanded for putting male lunatics two to a bed. Parkside Asylum, Macclesfield, opened in 1867, but quickly became overcrowded and as late as 1927 Arclid had to find room for 12 mental patients; see page 91.

Workhouse children were especially deprived, of their parents and of contact with the outside world. The school inspectors were critical of the lack of books, other than text books, and of toys and the general monotony of the children's existence. By the turn of the century the children were attending Brereton school. When they were apprenticed, often as young as ten or eleven, it was generally in their own Union since the settlement laws still applied and townships were not keen to take others' paupers. Sometimes boundaries were crossed; in 1884 Newcastle-under-Lyme Union wanted to place two boys in Alsager. The Congleton Guardians allowed one to be bound to John Askew, tailor, but blocked the other, citing the proposed shoemaker master as *"unsuitable"*.

In 1913 the workhouses became known as Poor Law Institutions, and remained known as such until their final disappearance when the National Health Service was inaugurated in 1948.

Hospitals.

There were two hospitals at which Alsager folk could be treated. The first to be opened was Hartshill Royal Infirmary in the 1830's. It was a voluntary hospital, initially endowed by the Duchess of Sutherland, but kept going with the aid of voluntary subscriptions. In 1839 the Board of Guardians of Arclid discussed becoming subscribers to it which would have qualified them to sent pauper cases there. Alsager supported the infirmary financially in several ways; the friendly societies subscribed, which entitled their members to hospital treatment there; special church collections, such as those at harvest festival, were donated; and between the wars a huge village carnival was held each summer to raise funds.

The Cottage Hospital in Crewe was built by the railway company, especially for the railway town, and was opened in 1896. That too was a voluntary hospital, dependent on fund raising efforts as well as the regular contributions from works and friendly societies.

To prove one's entitlement to treatment, a 'recommend' had to be obtained and signed by a clergyman or a J.P. In the early 1920's almoners were introduced into hospitals, to enquire into patients' means and to decide whether they could afford to contribute to the treatment.

The role of the Infirmary at Arclid was of great importance to the township, as an infirmary for the elderly and the chronically sick, right up to its closure. The workhouse from the start included an infirmary with twenty-six beds where the sick were tended by pauper women, not strong enough for manual work. They were however allowed extra food for their duties.

This infirmary was never large enough despite extensions carried out twice within a thirty year period. Finally, at the turn of the century a new two-storey, 100-bed, hospital was built, although at first there was only money enough to left to furnish the ground floor. The new building was provided with nurses' accommodation. In the late 1850's, when a paid attendant was employed, she had been untrained and her duties often doubled with those of dress-maker or seamstress. Once the cook was promoted to the position, and paupers were still employed on the wards as late as 1904. State registration of nurses started in 1919, and Arclid's first S.R.N. was possibly appointed in

1927. Steadily the importance of the infirmary grew in relation to the workhouse, and in time it was no longer called, 'a pauper hospital', but, 'a hospital for the poor'. One historian considers the medical services which the poor law provided as being the forerunner of the National Health Service.[6]

In the early 1920's accommodation for maternity cases, other than paupers, were accepted at a charge of £1 per week. Over half the 128 babies born up to 1949 were illegitimate; should the mother be under age she was considered a moral defective and sometimes kept in Arclid indefinitely. One such girl was known to have been there from the age of 16 until her death at 92.

The popularity of the motor car brought in more business, for a surprisingly high number of accidents occurred in the area, one actually demolished the infirmary's wall.

At the beginning of the second world war, in preparation for war casualties, five wooden huts were built in the grounds, and by 1941 there were 395 beds available, but they were used for evacuated patients rather than by the military. When, in 1948, the National Health Service was created, all hospitals, including former poor law infirmaries, were brought under the same organisation.

While the 1900 building and the war-time huts continued to be used for the elderly, the original building was used for mental cases as was the old workhouse. Much excellent nursing care was given over the years, but the buildings were old, and inconvenient, despite vast improvements carried out in 1970. At that time the Crewe Chronicle described it as the biggest and brightest of the Cheshire hospitals; but for the elderly of Alsager who had long memories, however bright it was, it never lost the stigma of being part of the workhouse. Arclid closed its doors in 1995 and now all that remains is the site.

Self Help and Friendly Societies.

To lessen the ever present spectre of illness, leading to pauperism and the workhouse, working men banded together to form self-help groups to give mutual support in times of hardship. Generally they were based at an inn where members would meet and pay in their weekly subscriptions. The following is a typical example of the aims and objects of such a society;-

> *"That this Society is established for the purpose of raising by voluntary subscriptions of the members thereof, a joint stock or fund for the mutual relief and maintenance. . . . in old age, sickness or infirmity. . . ."*

Hence the saying ,'on the club,' when a man was off work ill through illness.

---

[6] Gwendoline Ayres, *"England's First State Hospitals"*; At The Cross Roads 1971.

In Alsager the majority of members were small tradesmen, such as wheelwrights, smiths, carters, cobblers, and a sprinkling of smallholders and farm labourers; those who could afford the weekly payments. To distinguish themselves from plain burial clubs many of them adopted a name and became a 'brotherhood', with a certain amount of ritual, a kind of poor man's masonry. There were at least four such societies in Alsager and they flourished through the 19c. and into the 20th. Three of them were based on public houses, but the fourth, which had its roots in the temperance movement, met at the Primitive Methodist School. They were:-

The Loyal Order of Ancient Shepherds.

This had the largest membership and met at the Alsager Arms. The Society was founded in Lancashire in 1826 and spread to Talke o'th' Hill and the Potteries. The Alsager lodge was an off-shoot of the Talke o'th' Hill lodge, and probably started in the second half of the 19c.

The Ancient Order of Foresters.

Also founded in Lancashire, Alsager's Court spread from, and was known as the 'Bold Robin Hood'. It met at the Railway Inn in Audley Road, now inappropriately called 'The Yeoman'. Initially there were 23 members, with an average age of 23. It never had more than 40 members, yet it survived until 1930.

The Ancient Order of Druids.

The Society met at the Lodge Inn. Not much is known of it except that a banner was discovered in the attic of the Lodge during a change over of landlords in the 1960's.

The Independent Order of Good Templars.

The local branch was called 'Hope of Alsager Lodge'. Again little is known of its activities except for the information given in an advertisement of a club day during Stoke's Wakes Week in 1873. This proclaimed the first grand annual demonstration in a field in Alsager, and a special train was laid on from Stoke. All lodges were invited to attend, with members wearing their regalia.

Annual Club Days were held to proclaim the solidarity of these societies. There would be a procession around the village, with banners, decorated carts and many people in costume. The Shepherds wore large brimmed hats, their officers bore crooks and shears, and were accompanied by the minstrel carrying a tin harp, representing David in the Old Testament. Another member carried a live lamb. Their club day was held in the Potteries Wakes week, the first week in August, and was a great attraction to folk outside the township. In 1883 Rector Skene recorded that 3,000 people came down from the Potteries by train. Here is his report taken from the parish magazine in 1884;-

> *". . . . From early morning the township was astir. A brilliant procession with bands and horsemen and colours flying made its customary progress, ... A short service was held in the Mission Room at 10.45 the Rector conducting it, and delivering the address; and at 2 pm all sat down to dinner provided by Mr. Bates in a tent opposite the approach to the Brunds. Loyal toasts were proposed. . . . It would be difficult to describe the attractions on the Brunds. . . . A cricket and football match, booths and entertainment of every description, swings and hobby horses and the performance of acrobats; every kind of amusement and mirth was provided."*

The fair, held on Mr. Barkers land, the Brunds, later the sand quarry, was reached by the railway bridge in Talke Road.

The Druids held their club day entertainments on Fairview Field, now occupied by the central car park. Where the Foresters held their gala is not known, but their regalia included bows and arrows and costumes in Lincoln green. There were stringent rules to be kept and members who did not toe the line were fined.

After the birth of National Insurance in 1911 the role of the friendly societies lessened; although Lloyd George with his "9d. for 4d." scheme enlisted their support and their experience in collecting and distributing funds. Self employed men stayed with the friendly societies; others, such as the railway men, paid through their unions.

1946 saw the introduction of the compulsory National Health Insurance Scheme, the importance of friendly societies changed dramatically, and their membership declined. Some like the Shepherds are still in existence as bastions of thrift, but in a different form.

From the 1850's onward the social hierarchy of the village changed from 'farmers and cottagers', as Rector Skene quaintly called them, to working class and middle class. The wives and daughters of the new residents had servants, and time on their hands. What better way to use it than in charity work? The ladies of the church formed a Dorcas Society; they met once a month, at what made an agreeable social gathering, either at the mission church, or in Mrs. Ford's house and garden, at Heathfields in Dunnocksfold Road, to drink tea and sew useful garments to give to the 'deserving poor'. January 1st was the distribution day. The rector conducted a short service in the mission room for the Dorcas Society and *'those who had been selected to be the recipients of their bounty'*. In 1884 the report in the parish magazine read;-

> *"After the service a distribution was made (to such deserving poor as had received tickets) of sheets, flannel, underclothing for adults and children, also strips of calico to be made up at home. Over 40 families received seasonable gifts. . . . The ladies of the Dorcas who kindly devote their money, time and attention to this charitable work, give careful consideration to the wants of every case brought to their notice."*

By the 1890's a similar charity was being run, by a Mrs. Johnson, called the 'Mothers Help Society'. Whether it was an offshoot of the Dorcas or a rival to it is not clear. Alsager, unlike Barthomley, did not have a lying in charity to provide, or to loan out, equipment for a confinement.

Doctors and Nurses and Druggists

A resident doctor was a rarity in rural areas until the second half of the 19c., when G.P.'s began setting up practices in the developing parts of the parish. Barthomley township itself seems not to have had one. There are rare references to doctors' expenses in the overseers' accounts for the poor which seem to suggest that the parish looked to Sandbach for medical assistance. In 1685 a Dr. Daine of Sandbach treated 'Oakes lad', possibly a pauper apprentice, who had been scalded or burned and needed special attention.

"Jan. 28	*paid for carrying him to Sandbach to the*	
	Doctor	*1s.0d.*
Feb. 18	*ditto*	*1s.3d.*
Match 23	*pd. for Allom butter & meale for his feet*	
	& for dressing them	*5s.6d.*
March 25	*Pd. to Doctor Daine for curing his feete*	*5s.6d."*

The Alsager Town Book reveals that in 1759 Mary Hulse was given 1s.6d., *"To pay the Doctor for the cure of her leg"*, and in 1778 Dr. Millington's bill came to £2-3-11, presumably the annual account for the sick paupers.

In 1834 Alsager was placed in the Sandbach district of the Congleton Union with Dr. Charles Latham of Sandbach as its medical officer. He probably already treated private patients in the township. The Land Tax returns for 1795 show that a Mr. Latham of Sandbach came into possession of land at Day Green, occupied by Samuel Thorley, later he acquired Day Green Farm, occupied by Humphrey Lowe. Subsequently these properties passed to Dr. Latham, who is shown in the Tithe Award of 1840 as owning a total of 104 acres. In addition to the Day Green land this included eight acres acquired as a result of the recent inclosure of the Heath, on what is now the site of the University car park; this was occupied by a Widow Mason and included a house.

Dr. Henry Crutchley was the first G.P. to settle here and to start up a practice. Born in Market Drayton in 1840, he was awarded his medical degrees in London in 1861-62, he came to Alsager soon after and was still in practice when he died at the age of 84. His surgery was in Sandbach Road, attached to Holmcroft, the house adjacent to the war memorial, which he built. One of his biggest concerns was public health; a regular attender at the ratepayers' meetings from the early 1870's, he constantly brought up the need for a safe water supply and sewage system, so much so that the rector, with some resignation, reported in the parish magazine of March 1889 *"The well worn water question was discussed"*. In 1875 he urged that Alsager should adopt the recently passed Public Health Act, *"In consequence of the great increase of population and the general want of sanitary arrangements"*.

Crutchley was appointed Alsager's first Medical Officer of Health at the inaugural meeting of the newly formed 'Local Board of the District of Alsager' in March 1894, at a salary of £15 per annum. His first self appointed task was to go around with the workmen to disinfect the sewers, many of which were blocked, especially Shady Grove and The Fields, and he made a fine distinction between sewer gas and 'stink'.

He was a much loved physician and played an active part in raising money for the building of St. Mary's church. At his death in 1924 his patients and family presented the church with its bishop's chair in his memory. His practice was taken over by Dr. Percy Harpur, an Ulsterman who married Dorothy, a daughter of Adolphus Goss. He followed Dr. Kingston as Medical Officer of Health. After his death in 1956 this particular practice died out.

As the population continued to grow, another practice was started in the 1890's by Dr. Kingston of Avondale, Church Road. After his untimely death in 1922, Sir Francis Joseph included this story in his appreciation.

> *Whilst waiting for the train at Alsager station I heard a cripple maid of humble circumstances tell a friend: 'He was a good man to the poor. He doctored mother and father and would never let us pay a penny. Mother sometimes sent me for the medicine, when I asked; How much? he would laugh and say - Oh , five pounds'.* (Equivalent to about £100 in 1999)

After 1922 his practice was carried on by Dr. Frederick Lynd, another Belfast Irishman, whose famous brother was the journalist and cartoonist, Robert Lynd. The waiting room walls were adorned with his brother's amusing cartoons, all taking humorous swipes at the medical profession and patients. He was the official panel doctor and, during the war, was the Ordnance factory doctor also. In the 1930's the surgery was moved to Pool House, Crewe Road where today it still continues on a larger scale under the name of the Mere Medical Centre.

The third village practice was that of Dr. Matthew Hazlitt Sayers in Lawton Road, started sometime before the first World War. In the 1930's he took a young doctor, George Bates, as his partner. Dr. Bates became popular among mothers with families for his modern methods, his sympathy and his modest bills; for while the worker of the family was treated free by the panel doctor i.e. the doctor appointed to treat those who paid National Insurance, mothers and children had to pay for treatment. The practice relocated to Sandbach Road South in 1989 and is today known as the Cedars Medical Practice.

Simple operations such as tonsillectomies were performed on the kitchen table, with the kitchen decked out as a makeshift theatre. When, after a sudden death, a post-mortem was ordered, then that was likely to be carried out in the front room or parlour.

Druggists

There has been a long tradition of home and herbal remedies for most illnesses, these include comfrey, for sprains and bruises, foxglove, for relieving pain and goose oil for bad chests. A standard remedy in Alsager for ear-ache was a hot boiled onion placed in a sock and held to the ear. Quack medicines could be bought from travelling salesmen, or at nearby fairs. However, by 1850 an Alsager tradesman, John Espley, described himself in a gazetteer as a 'druggist and shopkeeper'. In later census returns he is listed as a grocer. In the 1881 census there was another druggist and chemist, John Priddin, aged 25. Both these men probably sold a range of patent pills and medicines, for prescriptions were not in general use. Doctors had their own dispensaries at their surgeries, and made up their own medicines for patients. In the 1930's the Co-op grocery department carried an impressive range of patent medicines which were kept locked in a large glass-fronted cupboard.

In Morriss's Directory of 1874 there is no mention of Mr. Priddin, but a chemist's shop was being run by Harding and Shields in Lawton Road, where Lloyds chemists is today. By the time of the 1881 census Mr. Shields, Westmorland born and aged 37, was, as well as running a druggists shop, also practising as a dentist. By 1914 the chemists shop was in the hands of John Lothian Potter, while Joseph Shield continued as Alsager's sole dentist for many years. By the 1930's there were two qualified dentists in the village, Arthur Fisher and Reginald Piggin, and Mr. Beaumont had succeeded Mr. Potter as chemist.

Nurses

Nursing did not become a profession until the second half of the 19c. care of the sick was undertaken by the family, with the aid of village women possibly having special skills. We have evidence from the Overseers' accounts, as seen above, of women, especially widows, being paid to care for others in the community. When smallpox broke out in 1771 Ann Robinson was paid to care for a victim.

There would have always been women who assisted in childbirth, but the first to be described as a midwife was Hannah Rhodes, in the 1871 census. She was a widow, aged 71, living in Shady Grove. Also in Shady Grove lived Samuel Hancock a widower aged 59, who was a licensed warden in lunacy. In 1881 he was caring, in his own home, for Levi Edwards, an imbecile aged 47, born in Weston. This was most likely a private arrangement. In 1881, Janet Macbeth aged 59, the widow of the former station master who had been tragically killed, was also listed as a midwife.

By 1914 there were at least three nurses, Mrs Taylor, Martha Done and Eliza Holinshead. Dressed in neat navy blue uniforms they were familiar figures riding their bicycles in an unhurried manner. In the 1920's and 30's the schools had Nurse Percival, known to the children as 'the nit nurse'. She was also on the district, visiting young mothers and babies in their homes; she organised a mother and baby clinic, which was held in St. Mary's school, run by a group of volunteer ladies.

In more recent times ancillary medical services, including child care, dentistry, district nursing and ambulance services, have been organised from the County Council Clinic and Ambulance station in Sandbach Road South.

By the beginning of the 20c. a more humane attitude to poverty was developing. Doctors, clergymen and enlightened industrialists, began to examine the causes of poverty and ill health among the working classes. A Royal Commission was set up, by Lloyd George, from which came the introduction of the old age pensions, in 1908, of 5s. a week at the age of 70; the opening of labour exchanges in 1911; and an insurance scheme for men in employment. This ensured workers were entitled to free medical care from the 'panel' doctor.

In 1929 the Public Assistance Division of the county council took over the administration of the workhouse, the Board of Governors was abolished, together with the word *'pauper'*, and Arclid became known as the Public Assistance Institution, but actually nothing changed, poor relief stayed the same. However, after almost a century of *"Intimidating the pauper into not being a pauper"*,[7] the end was in sight. The Beveridge Report, written and published in 1942 during the time of a National Government, planned a revolutionary social system but it had to wait until the end of the war to be implemented.

Following the National Insurance and National Health Service Acts, of 1946, the Welfare State came into being, on the 5th July 1948, providing unheard of security; free health care for all, and financial help in childbirth, sickness, unemployment, bereavement and old age. The Minister of National Insurance wrote of it as being a great day in the development of our social services. *"We have come a long way from the Old Age Pensions Act of 1908. This scheme is more than an Act of Parliament; it is an act of faith in the British People"*.

With all its flaws the National Health Service is more in the spirit of the charity of the old, parish orientated, poor relief, than was the Victorian union workhouse system, which prevailed from 1834 to 1948.

---

[7] Pauline Gregg, *A Social and Economic History of Britain 1760-1980.*

Chapter 6

A Religious Survey

It has already been shown that the earliest history of the church's activity in Alsager is unrecorded and unknown. But there is reasonable certainty that, from the middle years of the 13c., the township formed part of Barthomley parish, where the church of St Bertoline had been established before the Norman Conquest and where Alsager people had to trek to attend services, marry, christen their children and bury the dead. This situation continued until the establishment of the first Alsager parish in 1898, although the ties with the mother church were considerably weakened when Christ Church opened for worship in 1789, particularly with regard to church attendance, christenings and burials.

At Barthomley church officers were elected each year at a parish meeting, held on Easter Monday, and known as the vestry meeting. Two churchwardens and three sidesmen (one officer from each of the parish's townships) were elected in rotation. Alsager's man served as a churchwarden every third year, alternating with Balterley and Haslington, and as a sidesman the other two years. Barthomley and Crewe returned the second warden alternately. The position of these men in the parish was of greater importance than their modern counterparts because they, under the rector and lord of the manor, were the civil administrators, as well as being responsible for the running of the church.

A church rate was imposed on all parishioners; in the 17c. it was one shilling per plough (or Farm) and sixpence a cottage, and increased over the years. The money raised was used for repairs to the church, apart from the chancel, a never ending process; for wages paid for cleaners, parish clerk and bell-ringers, and the bread and wine for communion, the consumption of which seems to have been quite high!

A half-yearly report, called a presentment, was made to the archdeacon in Nantwich. This included a submission of the church accounts, reports of parishioners neglect of church attendance, the state of the building, and even the rector's misbehaviour. At the annual visitation in Nantwich the churchwardens, together with the rector, curate and sidesmen, presented themselves before the diocesan officials to be sworn in for their year of office.

This was invariably followed by a celebration, as in June 1690;-[1]

> *"payd the Court fees at the visitation   4s.0d.*
> *spent at the same visitation on*
> *parishioners and ourselves   £1.11.0."*

At the visitation of 1586 the curate became so drunk that he fell off his horse, into a pond, on the way home, and would have drowned had he not been rescued by the churchwardens.[2] At every visitation a copy of the church register for the previous year was submitted, and a list of recusants; that is, persons who did not take communion and who were suspected of being practising Catholics, was presented.

The earliest known reference to religious life in Alsager comes in 1578, when it is recorded that Robert Alger of Barthomley, husbandman, son of George and Elizabeth Alsager, and his wife Katherine were presented at the Metropolitan Visitation as being recusants.[3] If They were likely to have been fined 12d. but whether or not this was collected would depend on the churchwardens of the parish. Robert and Katherine can be identified with the Robert and Katherine Alsager of Alsager Hall, recorded in various deeds between 1548 and 1602, and whose marriage settlement is dated 1548.[4] They appear to have been indicted at the Quarter Sessions in 1582, for absence from church, but the court proceedings were relatively ineffective. Out of forty-one recusants, who were bidden to attend the quarter sessions, only five turned up to answer the charges, and it appears that these were dropped. Robert was presented again, as a non communicant, at the Diocesan Visitation in 1592, and as a trouble maker, at the Metropolitan Visitation in 1595.

Alsager folk had to bend before religious and political upheavals on a number of occasions. In the 1560's it appears that Robert Kinsey, the parson of Barthomley, was *'suspected to be a favorer of the masse and such papisticall tradicons'*, but it appears from the records that the main charge against this clergyman was one of sexual immorality. In the early part of the 17c. the form of worship at Barthomley appears to have been plain and simple, and to have continued in this Puritan form during the Commonwealth period. At the Restoration, in 1660, the restored former rector, Zachary Cawdrey, a conformist, or 'high churchman', appears to have reintroduced the prayer book, the wearing of vestments, and the practice of kneeling to receive communion, as required by the the Act of Uniformity in 1662, which

---

[1] Barthomley Church Wardens' Accounts 1663 - 1690.
[2] Edward Hinchliffe, *Barthomley*, 1856 p. 44 [Hinchliffe 1856]
[3] *"Elizabethan Recusancy in Cheshire"*; Chetham Society vol. 19. 1971. pp. 7, 8, 17, 41, 70 and appendix I p.139.
[4] Brit. Lib. Additional Charters; ref 53546.

precipitated the 'Great Ejectment'.[5] (Cawdrey had been 'sequestered' in 1649, see *'Barthomley, An Estate Village'.*)

The 1680's saw King James II, who was married to a Catholic, attempting to re-establish Catholicism in England. The church was unhappy, and six protesting bishops were put under arrest, only a fortnight before the queen produced an heir, for which the parishioners were instructed to say special prayers.

> *"1688*   *payd for a book for a day of thanksgiving*
> *for the Queen's being with child*   *8d.*
> *July*   *payd Mark Topping for an order for a*
> *Thanksgiving for the queen's safe delivery*   *8d."*

A further change of direction came with 'The Glorious Revolution,' in 1688. William of Orange, and his wife Mary, daughter of James II, were offered the English throne; the battle of the Boyne had been fought and won, and King James, his queen and baby son had fled to France. Popery was out, Protestantism was back again, and the parishioners were obliged to change direction with more special prayers.

> *"Feb 14*   *payd for a form of prayer of thanksgiving*
> *from popery & slavery.*   *8d.*
> *Spent on the Bell Ringers on the same day*   *2s.6d."*

The church accounts for the second half of the 17c. list a number of fascinating collections for good causes, some of which may have been compulsory, with the names from each township separately recorded. They were called 'briefs', and any town or persons who had suffered grievous loss could be granted one by Parliament, this permitted them to beg for financial help. In November 1671 a collection was made for captives in 'Turkie'. Mrs. Alsager of Alsager Hall gave 5s.0d; and Randle Poole of Cresswellshawe, 1s.10d. Seventeen contributions from Alsager amounted to £1-8-9. The whole parish collected £10. There was a 'brief' in 1682 for the relief of the "poore distressed French Protestants here in England"; and in 1689 and 1690, 'briefs' for the "distressed Irish Protestants here in England".

When the Lord Mayor of London appealed for relief after the Great fire, in 1666, Barthomley parish responded with;-

> *"Seven pounds and ten shilling . . . . collected on a fast day, 10 October*
> *1666 for those who had lost all in the sad fire within the citie of London."*

A further contribution was made in 1676, towards the cost of rebuilding St. Paul's Cathedral. Twenty-one Alsager men are listed as having donated between two shillings (Hugh Kent), and one penny (William Hardern and others).

---

[5] Barthomley Town Book 1664 records the purchase of a hood for Mr Cawdrey.

In the 17c. the church was responsible for collecting an annual tax called the 'Prisoners & Maymed soldiers money', for the relief of soldiers injured in the civil war; Alsager's contribution in 1676 was 9s.9d.

Occasionally parishioners were on the receiving end of parish funds; hedgehogs were thought to be a pest, sucking the milk from lactating cows, 2d. a head was paid by the churchwardens to those who caught them. It proved such a popular and lucrative sport, for there are long lists of hedgehog-catchers from 1671, that it is surprising that they did not become extinct!

> *"1678   For the heads of hedgehogs that were kild in Alsager*
> *which were forty-six   7s.8d."*

The churchwardens were paying out very large sums, compared to their income, and eventually the practice was stopped;-

> *"March the 28th 1692 being Easter Monday*
> *It is this day ordered by the wardens and Parishioners being mett That the*
> *Churchwardens for the future shall pay nothing for Hedge hoggs*
> *John Platt   John Smith   Ch. wardens."*

In addition to other taxes, all occupiers of property, even the tenants of the smallest croft, had to pay tithes to the rector. These payments constituted a significant part of his income, out of which he was responsible for the repair and upkeep of the chancel of the church and the rectory. In theory the 'tithe' was a tenth of all produce, every tenth egg, chicken, calf and produce of the land etc. Tithes were a vexed question and often led to bitter disputes between the rector and his parishioners. In the 16c. and 17c. several Barthomley disputes ended in the bishop's Consistory Court at Chester. In this parish, tithes were gathered in kind (apart from hay for which there was a modus), until 1840 when they were commuted to a sum of money. In 1705, in reply to an enquiry from the bishop, Rector Offley stated that the tithes were worth £150. In 1885 they amounted to £840; Alsager's portion of that being £240. Tithes continued to be paid up to the passing of the Tithe Act 1936 following which a redemption annuity had to be paid for a period of sixty years, which under the terms of the Finance Act 1962, had to be redeemed on the first sale of the property in question. The annuities were finaly abolished by the Finance Act 1977.

There was little sign of meaningful religious activity in the township during the first three quarters of the eighteenth century. The hamlet was dominated by the established church, the church of St. Bertoline, some three miles away, whose patrons and rectors were all members of the aristocratic Crewe family. Religious dissent too was almost totally lacking at this time; when in 1804, the Reverend Henry Babbington was asked for his comments, during a visitation enquiry from the bishop of Chester, he was able to deny all knowledge of any Papists, Presbyterians, Independents, Anabaptists, Quakers or any other sects. There was certainly no mention of Alsager in the

Nonconformist Ejections of 1660-62, although the list of dissenting ministers ejected or silenced did include clergymen in Barthomley, Haslington, Astbury and Church Lawton, suggesting a local nonconformist following. The hamlet appears to have figured in the Cheshire applications for licences to be granted under Charles II's 1672 Declaration of Indulgence to Congregational and Presbyterian ministers, in that licences were granted[6] to Ralph Alsager of Barthomley, possibly the same Ralph Alsager of Alsager, recorded as having one hearth in the Hearth Tax returns and referred to as 'brother of John Alsager' and 'yeoman', in the latter's will dated 1688; and to Hugh Kent of Barthomley. The latter is likely to have been the Hugh Kent, of Alsager, who died in 1686, and is described as 'gentleman' in his will. He is recorded as having four hearths in the Hearth Tax returns, his house has not been identified but evidence from a sale catalogue of 1889 makes reference to ground rents of 'Kent's tenement', with clues that this might be Town End Farm, now the Manor Hotel. By 1720, Bishop Gastrell's *"Notitia Cestriensis"* still contains no mention of Alsager, merely recording Barthomley as containing eleven dissenting families, and one Presbyterian meeting house; (this compared with Nantwich which had 5 Papists, 157 Presbyterians, 109 Anabaptists and 13 Quakers). Dissent was not completely moribund, witness the Quarter Session records of 1702 and 1726 respectively; these note that the houses of Jos. Hardhorne of Alsager, and Elizabeth Hilditch of Heath House, Alsager (situated in Well Lane), be duly registered as nonconformist places of worship.

What of the tide of Methodism? This was certainly making great inroads into the Anglican church's hold on the urban working class in North Staffordshire, witness the extracts from John Wesley's diary on page 125.

So far as Alsager was concerned the flame was flickering rather feebly, as Ian Sellars' introduction to Wesley Place Methodist Church centenary brochure bears witness;-

> *"John Wesley, though a frequent visitor to south east Cheshire, having preached at Congleton twenty-one times, at Nantwich seven, at Burslem sixteen, and more frequently at Astbury, Woore and Betley, probably never visited the township of Alsager. In his day this hamlet was in fact painfully remote, isolated and wretchedly poor, consisting of a few cottages on a vast expanse of soggy mossland, overgrown with furze and interlaced with sandy lanes which became impassable in wet or windy seasons."* (this description is not borne out by much of the evidence of this book!)

The dominance of the rectors of Barthomley was to be challenged in 1789, not by the power of John Wesley, but rather by the more subtle methods of three aristocratic ladies, the Ladies of the Manor of Alsager.

[6] F. J. Powick, *History of the Cheshire Union of Congregational Churches;* 1907.

A History of Christ Church.[7]

Christ Church, Alsager, has two unusual features, the style of its architecture and the manner of its creation. In its architecture it bears no resemblance to the gothic style of many other English parish churches; its antecedents are to be found in the basilicas of classical Italy and the renaissance designs of Andrea Palladio.[8] The instrument of its creation was also out of the ordinary, being a Private Act of Parliament dated 3rd February 1789,[9] whose preamble set forth the reason for the church's building;-

> *"Whereas the Parish of Barthomley in the County and Diocese of Chester, is very large, and a great part of it. particularly the Township of Alsager, situate at a considerable distance from the parish church of Barthomley aforesaid, inasmuch as many of the inhabitants are frequently hindered from attending Divine service there."*

The Act to resolve this undesirable situation was the work of the three Ladies of the Manor of Alsager who were given considerable powers;-

> *"An Act to enable Mary Alsager, Margaret Alsager and Judith Alsager to finish and complete a new Church or Chapel in the Parish of Barthomley. . . . and to endow the same; and to establish a Charity School within the said Parish, and vesting the Right of Presentation to the said Church in them and the future Lords and Ladies of the Manor of Alsager."*

This power, although extensive, was not without limitation. Thus the Ladies had the rights of Nomination and Presentation, and they alone could appoint curates and churchwardens to 'Christ Church, Alsager', as the new church was to be called; the Act saw it as a 'separate entity with a separate endowment'. However, it was to be a church without a parish, its clergy were to be known as 'curates', or, 'incumbents in charge of a proprietary or private chapel', and were not to be given the title of 'vicar' until 1946. There were also financial restrictions; although situated in the parish of Barthomley none of the Barthomley parishioners was to be responsible for Christ Church expenses' such as church repairs, churchwardens' expenses, and the curate's stipend. These financial burdens were to be met by pew rents, later supplemented by an endowment by which the benevolent ladies diverted rents, from their Brookhouse estate, to meet the cost of the stipend.

---

[7] For a fuller and illustrated account of the history of Christ Church, see; *"Christ Church Alsager 1789 - 1989"*, by T.R. Anelay. Staffordshire Polytechnic 1989.

[8] Pevsner; in *'Cheshire'* in his series *'The Buildings of England,'* Penguin Books 1971, attributes the design to Thomas Stringer.

[9] 29 *Geo.*III. 1789; CRO. ref. DMD/A/21

A further problem remained for the infant church as set forth in the 25th paragraph of the Act of 1789;-

> *"Provided always, and be it exacted and declared, That nothing in the Act contained shall extend to defeat or prejudice any Right, Title, Interest, Claim or Demand of the Rector of the said Parish of Barthomley, or any Tithes, Offerings, Surplice Fees, Oblations, Obventions or other Ecclesiastical Rights or Dues, arising within the said Parish, and belonging to the Rector thereof."*

In practice this paragraph meant that, from the moment of consecration, all baptisms and burials carried out at Christ Church were to be entered in duplicate in the Barthomley registers in addition to those kept at Alsager. Moreover, all churchings and burials at Alsager carried a double fee, half of which was paid to the Barthomley rector despite the fact that he had played no part in the Alsager services. It was not until the 18th August 1852 that this practice was terminated by an Order in Council which created a new District Chapelry of Alsager, also to be known as the Township of Alsager, bounded on north, south, east and west by the parishes of Sandbach, Audley, Church Lawton and Barthomley respectively. Furthermore, marriages were to be solemnised in Christ Church for the first time and the fees accruing therefrom given to the Alsager incumbent, as from 18th November 1852. This happy state of affairs was to last for only sixteen years when it was threatened from an unexpected source; from the London law courts, in the case of Fitzgerald v. Champneys, it was held that the power of assigning Districts did not extend to a Chapel regulated by a Local Act. This put the 1852 Order in Council aside; in giving his Counsel's Opinion on 29th December 1868, Henry Casson of Lincoln's Inn, stated that the case of Christ Church, Alsager, *"could not be distinguished in principle"* from the Fitzgerald v. Champneys ruling. In particular he stated that, *"If the Order in Council be, as I think, invalid, it would seem that a serious doubt would exist as to the legality of the marriages which have been solemnised in the Chapel."* The consternation caused to those persons who had exchanged marriage vows at Christ Church can readily be imagined, a consternation which was to last until 1881, when the Alsager Chapel (Marriages) Act legalised all Christ Church marriages in the following terms;-

> *"All Marriages so solemnised shall notwithstanding that the Order in Council of 18th August 1852 may be found to be invalid be as valid as they would have been if the said Order in Council had been validly made in pursuance of the above-mentioned Acts."*

Two years after the resolution of this marriage crisis a burials crisis now troubled Christ Church congregation. The quarter-acre burial ground, opened in 1789, was now full, and the Burial Acts Department of the Home Office had ruled that no further interments were to take place at Christ Church, other than in existing graves, i.e. relatives of those already interred. The problem was resolved in an interesting way; from 1847 to 1881 the position of curate at Christ Church had been held by two members of the Alsager family. Charles Alsager Tryon and William Archibald Sheringham. The latter incumbent, in his capacity as lord of the manor of Alsager, offered, at the Easter vestry meeting, to give half an acre of glebe land for the extension of the burial ground, on condition that his parishioners paid for the building of its boundary wall. This was duly carried out, a Mr. Samuel Davies of Alsager undertook to carry out the work at a cost of two hundred pounds, thus freeing another 800 grave plots and sparing the deceased's relatives the wearisome three-mile journey to Barthomley. In the midst of the rejoicing of the Christ Church congregation came a circular letter from the Rector of Barthomley, informing them of his right under the 1789 Act to claim burial fees for interments in any new Alsager burial ground. This brought to a head the simmering conflict between the Alsager incumbents and the Barthomley rector; already in 1867 there had been an unsuccessful attempt by Charles Alsager Tryon to get rid of the rectors' right to tithes. The adverse opinion by Casson in the Fitzgerald v. Champneys case, gave the Rector, Edward Duncombe, his chance to get rid of the Alsager 'lords of the manor curates'. In April 1881 the Alsager parishioners were stunned to receive the following statement, issued from the Alsager Parsonage.

> *"It has become my duty to inform you that the Rector of Barthomley, having been advised that the Order in Council considering Alsager a separate District is invalid, has intimated to me his intention to assume the personal charge of the people of Alsager as his Parishioners, and therefore I regret to say that my ministerial connection with you out of Church has come to an end. W.A. Sheringham, Incumbent of Christ Church, Alsager, April 1881."*

There were good reasons for the Barthomley rectors' dislike of the 1852 Order in Council, which had made specific reference to 'the consecrated church called Christ Church with its Ecclesiastical District consisting of the Township of Alsager'. The Order had made no reference to the tithes due to the rectors, hence Tryon's attempt to get rid of these in 1867. He saw the legal weapon which gave the rectors the power to interfere in Alsager affairs as a threat, and on the 1st June 1867 submitted a scheme by which one hundred and twenty pounds (or one half) of the annual tithe rent charge was to be surrendered by the rector to the Christ Church incumbent; there is no record of any positive response to the scheme.

It is likely that Sheringham's resignation was partly due to despair; George Skene, the new Barthomley rector, wrote that the Alsager incumbent had been informed by crown legal advisers of the impossibility of making a parish for Christ Church without another private Act of Parliament. This was confirmed when an Alsager deputation was sent to the Bishop of Chester 'praying that Alsager might be separated from the parish of Barthomley.'

Could the Archbishop of York solve the puzzle? Alas no. *"I found that the law officers of the crown had given their decided opinion that no scheme could be drawn up, seeing that Alsager was fenced round by an Act of Parliament - the private Act which had made secure the privileges of the Chapel."*

All attempts to break the deadlock having failed, the Rector decided upon direct action. Following William Sheringham's resignation, there was a period of five years without a curate at Christ Church, this at a time when the population of Alsager was increasing, with a new focus around the railway station, opened in 1848. How were their spiritual needs to be met? George Skene began by arranging services, first in the open-air, then in some private premises in Crewe Road and finally in a building to be known as either the 'Iron Church' or the 'Tin Tabernacle'. Contact with the mother church was to be effected by the publishing of the Barthomley and Alsager Parish Magazine in 1883. Still the embattled Christ Church congregation held out; at a meeting held in the 'New School' on December 29th 1885, it was proposed that a scheme to attach the 'Ecclesiastical Township of Alsager' to Christ Church be considered. The record reveals that speeches were made by Mr. Maddock in support of the proposal, whilst Mr. Craig and Dr. Crutchley opposed. When a counter resolution moved by Messrs. Mayer and Keen, to the effect that *"it is undesirable at the present time to separate Alsager from Barthomley, and that to attach Alsager to Christ Church without providing for a sufficient staff of clergy, would be disastrous to the Church work in Alsager"*, it was carried by the overwhelming vote of 114-6.

Hopes revived in the summer of 1886 with appointment of the Reverend Daniel Shaw as curate. In the autumn of 1890 he was summoned to Chester, along with George Skene, to meet the new bishop who was determined to settle the Alsager question once and for all; his scheme meant the creation of a new parish for Alsager, in which Christ Church would play no part, as follows;

> 1. advowson (or right of presentation to a benefice) to be purchased and vested in the bishop;
>
> 2. new church to be built in a situation to be fixed by the bishop, which shall become the parish church of the new parish;
>
> 3. new parish to be formed consisting of Township of Alsager, embracing within its area Christ Church, Alsager, and taking its endowments, including house and glebe, from the date of the next avoidance (or vacancy) at Christ Church;
>
> 4. Christ Church, Alsager, to become a chapel of ease; its burial ground remaining for the use of the new parish; and
>
> 5. a private Act to be obtained authorising the above proposals, so far as is necessary.

No opposition to the above scheme was to be tolerated, as the letter written from Chester to the Rector of Barthomley, on the 11th October, clearly bears witness.

> *"We are requested by the Bishop to inform you with reference to the various comments and representations received by him on the proposals for the establishment of a new parish, that he cannot accept any modification of these proposals, and particularly that the suggestion to constitute Christ Church as the parish church is not to be entertained on account of the structure and situation of that edifice, so long as there is any prospect of a new and more commodious building being erected in a central position."*

The bishop now moved speedily to implement his five point programme. By January 1891 he was able to write to George Skene thanking him for a cheque for two hundred and forty pounds with which to complete the purchase money necessary to obtain the advowson. February 1891 saw the signing of an indenture between the surviving trustees of the manor of Alsager and the Bishop of Chester, in which the latter was granted the advowson, pews, rights and privileges conferred upon the lords and ladies of Alsager, in return for the payment of five hundred and seventy six pounds. Although it was not until 19th December 1913 that the transfer received its official sanction, the bishop now had all the powers that he needed, including the perpetual right of nomination and representation together with the right or privilege of nominating and appointing churchwardens, clerks, sextons and clerks in holy orders for Christ Church, Alsager.

With all legal powers in the bishop's hands, the creation of the new church was now set in train. By September 1894 its foundation stone was laid, and on St. Peter's Day, 29th June 1898, the church itself, dedicated to St. Mary Magdalene, was duly consecrated. The problems manifest at the consecration of 1789 were not in evidence, the balance of the tithes formerly due to the Barthomley rector were to be surrendered to the incumbent of St. Mary Magdalene as vicar of Alsager and the patronage of the new Alsager benefice was now firmly in the possession of the bishop of Chester. Moreover the irritating duplication of fees for services carried out in Alsager but given to the rector was now a thing of the past. And the final blow to those optimistic Alsager congregation members who still hoped for a parish for Christ Church, came in the form of a Representation, drafted by the Ecclesiastical Commissioners, and signed and sealed by Francis John, bishop of Chester. This asked for a district chapelry to be assigned to St. Mary Magdalene, comprising, *"all that part of the parish of Barthomley. . . . which is comprised within and is coextensive with the limits of the township of Alsager."* The Representation was officially confirmed by an Order in Council dated 18th July 1898. It is interesting that this Order in Council appears to have made no reference to the 1852 Order in Council which had assigned the township of Alsager to 'the Consecrated Church called Christ Church.'

To the bishop it now seemed that the Alsager crisis was under control but the nemesis of clergy shortage was never far away. In October 1906 the Reverend Daniel Shaw, incumbent of Christ Church since 1886, died after a short but painful illness, with no obvious replacement in sight; to be followed by the resignation of the vicar of St. Mary Magdalene in April 1907. The problem was solved in an ingenious fashion, from June 1907 the Reverend H.A. Arnold was appointed in Alsager as the holder of two benefices, as Vicar of St. Mary Magdalene and perpetual curate of Christ Church. Now at last the Anglicans of Alsager were united under one leader and a period of peaceful progress could begin.

The Great War produced many problems for the united parish. Local affairs had to take second place to the young men fighting in France and a 'war working party' was set up immediately following the outbreak of hostilities in August 1914. Twelve months later saw the results of this group's Herculean efforts; it had sent to the Red Cross Society a total of 523 day shirts, 157 night shirts, 759 scarves, 903 pairs of socks and 73 pairs of mittens. The war took its toll of parishioners and clergy alike; Mr. Arnold had been replaced as Vicar of Alsager by the Reverend A. H. Waller, whose curate was soon on his way to join the Royal Army medical Corps. Three years after leaving Alsager H.A. Arnold learned that his son had been killed in France, whilst his nephew had been killed in a flying accident during training for the Royal Flying Corps. The news that the Rector of Church Lawton planned to join up as a forces chaplain meant a further reduction in Alsager clergy manpower, and Christ Church services were cut back to one evensong per month.

With the return of peacetime activities, progress could once more be resumed. In May 1919 a joint Parochial Church Council was instituted, whose membership consisted of the clergy, churchwardens and five other representatives from each church with meetings to be held quarterly. There was to be an annual joint Sale of Work, the proceeds of which were to be allocated pro-rata church seating - St. Mary 500, Christ Church 275. This period of comparative tranquillity came to an end in 1924 when the problem of overstretched clergy resources again came to the fore. Throughout the year no curate was available and Mr. Waller had to look after both churches practically singlehanded although his own health was not good. Ignoring a doctor's warning he went on his usual walking holiday in Scotland where he died of a heart attack.

The combined parish was again without an incumbent until February 1925 when the Reverend Arthur Lowndes Moir accepted the living. At last Alsager had the services of an ideal vicar, young, intelligent, able and industrious. All these qualities were sorely needed during the ten years of his incumbency, much of which was a lone battle against overwhelming odds. Like his predecessor there were staffing problems from the outset. His hopes of assistance from the Reverend E.C. Collier, who had assisted at Christ Church during the interregnum of 1924/25, were dashed when Mr. Collier, already a sick man, died in 1926. Each year saw the coming and going of curates, alternately raising and dashing the hopes of the beleaguered vicar. In October 1926 the Reverend P.L. Dickson was appointed, an experienced man and Canadian missionary, who promptly accepted a post at Huyton instead. In 1927 the Reverend Albert Maturin helped out for a time before being laid low with sunstroke and retiring to Harrogate. In 1929 a Reverend J. Bennett seemed to be the answer to Moir's problems; after serving for a few months he left in June en route for Canada. The main reason for the lack of long term curates was obvious; single candidates were hard to come by and there was no house available to attract a married man.

Arthur Moir struggled on in a hopeless situation. During 1927 he carried out no fewer that one thousand visits to his parishioners and planned to make visits to every house in Alsager in 1928. He speedily saw that the one hope for the parish was work with its young people, a work in which he had conspicuous success. He founded the Christ Church Children's Church as an exact copy of its adult counterpart, having Vicar's and People's wardens, sidesmen and councillors and having its own audited accounts. Arthur Moir inculcated practical Christianity in his young charges, in particular the care of those less fortunate than themselves. Thus it sent donations to the Cripples Home at Hartshill and the St. George's Boys Home at Chester, whilst overseas it supported the United Mission to Central Africa and the Society for the Propagation of the Gospel. Its special interest for S.P.G. was a cot in St. Catherine's Hospital, Cawnpore, India; beside the raising of money it sent nineteen dolls as Christmas presents for the sick Indian children.

In 1927 the Children's Church concentrated its efforts on the needy nearer home. In January its members visited Arclid Workhouse and provided an entertainment for its inmates, to be followed up by a gift service for the sick in Arclid Infirmary. During December Children's Church members again visited the workhouse bringing with them gifts for Christmas. The main sources of income for these activities were their own church collections and an annual garden party which the children organised themselves. In 1928 their Lenten collection was used to pay for the visit of forty Tunstall children to Alsager in July. The Christ Church children entertained them, organised games and sports activities and gave them ice cream, sweets and flowers on their departure. This activity was repeated in 1929, when forty poor children from Goldenhill were the beneficiaries. At the Vicar's wedding to Miss Aline Parkin, which took place in Chester Cathedral on 4th September 1929, one of his most cherished wedding presents was a solid silver rose bowl from Christ Church Children's Church.

The happy couple had scarcely returned from their honeymoon when new problems arose for the Reverend Moir. In 1929 he had managed to obtain the help of two clergymen, Messrs. R. Hughes of Colwyn Bay, and H. Grey, headmaster of Warrington High School, only to lose their services within a few months. The Vicar, being unable to obtain immediate replacements, took the only course which seemed available to him and conducted Sunday services alternately at Christ Church and St. Mary's. Once more, feathers, both ecclesiastical and lay , were ruffled; the rural dean, Canon Armistead stated that it was illegal to close the official parish church of St. Mary for even one single service. Without adequate staffing there could be only one brutal remedy; at a meeting of the joint Alsager Parochial Church Council, held on 3rd December 1929, the following resolution was passed to be forwarded to the Bishop of Chester;-

> *"that Christ Church be closed from the commencement of the New Year until*
> *such time as a curate can be obtained."*

The resolution, passed with only three votes in opposition, caused anger amongst the Christ Church congregation; a counter petition signed by nearly two hundred persons, asked the bishop for his help in seeking to prevent the closure of the church. Its adherents pointed out that Christ Church was in a sound financial position, despite having spent more than four hundred pounds on repair to its fabric. Moreover the church provided the bulk of the 'Sick and Poor Fund' for the parish, and its endowment formed the larger part of the vicar's stipend. All these pleadings were in vain; the closure went ahead with the bishop's agreement, saving only his insistence that Holy Communion should be held at Christ Church once a month.

The first six months of 1930 were bleak for Christ Church parishioners. Throughout this period the church remained closed as a crisis situation prevailed. The two church choirs were amalgamated and notices given to their choirmasters. The renowned Children's Church, together with St. Mary's Sunday School, were replaced by one United Children's Service at the parish church. However, in June 1930, a solution did appear to have been found, when the vicar was able to announce the appointment as curate, of Canon Francis J. Ashmall.

Could it be that at last the beleaguered vicar's troubles were at an end? 1930 was to see one final struggle in which the ghost of the 1789 Act was to make its unwelcome appearance, this time on the question of churchwardens, the appointment of whom was to be the prerogative of lords and ladies of the manor of Alsager, whose identity in 1930 was a matter of some conjecture. For some time the wardens had been appointed, one by the vicar and the other by the Parochial Church Council, and serving for a period of three years. The vicar had decided that, after two years, a change of Vicar's Warden would be beneficial, and accordingly nominated Mr. Vincent Brooke to this post in place of the incumbent, Mr George Ernest Barker, at the Easter 1931 meeting of the Christ Church congregation. As a temporary solution to the problem it was proposed that a Vestry Meeting be called to appoint two persons as acting churchwardens, pending the appointment of churchwardens under the Act of 1789. This proposal was unacceptable to both sides in the dispute; the existing wardens, George E. Barker and Thomas Edwards, flatly refused to accept the 'acting' label; their appointment would have no legal status, and they therefore appealed to the Archdeacon of Macclesfield for his opinion, which was *"Carry on as before"*. The archdeacon's support for the status quo was followed up by his May visitation, during which he duly appointed the rebel wardens from Christ Church, an act which infuriated the anti-warden lobby at St. Mary's. Sir Ernest Craig thought that *"Archdeacon Thorpe wants a sharp rap over the knuckles,"* whilst Sir Francis Joseph was astounded to hear of the archdeacon's action, stating that *"prompt steps must be taken to correct another illegal act in this parochial drama."*

The archdeacon was unrepentant, writing in June to the embattled churchwardens;-

> *"As to your own position as Wardens, I do not think you need be in any uncertainty. You were admitted last year by the Chancellor in due form and as no persons have been appointed in your stead you continue in office."*

Submission of the case for a legal judgment brought little comfort to the churchwardens opponents despite initial cause for optimism. On the one hand, Counsel, Kenneth Macmorran, agreed that in his opinion the right to appoint churchwardens was vested in the lords and ladies of the manor of Alsager. On the other hand, the Vestry Meeting which appointed Messrs. Barker and Edwards as acting churchwardens was 'entirely illegal', hence they were not properly appointed, however this did not mean that they were not properly constituted! They had been duly appointed without any objection by the archdeacon and the time for objection had passed. Nothing could be done until the next Easter Monday when *"the lords of the manor should appoint their own churchwardens"* for presentation at the Archdeacons Visitation. Counsel sagely concluded that *"the Archdeacon might admit more than one set of churchwardens and leave them to fight it out!"* In which event the lords of the manor appointees could bring an action against the rival claimants!

The debate rumbled on, providing a scenario which a W.S. Gilbert or Anthony Trollope might have relished; one can but agree with Arthur Moir's description of Alsager as *"having the most complicated system of any parish in the whole of Christendom."* Gradually passions died down and Canon Ashmall decided to take the lead in trying to ensure that both Alsager congregations lived together in harmony until some settlement was obtained. To this end he called meetings to bring about a Committee of Joint Co-operation which was in being by the time of his departure in July 1931, to be replaced as curate-in-charge by the Reverend J.R. Brunskill. Now at last could begin a period of peace for the troubled church ensured by an assurance from the bishop's solicitors that *"Christ Church, until its status under the 1789 Private Act is altered by legislation, must legally continue as a separate entity with a separate endowment."* There was still one problem to be overcome, that of inter-church clashes on the joint Parochial Church Council, in which the Christ Church representatives might find themselves an impotent and out-voted minority." The Bishop of Chester's solicitor devised a plan to allay these fears.

> *"The scheme should provide for Christ Church representatives on the Parochial Church Council being a sub-committee of the Council dealing with such matters as only concerned Christ Church, and that in all matters which concerned the whole parish, where there was a difference of opinion between them and the rest of the Parochial Church Council, then they should have a right of appeal to you (the bishop) or the Chancellor."*

By the end of 1934 both Mr. Brunskill and the Reverend Moir had left Alsager, the latter transferred to a less exacting living at Burleydam near Whitchurch. His farewell message to his parishioners read;-

> *"As you know, I have been obliged to resign the Benefice of Alsager owing to reasons of health. The responsibility and anxiety of trying to maintain the two churches, and all that this entails, have proved too great a strain."*

Arthur Moir's sadness was understandable, and yet it was during his vicariate that the struggle to safeguard the autonomy of Christ Church almost reached a satisfactory conclusion. When the Reverend Charles C. Potts of Altrincham was inducted as Vicar of Alsager and incumbent of Christ Church, it was to inherit a situation far different than that which faced his predecessor ten years earlier. Since October 1931 Christ Church had had its own Church Council under the chairmanship of the curate-in-charge, and its opening minutes record that "The Council was to be responsible for all affairs relating to Christ Church." Moreover the churchwarden previously nominated by the vicar was now to be nominated by the curate-in charge. A more tangible break with the past took place in 1934; the issue of pew name plates with its hint of social division, pew rents etc., was set aside with the issue of fifty cards sent to pew holders, asking their agreement to the removal of name plates from the pews.

The final irresistible force that was to drive Christ Church towards full independence came with the onset of World War II. During the dark days of December 1940 the vicar had noticed the sweeping changes which the war had brought to Alsager;-

> *"We are becoming familiar with the roar of street traffic. Empty houses are being turned into hostels, and soldiers, munition managers and workers are settling all over the village, while our old residents are overworked and tied down with new duties."*

At a May meeting of the Christ Church Council in 1941 the Reverend Potts expressed the wish that, if possible, a welfare worker should be provided to look after the large number of girls who would be coming to live at the 'hostel'. It was certainly true that the war was to change the village beyond recognition. First came the refugee children from Liverpool, shortly to be followed by the establishment of Britain's thirteenth Royal Ordnance factory at Radway Green. The munition workers who flooded into Alsager, urgently needed accommodation, quickly provided by an estate of four hundred 'flat tops' behind Lawton Road. Lastly came the Royal Navy, which launched a 'stone frigate' in the shape of 'H.M.S. Excalibur', an initial training base for naval entrants.

During the darkest days of the war Christ Church parishioners had not forgotten their dream of parochial independence. At a meeting of the congregation in May 1942 it was decided that all seats in the church were to be free for the first time; this considerable loss of church revenue was to be made good by the formulation of a freewill offering scheme. This was essential because division of the Alsager parish could not be considered without a guarantee from each church to pay a stipend amount of four hundred pounds per annum, a not inconsiderable sum for those days. In these negotiations Charles Potts played an important role tragically cut short by his untimely death in May 1944. Still the reformers pressed on, to be rewarded after two years of effort by an announcement in the 'London Gazette' dated 2nd August 1946;-

> *"We, the Ecclesiastical Commissioners for England . . . . have prepared the following Scheme for constituting a part of the parish of St. Mary Magdalene, Alsager, in the county and Diocese of Chester, a new parish. We are satisfied that a suitable endowment therefore will be provided. There is within the said area a consecrated church or chapel known as Christ Church which has been approved by us as suitable to be the parish church of the new parish. Now therefore, with the consent of the Right Reverend Douglas, Bishop of Chester, we do propose and recommend that as from this date there shall be a new parish . . . . the Parish of Christ Church, Alsager."*

The war had produced what years of legal wrangling had failed to accomplish. A dramatic increase of population from the three thousand souls of 1939 had produced a parish far too big for effective church management. All previous tribulations were forgotten on a gloriously sunny day in August 1946 when Dr. Douglas H. Crick, Bishop of Chester, formally inaugurated the new ecclesiastical parish; among the clergy present were the Reverends Bernard Pemberton, Vicar of St. Mary Magdalene since January 1945, and Dan Nicholas, ex-R.A.F. chaplain and first vicar of Christ Church, Alsager. It was the latter who, accompanied by his churchwardens, Messrs T. Edwards and P.J. Palfreyman, proceeded to the church tower, there to toll a bell in recognition that a new era was about to begin.

With the removal of all legal obstacles to its existence the new parish of Christ Church could now turn its attention to more practical matters. The first problem was that of a new church hall, to accommodate children's schools on Sundays, and social and organisational events during the week. But how could such a building be obtained in a Britain still trying to adjust from a period of wartime restrictions and construction controls? At a special church council meeting held in February 1946 the Reverend Dan Nicholas announced that *"the Ministry had told him that no building materials would be allowed for the next twelve months at least."* It was not until February 1951 that the quest for a new hall appeared to have met with success, by the purchase of two army huts from the former United States camp at Blythe Bridge. This was to prove only a temporary solution to the problem, for the church's occupation of these premises was to last for less that six months; they were sold in July 1951 for one hundred and seventy five pounds, a net loss of over three hundred pounds on the purchase price! Still the Parochial Church Council continued its search, undeterred by the death of its vicar, Dan Nicholas, who died in November 1951 after a short illness. His successor, the Reverend W. Gwynne John, continued his work and was able to announce a loan of some fourteen hundred and fifty pounds from the Chester Diocese, towards the estimated cost of some four thousand pounds for a new building. Despite some opposition the church council was finally given a mandate to proceed, by a meeting of the full church congregation on December 4th 1955; the building was to comprise a main hall, a kitchen and two small committee rooms, and on Sunday afternoon, November 24th 1956, the Dan Nicholas Memorial Hall was dedicated by the Bishop of Stockport. At last an essential venue for the church and its organisations was in being.

Another memorial to the work of Dan Nicholas was also in being. During his vicariate at Christ Church a new mission church had been created in the neighbouring village of Oakhanger and placed under the pastoral care of the Vicar of Haslington. Now it was proposed that the wishes of the Reverend Nicholas be realised and that Christ Church should take over the Oakhanger mission church. At a meeting of the Parochial Church Council, held in February 1952, it was unanimously resolved that this should be done and that application be made to the Church Commissioners for a scheme authorising alterations to the parish boundaries. By December 1952 the vicar could announce that by Order in Council the mission church of St. Luke, Oakhanger was to be linked with its 'mother church' in Alsager.

The next problem for the congregation was the provision of a suitable dwelling for its incumbents. There was a vicarage in existence at 17 Church Road, Alsager, bought at a cost of about three thousand eight hundred pounds.

After meeting the needs of Winston Gwynne John and his successor, the Reverend Thomas Griffiths Lewis, another clergy crisis arose with the departure of the latter in 1963. The vicarage, bought with such optimism in January 1947, was now in a sorry condition. At a crisis meeting of the Parochial Church Council, convened by churchwarden, Reginald Piggin, on May 7th, he informed his colleagues that *"three parsons had visited the parish and two had declined the living. In each case the reason given was the poor condition of the vicarage's kitchen and scullery."* This was supported by the Rural Dean and Diocesan Surveyor who saw the only solution as the provision of new premises. To carry on at the existing vicarage would mean the outlay of a considerable sum of money for redecorating and capital improvements, and a unanimous vote, taken at an emergency meeting, ensured that a new vicarage would be built. The new incumbent, the Reverend Hugh Llewelyn Williams, was to be housed in a Hassall Road bungalow until the building was completed. By 1966 he was able to move to the new building, erected at the corner of Church Road and Hassall Road, and described by the Diocesan Architect as one of the two finest vicarages built in the Diocese of Chester.

Mention has already been made of the internment crisis of 1883 when Christ Church burial ground was temporarily closed as no further plots were available; a crisis only solved by William Sheringham's giving, as lord of the manor, half an acre of glebe land for the burial ground's extension. By 1935 the churchyard was again full to overflowing and a further extension of its boundaries had to take place. The task involved the removal of approximately 12,000 bricks from the boundary wall, two-thirds of which were to be cleaned for re-use, together with a further 35,000 new bricks needed to complete a new boundary wall. Forty years on even this Herculean activity was found to be insufficient; the great increase in Alsagers population meant that a further extension of the burial ground was essential, but as with other problems there were legal obstacles to be overcome. As in 1883 the land in question was found not to belong to Christ Church, but as 'glebe' land was part of the personal benefice of the incumbent, the Reverend Cecil Siviter, newly arrived from Pott Shrigley in 1974. Once more a Gilbertian situation presented itself; in March 1976 Mr. Siviter was informed that if this glebe land was sold by him to the Christ Church Parochial Church Council then the consent of the Patron, the Parsonages Board, the Bishop of Chester and the Church Commissioners, would also be required! Moreover the question of loss of benefice income was raised ; Mr. Siviter replied that he was prepared to forego this seeing that it consisted of a yearly rent of five pounds only, paid by a local farmer for working the land! Still the ecclesiastical lawyers were unsatisfied. By October 1977, when all legal problems appeared to be surmounted, the Church Commissioners and the bishop's solicitors found yet another obstacle; there were apparently no deeds in existence for the area in question. Fortunately a stalwart witness was found, resident in the parish for more than thirty years, to swear that, during the whole of his period of residence the proposed churchyard extension was part of the benefice glebe land. Thus it was that, all problems solved, the new burial ground was consecrated by the Bishop of Stockport on 15th October 1978.

The last episode in this Christ Church saga takes us somewhat beyond the history's end date of 1974, but it has been included as bringing up to date an enterprise which began in 1956. It will be remembered that in that year the Dan Nicholas Memorial Hall was opened and gave good service to the church's organisations for the next forty years. Unfortunately it was now long past its best as the following survey reveals;-

> *"The roof was now in bad repair, not least as a result of damage by squirrels; the large window frames were rotting; the toilet and kitchen facilities were below basic hygiene standards; the heating system was on its last legs and the lack of insulation meant it was a fridge in the winter and a greenhouse in the summer."*

In 1989 the Reverend Harold Tate had retired, to be replaced as vicar of Christ Church by the Reverend John Varty. The new incumbent decided to treat the church hall as an important priority; as he wrote;-

> *"The work of the church especially amongst its young people was growing apace. . . . the Church Hall was not adequate accommodation for the numbers who were coming. With almost a hundred children, the layout was not flexible enough to accommodate the five groups, which frequently had to meet in homes. It was evident that we not only needed to renovate the existing building but were crying out for more space."*

The problems, not least those of the projected outlay, were immense; nevertheless John Varty decided to proceed. At the Parochial Church Council Meeting in July 1993 he distributed ideas and plans which he had drawn up; later architects were briefed, and by January 1995 plans were endorsed by the church council. In May 1995 a booklet was distributed to the congregation explaining the project, giving an estimate out-lay of some one hundred thousand pounds, later increased to one hundred and twenty thousand pounds. The parish responded to the challenge; by March 1996 the sum of ninety thousand pounds had been given or pledged with a further fifteen thousand pounds raised at a gift day on May 12th. The plans as agreed were to include an extension to form a parish office, a new kitchen, lounge and meeting room; alterations to the rear meeting rooms and the formation of a new room at first floor level; alterations to the toilets; a new gas central heating system; improvements to the electrical installation and complete re-roofing. With the contract signed, building work began in June 1997 and John Varty's vision was finally realised when a new church hall 'dedicated to the service of Christ's church in Alsager,' was officially opened by the Right Reverend Geoffrey Turner, Bishop of Stockport, on the 9th November, 1997.

The Church of St. Mary Magdalene.

When the Rev. Edward Duncombe, a member of the Crewe family, succeeded his cousin, the Rev. Edward Hinchliffe, as rector of Barthomley in 1850 he immediately found himself at odds with the Reverend Charles Alsager Tryon, a member of the Alsager family. He was a patron and incumbent of Christ Church, a chapel of ease, built as a result of the private Act of 1789 by the Misses Alsager. As patrons the Alsager family had the right to appoint the incumbents-cum-schoolmasters. They provided the appointee with a school-house, which was in effect a tied cottage.

Charles Tryon though, required a residence more suited to his position as lord of the manor, so he received permission from the trustees of the Alsager charity himself and three others, to convert the school buildings into a larger residence. Shortly after, Edward Duncombe automatically took over the ex-officio trusteeship of the charity from his predecessor, the rector of Barthomley, becoming a fourth trustee, and he objected strongly to the arrangement which had been made earlier, and he refused to allow it to proceed.[10]

But since alterations to the building were well in hand a compromise was reached; another school was to be built, Tryon would purchase the former school-house from the charity, and he would also take over the pastoral care of the township in return for the tithes due from Alsager Hall farm which amounted to £20 a year.[11] This arrangement was ratified by an Order in Council, making Christ Church an independent district church with the authority to solemnise marriages.

By 1867, following the rapid expansion of Alsager, the population had almost doubled and so had the pastoral care, Tryon rightly felt entitled to a larger share of the tithes, the residue of which were £230, but Duncombe categorically refused to agree to this.

Charles Tryon took legal advice as to whether the original agreement was binding and when it was declared invalid, he no longer felt obliged to carry out his pastoral duties. From then on, until he left in 1876, Alsager was, as Mr Craig described it, a spiritual desert.[12] The fact that the marriages performed during those years were also likely to be invalid did not seem to trouble either Duncombe or Tryon.

It seems as if in retaliation, Duncombe, who described himself as an impossible man, publicly accused the charity of mismanagement and disregard

---

[10] This quotation is taken from an unidentified newspaper report of the Parish Meeting held on Tuesday 29th December 1885. [29th December 1885, Parish Meeting].

[11] 29th December 1885, Parish Meeting.

[12] 29th December 1885, Parish Meeting.

for the wishes of the founders, in that the charity had been set up with fourteen trustees; eighty years on most of them had died and had not been replaced. By 1867 it was being run by a cosy group of four, one elected member, Mr. Randle Wilbraham of Rode Hall, and three clergymen, all ex-officio trustees, the Rev. Charles Tryon, the Rev. Edward Duncombe and the Rev. Edward Clayton, rector of Astbury, another member of the Crewe family and cousin to Duncombe; which left twelve vacancies.[13]

Duncombe cited the scandal earlier in the century over the Barthomley school charity, which had resulted in a very much reduced income for the schools, with the finger of suspicion being pointed at Mr. Twiss of Alsager and Odd Rode and Sir John Boughey, lord of the manor of Audley. The charities of Audley and Congleton had suffered a similar fate and, with this in mind, Edward Duncombe pressed for new trustees to be appointed.

When he got no response he printed and distributed copies of the 1789 Act, and followed it up with a pamphlet entitled *"Church and School Business in Alsager."*[14] In it he accused Tryon of *"landlordism and Lord-of-the-Manorism,"* citing that he was not only curate, but patron and sinecure schoolmaster. Thus, as lord of the manor, he was administering the charity and paying himself. Duncombe also alleged that the monies from the 33 acres of trust land were being used for purposes other than providing free education for poor children; and the school, he claimed, was not being run on non-sectarian and undenominational lines as the founders had intended. This pamphlet, which was put on sale price 6d at Beard's and the Post Office, caused quite a stir in Alsager.

Duncombe further infuriated the 'triumvirate' as he called them, by writing to the charity commissioners with his complaints. The accused called it a stab in the dark by a friend. The administration of the charity was in time sorted out and the full number of trustees was appointed in 1877. But it soured future relations between the Christ Church patrons and the rectors of Barthomley and ultimately, between the congregations of Christ Church and the future St. Mary's.

Charles Tryon left Alsager in 1877 and his successor was the Rev. William A. Sheringham, another member of the Alsager family. Duncombe retired in 1880 and another, thirty-five year old George Skene, inherited the Alsager problem.

On his arrival, George Skene came into an impossible situation though how complex he did not immediately recognise. The anomaly existing in

---

[13] The Act of 1789 sets out the names of the original trustees on p.8.

[14] A privately published pamphlet; Ref. [Duncombe]

Alsager was that of a township with many people, growing all the time, which was inside his parish, but so far removed from Barthomley church that its people could not have the same attention as those living close to that church; and yet not attended by the incumbent of Christ Church Alsager as envisaged by the 1789 Act.

True, the practical difficulties for a township within his parish, yet three miles from his church, were well known: it was these difficulties for people having to attend church at Barthomley which had led to Christ Church being built in the first place; but the needs and the forces which affected those people he had yet to learn.

It is clear that since his arrival in 1877, the Rev. W.A. Sheringham, incumbent of Christ Church, had attended to the pastoral needs of the Alsager people, outside his Christ Church flock, with no more concern than had his predecessor, the Rev. C.A. Tryon.[15] The *"spiritual neglect"* of Alsager had lasted for 12 long years since the Rev. Mr. Tryon had relinquished his responsibility, and it was into this situation that George Skene came in 1881.

Very soon after his appointment, the new rector received a visit from the Rev. Sheringham. Possibly, with Rector Duncombe gone, and a new man involved at the helm, Mr. Sheringham saw an opportunity to present a case to attain parish status for his church. In any event, George Skene was amenable to Mr. Sheringham's suggestions and was quickly persuaded that the best thing would be for Alsager to be attached to Christ Church. There would be merely a matter of surrendering a few tithes to Alsager and the matter would be solved.[16]

Alas, Mr. Skene soon found that the water in which he stood was both deeper and muddier than he thought. It was quickly established that it was not possible to constitute Christ Church a parish church without a private Act. Furthermore, the Rector was advised conclusively that it was not for him to promote such an Act, his part in the transaction would be merely the cession of tithes.

Presented with this situation by Mr. Skene and being asked whether he could promote the necessary Private Bill, Mr. Sheringham declined. He could not *"be responsible"* for it, though whether that meant financially or accountably is not clear. Further fruitless appeals to Mr. Sheringham left the Rector clear that he had but two options, he could abandon Alsager or he could undertake the responsibility for it himself; and he chose the latter.

[15] 29th December 1885, Parish Meeting.
[16] Skene's account of the meeting, published in the Alsager and Barthomley Parish Magazine, [Par. Mag.] July 1883.

Mr. Sheringham's response was immediate: he circulated an announcement of his future relations to the parish to all residents -

> *To my friends and neighbours, the inhabitants of the Township of Alsager.*
> *It has become my duty to inform you that the RECTOR OF BARTHOMLEY,*
> *having been advised that the Order in Council constituting Alsager a separate*
> *District is invalid, has intimated to me his intention to assume the personal*
> *charge of the people of Alsager as his Parishioners; and therefore, I regret to*
> *say that my ministerial connection with you out of Church has come to an end.*
>
>   *The Parsonage, Alsager,*   *W.A. SHERINGHAM*
>   *April, 1881*   *Incumbent of Christ Church,*

The 1852 Order in Council had been declared invalid in 1868 - thirteen years earlier. It is difficult not to feel that there was measure of pique behind Mr. Sheringham's action.

Skene now faced his task purposefully. Calling the parishioners to meet him in the parish room, an upstairs room opposite what is today Northolme Gardens in Alsager, he explained to them the facts that led to the township being still attached to Barthomley and he acknowledged the need for additional church accommodation. He emphasised the fact that there was no possibility of Christ Church becoming the parish church and that his actions had been taken after the finality of Mr. Sheringham's response, or lack of it, to his efforts. He resolved now to work to the end that when it became necessary to separate Alsager from Barthomley, it should have its own parish church in the heart of the township with ample provision for an increasing population.

The immediate need, however, was interim provision for Skene's Alsager flock and the Rector acted swiftly. With the help of village benefactors, there was erected, in the centre of the village, a corrugated iron chapel, examples of which, the work of the Liverpool manufacturer Isaac Dixon, may still be seen in this area. This 'Mission Room' was dedicated on 8th January 1882 by His Grace the Archbishop of York, who happened to be the Rector's uncle.

Seating over 350, this Mission Room served as the focus of all church activities for 13 years as well as being a meeting room and social centre for village life. Church life thrived: the record of the times shows constant activities, functions, fund-raising events and socials, and by the first anniversary of the Mission Room there was an amount of £1,150 available for Mission Room work.[17]

The 25th June 1883 saw a momentous decision taken by the financial committee at the Mission. It was *"unanimously and enthusiastically agreed"* that steps be now taken for the erection of a permanent church and for the

---

[17] Par. Mag.

securing of a site.[18]

In June 1884, the Rector called an important meeting. Fund raising had been going on continuously with events and subscriptions gradually swelling the building fund, while he himself had acquired something of a reputation as a 'notorious beggar' through his prolific letter writing for contributions. The time had come to make a start, and with commendable speed a site adjacent to the Mission Room was selected for the new parish church and a provisional agreement for its purchase made. Within weeks, the Lancaster firm of architects, Messrs Paley and Austin, were approached to approve the site and prepare plans, and the land was purchased.

Mr. Austin's scheme was for a church, with, adjacent, a schoolroom to seat 300, the latter to be built first in order to relieve the Mission Church of non-divine service. The new schoolroom would be secular, all could support it regardless of sect or party.[19]

The Alsager builder Mr. Gratton won the schoolroom contract and work commenced in May 1885. On 4th June, Mrs. Walter Palmer laid the foundation stone, using a silver trowel engraved for the occasion, and six months later, on 10th December, the building was opened. As a school and central hall for the township its 'quaint prettiness' was welcomed as 'a decided ornament'.[20]

The seeds of discontent, planted in the earliest days with the obligations of Christ Church to the Barthomley Rector, and sprouting through the years of uncertain cooperation, then neglect and withdrawal, had grown into a state of dissatisfaction and suspicion, much later to mature into very active rivalry, between the old Christ Church order and the growing new order promoted by Skene.

An example of the lack of harmony is seen in the Rector's reaction to the proposed gift by Mr. Sheringham of glebe land to extend the graveyard. Asking for a delay to allow a scheme of his own to be prepared, Skene was indignant when his request was ignored and his plans, possibly to protect his rights to burial fees, thwarted. A subsequent episode of his being prevented, on a technicality, from proceeding with a burial when at the graveyard itself gives an insight to the atmosphere of the time. With such thoughts in mind, we can understand how it was that the first public meeting in the new schoolroom was one of contention.

Within days of its opening, Mr. Skene called a great public meeting in the schoolroom to consider a development. The townsfolk present heard grave

---

[18] Skene's correspondence with the bishop. Ref CRO. P/102/3/1-44. [Skene Correspondence]
[19] Par. Mag, March 1885.
[20] Par. Mag, November 1885.

speeches and arguments provoked by a plan, proposed by the Patrons of Christ Church, to attach the Ecclesiastical Township of Alsager to Christ Church. Eminent voices spoke and while the plan was overwhelmingly rejected, it was clear that the muddy water had not yet cleared for Mr. Skene. The records of this period show constant references to *"the grave and anxious question"*, *"the burning question of the day"* and *"the calamity with which the township has been threatened"* in reference to the Patron's proposals. Rivalry and pettiness were rife, though it is difficult to look over the years and analyse the temperaments and motivations of the parties involved.[21]

For five years little happened outside the raising of funds, though 1888 saw the committee, needing to fan the flame of enthusiasm, planning a Grand Bazaar for the following year. For this event 10,000 tickets were printed, for a competition which the Rector made his own to organise and which occupied him in weeks of work throughout the nights.

The Bazaar lasted for four days in September, and was a truly remarkable event. It does not seem possible that there was anyone in the village who was not working for the effort, 20 stalls offered every conceivable attraction. The 'Foreign Articles' stall, for instance, offered items which had been donated to the Rector's appeals, from Nepal, Valencia, Benares, Cuba, Odessa, Pensacola, Pernambuco, Peshawur and Tokyo. A phonograph exhibition, a shooting gallery, photography, a display of automaton figures, and endless other novel enterprises were accompanied by entertainments and refreshments, and at the end the huge sum of £950 had been raised; and the Rector was so exhausted that he had to leave for a recuperative holiday!

The building project was now an accepted fact of village life; people could work for it without enduring the criticism and witticisms directed at its pioneers.

July 1890 saw the Rev. Skene writing from Barthomley to the Bishop with his scheme for the future of Alsager. It clarified the situation in the township, outlining its social and physical aspects and suggesting that his Lordship bear in mind that these factors, together with the unsuitability of an enlarged Christ Church, as that church *"would never form an efficient centre for church work in the face of the three chapels erected during the time of the church's inaction in the interests of the population."*[22]

The scheme which he proposed to the Bishop was to provide in Alsager a new church to be the parish church and, on its completion, to separate Alsager from Barthomley, making it an independent parish with its own vicar.

---

[21] 29th December 1885, Parish Meeting.
[22] Skene's correspondence, 11th July 1990.

Christ Church would become a chapel of ease within the new parish and, when next vacant, would provide its endowment, supplemented by the £250 of Alsager tithes surrendered by the Rector, to finance the new parish. It would be necessary to purchase the advowson, the right to present or appoint the priest at Christ Church, from the Patrons of that church and, to enable these things to be done, to obtain a private Act of Parliament.

The Bishop's reply was favourable. Mr. Skene's scheme gave promise of a very satisfactory solution, though he felt that the surrender of the total tithe was overgenerous. He recommended a reduction to £100.[23]

Fears of unease among the Christ Church people at the surrender of their rights and privileges dictated a cautious approach. The scheme was put to the Rev. Daniel Shaw, incumbent of Christ Church. He agreed, but was uneasy that his agreement might be seen by the more partisan elements of his church as a betrayal of trust. Fearing that he would be condemned for accepting any scheme of Skene, he hoped that the proposal could be presented as the Bishop's scheme. He could not be expected to resist his 'diocesan'. The scheme was duly presented to the people as the Bishop's.[24]

Still the unease was felt by the pew-holders of Christ Church at the surrender of their endowments and possessions for what seemed little gain. A final attempt by Shaw to alter the arrangements, complaining about the proposed site for the new church and suggesting again that Christ Church should be the Parish Church, met with a terse rebuff from the Bishop. There would be no modification of the plan; the line had been agreed and would be followed as proposed.[25]

The advowson was purchased and by January 1891, the Bishop was commending the work to the people with optimism. *"There had come down to the present generation of residents at Alsager a heritage of woe, or at least of perplexity,"* but he now prayed that the spirit of harmony may rest upon both wings of Alsager.[26]

March 1891 saw the site approved but though the fund stood at £2,145 there was no significant progress for nearly 3 years. August 1892 saw appeals renewed with some urgency, earlier enthusiasm had drifted into complacency.

By February 1894 the fund stood in excess of £4,200. At a meeting, considered to be the most important ever held in the township, it was agreed that funds were sufficiently advanced to justify a start to the carting of

---

[23] Skene correspondence, Bishop to Skene 15th July 1890
[24] Skene Correspondence, 31st July 1890
[25] Skene Correspondence, 22/9/90 and 11/10/1890.
[26] Bishop's letter in Par. Mag., February 1891.

materials ready for spring building and with the arrival in April of working drawings and specifications the work was put out to tender. Eleven tenders were received, with a margin of £2,000 between the highest and lowest and the work was given to Mr. Fielding of Alton.

At 11.00.am. on Wednesday, 13th June, 1894 *"unknown to many and unnoticed by all,"*[27] John Keen, the treasurer, put in a spade to turn the first sod, the work was begun.

On 20th September, at a great gathering, the foundation stone was laid by Lord Houghton who placed upon it an offering of £50. The scene was surmounted by a great decorated arch and the whole area was gay with bunting.

Under Mr. Hart, the foreman, building proceeded well. In December it was decided that the iron mission church should be sold. It was a sad decision. The Rector had written earlier that when it was gone *"we shall often recall its appearance as a scene of beauty."*[28] It was sold very quickly for £150 on 4th February 1895, and on 10th February, church services were held in the schoolroom for the first time. The Bishop's licence authorising the services and the administration of both Sacraments was read and for three years the schoolroom served both as church and village hall, with all articles and effects required for divine service being removed entirely when other functions took place. The arrangement was makeshift and posed many difficulties but with forbearance it seems to have worked satisfactorily.

Gifts came in various forms; a lectern, chairs and kneelers, linen, tiles for the floor and, usefully at this stage, the stone for concreting and infilling, from Mr. Frank Rigby.

As the building grew, the need for funds was more strongly felt and so, in September 1895 there was held the second four day Grand Carnival Bazaar. The anticipated cost of the church was £7,100 and the amount in hand now £6,100; and though the Bazaar was again ambitious it fell far short of the previous occasion with a sum of £450 raised.

It was not enough. In December it was accepted that the work had to pause, and so it was that by December 1896, the church stood ready for worship with a temporary tiled roof where its steeple should have been and an ugly brick wall screening the unfinished north aisle inside.

The opening and dedication was performed by the Venerable Archdeacon Woosnam on Friday, 8th January 1897. It was consecrated on St. Peter's Day,

---

[27] Par. Mag.
[28] Par. Mag., April 1894.

29th June 1898.

Very sparsely furnished at this time it gradually acquired glorious furnishings through the generosity of benefactors but it had to wait for forty years for the completion of its north aisle in 1937. Internally it is now complete, richly adorned with woodwork designed by the original architects and featuring outstanding stained glass by Powell's of London and Karl Parsons. It is built of Alton stone in a decorative style.

It is sad that externally the parish church of St. Mary Magdalene is still unfinished. The 'temporary' roofing is still in place after 100 years but even without the soaring spire of its original design it is a wonderful testimony to the dedication of those who brought it into being and particularly the remarkable George Skene. Its establishment did not immediately solve the problems of the past. The Bishop's 1891 hope *"that the spirit of harmony and generous achievement may abundantly rest upon both Alsagers"* was not fulfilled for some years but that is a story for another pen.

Origins and Growth of Alsager Methodism

There is no record of John Wesley, the founder of Methodism, ever visiting Alsager but there are records in his journals of a visit to Talke O' th Hill on March 18th 1738. He visited the surrounding districts on many occasions: Congleton 21, Newcastle 14, Nantwich 7 and Burslem 16.

Wesley was first an Anglican clergyman. Later, when he was banned from preaching in the established church, he went out on horseback and conducted services all over the country in a ministry which lasted for 50 years. He kept a personal diary of all his experiences and occasionally made frank comments about the behaviour of the locals. After preaching in the first Wesleyan chapel at Burslem he said;-

> *"I preached in the new meeting house but that was far too small to hold the congregation. Indeed this county is all on fire and the flame is spreading from village to village."*

Later he said;-

> *"Even the potters though they pelted me with stones are a more civilised people than the better sort, so called, at Congleton."*

The influence of his preaching throughout England must have had an effect on the North Staffordshire and South Cheshire locality. Wesley's impact across the whole area in the 18c. was enormous, not only in the growth of Methodism but also in giving working people, like the Potters, pride in themselves.

The above extracts from Wesley's Journal both point to the introduction and growth of Methodism in Alsager. The 'flame' certainly spread from North Staffordshire as an influx of families from the Potteries began to appreciate living in Alsager and the surrounding countryside.

Chapel Lane Methodist Church.

Methodism, in an organised form, first reached Alsager at the beginning of the 19c. at the house of Mary Cotton, the home of a weaving family. The house was situated off Close Lane and demolished around 1925. This house became the first Methodist preaching place in Alsager.

Benjamin White and John Mellor, of south Cheshire, who had proclaimed the Gospel in many surrounding areas first visited Alsager in 1804. They intimated to some of the cottagers that if any of them would open their houses for preaching a preacher would be regularly appointed to conduct services. These two worthy local preachers were credited with introducing Methodism here.

In 1807 Alsager was included in the Congleton Circuit but was later transferred into the Nantwich Circuit. There was no Sunday School and children had to go to Whittaker's Farm at Wheelock. Later Mr James Whittaker became the first class leader, he walked from Wheelock week by week to conduct meetings and exercise a pastoral oversight. He was followed by William Breeze, son in law of Mary Cotton, who was at one time clerk of Christ Church. The preaching at Mary Cotton's cottage started with a class of ten people and gradually increased. The weaving looms were pushed to one side but eventually worship became uncomfortable for the numbers attending.[29] In 1808 the first surviving plan of the Nantwich Circuit shows that Alsager had fortnightly services at 9.00 a.m. and 2.00 p.m., by the time of the next surviving plan, in 1825, there are services each week at 10.00 a.m. and 2.00 p.m.

As the cause progressed the original meeting house could not accommodate all who desired to worship. John Plant, a convert of Mr Breeze, sold a piece of his common or waste ground for the sum of "£5 of lawful English money." The land is described as being on heath land within the manor and township of Alsager and bounded by the road to Wheelock; later to be known as 'Chapel Lane' and then 'Hassall Road'. It was here in the summer of 1834 a one room chapel was opened for Methodist Worship.[30] The Reverend C. Jannion conducted the opening services and a Sunday School was

---

[29] Ian Sellars; *Place Mathodist Church Alsager";* Centenary Brochure 1969.
[30] *Hassall Road Chapel Magazine* **Date???**

begun with Thomas Holland in charge.

On Sunday, 30th March 1851 a record was taken of how many folk attended church in the first ever religious census in England and Wales. The survey also showed the diversity of churches and strength of the denominations outside the national Anglican Church. Alsager reflected the national trend of religious adherence in the mid 19th century. The Wesleyan Methodists, aggregated with Methodist sub-sects, figured second in the overall attendance returns. The figures for Chapel Lane, the only nonconformist place of worship in Alsager at the time the record was taken, along with the neighbouring Betchton Chapel were as follows:-

Chapel Lane, Alsager. Wesleyan Methodist (1834)

	Afternoon	Evening
Adults	66	75
Children	25	
	91	

Signed: Charles Latham 31st March 1851

Wesleyan Chapel, Hassall Green, Betchton (1829)

	Morning	Afternoon	Evening
Adults	45	82	22
Children	38	30	
	83	112	

Signed: John Holland, Roughwood Mill 31st March 1851

Since Alsager was very much out on a limb in those days an agreement was reached between the Tunstall and Nantwich Circuits to supply preachers on alternate Sundays. These arrangements continued until 1860 when Nantwich once again took over sole responsibility. In the meantime an adjacent plot of land was bought for £10. It was decided that the original plot was not large enough. The deeds state it was bought *"as a place of religious worship for the use of the people called Methodists in the connexion established by the late Reverend John Wesley."* The premises were enlarged in 1852, by a new building being erected at the side of the existing chapel, with the Reverend Dr. Beaufort being the inaugural preacher. This adjoining chapel was built to accommodate a steadily growing Society and Sunday School and it was apparently built complete with a gallery. Extensive renovation took place in 1912 and it is possible this work included the removal of the gallery. A further slice of land sold to the church by former trustee George Espley was eventually utilised by a modest extension in 1962. These premises became known as the Chapel Lane Chapel.

Notwithstanding these endeavours by the trustees to ensure that the chapel capacity was capable of fulfilling demand, a move to another location was contemplated. A site for a new chapel was purchased with this end in view. The land lay in Crewe Road, it is now occupied by nos. 119, 121 and 123; it formed part of the modest estate surrounding 'Beechwood ' in Chancery Lane, and was purchased in 1893 for £130 19. 0., from the estate of Thomas Sherratt deceased by Messrs. Wm. Chappell, Boot Manufacturer; George Hammersley, Master Potter; Wm. Bourne, Labourer; Thos. Bourne, Gardner; Henry Holland, Gardner; Alfred Holland, Farmer; and James Holland, Insurance Agent; all of Alsager. They in turn sold it to the trustees of the chapel in July 1895 for £130 19. 0. The trustees named in the deed being;-

William Witter	Wheelock	Farmer
Joseph Moulson	Haslington	Farm Labourer
Thomas Pemberton	Haslington	Farmer
George Espley	Alsager	Engraver
William Winnington	Admaston	Farmer
Alfred Holland	Alsager	Gardener
Henry Holland	Alsager	Gardener
Thomas Bourne	Alsager	Gardener
Joseph Holland	Alsager	Farmer
Daniel Hancock	Alsager	Grocer
Thomas Holland	Coppenhall	Labourer
John Cotton	Kidsgrove	Printer
George Moore	Alsager	Farmer
William Bourne	Alsager	Labourer
Peter Malbon	Alsager	Gardener
James Holland	Alsager	Agent
Ernest James Dean	Alsager	Joiner
George Holland	Alsager	Gardener
John Holland	Alsager	Gardener
Charles Frederick Holland	Hassall	Farmer

They appear to be the survivors of trustees appointed in 1880, supplemented by others appointed under a 'Memorandum of Choice' dated April 1895. The deed of purchase states, *". . . . And Whereas it is intended to erect upon the said plot of land a Chapel and appurtenances for the use of the people called Wesleyan Methodists . . . "* A further document in the same bundle,[31] dated May 1910, list the names of the surviving trustees appointed in 1895 and new replacements. Their names and occupations are of interest.

William Witter	Alsager	Gentleman
George Espley	Alsager	Engraver
Alfred Holland	Alsager	Dairyman
Henry Holland	Alsager	Gardener
Thomas Bourne	Alsager	Gardener
Joseph Holland	Alsager	Farmer
Charles Frederick Holland	Hind Heath	Farmer
James Holland	Alsager	Gardener
George Holland	Alsager	Painter
George Hamersley	Alsager	Flint Miller
William Cooper	Alsager	Baker

---

[31] Documents in the possession of Richard and Emma Sutton of 123 Crewe Road.

William Dixon	Close Lane, Alsager	Labourer
Joseph Bebbington	Close Lane, Alsager	Farmer
George Hilditch	Close Lane, Alsager	Farmer
Frank Edwards	Alsager	Window Cleaner
Samuel Birchall	Alsager	Engineer's Clerk
James Henshaw	Alsager	Insurance Clerk

Plans for the construction of the new chapel did not materialise and eventually, in October 1920 the trustees conveyed the land to Mr. Joseph Edwards who subsequently transferred it to Messrs. Joseph Edwards and sons.

The 1899 Conference included the chapel into the newly formed Sandbach and Alsager Circuit. A minister was assigned to live in Alsager, the first being the Reverend W.H.Wardle.

In the 1950s, it appears in certain documents, the church was already beginning to be called Hassall Road. By 1976, under the terms of the Methodist Church Act, the Church Council are now the managing trustees. Title deeds no longer hold any clues as to their identity, but Hassall Road has been served well by a succession of trustees through its first 140 years. The very first group were chiefly farmers and cordwainers (shoemakers) and included the names of Plant, Latham, Breeze, Holland and Cotton - families associated with the founding of Methodism in Alsager.

In the mid-20th century the trustees included Robert Arrowsmith, who lived at 'Far Heath', and gave his name to Arrowsmith Drive. Fellow trustees at that time included the names of Symms, Bebbington, Bruffell and Calderbrook. The former two, J.C. Symms and J. Bebbington, gave devoted service and officiated as organists for a number of years.

The following section is reproduced from *"Wesley Place Mathodist Church Alsager"*; written by Ian Sellars, B.Litt., M.A., for the Centenary Brochure 1969.

Wesley Place Methodist Church

After an opening section dealing with the coming of Methodism to Alsager and the establishment of the first congregation at Chapel Lane, to which reference has been made earlier, Mr. Sellars continues with the story of Wesley Place.

"By the 1860's the character of Alsager was beginning slowly to change. The railway had now arrived, bringing with it a number of wealthy persons from the Potteries who saw in the village an ideal site for pleasant residences away from the smoke and grime of the Five Towns, or even, in some cases, a congenial spot for a summer cottage! The east end of the village saw the erection of the great Victorian mansions which still give it its peculiar charm. Naturally this was a challenge to the Methodist people, for many of these newcomers were themselves Wesleyans. In 1867 after a lengthy debate it was decided that the Chapel Lane premises were too cramped and remote to cater for the new housing area, and the construction of a new edifice was authorised fronting the main road at the east end of the village. Mr Charles J. Baines, the moving spirit behind the venture, had the satisfaction of seeing the foundation stone of his new £2,900 project laid by Mr. Anthony Shaw, chief bailiff of Burslem, in June 1868.

A large marquee was erected on the other side of the road opposite the chapel, and here 1,400 people sat down for tea, a Foden traction engine supplying hot water. Flags and bunting decked the village, and the highlight of the proceedings was the arrival on a wagon pulled by two greys of a band playing "We're marching to Zion". Following the speeches, the prominent supporters, Messrs. Collinson, Ford, Hancock, Plant, Baines, Rigby, Burgess, Wildblood and Cope, laid purses on the stone, to a total of £41, and Mr Shaw added another £50. Within a year the building (architecturally unexciting but by no means ungraceful) was complete, and was opened on 1st June, 1869, by the Reverend Samuel R. Hall, President of Conference. The two Alsager Chapels, Big Wesleyans and Little Wesleyans as Wesley Place and Chapel Lane were now known, were separated from the Nantwich Circuit the same year and placed under the pastoral care of the second minister of the newly-formed Crewe circuit. Unfortunately the debt on the new building was grievously large, for these were the years when Cheshire was smitten by the terrible cattle plague, many farmers failed to honour their promises, whilst several wealthier members soon left the village to reside elsewhere.

The first thirty years of Wesley Place thus saw a grim struggle to pay off an intolerable burden of debt, which as late as 1880 still amounted to £1,150. In this year in fact the cause might well have expired altogether, but for the efforts of a certain supernumerary minister, the Reverend James Scholes, the first Wesleyan minister to reside in Alsager, who between 1876 and 1878 persuaded the people to make a valiant effort towards debt reduction. Huge bazaars and sales of work, plus the generous help of the Chapel Committee, saved the day, and by 1882 the crisis had been surmounted.

By the 1890's Wesley Place was a firmly-established cause in a rapidly growing community. It was also a most harmonious society, having never been rent by such disastrous schisms as overtook the Sandbach churches among others in 1834 or the whole connexion in 1848. Over the east end of the village the Wesleyans held undisputed sway, and one of the reasons advanced by Christ Church authorities in the 1890's why a rival St. Mary's parish church should not be built at the opposite end of Alsager, was that it could not possibly compete with the Methodists. By this time the population of the village had risen from 700 in 1860 to 1,148 in 1871 and 1,912 twenty years later. The ecclesiastical parish of Alsager was at last separated from Barthomley in 1895, and the "perpetual curate" of Christ Church became its first vicar. The Central School had been erected in 1885, while by the Act of 1894 Alsager became an Urban District in its own right, the same year as Cheshire County Council sanctioned the building of the Police Station.

Socially Wesley Place was an admirable melting-pot of the classes: potters and business executives rubbed shoulders with shopkeepers, domestic servants, and railway workers, the latter a very important section of the community, Only the farmers who now attended the more rural Chapel Lane, and the miners of Linley seem unrepresented: they gravitated to the Primitive Chapel in Crewe Road (founded in 1862) which ran a short-lived Mission station at Linley for their benefit in the 1890's. A community as lively, forward-looking and self-conscious as this had really very little in common with either Crewe or the Potteries from which in any case it was geographically remote, and much more with the old market town of Sandbach, with its deep-rooted Wesleyan traditions and easy accessibility by road and rail. In 1899 the inevitable was recognised by Conference, and the two Alsager chapels were separated from the Crewe circuit and transferred to Sandbach, to which circuit was assigned an additional minister who should reside in Alsager itself. A new chapter thus opened in the history of Alsager Methodism with the dawn of the new century.

The church to which the Reverend W.H. Wardle, B.A. came as the first minister in 1899 had 60 members and served a community of 2,600 souls. Class meetings were flourishing, there was a monthly celebration of the Lord's Supper and the evening service was of an evangelistic character, the Sankey Hymnal being in regular use. In addition to Wesley Place, Mr Wardle had pastoral charge of Chapel Lane, Rode Heath, Smallwood and Hassall Green, 'the country stations' as they were appropriately named. Among the most prominent Wesleyans in the village were Messrs J. Maddock, J. Bateman, J. Robinson, J. Arrowsmith, D. Richmond, T. Bourne, T. Cotton, C.W. Smith, J.J. Hancock, P. Merrick, W.G. Walker, W. Holland, the Houldcrofts, Sharpes, Higgats and Miss McKee. These were the folk who secured for their minister the spacious manse on Station Road, a few yards away from the Primitive Manse, attached to the Crewe Road Chapel. This building was to be enlarged with a curious agglomeration of outbuildings when the Reverend Gregory Renton arrived with a very numerous progeny as Mr Wardle's successor in 1902.

Following Mr Renton, the Revs. Cecil Groom (1905-1908) and Joseph Kewley (1908-1911) and Robert B. Saul (1911-1914) enjoyed successful ministries, considerable additions being made in these years to the school buildings at the rear of the church, and a useful link being made between

Wesley Place and the North Staffordshire Royal Infirmary for which collections were regularly held and to whose governing Board the church nominated one member. The war years were of course an extremely difficult time, though the number of young men who fell in the fighting was fortunately unusually small. The Reverend W.E. Russell who ministered from 1914 to 1918 probably did well to keep up the membership figures at a steady 60. His successor, the Reverend S. Paul Hadley, was however, too concerned with rehabilitation schemes after the war to be able to devote more than a modicum of time to the affairs of Wesley Place: his short and troubled ministry, distinguished only by the first and last efforts to provide Wesley Place with uniformed organisations, ended abruptly in February 1920.

In 1919 however, the Jubilee services had been held, and a special appeal for £100 had been launched, a considerable sum of money for a church whose quarterly assessment was then only £30. The names of the contributors to this fund and those of members appearing in the Leaders Minute Books of the period show that Wesley Place still embraced a good cross section of local society. Though the influential Huntbach family was no longer resident in the village, the pottery interest was now represented by the Websters, Weatherbys, Lucases, Dudsons, Bloores, Fords and Arrowsmiths. Local business and tradespeople included the Beards, Howletts, Walkers, Lawtons, Edwards, (on whose famous coal wagons the Sunday School scholars regularly departed for their treats), Cottons, Hancocks, Millwards, Deans, Colcloughs, Garlicks, Jacksons and Johnsons. There were still a few farming families, the Hollands and Leaches especially, attached to the congregation, but a most valuable contribution to the life of the chapel was made by a large number of gardeners and railwaymen then resident in the village.

It was one of the latter, Mr George Maddocks, a signalman, whose splendid leadership of the choir was to give the church its fine choral tradition between the two wars. The work of the Elsbys, Fosters, Hartleys and the two schoolmasters, Messrs Vodrey and Dale is also recalled with gratitude. The Reverend Frank A. Ashton (1920-1924) and Frederick L. Kinnings (1924-1928) are remembered by older members, the former for initiating a further extension to the church premises, the latter for his work among young people and formation of junior classes. Though the population of the village increased but slowly, by 1928 membership of Wesley Place totalled 109, and the quarterly assessment had been raised to £43. The Reverend T. Norris Roscoe (1928-1932) is remembered for his motor car (he appears to have been the first Alsager minister to have possessed this type of vehicle) and for another successful pastorate, with particular emphasis laid upon the development of the Wesley Guild.

Membership at the time of Methodist Union in 1932 stood at a total of

123. The union made hardly any difference to the life of Wesley Place, for though negotiations were begun with both the Sandbach United Methodist (Providence) and the Sandbach Primitive (Welles Street) circuits, all broke down, while Crewe Road Chapel determined to maintain its connection with the Tunstall group of churches. The Revs. M. Stanley Collins, M.A. (1932-1935) and C. Povah Bardsley (1935-1939) are remembered for two learned and studious ministries and the latter both for his remarkably fine preaching, and for his splendid pince-nez, an object of never failing amusement to some of the younger members of the congregation. (This was not the only pre-war curiosity associated with Wesley Place. A wooden shelf, now removed, was erected under the gallery by a certain gentleman who was tired of his bald head being the target for missiles dropped by irreverent Sunday School scholars from above.)

The dark years of the Second World War were made easier for the people of Wesley Place by the excellent ministry of the kindly ex-missionary, the Reverend E. Stanley Cheeseright (1939-1944) followed by the ministry of the Reverend G. Kenneth Eustace (1944-1949). Wesley Place emerged from the Second World War still strong, but with the class system moribund and still bearing the marks of being very much a rather narrowly circumscribed village cause. In the rapid expansion of Alsager which lay ahead, the chapel could easily have turned in on itself and become the spiritual home of a handful of diminishing old families suspicious and resentful of newcomers. That such did not happen is a tribute not only to the adaptability and vision of these families themselves, but to the wise pastoral guidance the church has enjoyed since the war.

The Reverend Horace Ibbotson - another ex-missionary (1949-1959) enjoyed a pastorate whose exceptional length is a mark of the sterling qualities which he brought to his task. Congregations increased steadily, a stage was erected in the large hall and a green "hut" put up to accommodate the extra activities connected with the church. Preaching of a high quality sustained the pastorate whose burdens were not eased when, on amalgamation with the ex-Primitive circuit in 1949 Thurlwood and Oakhanger were added to the Alsager's ministers care. The Reverend Eric Challoner (1959-1966) was an admirable successor to Mr. Ibbotson in every way. With pastoral concern as the keynote of his ministry, Mr. Challoner intensified the church's mission to the growing village, and to the College of Education; launched house groups and a stewardship campaign whose results in increased giving of time, money and talents proved of great blessing to the church, and encouraged a deeper committal to Christ on the part of the young and old alike. Other happy features of this ministry were the joint services held with St. Mary's parish church, the long delayed reception of Crewe Road Chapel into the Alsager circuit, and the launching of the impressive £12,000 building scheme whose completion was intended to coincide with the centenary of the church. The new extension would thus stand as both a symbol of the fruit of past endeavour and a gesture of confidence in the future of the church it was designed to serve. After the short ministry of the Reverend G. Buswell, M.A. (1966-67) who left Alsager to return to the teaching profession, the church was fortunate enough to secure the services of the Reverend Alan F. Barker under whose guidance it welcomes with humility and earnestness whatever fresh tasks the Holy Spirit will be pleased to lay upon it. In their fulfilment the people of Wesley Place will be paying the most fitting tribute to the pioneers of a century ago." [32]

Primitive Methodist Chapel, Crewe Road[33]

The second Methodist chapel to be erected in Alsager belonged to the Primitive Methodists and was built two years after the Jubilee of the denomination. The movement came into being at Mow Cop, and is commemorated by a memorial stone just below the castle. The first camp meeting, on May 31st 1807, saw thousands gathered there and arose out of the spiritual concern of North Staffordshire men like Hugh Bourne and William Clowes. The Wesleyan Methodists at their conference of that year considered camp meetings *"highly improper in England and likely to be productive of considerable mischief."* They disclaimed all connection with them.

If Christ Church was built of Mow Cop stone, it was the Mow Cop spiritual awakening of those evangelical revivalists that created the Primitive Methodist movement and subsequently the Crewe Road chapel.

The chapel was situated between 'The Burning Mountain', a name given to Mow Cop in a documentary by the Victoria Theatre Company of Hartshill on the life of Hugh Bourne, and his idyllic resting place in the Cheshire countryside at Englesea Brook, now the home of the Museum of Primitive Methodism.

On March 12th 1862 the Staffordshire Advertiser reported the laying of a memorial stone of the new Primitive Methodist Chapel at Alsager, and in its issue of July 13th 1862 it reported its opening at a cost of £550. It was built in the Italianate style in a biscuit toned brick, with accommodation for 200 people. One week later the paper reported a public meeting was held in a spacious tent near to the railway station attended by 400 people with a further £20 raised for the building fund.

Activities at the chapel were many and varied, and throughout its history

---

[32] Wesley Place Methodist Church Alsager, Centenary Brochure 1869-1969
[33] A. Hurlestone, *A Tribute to Crewe Road Primitive Methodist Church;* Cheshire Record Office.

it maintained an active Sunday School and youth section. The Children's Anniversary involved much preparation and gave pleasure to large congregations. This was followed by the Sunday School treat. Records for 1928 reveal the cost of visiting Rhyl as £8.6.0.

Methodists as a body were enthusiastic and industrious and formed themselves into circuits. At the time of the Methodist Unions in 1932 Crewe Road wished to remain in the Tunstall Circuit. They finally joined the Sandbach and Alsager Circuit in 1965.

By 1969, seven years after the chapel's centenary, finance and repair problems were brought to the attention of members at a society meeting. A commission, after visiting the two other local Methodist churches, came to the conclusion that the work of Methodism should be concentrated in two centres instead of the three existing ones. A letter was sent to all members from the superintendent minister, Raymond Warner, saying that;

> *"after careful consultation the Circuit Quarterly Meeting had decided to recommend to the District Home Mission and Chapel Committee that public services at Crewe Road be discontinued."*

It was a traumatic time for members as the doors finally closed and the last services were held in August 1969. Trustees at the time of closure were Mr and Mrs P. Baddeley, Mrs B. Heath, T.Davies and R.H. Eardley along with the serving officers at that time, B.Condliffe, R. Ledward, Mrs A. Stone and Miss K. Edwards who officiated as organist. A silver-plated communion ewer inscribed with *"in memory of the late Mary Asbury who was a consistent member and earnest worker from its formation"* is to be seen in the Primitive Methodist Museum at Englesea Brook. The organ was transferred to the Hassall Road Methodist Church.

The chapel is no longer in existence, the site being developed into shops and offices bearing the name 'Chapel Mews'. The work, enterprise and devotion which had for so long been put into the effort of maintaining this chapel are now but a fading memory.

Alsager Congregational Church[34]

After the building of three Methodist churches it was the turn of the Congregationalists to take an interest in planting a church in the village. A Christian denomination, formerly called Independents and founded in the early 17c. it had its roots in Puritanism and used the doctrine of democracy in the

---

[34] For a greater insight into the Congregational Church in Cheshire see F.J. Powicke, *History of the Cheshire Union of Congregational Churches.*

government of the local church. The Pilgrim Fathers who set sail for the New World could be regarded as primitive Congregationalists.

It was in 1870 that the Staffordshire Congregational Union called attention to the need for a church in Alsager, and by 1873 land was secured to build a small chapel, space being left for larger premises at a later date. An estimate of £1,000 was accepted for the building by Mr A. Davies of Alsager. To meet this target contributions were obtained from both the Staffordshire and Cheshire Congregational Unions together with a loan of £300 by Mr Maddock Senior. The foundation stone was laid in November 1876 followed, by tea in the Primitive Methodist schoolroom,[35] and by early summer, June 1877, the new chapel was opened for worship. By the end of the following year sufficient funds had been raised to clear the Church of all debt, which was no mean feat for a small congregation.

It was noted at that time by the Cheshire Congregational Union that the village was fast becoming *"a favourite residence of gentlemen engaged in business in the Staffordshire Pottery Towns."* Towards the end of the century the Church suffered a series of set-backs partly due to the new Anglican church of St Mary Magdalene. It was realised moreover that the religious accommodation in the village was greater than the demand. To counteract the marked drop in contributions and congregations the Church, in 1889, formed a joint pastorate with Sandbach and Wheelock which proved successful with increased membership and a reopened Sunday school. Regular collections to charities included the North Staffordshire Royal Infirmary and the London Missionary Society.

The church records reported *"considerable progress"* for 1895 whilst the following year is noted a year *"rather of quiet perseverance than of marked progress."*

Following the dissolution of the joint pastorate the Church regained its independence and entered a new and successful period of progress with the appointment of the Reverend Robert Hughes from Brecon College, at a salary of £100, an appointment which was to last until 1915. Among the improvements made during his ministry the church minutes records the following:-

> *"Mr Biggin proposed and Mr Gilman recorded that an organ be purchased for £210 net. £40 to be paid at once as deposit and the balance at the end of three months and that the instrument to be fixed in the Church in time for the Anniversary on June 21st 1903".*

The outbreak of the Great War 1914-18 had its impact on the Church; the Minister, the Reverend N. Burgoyne had succeeded to the pastorate but

---

[35] Crewe & Nantwich Chronicle, November 11th 1876.

was granted leave of absence to serve in France with the Y.M.C.A. Before his departure the last Sunday's collection was given to him to buy comforts for the troops. The 24 year old organist, Alfred Holland, joined up and his father, James, took over until his return. Later James' second son Bert took over and played until 1948 adding up to 35 years unbroken organ playing by the Hollands. After asking for a rise in 1925 Alfred was granted an 'honorarium' of £10 per annum. The organ blower received £2.

A number of Scottish families of Presbyterian persuasion settled in Alsager early in the 20c. and since the Congregational Church was nearest in outlook to them they formed a large part of its membership. They included the Chamberlains, Froods, Galloways, Thompsons and McKies. Most of them started off as travelling (or Scottish) drapers taking their wares round on a bicycle and accepting weekly payments. Later they set up shops and their style of business was a feature of the harder economic times right up to the Second World War. Between the wars two influential men were deacons; Mr Paxton-Barratt, a stock-broker who wore a frock coat long after it was the usual Sunday dress, and Mr Powell who was Registrar of Burslem. He was a friend of Arnold Bennett which would explain why his former bungalow just below St. Gabriel's church was called 'Bursley'.

Mr Pidduck, the Hanley jeweller, was prominent in the church in the 1930's. Devoted service was given by Mr George Clark who became a member in 1932 and completed 34 years as an officer of the church in capacity of either secretary or treasurer.

As worship and activities settled down to peace-time routine ministerial appointments were hampered by the church not being in a position to buy a manse. One outstanding minister in this period was Hartley Wareham who was a school teacher by day and his pastoral duties were done in the evening and weekends. The church felt it could not afford to pay him as a full-time minister as he wished and he eventually left to train in Anglican orders.

The 1927 Golden Jubilee was an outstanding event, special services being held by the then Moderator, the Reverend H. Carlisle. Fund-raising was earmarked to install electric lighting throughout the church premises.

In September 1933 the Reverend G. Markham arrived fresh from Paton College. He was popular and successful, but due to his impending marriage, he sought a transfer after three years, because of the lack of manse accommodation. Before he left a new vestry was built, evidence of the healthy state of the church life and it was formally opened by his successor the Reverend Tom Jones.

As the war clouds gathered in 1939 Tom Jones left to become an army chaplain and the end of hostilities found him languishing in a prisoner of war camp in Greece. The Church hall was used as an overflow reception centre for the Liverpool evacuees and for the distribution of gas masks. On the establishment of H.M.S. Excalibur naval camp the ladies of the Church opened a weekly canteen for the comfort and refreshment of service men.

The revival of religion experienced during the First World War was not reflected the same in the second conflagration. The leaderless church suffered a period of depression. With the young men enlisted for the war effort and the breakup of traditional family life the members remaining were of the older generation and numbers at services declined.

To retrieve the situation and as Congregationalism throughout the 20c. had begun displaying a more centralising tendency, the Middlewich Federation was established. It consisted of the churches at Middlewich, Alsager, Sandbach, Crewe and Wheelock, but the Alsager church withdrew in 1950 due to the financial burden involved in the cost of remuneration to visiting preachers.

The post-war years saw the Church struggling to maintain its witness when help came from the Reverend Gilbert Dash, a retired Methodist minister, who took charge successfully for seven years until his retirement.

A succession of evangelical ministers followed. These included Pastor Alan White and the Reverend Clive Tyler who arrived from the London Bible College and eventually moved on to South Africa. On the latter's departure the Reverend Harold Swindells of Congleton became Interim Moderator in 1964 and was able to secure a call to the church's first full-time ministry for 20 years, an event which signalled another and greater upsurge than ever in its vitality.

In 1966 the church was packed with visitors for the ordination and induction of Rosemary Shaw. Her pastorate, along with a responsible deaconate, saw the life of the church revived and membership strengthened. Afternoon Sunday School was changed to morning family service. An adult weekly fellowship and one of the first mother and under fives club were started and these continue to serve the community. The Alsager Council of Churches was initiated by Miss Shaw as its first secretary along with a Ministers' Fraternal. The fund-raising for Christian Aid Week was extended and shared by all the local churches. In 1970 the Minister's own wedding to Ted Hartley was held in the church and three years and one son later Rosemary Hartley resigned the pastorate.

In the early 1970's an important change took place. Discussions had been held for some time on the proposed union of the Congregational Church with the Presbyterian Church of England and Wales. In October 1971 the Alsager Church Meeting voted by an overwhelming majority (only one dissenting vote) to become part of the United Reformed Church which came into being on the 5th October 1972.

A plea for unity between the Church of England, Methodist and Congregational Churches twice failed, in 1969 and 1972, to achieve sufficient majorities in the assemblies of the Church of England.

In 1973 the Reverend H. Swindells was welcomed once again as Interim Moderator, although since 1966 he had oversight of Sandbach. So to help with the visiting and to take some of the services a retired minister was appointed Pastoral Assistant to the Church. The Reverend J. Charles was living near Congleton and accepted this appointment. Both ministers, along with past incumbents, took a prominent part in the year-long centenary celebrations of 1976 to 77, with the 101st anniversary service being conducted by the Reverend R.J. Hall, Moderator of the United Reformed Church, taking the Church into its second century.[36]

Catholicism in Alsager

The opening section of this chapter has already given some information as to early catholicism in the days following the reformation. The Church continued to be a proscribed organisation for many years and Roman Catholics were excluded from all public office until the repeal of the penal laws against them, termed 'Catholic Relief', begun in 1778. Under the terms of the 'Catholic Emancipation (Relief) Act,' of 1829, Roman Catholics were permitted to sit in Parliament and eligable for all public offices except those of regent, lord lieutenant, and lord chancellor. The passing of the Act vitually destroyed the government of Wellington and Peel.

Little is known about the organisation of the Catholic Church in Alsager before the 20c., there is no record of any place of worship in the township. The nearest churches are believed to have been at Congleton, Cobridge and Newcastle.

St. Gabriel's Church

During the early years of the 20c. only a few Catholic families, such as the Eardleys, the Regans and the Woods, lived in Alsager. Some of these are thought to have been of Irish origin. There was no Catholic church in Alsager at that time, St. John's at Kidsgrove being the nearest at a distance of 3 miles (5km). Catholics were obliged to travel to Kidsgrove, usually by walking, or to go to St. Mary's at Crewe.

In 1935 Dr Michael Aische converted an outbuilding at his home, 'The Cedars', into a chapel for the use of fellow Catholics who numbered about 20. This small congregation donated sacred statues, kneelers, altar rails and a confessional. Mass was celebrated by Fr. 'Tommy' Mulcahy. The chapel continued in use until 1939, after which time the statues and other items were

---

[36] Alsager United Reformed Church Centenary brochure.

stored away and members of the congregation reverted to their former practice of travelling to Kidsgrove or Crewe.

In that year the Royal Ordnance Factory was built at Radway Green. Thousands of workers were employed at the factory bringing many more people to live in Alsager. The population increased, from 2,852 in 1931 to 5,574 in 1951,[37] and consequently brought more Catholic families, by now 175 Catholics were living in Alsager.[38] Clearly, the lack of a Catholic church in the town was unsatisfactory.

In 1941 Fr. Albert Roberts came to St. Mary's at Crewe and realised that there was a real need in Alsager for the celebration of a Sunday Mass. First he, and his curate Fr. John Mortimer Lyons, used a wooden building at the Royal Ordnance Factory and later held Mass in Milton House which was being used as a workers' hostel. They later transferred to a new hostel opened on land formerly belonging to Heathside Farm (this was later to become the teacher training college).

However, these were only the first few of a string of different venues. Other sites included, the Ministry of Supply Community Centre in Longview Avenue, better known as Radway Club; the Working Men's Club in Sandbach Road South, and the Alsager Arms public house.

In his booklet, on the history of the parish church of St.Gabriel,[39] Davies describes how Mass took place at different times of the morning according to who was officiating. If it was Fr. Roberts it was at 9 or 9.30 a.m. because he had to return to Crewe for the High Mass of 11 a.m. But if the curate was on duty Mass was at 10 or 10.30 a.m. The celebrants were dependent on the services of Mr Rawlinson, a bank manager, who drove them to and from Crewe in his car.

When the Royal Navy training base, H.M.S. Excalibur, became a home to refugees in 1949 many among them were Catholics. Previous venues were now unsuitable and Mass began to be celebrated in the large assembly hall at the Excalibur site.

But even as early as 1946 Fr. Roberts had been giving serious thought to the provision of a parish church for the use of Catholics in Alsager. With this in mind land in Lawton Road had been purchased from Mr Snell, Chief Accountant at the R.O.F. The land was conveyed on 30th August 1946 but it was not until 1950 that Fr. Roberts was able to apply to the Alsager Urban District Council for permission to develop it. Plans were drawn up by the

---

[37] Census Returns, Public Record Office.

[38] Rev. E. M. Abbott, *History of the Diocese of Shrewsbury 1850-1986;* see entry under Alsager.

[39] W.R.Davies, *A History of the Parish of St. Gabriel at Alsager Cheshire in the Diocese of Shrewsbury.;* p. 9.

architect, F.G. Montgomery and these were passed by the appropriate authorities, but the church was not built. Perhaps it was too financially ambitious, as it would have been much larger than the present church.

In April 1952 Fr. Roberts again submitted plans drawn up by the architect F.X. Velarde of Liverpool and at last building commenced. The church was to be named St. Gabriel's but it was to be more than a year before it was ready for use, and worship continued throughout this time at the previous venues.

At last, on December 15th 1953, the church was opened and blessed by the Right Reverend John A. Murphy, Bishop of Shrewsbury. The ceremony was concluded with a Pontifical High Mass. It was undoubtedly a special day for Catholics living in Alsager and to mark the occasion the ceremonies were followed by a celebratory lunch at the Alsager Arms. Dishes on the luncheon menu were named after the church (Poisson Gabriel), the architect (Glace Velarde) and the builder (Pommes Tyson).

Five years were to elapse before a parish priest was appointed. This meant that marriages still had to be solemnised at Crewe although baptisms could take place, the first one being that of the daughter of Mr and Mrs Nicholls on Thursday 18th February 1954. The same year Fr. Roberts of Crewe was replaced by Fr. Wilfrid Kelly who, assisted by his curate Fr. McGowan, presided over St.Gabriel's until the summer of 1958. By this time parishioners were becoming increasingly anxious that a priest had not been appointed and Bishop Murphy was visited by a delegation to try to set matters right. During this difficult period it was only the efforts of a small group of dedicated people who kept the embryo parish in existence.

On August 28th 1958 Fr. Bob Fallon became St. Gabriel's first parish priest. This was also his first full appointment having served as a curate for 14 years. Several priests have succeeded Fr. Fallon each bringing something to contribute to the life of the church.

The first baptism at St. Gabriel's, that of May Josephine Dale, was undertaken by Fr. Fallon on October 5th 1958. The first marriage took place on the 18th October between John Gabriel Kelly and Mary Brown. The ceremony was conducted by Fr. Wilfrid Kelly. The following year, on November 18th, 32 candidates were confirmed by Bishop Murphy.[40]

With Vatican II (1962 - 1965) there was a complete change in the attitude of the Catholic Church towards other religious communities. Prior to 1965 it had been more like confrontation that cooperation. The attendance of a representative at meetings of the Council of Churches was now allowed but

---

[40] W.R.Davis, *Mini History of St. Gabriel's Alsager, 1992*

only as an observer. In Alsager this changed with the arrival of Fr. Kevin Byrne in 1968. He advocated full involvement with representatives on the committee. He also set up house groups in which parishioners met members of other churches in their homes. This whole-hearted taking up of ecumenism and closer cooperation with other churches in Alsager was to some minds the most important event in the history of St. Gabriel's.

Fr. Byrne also originated the idea of a school, and saw the project through the difficult initial stages of obtaining approval from the various religious and secular bodies. These plans came to fruition in 1975 when a primary school was erected in Well Lane.[41] Fr. Moorhouse his successor, did commendable work with the financing and construction of the school but he had to thank Fr. Byrne who, as it were, 'laid the foundations'.

These developments brought Catholicism in Alsager to a level of participation in marked contrast to those earlier years when members of the Catholic community had to follow their religious life outside the town.

[41] ibid.

Chapter 7

Education.

===

Early Education in Alsager.

Zachary Cawdrey founded his classical school at Barthomley rectory around 1660, and it is possible that children from the leading Alsager families would have been sent to this school. One former pupil, Sam Alsager, son of Ralph, went subsequently to St. John's Cambridge.[1] He later became Vicar of Sandon in Staffordshire and his daughter Mary married Roger Wilbraham of Dorfold, Nantwich. Their grand-daughters became the Misses Alsager who founded and built Christ Church. They were also responsible for obtaining the Alsager Act in 1789, during the reign of George III.

Bishop Gastrell, in his famous notes on his Chester Diocese[2] says of Barthomley:-

> "About anno 1675, a School was built here in y^e Church yard by the Rev.
> Mr Rich. Steel, and was afterwards endowed by him and others of y^e parish
> wth £13.2. for y^e Master, who is nominated by y^e Patron, Churchwardens and
> Rector. The School is free to y^e Steels of Claycroft Family and all other
> Parish^{rs} not having 10$^{li.}$ per annum in Lands or Tenements. Writings are in
> y^e hands of y^e Rectour."

Bearing in mind that at the time Alsager was one of the five townships that made up Barthomley parish the school must have catered for Alsager scholars.

The Alsager Act of 1789.[3]

An

A   C   T

to

Enable *Mary Alsager, Margaret Alsager,* and *Judith
Alsager,* to finish and complete a new Church or
Chapel in the Parish of *Barthomley,* in the County
of *Chester,* and to endow the same; and to establish

---

[1] *"Barthomley, The Story of an Estate Village"* p.193
[2] F. Gastrell. *Notitia Cestriensis;* Chetham Soc. 1st Series vol. viii p.213.
[3] 29 *Geo.*III. 1789; CRO. ref. DMD/A/21

> a Charity School within the said Parish; and vesting
> the Right of Presentation to the said Church or
> Chapel in them, and the future Lords and Ladies
> of the Manor of *Alsager,* within the said County.

The Act further recites that:-

> "**And whereas** the said *Mary Alsager, Margaret Alsager,* and *Judith Alsager,*
> intend, at their own Expence, to establish a School, near the said new
> Church or Chapel, for the Education of poor Children, of the said
> parish, or elsewhere; and to erect proper Buildings for that Purpose, and
> for the Residence of the Master of such School; and also to take in and
> inclose Part of the said Common or Waste Ground for the Use of such
> School-master, ..."

The Act specified that the area of land to be allocated for the school house and buildings should not exceed 30 acres and that this land should forever, after the decease of the Misses Alsager, be vested in trustees who were to include the Rectors of Barthomley and Astbury, the lord of the manor of Alsager, various specified local gentry and five occupiers of land in the township, namely; Rev. Richard Lowndes Salmon, John Ford, Thomas Rowley, William Lowndes and John Johnson. The trustees were required to ensure that the land and buildings vested in them were to be used for the purposes authorised by the Act and should:-

> ". . . . have the Government and Direction of the said intended School, and
> shall permit and suffer such of the Children of both Sexes, belonging to the
> said Parish or elsewhere (the Children of the township of Alsager always
> having a preference) as they shall think proper, to be therein taught or
> instructed in Reading and Writing, and such other Branches of Education,
> and until such Ages respectively, as they shall judge expedient . . . ."

The trustees also had the responsibility of appointing and supervising the conduct of the school master and providing him with a house. The Trust survives today as The Alsager Education Foundation.

In 1906 Mrs. McEwen wrote an account of life in Alsager[4] and she described the school thus:-

> " Up to 1847 what is now the Parsonage coach-house and laundry were the
> village school and there are those amongst us who learnt their letters there,
> and not without tears, for one may still hear of 'the tree of knowledge' in the
> Parsonage garden from which birch rods were cut to enforce learning and
> manners."

As the population of the village increased the old school buildings became totally inadequate, even after additions and enlargements. The original school had consisted of 12 scholars who received free education and some fee paying students. It was supported by the Trust and was supplemented by subscriptions. The school master was the clergyman. In 1804 the Rev.

[4] Mrs McEwen, *Alsager 1789-1906;* Longton 1906.

Babington made his reply to the Bishop of Chester's visitation enquiry and mentioned the Voluntary Charity School for the benefit of poor children of both sexes, which gave instruction in reading, writing, and catechism. By 1847 the number of children had increased to 227 in the mixed school and 129 infants and the decision was taken to provide new buildings on the site they now occupy, adjoining Christ Church, in Church Road. Sir Gilbert Scott was the designer of the new school which opened in 1848. The building is typical of the Victorian era and when first erected it sported a beautiful pointed bell tower, now sadly missing.

In 1847 the Rev. Charles Alsager Tryon became the incumbent of Christ Church. He was a member of the Alsager family and his arrival brought great changes to the education scene in the village. Bagshaw's Directory of 1850 stated;-

> *"Incumbent Rev. Charles Tryon B.A., Tithes are commuted for £240. In this chapelry a free school founded by Misses Alsager; for which they directed 30 acres of land should be enclosed, or that the school master should have the surplus of the profit by letting the pews, after deducting the repairs etc. of the church. The land has been enclosed but it is much the same condition as when it was common. Worth about £10 p.a. independently of residence of the teacher. Master teaches 12 children free."*

It is to the Rev. Tryon that the people of Alsager must direct their thanks for the elegant avenue of limes in Church Road. The verger of that time[5] wrote a poem about the trees, one verse speaks of the ill treatment of one of the largest trees at the hands of some of the school children; nothing changes! Charles Tryon was also responsible for the landscaping of the area around the Parsonage and the glebe fields and the woodland in the region of the Grig. Mrs. McEwen said of him "He left things better than when he found them."

It is very doubtful whether the Rev. Duncombe, Rector of Barthomley, would have agreed with Mrs. McEwen's valediction to Charles Tryon due to his acrimonious dispute with Mr. Tryon in 1860 over the management of the school, which was handled by the Alsager Free School Charity under Mr. Tryon's chairmanship. Mr. Duncombe published a lengthy pamphlet[6] on the subject in which he accused the Charity of possible misappropriation of funds and misinterpretation of the Act of 1789. He was also very concerned that the number of appointed trustees had a shortfall and did not comply with the original number required. Phrases such as *'stabbing in the back', 'being gloriously hated',* and *'not washing dirty linen in public but to wash it at home and impartially at that';* were found in the text. Not exactly the kind of language expected from men of the cloth!

---

[5] Charles Hemmings, verger over 30 years, *The Song of the Lime Trees by Christ Church;* 1890.
[6] Edward Duncombe, *"Church and School Business";* Spottiswood & Co., 1868

The following is taken from the pamphlet published by Mr. Duncombe in March 1869:-

Alsager 10th December, 1868.

Extract from the Statement of the undersigned Trustees of Alsager School with reference to the letter sent by the Rev. Edward Duncombe to the Charity Commissioners of England and Wales.

Clause 5. The Charity or Trust School is not a "nonentity". The School is in a very satisfactory condition, with 103 children on the books and under the conduct of a first-rate Teacher and School-mistress, subject to government inspection.

Clause 6. The original inconvenient School House has been sold by the Trustees with the sanction and under the powers of the Court of Chancery, and handsome and convenient School Room, Class Room, and suitable Outbuildings, besides a capital Residence for the Master have been erected from the plans Mr. G.G. Scott, Architect, with the money received from the sale of the original School House, largely augmented by funds provided by the Rev C.A. Tryon.

Clause 7. The office of Schoolmaster is held by the Curate of the Church under the powers of the Act of Parliament of 1789, section 18, who provides a deputy holding a certificate, and a school mistress, out of the surplus money paid to him by the Trustees largely supplemented from other sources.

Clause 10. We emphatically deny that there has been any "alienation" or misappropriation of Trust money or property in connection with the Trust, and are quite prepared to enter into an enquiry as to the truth of this statement.

Randle Wilbraham, Rode Hall, Lawton, Cheshire, Trustee.

Edward Clayton, Rector of Astbury, "ex-officio", Trustee.

C.A. Tryon, "ex-officio" Trustee.

With regard to clause 5. above, it is interesting to note that Joseph Finnemoore was far from happy with the state of the school when he took up his post of headmaster on Monday the 12th October 1868. His report in the log book can be seen in the extracts included at the end of this chapter. On Wednesday of the same week he complained bitterly to the Rev. Tryon about the want of discipline and the disorder.

In 1877 the Charity was reformed by the Charity Commission. Land vested in the trustees at that time included the Marl Pits, on part of which the Manchester Metropolitan University now stands, all the land around Christ Church, including the playing fields, the land called The Grig reaching to Sandbach Road and including the cottage on the junction of Sandbach Road and Lodge road. The Charity was again re-formed in 1956 when it became The Alsager Education Foundation; there are now 14 trustees under the ex-officio chairmanship of the Vicar of Christ Church. The objects of the Trust are to;-

(a). award Scholarships and Bursaries of Maintenance Allowances tenable at any school, university, or other place of learning, approved by the

Trustees;

(b). provide financial assistance, outfits, clothing, tools, instruments or books to enable beneficiaries on leaving school, university or other educational establishment to prepare for, or to assist their entry into, a profession, trade or calling;

(c). award Scholarships or Maintenance Allowances to enable beneficiaries to travel abroad or pursue their education;

(d). to provide, or to assist towards the provision of, facilities, of any kind not normally provided by the Local Education Authority, for recreation and social and physical training, including the provision of coaching in athletics, sports and games, for beneficiaries who are receiving primary, secondary or further education; and

(e). the provision of financial assistance to enable beneficiaries to study music or other arts.

The Trust, having bought land in Sandbach Road North from Mr. Candland, were able to build a new Infant and Junior school which was opened in 1900. This was needed to alleviate the acute overcrowding which by then affected the old school buildings in Church Road. From this period on the older buildings accommodated the senior scholars. The Trust still owns the Primary School, Sandbach Road, and the School and School House in Church Road.

Proceeds from the sale of property have been invested and provide an income to be used for the purposes of the Charity. Recent awards made by the Trust have included; the assistance in the purchase of books for university students; upgrading technical equipment and musical instruments in Alsager's schools; making available fees for playgroup pupils; and contributing to the costs of schools field trips and libraries.

The National School

From records preserved[7] details are known concerning early members of staff at the school and its management. On the 12th January 1863 Edward Sweeting took charge of the school as its headmaster. He had the full age range of children from infants to teenagers and his only helper was his wife, Mercy, who was uncertificated and only part-time. Within the school, as its log shows, there was a very mixed ability range and teaching was a formidable task but one that he was quite capable of tackling; as the inspectors report of June 1864 indicates.

"This school is very well taught and disciplined. The elementary subjects are thoroughly mastered and the general intelligence of the Scholars has been carefully called out. The Scripture knowledge is good. The catechism

---

[7] *Alsager Christ Church School Log Book 1863-1911;* Taken from transcription by Constance D. Jones 1992. (Manchester Metropolitan University, History Dept.).

needs to be more accurately taught. The repetition of Poetry has had a very
good effect on the reading."

In January 1865, Miss Ambrose joined the school as assistant mistress. On the same day six new children were admitted. Two of them were boarders who may have lived with the family of an agricultural labourer. In the 1851 census three children, from a pottery manufacturer's family, are recorded as lodging with such a family. One of them was Francis Creed Mayer, later prominent in Alsager society.

During the rest of Mr. Sweeting's time as headmaster he made his daily logbook entries, most of them concerned progress reports, curriculum subjects and domestic details. Among the interesting items was one that recorded the commencement of evening classes for the navvies working on the railway at Mere Lake: others recording a cricket match that took place between two elevens from the Boys Club, the choir trip to Liverpool, a school feast; and the fact that Mr. Sweeting received quarterly money from the Receiving Officer for pauper children. He was succeeded as headmaster on 12th October 1868 by Joseph Finnemore who made his first entry in the log book:-

"I took charge of Alsager National School.

State in which I found the School.

Scripture, very poor indeed, very few of the children able to answer the simplest Scripture question

Reading, rather poor also.

The Writing throughout the School seems very fair and also the

Arithmetic- with the exception of Stand. IV- the children working the examples very correctly.

Spelling very fair

Tables not very well known.

Composition very deficient for such large children. History, Geography and Grammar slightly known.

The discipline very lax indeed. In my opinion this being the worst thing about the school. The children change lessons & get their necessary apparatus very noisily and seemingly without any fixed method.

The books, slates etc in a very untidy condition & scattered thro' out the school.

Many things necessary for proper working of the school required as for instance- inkpots, chalk - books for Standards."

On Wednesday the 14th he complained bitterly to Mr. Tryon of the want of discipline and utter disorder.

In March 1870 the children were promised a half holiday in Mr. Ford's field, with scrambles for nuts etc., for regular attendance. Perhaps it was hoped that this would boost the numbers for the return in October. Sadly the numbers only increased by two. There had been a slight increase the previous year when Mrs. Lunt closed her school in Close Lane.

Under the 1870 (Forster's) Education Act figures were requested, in compliance with the Act and the return was as follows:-

"Thursday 27th October

	Boys.	Girls.	
N°. on Books	86	56	142.
N°. present on the day	69	40	109
N° not resident in the Parish	12	6	18"

In an earlier return the age range was from 4 years to 14 years, with the largest number in the 6 to 7 year age group.

Mrs. Sarah Ann Finnemore was responsible for the welfare and wellbeing of the girls who, it appears, were being taught in a separate room from the boys.

The financial return for this period was as follows;-

Pence for past year	£28.13.6½	*Boys*
	£19.18.4	*Girls.*
Total	£48.11.10½.	

Visits were often made to the school by Mrs. Wilbraham who showed a great interest in the girls. Other visitors included Mr. and Mrs. Craig, whose five children attended the school. The lord Bishop of Chester and his wife, with Randle Wilbraham also visited. They asked if there were any cases of absolute destitution among the pupils. The answer was "none". The Bishop expressed satisfaction with the way the school was run.

In June 1871 an Inspector of Schools came to visit and the head was asked about the number of labouring class families in the village. He answered that he thought there were 65 houses occupied by people who could not afford to pay more than nine pence. An entry in the logbook for 23rd June 1874 records:-

> *"Received cards from Mr. Clarke, Relieving Officer, for filling up with the weekly attendance of Pauper Children - also one from Crewe Relieving Officer, for Henry Steel."*

Government examinations were held and in 1873 the H.M.I. for the district, Mr. Williams, with the Rev. Tryon and the Rev. H. Smith were present when 55 children sat such an examination, 28 of the children were under 7 years of age. Two songs were sung, Men of Harlech and Home Sweet Home. The report of the event was good but it stated that more attention must be paid to the infants in the future. Drawing examinations were regarded as very important and certificates were awarded if certain grades were reached.

Religious education tests were set by the diocesan inspectors and the results were recorded in the logbook. Some parents objected to their children being taught the subject and requested that they should be withdrawn from these classes.

At this time the training of assistant teaching staff was very largely informal. The records of the school provide a number of illustrations of this. One of Mr. Finnemore's brighter and more reliable pupils, Elizabeth Latham, was chosen to act as pupil teacher and help with the teaching of younger children. It is not recorded if she had to undergo any training or examination to qualify. During the headmastership of Mr. Peacock, Mr. Finnemoor's successor, it appears that the headmaster's mother undertook needlework teaching. Mr. Peacock and his wife Hannah, were the school's only full time members of staff for many years but gradually this became extended. Due to the rapid expansion of education at this time there was a shortage of trained professional staff and a system was developed of using older children as monitors and pupil teachers who could qualify as assistant teachers if they passed an examination at the end of five years. There was an unnamed sewing mistress and in the government report of 1880 the name of S.E. Machin appeared as a pupil teacher; not a very successful teacher by all accounts, the headmaster noted that she did not know her lessons. She did however pass part of her exam later. Another pupil teacher was Thomas Bevan who was warned about lateness. A monitor, L. Price, a female, was also helping the Peacocks. It must have been extremely hard work to cope with the wide range of ability found in such a large number of pupils. The following tables help to illustrate the problems encountered and the methods used to relieve them.[8]

	Age	Wage	Job
Monitor	12	£6 a year	Helps teacher, gives out slates books etc
Pupil Teacher	13 - 18	£15-30 a year	During the day helping teachers, very often teaching themselves. In the evening, lessons from the headmaster
Assistant Teacher	18+	£60 a year	Normal teaching whilst working for a teaching certificate without which unable to become a head
Headmaster		£250 a year	Responsible for running of the school, also teaches and gives lessons to pupil teachers in the evenings

The older children were divided into classes, or standards, arranged by

[8] Cheshire Education Dept. *"The Alsager National School Booklet";*

age. The lowest Standard I, the highest Standard VIII. They were examined at the end of each year by the H.M.I. and if they passed they moved into the next Standard, if they failed they stayed where they were for another year. So in Standard III for example there would be children of different ages between 8 and 13. It is not difficult to imagine why so many children hated school when they might have been 12 and were in a class of 8 year olds. This grouping led to problems with accommodation. An inspector's report of 1889 draws attention to the biggest problem facing the school.

> *"The school is very crowded now . . . . In the upper standards the utmost working accommodation in seats is 90 and there are constantly 20 or thereabouts in excess of that number."*

And in 1899;-

> *"In the three upper Standards there are 86 children with desk accommodation for 50."*

The following table shows the curriculum for each standard and what had to be achieved by the children in order to progress.

	Reading	Writing	Arithmetic
Standard I Age about 8	Passage with words of one syllable.	Write on slate letters capital and small	Numbers up to 1000. Easy sums in addition and Subtraction. Tables up to 12x6
Standard II Age about 9	Passage from an elementary reading book.	Copy a line of print.	Division and multiplication
Standard III Age 9 - 10	Short passage from an elementary book used in the school.	A sentence from same passage, dictated	Money sums
Standard IV Age 10 - 11	A short paragraph from a more advanced book in the school	A sentence dictated from the same book but not the same paragraph.	Money sums.
Standard V Age 11 - 12	A few lines of poetry from a book in the school.	Sentence from reading book in the school.	Weights and measures.
Standard VI Age 12 - 13	A short paragraph from a newspaper or book.	Paragraph from same newspaper or book.	Fractions and decimals.

The Education Acts of 1876 and 1880 (Mundella's) decreeing compulsory education for all children did not take into account the accommodation problems encountered in village schools such as Alsager.   With the establishment of the new school in Sandbach Road in 1900 the problem was solved and the H.M.I. report for that year records;-

> *"The overcrowding difficulty having been successfully solved, better work has been done and the school is in a creditable state of efficiency, both as regards instruction and discipline. I am glad to recommend the higher principal grant."*

In May 1875 John C. Peacock had become headmaster of Alsager school. He was not happy with its general state; it is interesting to look back and note that Mr. Finnemore, when he took over from Mr. Sweeting, was of the same opinion ! Mr. Peacock said that the lower standards were very unsatisfactory, and some of the children did not know their letters, there were cases of truancy and producing poor home lessons.   A girl admitted from a 'private Adventure School' (whatever that was!) was found to be very backward.

A report dated April 1876 stated that Mr. Peacock appeared to be capable of effecting the desired improvement needed.   Some of these improvements are recorded in the logbook.

> *March 17th.   Tried new timetable.   Began Domestic Economy on Wednesday.*
>
> *October 20th. Reopened school in new room. Very much more comfort in working.*
>
> *Dec. 5th. The children of the day-school were invited to join with those of the Sunday school in giving towards a small present to Rev. Sherringham on his wedding.*
>
> *!885 Jan.13th. Mother refused to pay 4d. per week for son and was told to remove him or pay the fee.*
>
> *Feb. 17th. School used as polling station.*
>
> *April 6th. The Inspector of Nuisances called and took a sample of water from the school pump to be analysed. Result . . . . water good.*

Throughout this period the maintenance of discipline continued to be a problem. Amongst matters complained of were boys swearing, of using bad language on the way home from school, and of lying. Such things were not new to the school.   Earlier logbook entries indicate pupils were noisy and untidy, ill-used school equipment, and even that boys were punished for setting fire to exercise books in the lane outside school. Behaviour away from school seems to have been no better. Evidence from the log details punishment for pulling up tree roots on the roadside, tampering with newly laid gas pipes in the village, damage to cornfields in the summer holiday, together with a host of minor misdemeanours such as loitering, lateness, fighting, stone throwing, trespass, apple stealing, vandalising trees, running off at playtime and making gaps in hedges. In October 1883 a boy was sent to an Industrial school by the magistrates. It would appear that children's behaviour is very much the same as it always was !

A constant anxiety during the later years of the Victorian era was that of maintaining attendance. In 1874 an entry in the log reads:-

> *"Mr. I. Yates came to school regarding sending Sam Hilditch to school, under the Workshops' Regulation Act, ... he being employed at Yates' Brick Bank must attend 10 hours per week at school . . . ."*

and again in 1885:-

> *"I complained to the Attendance Officer at his visit about the great numbers of children away, or attending irregularly. During the last fortnight the attendance has been 66 per cent of the numbers on the registers and has seldom for the last few weeks risen above 75 per cent. A good many children make a constant habit of staying away two and sometimes three times in a week."*

Attendance suffered also when both boys and girls were absent from school during the potato picking season, the setting of crops or harvesting. Souling[9] featured in the yearly calendar of events, as did fêtes and garden parties; all these, according to the logbook, affected the attendance figures and caused concern. The main cause of concern however was illness. In some instances the school had to close for a number of weeks, as was the case in October and November 1902, when measles became very prevalent. There were recorded incidents of something called the 'itch', it appeared difficult to cure as it was mentioned over a period of time. The usual childish ailments listed were;- scarletina, diphtheria, whooping cough, chickenpox, mumps, and influenza, all of an epidemic nature. Also noted were cases of fits and of St. Vitus dance, a disease not often mentioned today.

In 1895 the headmaster recorded notice of an outbreak of scarlet fever in Red Row, a group of cottages in Audley Road; as a result 12 children were not allowed in school. The head was told by the Sanitary Authority that he must obey the order. There were other occasions when the whole school was closed because of illness.

Despite the good H.M.I. report in 1900 Mr. Peacock continued to be most concerned with the problem of absenteeism and mentioned it a number of times in the records of the next few years. Children stayed away to attend Band of Hope trips, flower shows, Forester Club parades, church and chapel treats, and Church Lads Brigades camps. One entry in the logbook records that there was a very smart wedding in the village and parents kept their children away to watch it. The authorities were as concerned as the headmaster; two parents were fined for allowing their offspring to skip school.

[9] When children called at houses and sang for *soul* cakes or sweets.

The Victorian era drew to a close on the death of the Queen in 1901. Despite the problems with curriculum matters and severe overcrowding etc., the children of the village school enjoyed social activities such as treats and tea parties. In some cases these were used as a bribe to get the children to participate in fund raising activities. The girls attended sewing parties organised by Mrs. Tryon and Mrs. Wilbraham, at school and in the homes of both ladies. The Dorcas Society benefitted from these activities as is described elsewhere. The boys were well catered for with their drum and fife band, the Boys Club and sporting activities, resulting in matches against other teams. The Edwardian era began and in June 1902 Alsager school celebrated the coronation of Edward VII with a week's holiday.

At the turn of the century fees for elementary education had been virtually abolished, even though these had been only a few pence per child they represented a major outlay in a poor family with several children. Poverty is reflected by one logbook entry at least. When George Anderson, one of the boys, drowned in the Marl Pits one Saturday night, the other pupils collected 24 shillings to help his parents, who were very poor, to meet the funeral expenses.

In 1901 Mr. Peacock recorded that some pupils went to Congleton to be examined for Labour Certificates. These were *'blue forms'* that stated that the recipients had reached a certain standard in the '3 R's' and were therefore entitled to leave school at 13. In some cases pupils under this age were allowed to work part-time, whilst attending school, as is shown in the case of Sam Hilditch who was working on Yates' brick bank in 1874.

By 1904 the staff of the National School comprised;- Headmaster, John C. Peacock; Assistants, Moses Corfield, Maria Birch, Mabel J. Tinsley, George S. Jacobs, and Myra Whittaker. The sewing mistress was Agnes Peacock and gardening was taught by George Sargent.

Practical work in the school garden may have come as a welcome relief to the boys from written work but on one occasion they got so wet they were sent home to change. At another time they were allowed out of school to attend a ploughing match at a local farm. Agricultural interest was being stimulated and it was duly noted by the authorities. A Mr. Dymond from The Board of Education called at the school to enquire into the method of teaching gardening. He was interested in both the theoretical and practical work being carried out and said that it was first school he had been to where a practical gardener was employed to teach boys.

Also on the time-table were lessons on general health matters. The boys were already being instructed in the value of fresh air and practical work. The girls too were being encouraged to take an interest in their personal appearance. Talks were given on the laws of health, personal cleanliness, general health and baby care. They were attending cookery classes in St. Mary's schoolroom and being instructed on food values etc. Temperance was another subject which warranted attention and talks appeared on the time-table, resulting in the writing of essays for which certificates were awarded.

In 1911 a nurse visited the school and later in the year there was a visit by the Medical Officer. He inspected the children and, according to the records, he disrupted the time-table for two days. This was probably the first of many school medical and dental inspections.

It is worth recording the details of those members of the staff of the school who have left their mark on Alsager society during the greater part of the twentieth century.

Moses Corfield; a former student of York Teacher Training College (The College of St. John York?) he began his teaching career as a certificated assistant at Alsager in 1901 and later, on the retirement of Mr. Peacock, became headmaster.

Miss Maria Birch, who came to the school as a pupil teacher in 1899, was described by Mr. Corfield as 'one of his most valued members of staff'. According to the logbook she *"served loyally and devotedly in the school for over 44 years";* when she left she was presented with an electric reading lamp and a sum of money by the vicar, the Rev. C.C. Potts, on behalf of the managers and scholars. One sad note, before she retired, Miss Birch was moved to the Junior School by the Education Authority and was forced to end her career away from the school she so dearly loved.

Mr. J. O. Hughes; had been headmaster of Rode Boys School and was transferred, with his assistant, Miss W. Holmes, to Alsager on the closure of his school. He succeeded Mr. Corfield as head and Miss Holmes became his deputy.

More recently James Crabtree was appointed woodwork master and Helen Timperly home economics. Mr Fred Morris, organist at Christ Church joined the staff as music master in 1950. In September 1954, when appointments for teaching staff were already being made in preparation for the move into the new buildings in Hassall Road, the staff consisted of Mr. J.O. Hughes, Miss W. Holmes, Mr. F. Morris, Mrs. M. Bebbington, Miss M. Williams, Mrs. J. Penketh and Mr. M. Hollinshead.

In 1948 the County Architect had produced a plan for Alsager C of E (Modern Secondary) School giving the positions of the proposed new H.O.R.S.A. hut, sited on the glebe land, which was to house the home economics and handicrafts departments. The plan also showed the new canteen in Hassall Road.

Pupil numbers continued to increase and the life of the school turned full circle when the Parsonage building was once again used for teaching purposes.

Mr. Hughes had his office in the room which was once used by the vicar as his study. It was the usual practice, for the staff in the old school, to send a boy, or girl, to warn Mr. Hughes of the approach of visitors. The messenger could run through the shrubbery, over the ha-ha, into the garden, and round to the study more swiftly than the car carrying the visitor could make its journey.

The new building opened in 1955 under the headship of Mr A.J. Hawkes. Mr. Hughes remained as joint deputy head with Miss Holmes until his retirement. The new school absorbed schools in the surrounding areas including Barthomley, Smallwood, Rode Heath, and Mow Cop with children aged 11+ being transferred to Alsager Secondary Modern School. Many of the schools affected had their staff and older pupils transferred with their buildings remaining as primary establishments. It took some time for the children from the outlying schools to settle down in their new surroundings. The atmosphere in small village schools had been very different to that of a larger establishment, with many specialist rooms and long corridors. The pupils were no longer taught in form groups under one form teacher but moved from one department to another. Apart from the emotional upheaval the physical toll on the younger children was immense.

Mr. F. G. Parker followed Mr. Hawkes as headmaster and Miss Holmes continued as his deputy. The curriculum then was based on five broad subject groupings, Technical (Boys), Technical (Girls), Commerce, Rural Studies and Practical. Within this framework the subjects offered were; English, maths, history, geography, science, music, woodwork, metalwork, technical drawing, cookery, needlework, typing, rural studies, art and physical education. Within the groups there was a certain amount of mixed ability teaching but there was streaming in English and maths. No external examinations, such as CSE's or 'O' levels were taken until a few pupils stayed on at school on a voluntary basis to take CSE in the late 1960's prior to the Newsome Report which recommended that the leaving age be raised to 16 by 1965. The Act that followed, known as the ROSLA, (Raising of the School Leaving Age) meant that schools such as this were able to offer examination courses for CSE. and 'O' levels to pupils at the beginning of the 1970's. On the retirement of Miss Holmes in 1966 Mr. John King was appointed deputy head.

Mr. Parker left the school in 1968 leaving Mr. King in charge until the appointment of Mr. J. J. Andrews in 1970 by which time there were 580 pupils registered. In September 1971 Alsager Secondary Modern School ceased to exist and Alsager Comprehensive School came into being. In July 1993 Mr Andrews retired and handed the school over to Mr D. Black, with Mr. P. Clarke, Mr. H. Austen and Mr. L. Purcell as his deputies.

Other Early Village Schools.

In the early years there is very little documentary evidence available with regard to educational establishments but it is known that there were dame schools in existence and it is more than likely that Alsager could lay claim to one or more such institutions. The Victoria County History of Cheshire, vol. III, page 202 states, in connection with the funding of early schools;-

> *"In some places a rather different form of bequest gave a school a fixed annual sum, for instance £42 a year at Alsager and £13. 2.s. at Barthomley."*

The reference to Barthomley clearly relates to the school referred to by Bishop Gastrell but it is unclear what the Alsager reference alludes to or the date at which it was applicable.

In her book, *"The Victorian Country Child";* Pamela Horn[10] best describes such a school:-

> *"Perhaps the worst offenders were the dame schools which still survived in many localities, where mothers sent their youngsters for a penny or two per week and which were little more than child minding institutions . . . . The greater part of the private dame schools are held in dwelling rooms . . . . frequently spending a great part of the school hours sitting on forms round the kitchen, with dog-eared pages of spelling books in their hands, from which they are supposed to be learning, while the 'school-mistress' is engaged in sewing, washing and cooking . . . ."*

With the housing development taking place in Alsager after the coming of the railway, there came a need for educational establishments for the children of the new families, many of whose parents were professional people or industrialists from the nearby Potteries. It was said at the time that the children of these families needed the purer air of Alsager to survive. Alsager at this time acquired the name of 'Mug Town', after the influx of the potters and their offspring.

The more 'well to do' farming families also welcomed the move towards the establishment of private schools.

But it was not only the village schools that interested parents. Some non-conformists objected to their children being taught the catechism, especially at the National School. They sent their offspring to the Hassall Green Wesleyan day school. One of those children, James Holland Lunt, wrote in his autobiography of 1912;-[11]

> *"From nine to ten I received my last elementary education at Hassall Green Wesleyan School along with my two cousins Henry and Alfred Holland. To reach school we had to walk about two miles each way, taking our dinners*

---

[10] Pamela Horn; *The Victorian Country Child;* Alan Sutton 1990

[11] Unpublished account of his school-days by James Lunt, in the possession of Mrs. S. Fox.

*with us. At the time I left this school I was only ten years of age. Another
two years of education would have been of great value to me."*

An entry in the National School log book records that 4 pupils from the
Hassall Green register were admitted, so it seems that the distance became too
far and inclement weather too much, or some dissatisfaction with the teaching
had occurred. James Lunt was the grandson of Samson Holland who kept the
Plough Inn. His uncle was Thomas Holland the miller at Alsager mill and the
first superintendent of the Sunday School at the new Wesleyan chapel, situated
in what is now called Hassall Road; which opened in 1834. James himself
was a local preacher on the Talke Circuit.

Some early personalities involved in education are recorded in the census
returns of the nineteenth century. In 1841 the Rev. Thurston Forshaw, living
at Heath House, had only one boarder staying under his roof, though it is
quite possible he had other classical scholars studying on a day school basis.
In 1851, a science mistress, Mary Webster, was also teaching at Heath House.

It is recorded in Bagshaw's Directory, 1850, that Francis W.H.Stonehewer
was the master of the Free School and yet in the 1881 census it states that Mr.
Stonehewer was headmaster of the Grove House School, aged 61, living with
his wife aged 62, and three children aged 23, 21 and 13 years old. One of the
children is registered as a bank clerk. There was a G.Shenton on the teaching
staff but no boarders were recorded. It is interesting to see that in February
1874 Mr. Stonehewer signed a form appertaining to a drawing examination
paper in company with the Rev. Tryon and Mr. Finnemore who succeeded
him as headmaster of the Free School. Mr. Stonehewer died in 1885.

Elizabeth Ann Hamilton, in 1851, was a governess employed in an
agricultural labourer's home, to teach three children from a pottery
manufacturer's family who were boarders there.

In all there were 12 school teachers recorded in the 1851 census, but
sadly, we do not know where all were employed. However we do know
where Miss Agnes Broady taught. Her name appears in the 1861 census. She
advertised a boarding school for ladies in the Morris Directory of 1874. This
was situated at the 'Firs' in Sandbach Road. Mr. Stonehewer's boarding school
is also mentioned in the same edition.

The census of 1881 reveals more information regarding private education
in Alsager. There was a ladies, boarding and day school at Ashville; Agnes
Broady was the school mistress and her mother was the housekeeper. In 1883
the Temperance Society used four class rooms at the school for meetings, they
continued to do so until St. Mary's schoolroom was built. In 1891 Miss
Broady and her mother were living in Lawton Road, near to Shields, the
chemist. There is no record of the date when the school re-located to Lawton
Road.

The earliest reference to Field School was in the census of 1871 which stated that Margaret Bragg was a governess there. Later, in 1881, a school is recorded at Field House in Fields Road. The headmaster was Samuel Bray, it would appear in name only, as he is recorded as being unemployed. His wife Mary, aged 44, was boarding school mistress and their daughters, Amelia 24, and Elizabeth 22, were also recorded as boarding school mistresses. There were three boarders, aged 14, 10, and 8; they came from Burslem. A Lucy E.Eardley was also a member of the teaching staff.

In the same year, 1881, a Mrs. Kathleen Bastards of Greenway Cottage was a governess with one pupil who was a boarder. In the same house lived her brother Richard Johnson, an engraver. One wonders what circumstances brought a Frenchman, born in Paris, to live in Audley Road in 1881. His name was Thomas Chatnetet and he taught French, music and singing. Also in 1881 Francis Randle Wilbraham of Cresswellshawe House employed a governess.

The Parish Magazine for August 1887 records that in the absence of the Rev. G.W.C. Skene, Rector of Barthomley, on holiday, Mr. Grant, headmaster of Alsager High School, took morning service at St. Mary's Church. This is the first reference we have to a high school. In March 1888 there is a further account concerning the school;-

> *A very successful entertainment given in the public room by the scholars of the High School. Mr. Craig was to have presented the prizes but he was away on the continent. Names of pupils receiving prizes: T. Bibby, S. Bailey, E. Barrett, N.G. Rigby, A. Edwards, A.E. Barker, H. Watson, R. Sant and H. Dudson. Some of the boys obtained certificates at the Examination of the College of Preceptors in December 1887.*

Mr. Grant's father, a retired clergyman, was living with them and possibly taught classics to some of the boys. The school was still in existence at the time of the 1891 census when it was situated in Sandbach Road, at the Firs and was known to have taken boarders.

In 1891 a Miss Kate Saunders ran a school for young ladies somewhere in the village. The 1906 Porter's Directory made reference to Alsager High School situated at The White House, Crewe Road, the building to the right of the Hall Drive. The headmaster was R.T. Thistlethwaite B.A., a graduate of Keble College, Oxford. The staff consisted of Mr. J.J. Ashton, drawing and science; Mr. H. Smith, music; and Miss Hall, preparatory mistress.

Miss Hall, with the help of her sister, eventually opened her own preparatory school in the Institute. The two sisters lived in Station Road. They taught reading using the phonetic method and some of their pupils have been heard to say that they have never been able to spell successfully. The school closed sometime in the 1930's. Around this time there was also a school in the Christian Scientist's Church, held in a wooden hut on the Mere side of Sandbach Road, next to where Coranation Gardens are today. This was demolished around 1937.

The Newer Schools.

The Alsager C of E Primary School

The school is situated off Sandbach Road, down the narrow lane which leads to the Institute and bowling green. The building is owned by the Alsager Education foundation.

The school was opened in 1900 to relieve overcrowding at the Church Road school, which it achieved by removing the younger pupils to the new school. Miss Peacock was the first headmistress, she was the daughter of J.C. Peacock, headmaster of Alsager School in 1875; Miss Yearsley, Miss N. Williams and Mr. A. H. Molyneux were also in charge of the school at some time and are remembered with affection by their former pupils. Among the staff in the early days were Miss Voight, Miss Rock, Mrs. Bennett, Mrs. W. Sheppey, Mrs. L. Armstrong and Mrs. E Penketh.

Overcrowding was always a problem and at one time Mrs. Sheppey had to teach her class in the Primitive Methodist schoolroom on the site of what is now Chapel Mews, in Crewe Road. Mrs Penketh also suffered the inconvenience of teaching in the Army Cadet hut adjacent to the Institute. During the time Mr. Molyneux was headmaster, the Infant classes were transferred to Excalibur, the former ROF. hostel in Fields Road. Miss G. Stubbs was in charge of the Annex at first but later Mrs. N. Miller took over as deputy to Mr. Molyneux. Among the staff who taught there were Miss M.E. Parry and Mrs E. Penketh, whose class consisted of the children of displaced persons who were temporarily housed on the Excalibur site.

Security at the Annex was always a problem and on one occasion some children broke in and played at "sitting round a bonfire". The whole building was set alight. According to Mrs. Miller, the Parent Teacher Association saved the day with invaluable help and made themselves responsible for clearing up the debris and restoring order. Apart from their manual labour they also gave financial help. After this incident they became very vocal about the overcrowding and unsuitable accommodation until in 1965 the new school at Ivy Lane opened and became Alsager Excalibur County Primary School. Mr. Molyneux continued as headmaster, Mr. Worrall was his deputy and the staff of the Infant Department were Mrs N. Miller, Mrs. I. Beck and Mrs. P. Elkin. The Junior Department was staffed by Mrs C.M. Bates, Mrs. C. Creed and Mrs. J. Molyneux.

The number of pupils attending the school on the opening date was 296. There was a rapid increase in numbers over the next few years due to the expansion of Alsager from village to small town. In 1969 the average class size was nearing 40 and it was obvious that further accommodation and staff was needed. In the summer of 1971 there were 186 infants and 234 juniors registered. Mrs. V. Band, who joined the staff in May 1972, and Mrs. J.L. Illing were known as 'floating teachers'. Some of their lessons took place in the cloak room or wherever space was available. Further accommodation was built and in 1972 there were 393 pupils being taught by 13 teachers. Mr. Molyneux retired at Easter 1980 after 27 years as headmaster of Alsager C. of E. Primary School and Excalibur County Primary. The present head teacher is Sheila Dentith.

Alsager County Primary School

With the building of Radway Green Factory in 1939-40 and the extensive housing estate for its workers, the number of school age children rose rapidly and immediate action was necessary to cope with overcrowding in the existing primary school.

Two flats in Bankside Court were converted into an emergency school. A corridor was built down one side of the building, giving access to all the rooms facing the open country. Miss D. Hale was the head teacher and she remained at the school until 1948 when she became the first female lecturer at Alsager Training College; later to be appointed deputy principal. Mr. R. Highfield, who was teaching at the senior school at the time, was appointed temporary head teacher, later confirmed as head. Among his staff were Mrs. E. Harrington, deputy; Mr. L. Houghton, who later became deputy and did not retire until 1978; Mr. J. Doran, Miss Luckman and Mr. Mellor.

By 1964 overcrowding had become so great that further classrooms and a hall and dining-room were built. The former C. of E. Primary building was also taken over as an annex and is still in use today. Mr. Highfield retired in 1974, after a teaching career of devotion to the children in his care and to the teaching profession in general. He worked tirelessly as a union representative for the N.U.T. It was a fitting tribute paid to him when the school moved into new premises and became Alsager (Highfield's) Primary School, opened in October 1988. Mr. Bickerton was appointed headmaster on Mr Highfield's retirement and he in turn was succeeded by Mr. Girbow.

Pikemere County Primary School

Opened in January 1969, Mr. D.R. Harris was appointed headmaster in 1968, before the autumn term and took up his appointment six weeks before the school opened. His deputy was Mrs. C. Marshall. In the Infant Department staff members were Mrs. K. Burns, Mrs. P. Lodey, and Mrs. M. Turner. The junior age group were taught by Mrs A. Jones, and Mr. C.

Woolridge.   Later Mrs Y. Cresswell was appointed head of the Infant Department.

Mr. Harris introduced a new and revolutionary method of vertical streaming into the school, which at first was viewed with scepticism, but which proved to be highly successful. The school building was set in green fields and the rural aspect was conducive to the study of wild life. Animals such as pigs, sheep and rabbits were kept, and cared for by the children, on the school premises.

It is interesting to note that Mr. Stonehewer, former headmaster of the Free School, was the owner of a private school situated at Grove House, which overlooks the grounds of Pikemere School. Education in that corner of Alsager continues to flourish and grow. The school's present head teacher is Mrs. A. Lees

Alsager Cranberry County Primary School

The school was opened in 1962. The first head teacher was Miss G. Stubbs who had formerly had charge of the infant children at the Excalibur annex of the C. of E. Primary School. Her deputy was Mr. J. Capewell. The original staff consisted of Mrs. W. Sheppey, Mrs. H. McWaters, Mrs. B. Morgan-Parker and Mrs. Singleton-Green; Mrs S Adams joined the staff a year later. Miss Stubbs left in 1967 and Mr. F. K. Hargreaves was temporarily appointed head assisted by Mr. D. Romano. Mr. P. Llewelyn was finally confirmed as head in April 1968.

In May 1975, further building having taken place, two separate schools came into being; **Alsager Cranberry Junior School,** under the headmastership of Mr. Llewelyn, later succeeded by Mrs. B. Littler. Mrs Hennessy-Jones is the present head and Mr. S. Reader as deputy; and **Alsager Cranberry Infant School** under the headship of Mrs. B. A.Finlayson. Mrs P. Dickenson is the present head teacher with Mrs. C Davies as her deputy.

St. Gabriel's R.C. Primary School

Situated in Well Lane and not opened until 1975, after the period covered by this history concludes. The first head teacher was Mrs. P. Hall and the deputy Mrs. R. Lockyer.

Alsager Training College. 1947 - 1960.

James A. F. Christie B.A.(Hons) Dip. LIS., ALA., wrote an informal history of Alsager Training College between 1947 and 1960 and his opening paragraph was as follows:-

"Oaks from Acorns grow - this is one way of looking at Alsager Training

> *College between 1947 and 1960 as it grew from a wartime hostel on the outskirts of a small rural town in South Cheshire to become one of the country's larger training colleges. Consequently high academic standards distinguished it and both students and staff of those years remembered their time in residence there as some of the happiest days of their lives."*

The aim of the college was to train ex-servicemen, recruited by the Emergency Scheme, in accordance with the 1944 Education Act and the McNair Report. With this goal in sight the Alsager Emergency Training College was brought into being. Students were housed in the former Ministry of Works hostel which had been built to accommodate munitions workers at Radway Green.

In September 1949 the college was renamed The Cheshire County Training College, Alsager; and the two year certificate from Liverpool Institute of Education was awarded to successful students.

The first principal was Mr. S.H. Woodiwiss, who was, according to James Christie:-

> *"An authoritarian of the old school, he was however very broadminded, considerate of student problems and moderate in discipline."*

Mr. Woodiwiss retired in 1960 and Mr. Reuben Wesley, who had been a founder member of the Emergency College staff, returned as principal. In the same year the national Three-Year Certificate of Teacher Training was introduced. The college now had 315 students and a staff of 32.

The old pre-fabricated buildings were replaced with buildings more suited to the technological age of today but described by Pevsner as *"Remarkable for quantity but not quality - architectural quality:"*[12] and the college became a College of Higher Education offering, in addition to teacher training, a wide range of degree courses. Now it has become part of The Manchester Metropolitan University. Truly those small Acorns have become sturdy Oaks!

Extracts from The National School Logbook and Scholars' Recollections

Parliament decreed that from 1862 every school receiving grant aid should keep a logbook. On the 26th January 1863 Edward Sweeting, headmaster of Alsager Christ Church Day School made his first entry.

> *"1863 January 26th.*
>
> *I took charge of Alsager National Mixed School on Jany 12th 1863. The attendance was very small owing partly to the unfavourable state of the weather. I could not form any plans for carrying on the school work with so small a number. Those who attended were very backward in everything,*

[12] Pevsner and Hubbard; *The Buildings of England; Cheshire.* Penguin Books 1971.

about 12 of them did not even know their letters. I devoted most of my time to these to teach them to read, and get them on the 'Primer'. I have now reduced the number to three children who are not certain of their letters. They are unable to write the easiest of letters on their slates and have no notion whatever of numbers. The First Class (Girls and Boys) read very monotonusly. The writing is only moderate and their spelling with one or two exceptions is very bad. The Arithmetic is much too low for a First Class. The Scripture is very much confused (in facts), and they have but a faint knowledge of either History of Geography.

The same be said of the second class, and also that there is too great a gap between them & the first, especially among the girls.

The third and Fourth Class are under the care of my Wife during the morning and are with me in the afternoon. The third can only read words of one or two syllables. Some of them write very fairly on slates. The boys began to do addition sums today for the first time.

The Fourth Class can scarcely do anything."

During the first week of Mr. Sweeting's headship the number of pupils attending the school had risen to 55, so one presumes the weather had improved. Religious instruction appears to have featured very strongly in the early weeks of the log's existence, the vicar, the Rev. Tryon being a frequent visitor. The following entries in the logbook give an insight into the curriculum and assessment.

"1863 Feb. 9th.

Parable of the Prodigal son very well said. Whole of the XVth Chap. of St. Luke to be said next Monday. Gave Classes 1 & 2 a piece of catechism to write on slates. First Class did it fairly, but second made most absurd mistakes in the Lords Prayer. e.g. "Our Father charter heaven". Had girls to do arithmatic in the afternoon. Read pieces from the newspaper for Reading lesson.

Tuesday 10th.

Gave English History lesson on Alfred the Great to classes 1 &2 and gave them for home lesson an account of it to be written. Took third Class in Numeration, only able to put down numbers correctly up to twenty. Took fourth class in counting. Some of them able to count twenty correctly.

Wednesday 11th

Gave Grammar Lesson to 1st & 2nd Class on Parts of speech, and explained the noun and pronoun. Dictation on paper done very badly. Eight of the second class not to do it again for some time, but transcription instead. Took 3rd and 4th in Scripture (Life of Moses)

Thursday 12th

Began to teach five of the First Class boys to do Algebra. Second Class doing Compound Addition and subtraction. Most of them seem to understand it. Others in the second class only doing (beginning) simple subtraction. In the afternoon I took Fourth Class in Reading and Counting. Third Class wrote a copy of Capital letters.

Friday 13th

Gave Lord's Prayer and Belief to be written on slates by 1st and 2nd Class. Done much better this week than last. 6 were marked good. Read English History (Edgar - Ethelred the unready) Taught the whole school to sing the Multiplication Table.

Monday 16th

XV Chapter of Luke said very well, especially by the Girls. Began to give tickets for home lessons well done. Read English History (Life of Canute) subject for home lesson. Second arithmatic Class began to do Compound Multiplication.

Tuesday 17th (Shrove Tuesday)

Book Hawker visited the school. Bought two Reading books for the use of the school viz. Gulliver's Travels and Childs companion. Afternoon a half holiday.

Wednesday 18th (Ash Wednesday)

Morning Service in the Church. 3rd and 4th Classes stayed in school, former did transcription and latter were taken in counting numbers up to twenty.

Thursday 19th

First Class did dictation on paper and 2nd did transcription on paper. only moderately done on the whole; writing Very Fair but spelling Very Bad. Second Class in arithmetic began Multiplication (compound) by nos. where factors cannot be used. Gave some to be done at home. Five out of the class brought them done correctly. Took the 4th Class in Reading in the afternoon and wrote. down figures on the black board from 1-20 for them to learn.

War casts its shadow over the so called 'happiest time of a child's life' and this was one account by a pupil of that time, recorded during the Alsager Arts Festival of 1990 when older residents recorded their memories on tapes whilst visiting the 'Alsager Remembered' exhibition. Miss Win Holmes talked of her school days before and after the 1914-18 war.

She remembered being taught in a classroom where there were two classes being taught at the same time by two different teachers. Hymns and prayers started every day and the tunes were taught by tonic sol-fa. Everything had to be learned by heart. She remembered writing the Lord's Prayer, properly, with every full stop and comma correctly placed. The Creed was also learned and written down. The Diocesan Scripture Examinations were frequently endured by all the children. Tables were chanted and learned every day. Poems were memorised and, what is more, remembered! She recalls that there were no books , no paints, no crayons and drawing was on the back of wallpaper. Instruction, rather than discussion was the order of the day.

Miss Holmes benefited from her education by such rigid methods, as she won a scholarship at the age of 11 and went to Crewe Grammar School. She later became a student at Crewe Teacher Training College. Her first teaching post was in Smethwick. She later became assistant teacher to Mr. J.O. Hughes at Odd Rode Boys School, when this closed she moved with him to Alsager Secondary Modern and later became its deputy head.

Another former member of the Infant and 'Big School', or as he called it 'Whitewash College', at this time, remembered Mr. Peacock, the headmaster as being a tall white haired man, with a propensity towards corporal punishment. Despite the strict regime he enjoyed his school-days. He remembered Miss Birch very clearly, as being very austere and wearing dark clothes. His memories of a Scottish lady, called Mrs Frood, were a little warmer. She was a widow with two small boys and was partially disabled. He left school at 14 and went to work at Settle Speakman.

The pupils helped with the war effort by their blackberry picking. In August and September the whole school marched down to the Peat Moss and gathered the fruit, which was then boxed and despatched from Alsager station to the fruit factory, for consumption by the troops. He remembered the station platform and the children being covered in red juice.

The boys played their part in the vegetable garden at the school, the play area was dug up to provide extra plots to grow more and more food. He shared a plot with another boy and recalled the pride he felt when he took his first crop of broad beans and new potatoes home to his mother.

Mrs G. Davies, recounts her school-days, during the period 1915 - 1924, as follows:-

"My school-days began in 1915. George V was on the throne and we were at war with Germany. The one thing uppermost in my mind at the time, and which appeared far more frightening than the war, was the prospect of having to start school and having to leave behind a wonderful home adjacent to the Mere which, like a huge mirror reflected all manner of shapes and changing skies. It was on a September morning, when, dressed in a white 'pinny' over a long black dress and wearing my black shin-high button-up boots, my mum walked me up to the Infants' School in Sandbach Road North. The brick building seemed remote and foreboding. The walls within were whitewashed and there was a revolting smell of carbolic. Desks were of oak and made to accommodate four to six pupils with inkwells set at equal intervals. The cold, hard benches on which we sat were also of oak, ornate iron legs attached them to the desks. The teachers looked very austere in their cotton blouses, severely tucked into the waistband of their black, long skirts; suddenly I felt very much afraid.

The Babies' Class, First Class and Standard 1, marked the first three years of a pupil's school-days. At the age of eight, we were marched - boys and girls together - down to the other end of the village into Church Road, where the church school nestled almost beneath the imposing tower of Christ Church. The war had just about ended, the teaching staff at the school were of the highest calibre available at the time but the conditions under which they and the pupils had to work were far from satisfactory. The only source of heating throughout some of the coldest winters on record came from dark-looking, triangular shaped, coal-burning fireplaces, of which there was one in each room. Sore throats and swollen glands with all their complications were prevalent, particularly amongst those children seated away back from the warmth, and necks bound with old stockings inlaid with goose oil were the order of the day.

Discipline was severe. The cane was used every day and if any pupil committed an offence, such as damaging property, and failed to 'own up', the whole class got the stick! That way the master was sure to strike the real culprit.

Very few scholarships were available to Grammar Schools. The poorer children and the poorer scholars stood a very slender chance of obtaining one, If one was no good at arithmetic (I was one of them) other subjects, such as English, art, history, geography and scripture seemed to count little. However, the lessons we did learn held us in good stead for the times ahead and it was with mixed feelings that I left school in 1924, at the age of 14, to go out into the world to earn my living."

Another former Alsager school-girl, Margaret Bebbington, relates her educational experiences which followed those of Mrs Davies.

At the age of five, in 1929, I attended the Infant School. The head mistress was Miss Yearsly and one of her assistants was Mrs. Voight. I remember Miss Yearsley as a tall, thin lady who always wore black. She may have been small, but to a five year old she is remembered as being very tall. Her hair was scraped back into a bun. She rode a bicycle, described in those days as a 'sit up and beg', it had a network of strings over the back wheel to prevent her long black coat from getting tangled in the spokes. Her outfit was topped off with a black, brimmed, felt hat.

I remember sitting in a double seat desk which had an iron frame, very painful bruises resulted if you didn't sit down carefully. The writing area of the desk was roughened, so each child had a square of dark green linoleum on which to rest exercise paper. There were sand trays on which letters could be written as the alphabet was learned. The class used pencils to write and no ink was used in the Infant School, that 'dubious treat' was waiting in store for us when we reached the 'Big School' and learned 'joined up writing'.

We took a ha'penny to the class teacher to pay for a cup of Horlicks to drink at playtime. One day, the boy sitting next to me, swallowed his ha'penny. Great panic ensued and he was duly conveyed to the surgery of Dr. Sayers, the local G.P. I can see him now, quite plainly, swaying too and fro on the back of Miss Yearsly's bike as she peddled up the road past the Institute. It was about two weeks before the coin appeared again to be passed round an admiring group of children. A very exciting moment, never to be forgotten, occurred when the airship, the R100, passed over the school. We all stood on the playground, looking upwards in amazement.

At the age of eight we moved to the senior school and were taught in the room at the side of the main building by Miss Rock who had moved from the Infant School. There was a fire in this room, with an oven at the side and any child who wished to remain at school at lunchtime could bring food to be heated. It had to be clearly labelled with the name on a little flag. My mother always washed on Mondays, so I brought a pie to be placed in the oven, and duly eaten off the top of the desk using my own knife and fork.

In 1933 I moved into Standard IV, to be taught by Miss Birch, who was a child in the Victorian Era, and who became a pupil teacher under John Peacock before the beginning of the twentieth century. She was a rigid disciplinarian and could administer a very painful rap to the arm when provoked. Whenever there was a funeral at Christ Church, Miss Birch would sit on the fireguard, this gave her an uninterrupted view of the proceedings. and woe betide the child who rose from its seat during the event!

The school day began with prayers and a hymn. Mr. Corfield, the head-master. always stood in the central doorway, hands holding his cane behind his back! After this assembly we began lessons with the chanting of tables followed by mental arithmetic. Geography consisted of lessons about the British Isles; we learned about the bogs and rivers of Ireland, the regions of Scotland and about industries, especially the coalfields. History notes were copied from the blackboard, we drew Stonehenge and Roman urns and swords. Following information on the English, the Vikings, Alfred the Great and the Normans, Magna Carta was mentioned. Natural history lessons followed the seasons of the year, with drawings of spring flowers and autumn leaves. The history of the bee and the frog occupied a few weeks, as did the story of the cuckoo. At the back of our 'best book' we copied such sayings as 'Wisdom is better than Rubies', and 'A Thing of Beauty is a Joy forever'.

I shall always be grateful to Miss Birch because she taught me to love poetry and we learned poems by heart, I still remember them today. I left to go to Grammar School in 1935 but I returned in 1954 to teach in Miss Birch's room and to fulfill my childhood ambition . . . . to sit on the fireguard.

Former pupils when talking of their days at school always mention 'playtime' and the mystery of games and their season's. Robert Louis Stevenson, writing in Scribiners Magazine,[13] wrote:-

> *"boys and their pastimes are swayed by periodic forces inscrutable to man; so that tops and marbles reappear in their due season, regular like the sun and moon".*

The weather would sometimes be responsible for the change of game, tops, with their brightly chalked circles, would be impossible to whip in deep snow; but the reason why currently fashionable activities became suddenly unpopular is an unfathomable mystery. One day the play area was alive with certain sounds associated with a chasing game and then suddenly it became full of whirling skipping ropes and chanting . . . .

> *'All in together girls,*
> *This fine weather girls,*
> *When I count twenty.*
> *This rope must be empty . . . . one, two . . . .'*
>
>   *or*
>
> *'Oliver Cromwell lost his shoe,*
> *At the battle of Waterloo,*
> *Salt, Mustard, Vinegar, Pepper.'*

With the last line the rope twirled faster and faster and then came the shout "All Out".

---

[13] *"The Lantern Bearers";* Scribiners Magazine 1888.

Suddenly a further change of scene and maybe Hop Scotch took over. The playground would be covered with chalked or scratched diagrams through which a piece of tile would be moved to score in the game. Ball games and chasing games were always popular and Marbles took its turn. Many children would be late home for tea because they had played 'merps' on the way. In the autumn conkers were soaked and hardened to fight playground battles.

Mr. Les Cowden remembers taking his iron hoop to be repaired by Mr. Rathbone, the blacksmith, at the smithy in Audley Road. The charge for repair was a penny. It took great skill to bowl a hoop along the sandy tracks and uneven roads of the village in 1914.

Playground games appear to have lost their appeal these days and to have been replaced by more sophisticated electronic activities, though having said that, football is ever popular, but who can explain the game of 'Prison Bars', played on Prison Bars Field, formerly on the site of the present day Hall Drive.

From, *'The Song of The Lime Trees by Christ Church'*

We are nineteen trees in number
And we are reckoned very fine,
All alike in height and colour
Standing in a long straight line.
Yes! we know we're very pretty,
Folks have said it time enough,
But we'll warrant we've a temper
When the wind's a wee bit rough.
We can shake and howl and blubber
Like the youngsters that pass by,
Or, we'll stand as stiff as plimbobs,
Softly, heave a gentle sigh.
How we'd like to whack those youngsters,
For they've tried their best to mar
Every bit of beauty in us,
Little rascals that they are.   *(Charles Hemmings 1890)*

Chapter 8

The Inclosure of Alsager Heath in 1834.

Enclosure of land which hitherto had been either common or held in open field arable husbandry was an established concept centuries before the Alsager Award.[1] Whatever its genesis it received nationwide approval in 1235 when the Statute of Merton allowed a lord of a manor to enclose common land provided his tenants retained grazing sufficient for their needs.[2] In the second half of the eighteenth century the pace quickened: between 1760 and 1797 Parliament passed about fifteen hundred private Enclosure Acts which had evidently become the accepted means of preventing runaway change to the agrarian and landowning communities. From 1801 legislation of a general character made the granting of permits for enclosure simpler and less demanding of Parliamentary time, until in 1876 a more enlightened approach actually prohibited enclosure unless commissioners, appointed with Parliamentary approval, were satisfied that it was to the benefit of the local community as a whole.

Enclosure of heath, common or waste involved extinguishing the rights of the commoners over the land in question. In the case of Alsager the Heath was owned by the lord of the manor but it was not his to do with as he wished, his ownership was subject to the interests of those who held such common rights as pasturing, the digging of peat, the taking of wood and other rights on the land. Those who had the benefit of these common rights were "the commoners", they were freeholders in the township and are referred to as "the proprietors" in the Award. These rights would almost certainly be exercised by their tenants who occupied the farms and they would have been very carefully defined with individual farmers being able to pasture a specified number of animals on the heath. The long lanes leading northward from the farms lying to the south of the railway probably functioned as cattle roads for stock pastured on the heath. Brook House Road is a typical example of this. Enclosure came about because the commoners or freeholders could see more profitable ways of using the land than leaving it as open heath. When the

---

[1] By Act of Parliament 2 Geo IV., 1821. Ref. CRO.QDE/1/31
[2] Richardson p. 19.

common rights were extinguished by an enclosure Act and Award the proprietors who held them were compensated by being awarded portions of the freehold interest of the land enclosed, proportionate to their freehold interest in the land from which their common rights arose. It was therefore in their interests during times of agricultural prosperity to co-operate with one another to secure enclosure. The losers of course were the tenants of the freeholders who lost the right of commoning which had previously accompanied their rented holdings.

The *Alsager Inclosure Award* cites the Act of 1821 by which two commissioners, Charles Heaton of Endon, representing the lords of the manor, and Joseph Fenna of Baddeley representing the freeholders, later to be replaced by Thomas Smith, were appointed who began work in the same year. The Surveyor was Charles Smith of Endon, possibly an associate of Charles Heaton. In its opening paragraph the Act, which was presumably typical of many, reveals the social structure of the time and the paramount importance of land as a source of wealth, power and influence:-

> *".... whereas Margaret Williams and Susannah Williams, spinsters and Catherine Sheridan, Widow, are the Ladies of the said Manor, and as such are Owners of the Soil of the said Commons and Waste Grounds, and all Mines and Minerals within and under the same and whereas the Right Honourable John Lord Crewe is the Patron of the Rectory of the said Parish of Barthomley and whereas Willoughby Crewe, Clerk, is the Rector thereof: and whereas the said Margaret Williams, Susannah Williams and Catherine Sheridan, the said John Lord Crewe, with Randle Wilbraham Esquire, John Latham Doctor of Medicine, Thomas Twemlow and certain other Persons, are proprietors of and claiming to be interested in the said Commons....And whereas it would be of great Benefit and Advantage to the several Persons who are Proprietors....if the same were divided and inclosed, and specific Parts and Shares thereof assigned and allotted unto the several Proprietors..."*

Thus in its very beginning the Act records the status of named individuals and without question confirms formal recognition, by the highest possible authority, of their title and rights as existing proprietors. Karl Marx traces this procedure back to the forcible occupation of common lands by feudal lords frequent in the late fifteenth and early sixteenth centuries and brands the enclosures of the period from say 1760 and the following hundred years as *"the Parliamentary form of robbery (which) is that of Bills of Enclosure by which landowners grant themselves the people's land as private property,...setting free the agricultural population as a proletariat for the needs of industry."*[3]

---

[3] Karl Marx *"Capital, English Edition:* Pelican 1976, Vol. I, pp 885-886.

The motivations behind the many enclosures throughout the country do not lend themselves properly to such a sweeping generalisation. They must surely have been influenced by local conditions, eg. the profitability of agriculture, population, type and size of agricultural holdings, proximity to large centres of population (which would be markets for farm produce as well as industrial areas beckoning labour by higher wages), the state of communications, the extent of owner-occupation, and the ambitions and foresight of existing owners. These and no doubt many other considerations and indeed the effects of enclosures on the lives of the people have been the subject of great debate among scholars producing widely divergent conclusions.[4]

The handsome calf-bound book, finally published in 1834, which can be seen in the Cheshire Record Office[5] has an accompanying coloured plan entitled *Alsager Heath Inclosure* which does not include the village of Alsager as it then was but covers the greater part of today's Alsager north of the railway. The plan shows the full extent of the 350 acres referred to in the Act. Starting in the east, in Lawton Road, the Heath included a narrow strip on the Lawton side of Fields Road, it then followed the line of the road turning into Ashmores Lane with the Pinfold and a small piece of land where the station is today. It returned along the line of Sandbach Road and Station Road, cutting through what are now the house plots on the southern side of the latter; turning into Crewe Road it passed the end of Hassall road to Close Lane, with one or two small coppices on the southern side. From the end of Close Lane it followed the boundary with Haslington as far as Dunnocksfold Road where the boundary left the road and cut across to Heath End Farm then following Pikemere Road to Sandbach Road North, turning left and then right following the rear boundary of Avon Court to about Wilbraham's Way; skirting Moorhouse Farm and Shady Grove it re-emerged into Lawton Road a little further east than the starting point. Some pieces of the Heath had already been enclosed before this award, the site of the school set up by the three Alsager sisters under an Act of 1789 which also provided for their financing the building and endowment of Christ Church was one: this approximated to the site of Alsager School today. Others are described on the map as *"Old Inclosures"* and include lands fringing Sandbach Road South, an area between Bank Corner and the Mere and another between the former Lodge Inn and the Mere, the area of Moorhouse Farm in Shady Grove, the

---

[4]G.E.Mingay: *Enclosure and the Small Farmer in the Age of the Industrial Revolution;* Economic History Society, 1968.
[5] CRO. LUAs/3190/1

area of Cranberry Moss and small areas adjoining Manor and Heath End Farms. These areas are excluded from the Commissioner's Award.

Before dealing in detail with the allocation of land the Commissioners were required by the Act to survey all public roads and footpaths and if necessary to divert or make new roads. All roads included in the survey were to be *"kept in good repair by the owners and occupiers of Estates in the Township of Alsager."* There is no record of any of these roads being turnpiked[6] and in theory their upkeep was still the responsibility of the Parish under the Highways Act of 1555. The Commissioners instruction here transferred this duty to a more closely defined group of individuals and in the following year the 1835 Highways Act introduced the new principle of Highways Authorities to amalgamate groups of parishes for the more effective maintenance of the road system for which a special rate could be levied.

The following roads are named in the Alsager survey:-

Public Carriage Roads 30 feet wide.

Barthomley Road. (now Crewe Road and Lawton Road)

"over Alsager Heath into the Ancient Lane near a house in the occupation of Joshua Farroll...towards Church Lawton." (There is no mention of the nearby turnpiked road from Talke via Church Lawton to Cranage, authorised in 1730.)

Alsager Lodge Road. (now Chancery Lane, Lodge Road and part of Sandbach Road North)

"...into the Ancient Lane which leads towards Smallwood." Sandbach is not mentioned. In the Award parcel No.45 is allotted to the Trustees of Alsager School *"In respect of Land given to widen Alsager Lodge Road".* (Reference to the map suggests that Lodge road may at one time have run closer to the Mere than it does today and that it was much narrower.)

Hassall Road.

"...over Alsager Heath into the Ancient Lane near a Farm House formerly in the occupation of William Thorley now Samuel Hargreaves...towards Hassall." (the farm house referred to is Heath End Farm)

Church Road.

Alsager Road. (now Sandbach Road South)

"...leading out of Barthomley Road near a house in the occupation of John Pimlot (at Bank Corner) *over Alsager Heath into the Ancient Lane near a house in the occupation of Samuel Warburton, Wheelwright,...towards the village of Alsager."* (Samuel Warburton's house was close to what today is the "Yeoman Inn", this places the village centre of Alsager between the Yeoman and Town House and Town End farms (The Manor Hotel). **The Pinfold or pound,** (the enclosure used to pen straying animals, probably from the Heath, was in Alsager Road in the area of the station.[7])

---

[6] *Transactions of the Lancashire and Cheshire Antiquarian Society.* Vol.X. p.237.

[7] Tithe Apportionment Map of Alsager 1840, CRO. ref. EDT.12/2

Occupation Roads 18 feet wide.

Sandhole Road. (Station Road)

"... leading out of Alsager Road (Sandbach Road South) *at a house now or lately in the occupation of John Wildblood."*

Hole House Road. (Cross Street and Well Lane, extending to Hole House Farm, now the Willow House Hotel.)

Bankhouse Road. (marked Brook House Road on the map and now Brookhouse Road.)

"...from the Bank House (the farm)...*across Sandhole Road* (Station Road) *into Alsager Road* (Sandbach Road South) *near a house in the occupation of John Holland."*

Back o' th' Meer Road. (Sandbach Road North)

leading out of Barthomley road (Bank Corner) *near a newly erected house belonging to the representative of Samuel Barnet deceased...into Alsager Lodge Road near a cottage lately in the occupation of Thomas Bosson deceased."*

Haslington Road. (Close Lane)

(The map and text show that Haslington and Wheelock were approached from this road which was on the boundary between Alsager and Haslington townships.)

School Road. (probably on the line of the modern school drive off Lodge Road, continued to Hassall Road)

"...to be kept in repair by the Trustees of Alsager School or their tenants." (The Reverend John Richardson, *"Minister of Alsager,"* is mentioned as one of the occupiers of adjoining land.)

Twemlow's Road. 15 feet wide. (probably the route through the University site leading to Manor Farm, owned at the time by the Twemlow Family.)

"...opposite School Road aforementioned...set out for the use of John Latham Esquire and Thomas Twemlow."

Public Foot Roads or Ways 4 feet wide.

Lettered **A** to **E** on the map and described in detail similarly to the other roads. They were to be kept in repair by the owners of adjoining land in proportion to the value of their allotments in this Award.

The frequent use of the expression *Ancient Lane* to describe the continuation of the named roads beyond the Alsager township boundary and the lack of any reference to such places as Sandbach, Tunstall or Nantwich may give the impression of a population having a very limited view of the outside world. Perhaps this is misleading; the population of Alsager township was 359 in 1821 and had risen by 24% in 1831 with the number of inhabited houses rising from 66 to 83 in the same decade,[8] contrary to Karl Marx's theory. An increase in the number of small occupiers, not necessarily tied to agriculture, as one result of enclosure, and the growth of locally generated wheeled traffic would make the demands of road maintenance ever more urgent. It seems possible that the arrangements for implementation of the Commissioners' order for road repair were inadequate but it was not until

---

[8] Census Returns, PRO and VCH. Ches. Vol II. pp.203-205.

1862 that Parliament moved to strengthen the 1835 Highways Act by making Highway Authorities compulsory and two years later the dissolution of the Turnpike Trusts began. The viability of the trusts had declined with the advent and build up of first canal and then rail transport leading to a dramatic reduction of long distance road traffic and a consequential drop in revenue making it difficult or impossible to maintain roads in accordance with the improvements introduced by engineers such as Telford, Metcalf and McAdam during the previous hundred years or so.

Allotment of Lands.

The enclosed land was divided into lots or parcels which were identified by number on the plan and in most cases described in some detail in the text. These were then awarded to the proprietors and freeholders, or sold at auction to defray the costs of the Act and executing the Award. Allotments from the waste were made to eight freeholders only, the proprietors of common rights, and to Mary Tryon and Robert Pollock as joint lords of the manor.

Freeholder./Proprietor.	Acres.	In respect of:
To Mary Tryon and Robert Pollock	22.	as Lady and Lord of the Manor.[9]
jointly to Mary Tryon and Robert Pollock.	78½	as freeholders of the remainder of that part of the Alsager estate entitled to common rights.
Reverend John Richardson, Curate of Alsager.	18	as holder of glebe land at Brookhouse.
John, Lord Crewe.	1½	as holder of land at Aspenhurst, T.A.refs.467, 468, 469.
John Ford Esquire.	21	as freeholder of Hole House Farm.
John Latham.	18	as freeholder of Day Green Farm.
Thomas Twemlow	16	as freeholder of Manor Farm.
Trustees of the School.	2	in respect of the trust interest in former heath lands.
Randle Wilbraham Esquire.	44	as freeholder of Lane End and Cresswellshaw Farms.

Section XIX of the Act required the Commissioners to;

> "*set out ...parts (of the lands) for the general use of the proprietors...for the getting of Stone, Marl, or Clay for Bricks, Gravel, Sand and Earth to be used upon the Lands...inclosed, or for the making and repairing of the*

[9] Tryon and Pollock were the heirs to the Alsager Estate, the three ladies cited in the Act having died before the implementation of the Inclosure Award.

Bridges, Highways and Roads...; which said Allotments and the Herbage growing...upon them shall be vested in the Surveyor...of the Highways of the said Township..."

Only one lot, No.4, was allotted in this way. This included the marl pit in Hassall Road, near Heath End Farm, now the site of the recreation ground.

The record gives details of two auctions held at the Lodge Inn, then at the corner of Lodge Road and Church Road on the site of West Mere Lodge. On the 29th November 1821 a total area of 69 acres 33 perches was sold for £1,258.10.0 to thirteen buyers. On the 4th August 1826 a further 39 acres 3 roods 19 perches were sold for £597.10.0 to eight buyers.

29th November 1821.

Buyer.	Lots.	acres.			£. s. d.
William Barker.	66.	0	2	36	21. 0. 0.
John Brereton.	65.	1	0	17	31.10. 0.
James Bradley.	50.	1	2	31	45. 0. 0.
	57.	5	1	11	118.10. 0.
(lot 50 resold to Wm. Bourne, lot 57 resold to Thos. Thornhill.)					
Thomas Beech.	49	11	1	3	175. 0. 0.
Samuel Barnet.	56.	4	2	9	110. 0. 0.
Joseph Edwards.	48.	8	2	19	115. 0. 0.
John Holland.	64.	0	2	8	13. 10. 0.
Lawrence Plant.	29.	1	3	2	44. 0. 0.
John Plant.	28.	0	3	14	21. 10. 0.
John Pimlot.	63.	0	2	11	50. 10. 0.
	55.	1	1	18	
? Shakeshaft.	39.	11	1	24	145. 0. 0.
(resold to Joseph Edwards)					
Thos. Smith, Trustee for Thos. Heaton.	62.	0	2	29	18. 0. 0.
Joseph Yarwood.	43.	8	2	12	350. 0. 0.
	10.	10	0	29	

(lot 10 resold to Jos. Dean.)

4th August 1826.

Buyer.	Lots.	Acreage			£. s. d.
Samuel Barnet.	58.	1	0	1	22 0. 0.
Thomas Bourne.	52.	0	3	5	30. 0 0.
Joseph Edwards.	41.	5	1	5	84. 0 . 0.
John Holdcroft.	14.	6	3	37	96. 10. 0.
Josiah Nathanial Mayers.	9.	7	2	16	89. 0 0.
Thos. Smith trustee for Thos. Heaton.	60.	0	3	38	23. 0. 0.
Robert Shufflebotham.	8.	6	0	6	63. 0. 0.
Joseph Yarwood.	40.	6	3	6	140. 0. 0.
	42	4	1	25	50. 0. 0.

(lot 42 was resold.)

Some of the land purchased at these sales has remained in the hands of the purchasers' families to the present time.

There was to be no free-for-all exploitation, of land awarded or bought, by freeholders and purchasers. Before the final execution of the Award;

> *"...after the passing of this Act...no person...shall cut, dig, pare, flay, get or carry away any Turf, Clay, Soil, Stone, Gorse, or any Dung in, upon, or from the said Commons...without Leave or Licence of the said Commissioners..."*

The Commissioners were also to;-

> *"...set out, order and direct such new Ditches, Drains, Watercourses, Tunnels, Watergates, Banks, and Bridges to be made of such Depth and Breadth ...as they shall think proper...for the Purpose of effectually draining...the Lands...and the several Bogs and Turbaries thereon..."*

together with the appointment of the persons who were to pay for these works and their future maintenance. No sheep were to be pastured, for seven years following the completion of the Award, on any of the enclosed land which would be fenced at the new owner's expense with fencing material that was to be quickset hedging, unless the hedges were protected by other adequate fencing.

The Rector of Barthomley would not have been pleased with one provision of the Act which relieved allotted lands from Rectorial Tithes for a period of seven years.

Further perquisites for the Ladies of the Manor or their successors were the confirmation of their ancient rights including forfeiture of the goods and chattels of felons and fugitives and their title to the;-

> *"Mines, Beds, Veins and Seams of Coal, Cannel, Slack, Ironstone, Limestone, Salt springs...in or under the said Commons..."*

adequate compensation being due to the occupiers if any workings were installed for extraction of these minerals. Also;-

> *"Alsager Mere, with a border round the same, of the width of Nine Yards from the Highwater Mark together with all convenient Roads or Ways to the said Pool, shall remain vested in the Ladies or Lords of the Manor..."*

After 1834 there were approximately thirty owners of land in the area enclosed under the 1821 Act where previously only common rights had existed, the ownership of the soil being vested in the lord of the manor, and the new owners of the land sold at auction held only about 33% of the enclosed area. The population of the enclosed heath lands appears to have been approximately 100 in 1841 although the number cannot be regarded as being completely accurate due to a number of inconsistencies between the various records and the apparent high mobility in population, judged from the evidence of the 1840 Tithe Award and the 1841 Census. However, the resultant figure is sufficiently close to the increase recorded in Alsager's population by the 1821 and 1831 census returns for the enclosure of the heath land to be a plausible reason for this increase.

Much of the land auctioned at the 1821 and 1826 sales[10] lies on the northern and northwestern side of the Heath, bordering the better grade of land of Heath End, Manor and Dunnocksfold farms, most of which remain in agricltural use to this day.

Those plots which might, by their size and location, be considered to have been bought primarily for agricultural use were taken by 7 buyers at the 1821 sale at an average price of £16 per acre and by 5 buyers in 1826 at an average price of £14 per acre. These were broadly speaking larger areas than those in another group of plots, which may account for the lower unit prices.

In this other group 16 plots on the south of Lawton Road and in what we may well name the golden triangle bounded by Ashmore's Lane and Station Road with Sandbach Road South through its middle were sold to 8 buyers at an average price of £24 the acre in 1821 and 3 plots went to 3 buyers in 1826 at an average £27 per acre.

It is worth noting at this point that the roads surveyed and described in the Inclosure Award and lying essentially on the Heath (only one "Ancient Lane", Audley Road today, passing through the hamlet of Alsager as it then was) remain our "through roads" today. Their existence, many of them "Public Carriage Roads 30 feet wide", at that time suggests a well-established traffic not only between the outlying farms and the Heath area in which commoners' rights were enjoyed, but also between Barthomley, the parish centre, and places further afield such as Nantwich, Sandbach, Congleton and Tunstall and the important 'national' road, the turnpike through Church Lawton running north and south.

The buyers of land with frontages on these main roads, even if they intended to farm as smallholders, may have had the foresight to see Alsager developing far beyond its character at that time; land even in small amounts could be seen as a hedge against the uncertainties of a country emerging from the aftermath of the Napoleonic wars. Some purchases may be seen as speculative: Joseph Yarwood for example resold 10 acres between Dunnocksfold Road and Manor Farm, presumably at a profit, to Joseph Dean, and a Mr Shakeshaft resold 11½ acres on Hassall Road opposite Heath End Farm to Joseph Edwards.

The few sale prices mentioned in the Award are too small a sample to

[10] CRO. Ref. D5251/5&6.

allow general conclusions about market values but do give us some idea of the motives and trends of that period in that place for comparison with those of a later date.

The North Staffordshire Railway came to Alsager in 1848 and a generation later the village was becoming popular as a dormitory for the industrialists of the Potteries and a place of opportunity for skilled artisans, traders and domestic servants. The 1871 census recorded a township population 1148. Property development and house building offered new wealth to those with enterprise and capital. The sale of the Alsager Estate in 1876-1877, by which time the area owned by the heirs of the Tryons and the Pollocks was such that more than 500 acres and many buildings were put up to auction, provided sites ideal, in the words of the agent's catalogue for "villa residences". The sale catalogue[11] cited an indenture of 1819 and the 1834 Inclosure Award to establish the Alsager heirs' title to the property.

50 years on from the auction of enclosed lands on the Heath, Alsager was a very different place. Still part of Barthomley parish even though Christ Church was approaching its 90th anniversary, in the mid-1870's the population of the township, essentially the area of today's civil parish, was around 1400 having doubled in the previous 15 years (as it was to double again by the first decade of the 20th century). Changes in the structure of society and attitudes to economic matters were inevitable.

On the 5th July 1876, the day of the first auction of parts of the Alsager Estate, previously announced in the Staffordshire Sentinel, that journal reported the coming of the Telephone to London. Samuel Morse had invented the electric telegraph in 1832 and transatlantic communication was successfully established by submarine cable in the 1860's, but national and particularly local newspapers remained the essential medium for dissemination of "intelligence" to the population at large.

Typical reports of the day:-

> Mr Disraeli told the House of Commons that the Servians had crossed the Turkish frontier and the Prince of Montenegro was at the head of his troops...

> The Alsager Druids announced their Annual Fete, " a band will play for dancing and there will be a variety of amusements."

> A new Clydebuilt iron ship had sailed from Greenock for Brisbane providing free passage to Queensland for 133 single men, 66 single

---

[11] ibid.

women, 32 married couples, 48 children and 7 infants. Press advertisements of the period sought "skilled artisans and servants at wages about double English rates. Farm labourers £30-50 plus board and lodging."

In the Education Column:

"Greenway Cottage, Alsager. MRS BASTARDE will resume the duties of her establishment on the 25th July."

The Macclesfield Courier reported the celebration in the U.S.A. of the centenary of the Declaration of Independence and the annihilation of General George Custer's command by an overwhelming force of Sioux under Chief Sitting Bull.

And a Hanley tailor advertised:-

"The Cricketing season.

Trousers 13s/6d ready made or to measure."

A part only of the Sentinel's report of the Sale on the 5th and 6th of July 1876 survives in somewhat tattered form on microfilm in the Horace Barks Library in Hanley. The sale was held at the Royal Crewe Arms Hotel. The catalogue's plans show that the main residential area of Alsager had moved from its former situation as a hamlet in the 1820's in the vicinity of Town House, which still stands in Audley Road, to the area of Ashmore's Lane, Sandbach Road South, Station Road and the south side of Crewe Road as foreshadowed in the 1821 and 1826 sales described above.

The property on offer included several farms: Dunnocksfold, Heath End, Town House (*"an exceedingly good house, suitable for a large family"*) and Alsager Hall Farm and Corn Mill (*"parts of the farm are much elevated and admirably suited for Residences"*). Except for Town House Farm, the greater parts of these farms are still cultivated today.

The Alsager Arms Hotel, *"A long established Hotel adjacent to Alsager Station doing an excellent business and the land most desirable for building."*), the Plough Inn (*"this is a well accustomed Inn"*), the Lodge at the corner of Lodge Road and Church Road, no longer an inn as it had been in 1826 but now *"capable of being converted into one of the most beautiful Residences in the County"*, the *"far-famed Alsager Mere"* and the lands surrounding it were also among the 47 lots in the 1876 sale. The catalogue noted that *"the farms are yearly holdings"* and that the tenancies would not be affected by the

Agricultural Holdings Act of 1875[12] which provided for tenants to be compensated for "improvements" they had made in their holdings in the event of termination of a tenancy. Landlords would be entitled to compensation at the same time in cases of neglect or breach of contract by their tenants. It is interesting to note that disputes arising in the application of this Act were ultimately subject to the authority of the Inclosure Commissioners for England, an office which we might have expected to be defunct by this date. This Act was one step in the gradual codification of the legal relationship between landlord and tenant, no doubt to the advantage of both sides in the long run, but in the case of annual renewals, as here, not appropriate.

Buyers were required to pay additional sums for any "timber, timber-like trees, underwood and plantations" on their purchases.

Agriculture was thus at this time a reduced but still probably the most important single feature of Alsager's life, judged by the area of farmland offered for sale in 1876/7 namely 80% of the total sale area or about 22% of the whole township, and the proportion of the population actively engaged in farming and its supporting trades or as landlords, about 11% of the total, 1,148 at the 1871 census.[13]

But the most significant change in Alsager's society since mid-century was in the range of occupations or sources of livelihood of its residents. Retail traders and skilled artisans apart, professional arrivals included solicitors, accountants, house agents and by 1871, a doctor of medicine. Already in 1861 there were recorded 6 Manufacturers, 6 Proprietors of Houses and one Landowner, several Managers and Farm Bailiffs. In 1871 the structure of Alsager's society could be said to be completed by a Florist, an Organist, three Gentlemen, a Toll Collector and a Pawnbroker! Seven employees of the North Staffordshire Railway attest the importance of rail travel to the daily commuters from Alsager to Kidsgrove and the Potteries. The village was ripe for further development.

Amongst the earlier lots sold was Dunnocksfold Farm of 91 acres, bought by William Rigby for £7000 an average price of £77 per acre (or £190 per hectare). Smaller lots, from 10 to ½ an acre sold for an average of around £140 per acre (£346 per hectare), but with a wide variation depending on location and individual characteristics. Throughout the catalogue emphasis is

---

[12] Keele University Law Lib. Ref. KC.35.A1P8

[13] See Chapter 10, 'From a Sleepy Village to a Thriving town', for a fuller description of 19c. Alsager.

on suitability for building, particularly for "villa residences", which gives us a picture of well-to-do families with live-in servants.

By no means all the lots were sold at the 1876 auction. Just a year later 29 lots were reoffered. The only record we have is of the purchase by John Scott of Bradley Green in Staffordshire of 23½ acres including Cranberry Moss and extensive frontage on Crewe Road for which he paid £1,540, an average price of £65 per acre (£161 per hectare).

With some caution we may compare the value of land in Alsager in 1821 and in 1876 and must first consider the changing value of the currency. Many different criteria have been used in compiling tables of the cost of commodities over several centuries; many causes of temporary peaks and troughs along the way are cited such as the Napoleonic wars, good and bad harvests, the world supply of gold, rapid rises and sometimes falls in population, imperial adventurism partly funded by new taxes: there is however agreement that prices of consumables fell between 1820 and 1850, rose to a second half-century peak in 1874 before falling again until the turn of the century. These swings are accepted by scholars as one indicator of inflation or deflation of the currency and in July 1876, at the time of the first auction sale of the Alsager Estate, we may assume an increase in prices generally, due to inflation, of 15% compared with those of 1821.

The coming downturn in agricultural prosperity would not yet have been anticipated and the better grade of land was still farmed - and remained so long after the sale - lending a measure of stability as a background to the social and economic changes discussed above.[14]

The wealthy manufacturers, the property developers and speculators, the managerial and professional classes, even commercial interests from far afield (W. A. Gilbey, wine merchants of London paid £3,150 for the Alsager Arms) were ready to pay up to well over £200 per acre (£500 per hectare) for building land, 700% and more above the prices paid for similar plots 55 years earlier, the 15% inflation noted above being relatively insignificant.

Such was the measure of the changed character and status of Alsager over 50 years.

It is worth considering what effect enclosure of the Heath had on the Alsager community in both the long and short term and what might have been the result had it not taken place. In the short term it brought more land into

---

[14] For further reading on this topic see John Burnett, *A History of the Cost of Living;* Pelican 1969.

agricultural production and appears to have led to a swift and significant increase in population. It is the poorest quality land in Alsager, as anyone who tries to garden it knows! It was the last land to go into production and the first to come out. This may have been due partly to its quality but also partly to the fact that much of it was occupied by small freeholders who could and did develop it for housing and associated uses or else sell it to others to do likewise. When the railway came there was a ready supply of land available on which to build an urban settlement. Had the whole area of the former heath remained in the hands of a single owner and been subject to either commoners rights or else valuable agricultural land it is very possible that the modern suburban town that we know today might not have come into existence. It is not mere chance which resulted in the older established traditional farms remaining largely intact until the latter part of the twentieth century but the fact that they occupied better land. We should look back at the Alsager Inclosure Award and consider it to be the charter document of our present day community.

Chapter 9

Communications

Highways and Roads

The roads in Alsager township at the time of the Enclosure of the Heath in 1834 had probably existed as paths or tracks for centuries, although there is little written evidence to confirm this. Signs of anitiquity are still evident in the lengths of sunken lanes, referred to at the enclosure as ancient lanes, on slopes on or near the town's boundaries; at Mere Lake and Lawton Heath End and the abandoned section of road below the site of the former Lawton railway station.

Documents in the Public Record Office relating to transfers of land in the township in the 13c. and 14c. mention the *"highway to the Witemere"*[1] - wite meaning either a curving bank or a place of punishment; the lane leading from Alsager to the park at Audley;[2] and a lane near the Barthomley border.[3] A Church Lawton deed of the same era refers to the *"highroad leading from Nantwich to Leek"* of which the present Crewe and Lawton Roads were a section. These documents record land or properties but apart from reference to the mere it is difficult to identify them with present day sites.

Although it cannot be said with any certainty that prehistoric tracks existed in the immediate area, yet the Neolithic and Bronze Age burial sites at Gawsworth, Lawton and the Bridestones, with isolated finds of pottery and other articles, are an indication of earlier settlements in south-east Cheshire. Finds of sophisticated stone tools, which originated in North Wales and the Lake District, and artifacts of Irish origin, indicate movement of materials which could include salt and copper found in the area. Such movement demanded recognised routeways, if not formal tracks.

In order to establish links with Chester, their main port and base, the Romans built their military roads from the South-East following the line of the Trent valley, a direction followed later by turnpike, canal, main-line railway and motorway. Chesterton is the nearest Roman site to Alsager, and was a military camp. The village of Red Street derives its name from 'strata',

---

[1] PRO. C146 4929, late 13c.
[2] Brit. Lib. Add. Ch. 53534, 24th May 1356.
[3] Brit. Lib. Add. Ch. 53535, 24th May 1356.

the Latin for road, and perhaps 'rad', O.E. for road. The route linking it to Chester is not certain, but it could have passed within the eastern boundary of Alsager and afterwards followed the line of the present A50; a stretch of which, at Rode Heath, is still known as 'Street Lane'. These well constructed roads needed constant maintenance, and by the time of the Anglo-Saxon settlement they had fallen into disuse and disrepair. The newcomers who did not use carts like the Romans had little use for them. Generally their goods were carried by pack horse while people travelled by horse or foot along earth tracks which were often at the side of the crumbling roads.

After the Conquest, the Normans, like the Romans, needed to improve the tracks between the communities in order to achieve effective domination in a hostile country. The lord of the manor who administered government at local level, was made responsible for the construction and maintenance of the highways and bridges and empowered to raise the necessary labour and resources for this.

There was a great monastic revival under the Normans and as these monasteries acquired a considerable amount of land and estates through endowment, the Church took over much of the responsibility for the roads and bridges. There were monasteries at Vale Royal, Combermere, Abbey Hulton and later Dieulacres at Leek, an area of Staffordshire increasingly dominated by the Earls of Chester. (An early medieval thoroughfare, probably an earlier salt track leaving Cheshire near Congleton and going towards Leek was called Earlsway). Consequently the track from Barthomley to Lawton would be in frequent use by those travelling between Dieulacres and Nantwich and between St.Werburgh's Chester and Church Lawton, a parish attached to that monastery.

Several of today's footpaths now used exclusively for leisure were once as important as the present day main road. As far as Alsager was concerned the thoroughfares most in use would have led to the church, the mill and township centre (Town End area). Today's maps show a number of paths converging on the mill and Town End whilst the shortest route to Barthomley church is the path from Fannings Croft, past Brookhouse and Bank House farms, and Alsager Sprink to the Barthomley boundary near Bank Top Farm at Radway Green. It then passes Foxley and Flash farms to join the Radway Green to Barthomley road near Cherry Tree farm. This 'coffin road', over higher ground bordering Staffordshire, could have been in regular use until the 19c. Before the consecration of Christ Church, marriages, funerals, church baptisms and divine service could only take place at St. Bertoline's, although there is evidence that some families near the border used Audley and Lawton for baptisms.

Markets and fairs played an important part in local life where a large variety of manufactured goods were on sale as well as surplus produce. From the 12c. onwards charters were granted for weekly markets and fairs to be held on church feast days such as Lammas, Michaelmas and Ascension. Newcastle-under-Lyme (charter 1172) would draw people from Alsager and beyond. They would travel along the Mere Lake road, which was the shortest route to the main highway south, with their animals and produce. Other local markets were Congleton (1272) and Betley (1299); Nantwich received its charter in 1319. For a time there was a market at Brereton but it was small and could not compete with Sandbach (1578) and by the 17c. had ceased.

Congleton and Sandbach held regular fairs and were the most convenient for Alsager. They would generate additional traffic on the road by Cresswellshawe, to Betchton and Smallwood, enhancing its importance. The route to Audley would have acquired more significance with the extraction of coal in the townships beyond the county boundary.

By the end of the 15c. upkeep on the main roads could barely keep pace with the wear and tear caused by this increased traffic and trade. Following the dissolution of the monasteries around 1540, when their land and estates were seized, the Church lost overall control which was disastrous for the road system, and led to a state of appalling neglect.

The 1555 Highways Act attempted to remedy this by transferring road maintenance from the manor to the parish and making it responsible for roads within its boundaries, but it brought little improvement. To cover the cost a levy or lay was imposed. Two men in each township were appointed to organise labour and materials for the repair and maintenance of its roads and bridges. It was not a popular appointment since they were responsible for seeing that all men, whose income was less than £50 per annum, spent six days of the year in maintenance and repair work. The wealthier townspeople could provide a horse and cart in lieu.

Towards the end of the 18th century Richard Lindop, a farmer from Coppenhall recorded:-

> *"At a convenient time the surveyor gave the (parish) clerk orders to publish for a day's work. On the next Sunday the clerk, rushing out of church at the end of the service cries: 'Oyez! Oyez! This is to give notice that the inhabitants are to meet on Wednesday morning at 8 o'clock with picks and shovels in order to repair the highways. God Save the King' ".*

No doubt something similar occurred at Barthomley Church.

The Overseers of the Highways, as they were called, were elected at the vestry meeting at Barthomley Church on Easter Monday, until 1676 when by Act of Parliament it was altered to Christmas. Although they are listed in the churchwardens' accounts from 1667, separate expenditure is not itemised until

1725. Ralph Alsager de Halls was one of those who served in 1667. It would appear that apart from labour, little was spent on road maintenance until the first half of the 18th century. It became the practice for overseers to serve according to the property they held, and there are a number of women, presumably widows who took office.

1719   Elinor Steel
1783   Widow Fox
1804   Mary Thorley

Two others who served in the 19th century were Julia Barker of Oak Farm and Mrs Beresford. From 1776 only one overseer was appointed.

Long distance travellers coming from the north or south would turn off the main route at Lawton (Red Bull). There are 17c. records of friends and former students of the rector, Zachary Cawdrey, visiting him. He was a former Proctor of Cambridge University and fellow of St. John's College and highly respected in clerical circles. (See *Barthomley, an Estate Village*). Henry Newcome wrote in his autobiography:-[4]

1675   *"I went away to Barthomley and found my beloved tutor at home".*

1681   *(When travelling from Manchester to Woburn) "I came that night in safety and season to Mr Cawdrey's where I kept the Sabbath".*

1682   *"Amid floods we came to Lawton and so to Barthomley".*

At about this time the presenters' reports on the highways usually note that these are in good repair but then frequently add the rider; *"According to the season of the yeare".* The only noticable lapse was in 1693 when the township as a whole was fined 10s. *"For not repairing their highways".* In October 1698 the record reads, *"We present Randle Hilditch for not repairing the Brun Lane and give him untill the 25th March and a merce him in 6s.8d."* The hundred court estreat confirms *"Randle Hilditch for not repairing the Brun Lane pursuant to an order of this court amerced vjs.viijd."*[5]

From medieval times the lanes were levelled off each spring by using a large plough to remove the ruts formed over winter. On steeper slopes the mud had to be removed. Over the years this gradually lowered the level of the road as more and more mud was dug out which is how many of our ancient sunken lanes came about.

In the first half of the 18c. the surveyors began to buy in quantities of stone and to pay for labour. The practice was to make a stone causeway for pedestrians and horses two or three feet wide, with a track of earth alongside

---

[4] Chetham Soc. Series I, Vols. 26 & 27 1852.
[5] CRO. DCH./Y/6

for carts and carriages; but the stones were very uneven and treacherous and the cartway often held inches of muddy water. Lindop of Coppenhall claimed that deep ruts in the cartway so hindered transport that it sometimes took nine horses, one behind the other, to haul one ton of coal. Rector Hinchliffe, writing in 1850, described the roads as formerly being either of deep heavy sand or of stone dragged at great expense from Mow.

According to the overseers' accounts payment was made for stones from fields as well as from Mow Cop.[6]

> "1728   *Paid for 4 tun and a half of stones at 5s a tun*   £1-2-6
>
> 1729   *Paid John Twemlow for Mow stones*   7-6
>
> 1731   *Paid for 16 tun of stones at 5s a tun (my own 11½ tun,*
>   *John Leversage 2 tun, George Maddock 3 tun)*   £4-0-0"

Yet in 1783, 72 tons of stone was bought in at 10d. a ton, possibly of inferior quality. Bricks cost 14s. per thousand and would be locally made in Close Lane, Audley Road or possibly other sites.

In 1731 men were paid 1s.1½d. per day for breaking stones; so too was the man who weighed them. In 1787 Saml. Thorley was paid 1s. for a ton of boulders, and for carrying the scales to Saml.Thorley someone earned 6d. William Brereton, surveyor for that year, paid himself 1s.8d. a day while other workers got 1s.2d; a boy's rate was 6d.

Pavers, or paviers, seem to have been paid by the length of work completed and, since it was thirsty work, *"Ale for the pavers"* is a frequent expense. In 1783 the pavers cost £6-7-2½ with 4s. for ale. Quantities of wood were used;-

> "1733   *paid for wood to lay over the foot causeways 2s.*
>
>   *paid for a waggon load of yew and other woods to repair the*
>   *roads 1s.6d.*
>
> 1773   *To timber for supporting the horse causeway leading to Foxes*
>   *5s."*

In 1783 5s. was paid for 'oil and paint and painting the stumps;' these were to stop waggons from encroaching on to the footway. That year 5s. was spent on a copy of an Act of Parliament, no doubt relating to the upkeep of roads.

The surveyors sometimes journeyed beyond the boundaries on business:- to Audlem, Newall, Nantwich and Wrenbury, at the township's expense. In the repair of bridges, gorse and broom were used, presumably for securing a firmer foundation in soft boggy areas;-

> "1725   *Pd. For Broom and Gorse for stoops*   5s.8d."

---

[6] CRO. Barthomley Town Book, ref. P.C.2.

In 1729 Abraham Hulse earned 2s.6d. for *"splitting a tree for two bridges"*, and in 1733 the cost of *"putting a bridge over Larwood"* was 2s.6d., possibly that also was made of wood.

Townships shared the cost of bridges on the boundary. In 1764 the Barthomley - Alsager bridge was replaced by a brick one, and half the cost of the 'Radway Plat' was £2-3-0. The shape which was used to support the brick arch during construction was sold to another township:-

> *"Received for half the centre that was sold at Radway Green   1s.6d."*

Eighty years on, in 1848 the overseers of Barthomley were again meeting to discuss the rebuilding of that bridge, and it was finally carried out in 1850.

In 1853 a proposal was made for the construction of a bridge at Cresswellshawe *"if Betchton township would be willing to share the cost"*, but was it built? For in 1895 Alsager Urban District Council shared the cost of repair to two foot bridges at Cresswellshawe with Congleton Rural District (which superseded Betchton). This suggests that perhaps there was still only a ford at Cresswellshawe. The upkeep of roads not repairable at public expense was the responsibility of the landowner. If in default, he was answerable to the Manor Court, and he could be fined;-

> *"1731*   *"We present Richard Steele for not repairing his stiles in the footway leading to Alsager Heath and order him to lay open the said way and put the stiles in good repair before Martinmas, subject to a fine of 5 shillings."*[7]

Some places such as Mere Lake, the sunken lane to Talke, are named in the accounts. In 1772 repairs to its bank cost 12s. and more money was spent on it the following year. Day Green Lane was levelled in winter that year by George Mottershead.

Hooze Hollow, which was variously spelt Ouse, Oose, Woos, Hooles and Hools, was a continuing source of complaint and expense up to this century. It can be located on the low ground where a stream forms the boundary between Alsager and Lawton, and where the Caradon (Twyford's) factory entrance has now replaced the Brunds farm track.

Its very name conjures up a muddy area and quite possibly it was still a ford in the 18c., with a wooden foot bridge at the side for pedestrians. In 1784 the surveyor, John Cookson, was summoned to the Quarter Sessions at Knutsford to answer the charge that Alsager had *"failed to keep the King's Highway from Nantwich to Leek in good order at Oose Hollow."* The township was also told that the highway passing within its boundary was too

---

[7] From the Betchton Manor Rolls, see unpublished work by H. Buller, *'Annals of Alsager'* SECSU.

narrow and ought to have a *"breadth of eight yards and upwards."* [8]

> *"1784   Repairs to Wooshollow Brook   6d.*
>
> *1784   paid Ralph Waller for stone for two men and two teams one*
> *days cleansing Hooshollow Brook   3s.*
>
> *1826   Repairing a plat at Hooze Hollow   3s.*

Turnpikes and Carriers

Cheshire's roads were considered by one 18c. traveller as being among the most detestable in the country. There had from the 14c. been limited, slow moving waggons, but salt and wool was still being carried by pack-horse. It took the Crewe family's coach 5 days to reach London, and most long distance travellers still rode on horseback.

In an effort to improve the major routes various turnpike trusts were set up to be responsible for raising funds to maintain a length of highway. In fact they were renting a piece of road and exacting tolls from users to defray the cost of upkeep. Those which possibly benefitted Alsager most were the Tittensor-Talke turnpike trust which was established in Staffordshire in 1714, and the Cranage to Lawton (Red Bull), part of the road from London to the north-west, turnpiked in 1730. In 1763 the road from Burslem to Red Bull was turnpiked.

Between 1817 and 1822 the Talke turnpike road was re-aligned from the Dimsdale in a more direct line to Talke, afterwards crossing the Alsager boundary at Linley Wood. A tollgate was established at or near the present Tollgate farm. The new road then continued into Lawton, joining the Cranage turnpike at Lawton Gate. Turnpiking gathered pace in the second half of the century and the number of carriers operating grew substantially and pack horse transport declined.

An Alsager man who took advantage of the opportunities which presented themselves was John Twiss of Town House. He developed a thriving business. As stage coaches and carriers swelled the traffic on the turnpike roads, so coaching inns proliferated where bed, board and a change of horses were to be had. Talke was particularly well known to waggoners, drivers and travellers for its numerous inns. The Lawton Arms was well situated to benefit from passing traffic.

In 1828, Thomas Holland, of the mill, was charged at Knutsford Quarter Sessions with;-

> *"riding in his cart on the turnpike road in Haslington without a person to*
> *guide same".*

---

[8] CRO. QJB/Mf. 200/13.

At the Enclosure the town roads were classified into public carriage and occupation roads with standard widths; full details are set out in Chapter 8.

In 1848 the administration changed. The March vestry meeting to elect the current year's officials was called a meeting of the ratepayers and was held at the (old) Lodge Inn, alternating with the Plough Inn and later the newly built Alsager Arms. For the first time there were minutes of the meeting as well as accounts. A rate of a shilling in the pound was agreed upon for the upkeep of the roads and a standing surveyor, Samuel Faram, was appointed at a salary of £10 per annum. A few years later this appointment was referred to as Waywarden.[9]

Hoose Hollow was again causing problems. Randle Wilbraham Esq. and his son, Randle Wilbraham Jn., wrote complaining of the state of Barthomley Road where it ran into the Lawton Township at Hooles Hollow. These two worthy gentlemen sent a donation of £5 each towards repairs and *"the best thanks of the meeting was tendered for the gentlemens' most generous subscription."* The clerk was instructed to assure them that the *"inhabitants of Alsager were fully prepared to carry out their wishes in regard to putting the said roads of the Township in good & efficient repair in as short a time as possible."*

On July 1st 1848 a statement of repairs carried out, including Hoose Hollow, was laid before the meeting at the Lodge, and it is clear that the new road-making method of MacAdam had been adopted. This involved removing the old central paving, laying down on soil a good, well packed, layer of stone to a depth of 6-12 inches and topping it with a layer of finer grained stone. This would compact to form a solid surface. MacAdam's method was an improvement on those of Metcalfe and Telford, being both cheaper and quicker.

> *"29½ roods of pavement taken up & macadamised at Hooles Hollow*
> *10½ roods of pavement as above near Mr. Thos. Lowe's*
> *11 roods of New Road forming coping & fencing near Hools Hollow*
> *40 tons of Broken stone laid down on the Fox branch of road for repairs*

Cost of the above		*60- 0-0*
To 160 Rood of pavement Macadaming		*80- 0-0*
to cinders		*40- 0-0*
to fresh stone		*20- 0-0*
wages		*40- 0-0*
Due to Jos. Edwards		*4-15-0*
	total	*244-15-0*

In 1874 Dr. Crutchley again highlighted the problematic Hoose Hollow. He proposed an alteration to the road at the boundary with Lawton where

[9] Alsager Vestry Minutes. CRO LUAS 3134/8

there was a sharp double bend close to the level crossing. The estimated cost was £300, and after consultation with Lawton township and the Highways Board, it was agreed in January 1875 to take action. A new stretch of road was laid on the Lawton side, running in a straight line from the hollow to the level crossing. The redundant piece of road was abandoned and became part of a footpath from Lawton Station to Alsager Station. It can still be seen as a shallow depression in the field alongside the modern road.

By modern standards the road was still narrow and winding. Seventy years later it was again the cause of trouble during the severe winters of 1939-40 and 1946-47. The hollow was blocked by snow drifts for several days, virtually cutting Alsager off in that direction. After further widening, made necessary, possibly to accommodate the Twyford's traffic, Hooze Hollow is but a name on an old map.

In 1850, footroads in the vicinity of the Parsonage were altered. They would be the paths used by the children when it was the village school, and perhaps were passing too close to the curate's newly converted residence.

In 1854 potters shards were spread on the 'New, or Sandy Lane' before laying any stone. This new road gave a more direct approach from the Lawton end of the village to the six-year old railway station. While older residents still call it Sandy Lane, officially it is Ashmore's Lane.

In 1894 the Town Council became the Urban District Council and one of their first moves was to have the roads inspected followed by strenuous efforts to improve them. Instructions were given for the purchase of 80 tons of Gawsworth stone, 300 tons of Penmaenmawr stone, 25 tons each of furnace cinders and broken limestone from Froghall to surface the bye-roads, and 80 loads of ashes from the waterworks and the railway for the pavements; but the roadmen were not happy. They brought it to the notice of the board *"that in all Local Board Districts workmen are provided with tools, whereas the Alsager men have to find their own"* - a surprising revelation, for in 1848 the township had its own tools, albeit basic;-

> *"Lady Day 1848*
> > *1 wheelbarrow and 1 new ditto*
> > *8 stone hammers for breaking stones*
> > *1 pick and 1 new ditto*
> > *2 spades 2 rakes 2 scrapers"*

The above list was supplied by Charles Ollier, a labourer usually employed on the roads.

By 1894 a steam roller was being used to compact the newly metalled roads. Though vastly improved they could be unpleasant in dry and windy weather when swirls of white limestone dust blew about, and only the use of a water cart and sprinkler would settle it. Nor was the council popular when it spread the cinders on the roads and paths. Miss Gertrude Craig wrote an ode of lament which was published in the parish magazine, July 1905;-

DUST AND ASHES
The village once was sweet and clean -
alas! and alack!
For all its pretty roads have been
Edged with rims of black!
With a Quack! Quack! Quack!
In council they meet,
To give us a treat
In ashes, dry, dusty and black.

However the township had to wait at least two more decades before the main roads were tar macadamed.

In July 1895, at Alsager's request, the County Council took over the maintenance of Barthomley Road from the Plough to Sandy Lane, and from Betley Place (Bank Corner) to the railway station.

The subject of street lighting was first broached in April 1894.[10] It was suggested that the Kidsgrove Gas Company be asked for an estimate per lamp, *"if lit from sunset to 11pm for 8 months of the year, moonlight nights excepted"*, but the project was shelved for 12 months. A motion to install electric lighting was rejected because of the unsightly overhead wires it would require. Finally gas lamps were installed in 1896 by James Edwards, at £2-14-6 per lamp, and a lamp-lighter was employed at 12s. per week.

His equipment was a long handle fitted with a metal container at the end, to hold the carbide and water, which produced the carbide flame, and a wind shield. He would poke this through a small gap at the bottom of the four-sided glass lantern to turn on the gas tap, and apply his 'torch' to the incandescent gas mantle.

After a few months he applied for a rise, owing to the *"arduous nature of his work"*, possibly because the village youths had discovered new targets to aim at, and he had to replace the broken gas mantles which were very fragile. As the numbers of lamps increased so did the vandalism, and in the winter of 1900, handbills were distributed offering rewards for *"information leading to the conviction of persons interfering with or damaging the lamps."* Early in the 1930's gas lighting was replaced by electricity.

At the turn of the century the Barthomley road, once a desolate heath track, was lined with a variety of villas and houses. The Avenue was a private road with a gate to the main road. The Craigs at Milton House, for

---

[10] Alsager UDC. minutes 1894-96. CRO. LUA's/1/1.

the sake of privacy, had built an unsightly high wall which stretched from the top lodge to the bottom lodge. Alsager centre was much improved when it was pulled down and Milton Gardens opened to the public. The new Police Station was built in 1894, opposite to a little general grocer's shop which had been there before the tithe apportionment. Latterly it was occupied by an eccentric member of the Goss family who drove a gas-fuelled car during the Second World War. The building was demolished in 1954 and the site is now occupied by the telephone exchange. The Fields, as Fields Road was then known, became a through road and further houses were built in the 1880's. Shady Grove petered out into a path at Moorhouse Farm. Pikemere Road was narrow, with clumps of yellow bird's foot trefoil growing up the middle, giving it the nickname of "eggs and bacon road". The old Police Station was situated at its junction with Sandbach Road North. Talke Road was unadopted beyond the Audley railway and there was no access to the Newcastle road until after the Second World War. Proposals for reconstruction were not always welcomed by the residents who would have to bear the cost. Opposition was met with compulsory orders obtained at Sandbach Magistrates' Court.

Older villas in Alsager have stables and coach houses indicating that private carriages were kept. The bicycle became very popular: Adolphus Goss was an enthusiastic member of the Cyclists Touring Club. Furniture was removed locally on a hand cart, farm waggons were used for excursions and for Gala Day processions. However, with the station capable of receiving all manner of goods, there was an opening in the carrier line for someone with enterprise and William Band was the man.

He walked from his native Macclesfield to work in Alsager around 1860 and in the 1861 census he was listed as a cordwainer (shoemaker). He later worked as a railway porter at the station where he noticed a gap in the distribution of goods arriving there. He developed a horse-drawn transport system which served the surrounding countryside, and operated from Fair View at Bank Corner. By the turn of the century William Band and his family had a fleet of horse-drawn vehicles to transport all manner of goods including coal. There were extensive outbuildings, stabling and pasture for the horses where now the Fairview carpark is, with the carriages suitable for all occasions, white horses for weddings, and black horses for funerals. The drays and waggonettes were used on Friendly Societies' gala days and for taking people to Sandbach market.

In July 1905 eight of Mr Band's waggonettes set off for Queen's Park, Crewe, with 200 Sunday School children and their teachers packed into them. They were described in the parish magazine as *"making an imposing procession."*

When the vicar first began holding open air services near the Alsager Road railway station at Linley in 1904, prior to the Linley Mission being built, Mr Band's 'lurry' was pressed into service. A harmonium and seats were loaded onto it and transported each week during the summer months. The 'lurry' also made an excellent platform for the preacher. As petrol driven vehicles came into use, the next generation ran a taxi service until 1953.

Fairview was bought by the Urban District Council in 1935 for their operational centre. It was the rate office, the depot for the fire service, and during the war the Food Office as well as the A.R.P. centre, with the air raid warning siren on the roof. It was demolished around 1970 to make way for the Civic Centre and Library.

In the early 1940's the Radway Green Estate was built, the two principal roads, Longview Avenue and Moorhouse Avenue, perpetuate the names of the two farms on which the estate was constructed.

Since the war there have been many housing developments with numerous new roads. Some of their names reflect their local and county associations; but whatever they are called, nothing can detract from the tradition associated with the old roads.

Postal Services

A postal service between important towns had been established in the early 16c. to deal with government dispatches and in 1629 it was reorganised to take private mail. The first letter office opened in London in 1631. To begin with letters were carried by mounted post boys on the main routes. At junctions with minor roads they were met by post boys on foot, who took the letters the comparatively short distances to the near-by villages. Often it was more convenient to send a manservant as did Henry Newcome when trying to secure Acton vicarage for his clergyman son. He dispatched his footman from Manchester to Chester with a letter for the Bishop but the Bishop was not at home;-

1678   *"...but when he (the footman) returned with the letter I was not satisfied and sent him again, to Barthomley, to be directed by Mr. Cawdrey whether to go to Weston or no"...*

Newcome's son did get the appointment.

The first Royal Mail coach ran in 1784 between London and Bristol and within two years Cheshire was benefitting. There were designated collection points along the route. Alsager's was Red Bull, as shown in the Alsager Overseer's accounts of 1828;-

"paid for leter	*3d.*
paid for a leter to the Ouse of Comens	*1s.0d.*
May (my) Joney to Red Bull to put the Leter in the post	*1s0d."*

Penny post, a standard rate intoduced in 1840, brought in a considerable reduction in cost.   The development of the railways brought rapid improvement in the service, for as soon as a railway line opened between centres previously served by long distance mail coaches, it took over. Mail coaches had had their day, and were soon to be discontinued, but in this area, the North Staffs. Railway and the Post Office could not at first agree on terms. So the mail was carried on the L.N.W.R. to Whitmore, taken the 5 miles to Newcastle by road and from there distributed to the local points. Accordingly Alsager's letters continued to be *"received through Lawton"* as the Post Office Directory for 1857 stated.

The first reference to a local post office, savings bank and postmaster, Joseph Baddeley, is in a directory of 1874. It was located in Station Road close to the present Lodge Inn and is marked on the Ordnance Survey map of 1875. The post box was emptied at 8pm. but letters could be left at the post office up to 8.30pm.

By 1878 the post office, now a telegraph office, was sited at the Poplars in Alsager Road (Sandbach Road South). The postmaster was Joseph Barratt, he and his wife also kept a confectioner's shop. They catered for numerous church and other events including Friendly Society galas. In 1895 the council made a request to the G.P.O. for Alsager to have a delivery of post on Sunday, but the G.P.O. declined. Mr. Barratt died in 1890 and Mrs. Barratt kept on the post office until the 1920's.

The post office then moved to 48 Crewe Road, with Mrs. Bertha Heath as the sub-postmistress. She was an energetic figure behind the counter until the middle 1950's. It was also a chemist's shop. When Mrs. Heath retired the post office once again moved, this time further up Crewe Road next to Joseph Edwards, undertakers, with Mr. Smith as sub-postmaster. Since then it has had two different locations in Lawton Road.

Another sub post office opened in Audley Road, possibly after the First World War. It has been in three different locations, all close to the railway station but it has been at the Railway Stores since the 1930's kept for many years by another Mr. Smith and then his successors.

When the telephone came into general use, an exchange was set up in the front room of a private house in Crewe Road. It was originally operated by Mrs. Hughes and later taken over by Mrs. Clowes who ran it for many years. With the increase in demand for telephones after the war, and the dialling system being introduced, a new telephone exchange was built in Crewe Road, in the 1950's, opposite to the Police Station.

In about 1900 there were 10 subscribers;-

6	Barrett T. Paxton	Rosedale (Station Road)
9	Birks Jn.	The Wood (Sandbach Rd. N.)
3	Corn W & E	White House (Crewe Rd?)
7	King H. B.	Hope House (The Fields)
1	N.S. Brick & Tile Co.	Alsager
0200	Parkes A.	Alsager Arms (Station Road)
2	Rigby F.	Westmere Lodge (Lodge Rd.)
4	Rigby & Co. Ld.	Bunkers Hill (colliery)
10	Rigby R.	The Grove Lawton (demolished)
5	Settle J.	The Hill (burnt down)

The Canals

During the early years of the 18c. various schemes were put forward for improving the navigability of England's natural water-ways with varying degrees of success. If effective, heavier and bulkier loads could be moved as quickly and more cheaply than on most parts of the existing road system, to the benefit of the country as a whole.

In Cheshire efforts over many years to maintain Chester as a major port had not achieved lasting success but tributaries of the River Mersey, particularly the lower Weaver, were markedly improved enabling sizeable loads to be carried inland as far as Northwich and Winsford. Rivers, however, are subject to variations in levels and flow due to tides, currents and weather and although the advantages of still water conditions were generally appreciated the principles of achieving them were not fully understood.

By 1761 however the Sankey (St. Helens) and Bridgewater canals had been constructed and the great success of the latter had re-invigorated the interested parties in North Staffordshire who had considered a waterway running through the developing Potteries area and linking the Trent and Mersey rivers. Surveys of possible routes had already been made including one by James Brindley of Turnhurst, in 1758, before he was employed by the Duke of Bridgewater as engineer for the canal project for transporting coal from the duke's mines at Worsley into the neighbouring town of Manchester.

Rival schemes were debated and in 1765 the 'Company of Proprietors of the Navigation from the Trent to the Mersey' applied to Parliament for authority to proceed. The Company of Proprietors included the Duke of Bridgewater, John Sneyd, Josiah Wedgwood and numerous local landowners, merchants and manufacturers. Josiah Wedgwood was appointed treasurer and James Brindley engaged as engineer for the project. Construction was authorised and began in 1766.

The canal, as surveyed and planned by Brindley, left the Trent at Wilden Ferry between Nottingham and Derby, roughly followed the course of the river upstream to north of Stoke where it crossed the watershed in Harecastle tunnel before descending into Cheshire, proceeding via Rode Heath, Wheelock, Middlewich and Northwich to its junction at Preston Brook with the extended Bridgewater canal giving access to the Mersey at Runcorn. The total length of the Trent and Mersey canal was 93 miles and Brindley who envisaged it as part of a wider scheme with connections to the Severn and the Thames preferred to call it the Grand Trunk Canal.

Due to difficulties and delays involved in the construction of the Harecastle and Preston Brook tunnels the canal was not completed and through working achieved until 1777, five years after Brindley's death. He had been involved in other projects up to the time of his death including the Caldon canal, linking the limestone quarries between Leek and Ashbourne with Etruria.

The canal gave a tremendous boost to the Potteries area and many other localities along its route, and can be regarded as a major event in the development of the Industrial Revolution in Britain. Over the following half century canals were developed on a large scale despite improvements in road construction. It was not until the railway era was established that fresh construction virtually ceased.

Although many places adjacent to or near a canal developed rapidly, Alsager was not among them. At its nearest points between Hassall Green and the aqueduct on the A50 at Church Lawton, the Trent and Mersey canal is within half a mile of the township boundary but it had little noticeable effect industrially or commercially. The development of the salt works at Rode Heath may have created some local employment as may the construction of wharfs and warehouses in that village. A directory for 1851 covering Barthomley parish has boat builder and boatman among the occupations listed, and the parish registers confirm that some of those so described lived in Alsager. The main benefit, from the canal, locally, would have been in the supply of non-perishable goods, such as coal, china-clay, salt, earthenware and other manufactured products in general use; lime and manure for the farming community and the bulk dispatch of agricultural produce, such as potatoes and grain to the rapidly expanding industrial centres

The notice placed in the Staffordshire Advertiser in 1821, by the trustees of the Alsager Heath Inclosure Award, advertising land for sale by auction makes reference to the proximity of the canal as an inducement to prospective purchasers. John Twiss, the Alsager carrier, with interests in Stafford, Stone and Manchester, is recorded as being a member of *'The Inland Navigation Association for the Apprehending and Prosecution of Felons'*, an organisation based at Stone and which had a Mr. Pickford also amongst its members. Twiss no doubt had business interests at local wharfs the nearest being Butt Lane, Rode Heath and Wheelock.

Aerial View of Alsager in the mid 1950s.

The Rev. Charles Alsager Tryon, Incumbent of Christ Church 1847–1877 and Lord of the Manor.

The Mere 1892, taken from a point opposite Northolme Gardens, Crewe Road.

Old Cottage in Well Lane (possibly Heath House Farm).

Fair View, Bank Corner, with Council Offices beyond, 1969.

Alsager Mission Church (The Tin Tabernacle), Crewe Road, 1881–1895.

The Rev. George Skene, Rector of Barthomley 1880–1923.

Original deed, dated 1302, relating to land at Aspenhurst, Alsager (ref. CRO.DVE.1/A1).

Ref. CRO. DVE.1/A.1. (original 20.5cm x 8cm)

Translation.

Know all men present and future that I Adam, son of Nicholas of Alsacher, have given, granted and by this my present charter I have confirmed

to Randle de Praers of Bertomelegh a certain piece of ground that is called Aspenhurste, with appurtenances, in Alsacher, as is enclosed and encircled by a certain ditch as far as the bounds with Bertomelegh, with a certain stream adjacent to the same

land, within the aforesaid boundaries. To have and to hold to the said Sir Randle and his heirs and assigns from the chief lord of that fee.

freely quietly, well, wholly in peace and by heredity forever with all freedoms, profits, free commons and easements in the waters, moors, marshes, ways, paths, fields, pastures, rights of pasture and in all other places wheresoever pertaining to the said land and to the township of Alsacher.

Paying therefor annually to the chief lord of the fee a pepper corn on the feast of saint Martin in winter for all secular services, payments and demands everywhere pertaining to the said land. Truly, I, the said Adam and my heirs will warrant, acquit and

defend everywhere, forever, all the aforesaid land of Aspenhurst with the stream aforesaid adjacent to it and all its other appurtenances, to the said Randle and his heirs and assigns against all people. In witness whereof I have placed my seal on this present charter.

These being witnesses; Richard de Mascy, William de Brereton, knights; Robert de Brescy, then sheriff of Cheshire; William de Praers, Patrick de Crue, William de Alsacher, Thomas de Ordeswyk, John del heth, Nicholas the clerk and many others.

Translation of the Aspenhurst deed. Aspenhurst is sited at Map Ref. 788540.

Poster advertising the Club Day of the Independent Order of Good Templars, 1873.

Procession of the Ancient Order of Druids outside The Old Villa, Sandbach Road South, 1890s.

Diamond Jubilee Procession 1897, outside the Lodge Inn, showing Church Road.

Alsager Station 1899.

Crewe Road, about 1900.

The Post Office at The Poplars, Sandbach Road South, early 20c.

Children out from School, by Christ Church.

The Bands' Carriages, opposite Lynton Place.

Hancocks Bakers, Bank Corner (corner of Lawton Road and Sandbach Road South).

Dedication of the War Memorial, 19th June 1920.

Alsager's Home Guard Platoon, World War Two.

Alsager Social Club, Sandbach Road South (now the site of Homeshire House), 1984.

The Old Parsonage and Schoolroom, Christ Church, taken in 1964.

Cresswellshawe Farm, on the site of the Wilbraham Arms.

A true and perfect Inventary of all the goods
Cattells and Chattles of Quick and Dead Moveable and
unmoveable whatsoever of Thomas Sidway late of
Allgare in the County of Chester yeoman deceased taken
the Nineteenth day of ffebruary Ano dni 1661 viewed
and appraised by us whose names are underwritten

Inprimis Eight Cowes foure twinters & foure Calves — 55 = 03 = 04
Item two Mares and one Nagg — — — — — 12 = 10 = 00
Item Tenn Sheepe — — — — — — 03 = 00 = 00
Item two Swine — — — — — — — 01 = 04 = 00
Item Poultery — — — — — — — 00 = 11 = 00
Item Muck in the Midding — — — — — 00 = 05 = 00
Item a lease of certaine Acres of Lands lying in Lostly
    yet in being — — — — — — — } 170 = 00 = 00
Item Corne in the house and barne & growing in the
    feild and hay — — — — — — — } 32 = 00 = 00
Item Waine timber & plow timber with Carts & plowes
    harrowes and boards — — — — — } 15 = 07 = 00
Item all husbandry ware and Iron ware — — — 03 = 10 = 04
Item all the beds and bedding with all y furniture — 29 = 00 = 00
Ite woollen Cloth butt ffynon Cloth Sheets & Naggary 10 = 14 = 00
Item Cord and yarne — — — — — — 01 = 13 = 04
Ite Coffers Chests boxes & one presse — — — 02 = 16 = 00
It Beefe Bacon Butter Cheese and all other provision
    in the house — — — — — — — } 10 = 13 = 04
Item Chaires Stooles quissions & wooden ware — 03 = 03 = 00
Item Brasse pewter Maslin one Mortor & pestill — 12 = 03 = 10
Item one Bible and other bookes — — — — 00 = 10 = 00
Item Six dozen of Trenchers and other small
    things for houswifery — — — — — } 01 = 00 = 00
Ite Silverplate and Spoones two gould Ringes
    & two Silver Ringes — — — } 13 = 05 = 00
Ite monyes due by bond lent monyes and other
    monyes due to the Testator — — — } 11 = 00 = 00
Ite his apparrell and monyes in his purse — — 10 = 00 = 00

The totall is- 309 = 10 = 06

Viewed and appraised by us
Thomas Rawson his mark
Samuell Dickonson -
Raph Shawe
Thomas Cooke

Esta probata et dc ..... 22 Maij 1662

An example of a 17c. Inventory, Thomas Sidway, 1662, see page 248.

THE RAILWAY AGE

At the beginning of the nineteenth century, through the discovery and harnessing of the steam engine, the railway revolution had begun in North East England. By 1830 the Liverpool to Manchester line had opened for business, it was one of the first in the world to operate a timetable for passengers and goods. The eventual success of this venture was to speed railway mania throughout the land. This fostered many plans for routes between the major cities and changed the life and landscapes of Britain. There were going to be many Acts of Parliament and company board meetings but within the next twenty years Cheshire and North Staffordshire had the railway tracks serving their towns and countryside. During 1848 the iron rails had crossed Alsager's acres severing the fledgling township from the heath.

A plethora of railway companies was formed, but it was the London - Birmingham Railway that built the line from the capital's terminus at Euston to Birmingham. As the tracks of the Grand Junction Railway forged towards the North West, through Stafford, towards Warrington, the route met with considerable differences of opinion. This pioneering north-south artery was to shape the future rail systems of the countryside through which it passed.

It was inevitable a Cheshire junction be created. Projects to Chester and Birkenhead were planned and the competing rivalries of Manchester and Liverpool were proposing more direct links with the main London line. Crewe was selected as the location for this junction against the strong contention of Nantwich, which was already the road centre of south Cheshire and by 1831 possessed canal communications to most parts of England and Wales. The first station at Crewe was built in 1837 where four tracks merged and the town of Crewe owes its existence to the railway lines (it was recorded in early census returns as Church Coppenhall). Later the growth of the town was enhanced by the establishment of an engineering works.

But all was not well in the area. Annoyance was felt in North Staffordshire by persons who had interests in the original scheme that the line had omitted altogether any communication with the Potteries.

The North Staffordshire Railway.

The Potteries fought hard for a railway system due to the Grand Junction Railway being routed from Birmingham and Stafford to Crewe. This line should have passed through the Potteries on its way to Crewe but due to influences, agreements and compromises between various promoters the 28 miles of track between Stafford and Crewe passed through fields and villages that had no special need for it - hence the Potteries had to construct a railway of its own. Basil Judah quotes The Illustrated London News of that time as saying;-

> *"Before the formation of the North Staffordshire Railway,*
> *a large tract of the country was wholely destitute of railway*
> *accommodation. Although it contains nearly half a million*
> *inhabitants and includes the manufacturing districts of the*
> *Potteries, Leek, Congleton and Macclesfield and the towns*
> *of Uttoxeter, Stone, Cheadle, Newcastle-under-Lyme, and*
> *Ashbourne, all of them centres of business for the agricultural*
> *population of the surrounding villages. No inconsiderable*
> *portion of this large tract also abounds in mineral wealth -*
> *limestone, coal, clay, and iron being found in abundance."*[11]

The formation of the North Staffordshire Railway was born out of the fact that the area was devoid of railway construction by the railway politics of an earlier decade. From 1846 to 1923 the North Staffordshire Railway Company provided a railway service linking this area to the rest of the country. Its distinctive motif, the Staffordshire Knot, earned it the nickname "The Knotty". In its early formation years the N.S.R. Company acquired the Trent and Mersey Canal enabling it to control its main competition.

Throughout its existence the company was fiercely independent and earned its place in history in the formation of England's railway system.

Stoke to Crewe Line

The first Director's Report given in September 1846 shows the Railway Act for the Derby to Crewe line via the Potteries was one of three obtained by the N.S.R. in June 1846. The line, being one of the back bones of the N.S.R. system, became known as the Knotty main line, as it connected the East Midlands with the emerging railway centre at Crewe. The Crewe line met with legal difficulties created, by Lord Crewe, which caused a three mile deviation. Parliamentary sanction was needed in July 1847 to enable the line to rejoin its original route at Radway Green. Even 60 years later the 1908 official 'Illustrated Guide,' in which the N.S.R. featured in trying to improve its image, stated;-[12]

> *"there are as many manufacturing centres as bad, or worse than the*
> *Potteries. Leaving Stoke the line continues through the same industrial*
> *scenery. After passing Harecastle pleasant country accommodates the line*
> *to the L & N.W. Junction at Crewe."*

Alsager, through its geographical position, found itself astride the stratetegic line from Derby and Stoke leading to the emerging railway centre

---

[11] Basil Jeuda, *The Knotty;* Lightmoor Press p.4.
[12] ibid.

at Crewe. An engineer by the name of Merritt[13] was responsible for the construction of both the Crewe and Sandbach lines. A work force of 540 men with 30 horses and 110 wagons were needed to lay the tracks. The line opened on 9th October 1848, at the same time as the handsome Stoke Central Railway Station, and the main branch line from Stoke to Congleton. The Staffordshire Advertiser of 14th October described the weather *"as most unpropitious for out of doors manifestations"* but the event was celebrated throughout the area with crowds of spectators thronging the bridges, the approaches and almost every advantage point to see the trains pass by.

The opening of the Crewe and Congleton branches was celebrated by a public dinner at Congleton Town Hall given by the Mayor and Corporation of the town to the Chairman and Directors of the N.S.R. In its report of the opening, printed on October 14th 1848, The Staffordshire Advertiser reported the Mayor;-

> *"calling attention to the important event they were assembled to celebrate and that it was the first link of the chain of railway communications that would join the neighbouring towns."*

The running of Sunday trains became controversial and generated a correspondence, for and against, in the August editions of the Staffordshire Advertiser of 1848. One such letter addressed, to the directors of the North Staffordshire Railway, was signed by the clergy, magistrates and other inhabitants of the parishes of Barthomley, Lawton, Audley etc. It stated;-

> *"The continued observance of The Lord's Day should be promoted and to secure for all classes the advantages of a weekly cessation from labour, and respectfully call your attention to the evils likely to arise from running trains on Sundays."*

This was reinforced by a letter from Haughton Rectory (Staffs). which included the following;-[14]

> *"I have seen with much pleasure the very Christian protest . . . . against the Sabbath desecration upon the North Staffordshire Railway . . . . No wonder at our gaols being filled! No wonder that crime should increase if Christian people do not lift up their voices and use their energies to put a stop to that which is so hurtful to those who are engaged in it, so evil in its example, and so likely, 'if not timely remedied,' to draw down Divine vengence upon our Queen, our country and ourselves."*

Mr. Downes Banks of Manchester wrote;- [15]

> *"I . . . have seen with regret an attempt on the part of several clergymen to saddle the directors of the North Staffordshire Railway with the utter ruin of the British nation, both morally and politically if they lend their sanction*

---

[13] This information has been taken from a leaflet produced by Congleton Borough Council.

[14] *Staffordshire Advertiser* 5th August 1848 p.3. col.1.

[15] ibid. 12th August 1848. p.8. col. 5.

*to the running of cheap trains on the Sabbath day . . . . These cheap trains
. . . . are mainly intended for the use of the poorer classes, for that large
body of the inhabitants of the Potteries, who fully employed during the week
have only leisure for one day of rest . . . ."*

Alsager Railway Station

When the railway reached Alsager it helped to put the remote hamlet on
the map, and became a catalyst that nurtured its growth into a thriving village.
The line opened on the 9th October 1848. The service commenced with two
trains each way but by 1850 there were five trains daily, between Crewe and
Derby, calling at Alsager. The service between Stoke, Alsager and Crewe
gradually developed enabling people to become more mobile. It was by
chance of its geographical position that Alsager found itself astride the
Knotty's main-line track, the iron rails crossing the sandy lane that led down
from Alsager township towards the heath. The station was built on the site of
the old pinfold. The original buildings have hardly changed over a century
and a half, on both platforms were passenger waiting rooms; there were
reception areas for goods and parcels, and an office for the issue of tickets.
The two long platforms were a source of beauty as the gardens were
meticulously maintained. This was stimulated by the Railway Company
themselves making awards for the best kept country stations and the staff
contributed over many years in maintaining well kept flower beds and borders.

Not only did it provide a social service but it started to create
employment. One local family, in its early years, awaited the trains with a
horse and dray, and distributed the goods into the surrounding areas.

The signal box was on the other side of the crossing from the Station
Master's house. The 'box', now demolished, was served by generations of
signalmen who controlled the track by a number of levers which operated the
signals and the crossing gates were opened and closed by the signalman in his
box. The "clang" of the signal box bell heralded the imminent arrival of a
passenger train. A small goods yard opposite the signal box has also
disappeared. It received regular consignments of coal and other minerals
which the railways were so adept in carrying. Old folk-lore had it, if one
could hear the rumble of the train approaching from Crewe it was a sign of
rain.

Alsager station became the hub of village life, the centre of news, gossip
and advice. It was the home of a bookstall and the telegraph office. People
met and mingled - the Royal Mail and newspapers arrived on time and with
consistent regularity. During the 1939-45 war even the cash arrived to pay the
workers at the Royal Ordnance Factory, Radway Green. It became a gateway
to school, work and leisure. Many excursion trains left for the seaside and
country. The North Wales coast, Blackpool and Uttoxeter Races became

popular destinations. The cost of a workman's return to Stoke in 1940 was 10d. (4p.).

By the time the station had completed its first hundred years many of the local inhabitants had passed through it, in endless profusion, on a variety of missions. It was a place of motion and emotion, parting and reunion, arrival and departure. One emotional departure was enacted when three people left in 1911 and joined a larger party at Crewe station; they had answered the call of the New Zealand Railways for experienced personnel. A larger crowd gathered in 1919 to say farewell to a farming family emigrating to Canada.

Many of Alsager's conscripted young men left the station during the years of war, clutching their call-up papers and a free rail pass, as they made their jouney to the recruiting destinations. The 1939-45 war years saw the platforms at the station accommodate the arrival of four distinct waves of new-comers that lapped over the village. At the commencement of the conflict a train load of 250 evacuees arrived from Liverpool. Throughout the next few years many young female workers, from all over the U.K, arrived under the directed labour scheme to reside at the hostels and work at the Radway Green Munitions Factory. Later in the war one of the hostels (Fields Road) was taken over by the Royal Navy as a training camp. Regular intakes of naval recruits arrived and departed. Today this is the Excaliber industrial estate. Finally after the cessation of hostilities a 300 train load of young people and women arrived. These people were of Baltic nationality and known as displaced persons who had no wish to return to their native lands.

After this period of great activity the station quietly reached its centenary in 1948. Shortly afterwards petrol rationing ended, which together with Government reluctance to conceed to the railways full commercial freedom, made the decline in public transport inevitable.

On July 1st 1923 the North Staffordshire Railway had merged with the London, Midland and Scottish Railway Company. On 1st January 1948 the railways were nationalised under British Rail. The long decay of the railway system, over quarter of a century, resulted in the introduction of the Beeching Plan in the 1960's when many stations and branch lines were declared redundant and closed. In 1995 the system was broken up into regional entities and preparation made for it to be sold back to private enterprise.

Alsager station became an endangered species and by the end of the 20c. became the focus of conservation. To close and demolish the station would significantly diminish the life of a town. It would bring the curtain down on a stage which has witnessed many dramas, comic and tragic, and has mirrored the changing times. In its own way the station has played a vital part in Alsager's past and growth, and still has a role as the twenty-first century approaches.

The Salt Line

The line from Lawton Junction to Wheelock was opened for goods traffic on 21st January 1852 but the first passenger service was not provided until forty-one years later on 3rd July 1893. How different its passenger fortunes might have been if the proposed extension of the North Staffordshire Railway system had been built from Wheelock to Liverpool.

The line was a single track and skirted the Alsager township boundary following the contours of the Wheelock Valley. It was the only branch line of the North Staffordshire Railway to be completely built in Cheshire, and was eventually extended to Sandbach by 1858. A station at Hassall Green was opened on April 17th 1905. The construction of the line was helped by the proximity of the Trent and Mersey Canal which the N.S.R. controlled. It proved vital in the construction of the track as many of the bulky materials were transported by narrow boat. The line became known as the Salt Line, as it transported salt from the Cheshire workings to the Potteries and beyond.

The sparsity of passenger traffic is shown by the takings at Lawton Station which averaged £150 a year over the four years following its opening in 1893.[16] A note in the public timetable requested passengers *"To provide themselves with suitable change to pay for their tickets as the Company's booking clerks are not able at all times to give change."*

Bradshaw's 1910 copy of the train service shows a passenger service of three trains a day, with an extra train on a Thursday, presumably for Sandbach market. Lack of passengers and infrequent trains saw the service closed on 28th July 1930, and freight transport finally ended on 4th March 1964. Before its closure the line was used by freight traffic to ease congestion around Crewe during the period of electrification during the early 1960's. On occasions it was used by the Royal Train for overnight stabling as it was deemed a good security position. Two surviving examples of N.S.R. architecture can be seen at the crossing keepers' houses at Lawton and Hassall.

Today these two disused commercial transport arteries of railway line and canal, which virtually meet at Hassall Green, are intersected by the M6 motorway. All three interweave just beyond the northern extremity of the former Alsager Urban District boundary. One can observe a wealth of old and modern transport history from the vicinity of Hassall Green Station. The modern motorway symbolising a new wave of transportation which followed the demise of the rural branch lines and canals.

---

[16] Christienson and Miller. *The North Staffordshire Railway;*

The Alsager to Keele Line

Alsager's second railway station was situated at the Linley end of Talke Road and was known as Talke and Alsager Road, it was opened in July 1889. In later years, 1902, the 'Talke' was dropped. The line had been opened on 24th July 1870, a late date in the history of railway construction and was authorised by an Act of Parliament in 1864 which covered the development from Alsager to Keele.

Alsager Junction was the start of the line which became the scene of busy activity. This area of the Knotty Railway eventually saw the start of an industrial complex and was the site of an engine shed, the second largest after Stoke, a station with staggered platforms and a network of sidings. It also attracted the wagon building and repair works of Settle Speakman & Company.

The line left the Stoke-on-Trent to Crewe track near the boundary with Church Lawton and climbed steadily towards Audley. It crossed the county boundary at Mere Lake and cut across the route of the A500, the lineal road that connects North Staffordshire and South Cheshire. The track proceeded for seven and a half miles before joining the Stoke to Market Drayton line west of Keele Station. It passed through part of the North Staffordshire coalfield serving the many collieries in the Audley area, and had many spur lines as a result.

At the begining of the 20c. the Audley branch line had passed the peak of activity. As an unbroken line of pits and an ironworks closed down, mineral traffic became less. Passenger traffic declined as road transport developed, and the last passenger train ran on 27th April 1931. Mineral traffic continued to run for a few more years with the line finally closing on 7th January 1963.

After the closure of the Salt Line and Audley branch line the permanent ways were dismantled and the embankments and cuttings were turned into interesting walkways. Now the two disused tracks provide attractive ways into the Cheshire countryside allowing horse riders, cyclists and walkers, free from traffic, to observe a wealth of wild life and habitats that have evolved down the centuries.

Settle Speakman & Company Ltd;[17] Railway Wagon Works [18]

The above works was built during the 1920's to maintain the fleet of railway coal wagons owned by Settle Speakman to transport coal from the

---

[17] For a full account of the history of the Company see *"!860 - 1960 Settle Speakman & Co., Ltd."* Published by the Company. SECSU. Library.

[18] This section has been contributed by Mr. Douglas Allen of Alsager.

North Staffordshire pits, which they also owned, to their customers, mainly in the North-West and Wales, and also to Garston Docks at Liverpool for shipment to Ireland. Prior to nationalisation of the pits in 1948, Settle Speakman owned the following collieries in North Staffordshire:

> Stafford Coal & Iron Co. Ltd. Trentham;
> Stirrup & Pye Ltd. Longton;
> Glebe Colliery, Fenton;
> Mossfield Colliery, Longton;
> Bignall Hill Colliery, Jamage;

The railway wagons from these collieries, together with the wagons which were lettered SETTLE SPEAKMAN, were maintained at the Wagon Works at Alsager and were used, as stated above, to transport the coal to the various customers and, when empty, were returned to the above mentioned collieries. When World War II broke out in 1939 all coal wagons in the country were 'pooled' and the empty running back to specific pits ceased, which was a great saving for the railways. As a result of this 'pooling' railway wagons belonging to all sorts of companies came into the wagon works at Alsager for repair. When the war ended this situation continued, and eventually, with the nationalisation of the railways and the collieries, both assets passed from the control of Settle Speakman.

During the immediate post-war years repairs to steel constructed wagons, as well as the conventional wooden wagons, were undertaken at Alsager and this continued until the 1960's when British Rail kept the repair of wagons to themselves and ceased the practice of allocating work to independent repairers. For several years after the cessation of wagon repairs, general engineering was undertaken at Alsager, steel fabrication being the main item. When this transition ceased to be viable, in 1970, the works closed and some 200 employees were made redundant. The buildings were then leased for storage, the only remaining Settle Speakman connection being the Fuel and Transport Department. This remained in the garage and office at the works until 1974 when it was demolished and new storage was built for Indesit Ltd. - the Fuel and Transport Department having by this time been sold.

The site at the present time is occupied by Cardway plc for the manufacture of cardboard cartons.

Alsager Loco' Sheds

To cope with the expected increase in freight when the Audley branch line opened in 1870, an expectation which increased further due to a demand for coal from the French during the Franco-Prussian war of 1870-71, a servicing area was established at Alsager junction. First a water tank was installed, and later in 1886 a sand furnace was added beneath it. Dry sand was needed to assist locomotives braking and gripping on wets rails and on inclines. There was at this time no accommodation for locomotives to be based at the yard but possibly standby arrangements were made in advance with the depot at Stoke.

In January 1890 plans were made to build a permanent depot, which became known as 'Alsager Locomotive Sheds', and which was in operation early in 1891. The engine shed, built to a LNWR design, contained four 'roads' and remained unaltered until 1945, when the roof was replaced. The depot was equipped with a new water tank, with the water being pumped from the canal at Lawton, with mess rooms, with an oil store below, new sand drying facilities and a turntable. The marshalling yard was made up of fourteen sidings, five of which, with additional watering facilities, were exclusively for the use of the Audley line. The yard received loaded trains from the collieries which were then marshalled for forwarding to their various destinations. Night-time shunting could be noisy and audible over a considerable distance, depending on the weather conditions. By 1900 there were sidings on both sides of the Crewe-Harecastle tracks and the waggons, which were the property of the collieries, were again shunted, this time for return to their various pitheads.

Although it is not known how many engines were based at Alsager in 1891, ten years later there were fifteen, with extra ones being brought in when required. In 1950 there were seventeen; ten tender engines (0-6-0), four tank shunters (0-6-0), and three 2-6-4- tank engines which were mainly for working passenger trains from Radway Green. A large dump of coal for fuelling was stored in the yard as a precaution against supplies drying up through emergencies. The covered coal stage was an island platform with coal trucks drawn up on one side and engines to be serviced an the other. At first the loading was done entirely with shovels; later a hand crane was introduced but coal was still partially loaded by hand; in 1935 the ailing crane was replaced with an electric one.

When the depot opened key staff were initially transferred from other depots at Stoke, Uttoxeter and Burton. In some cases the North Staffs Railway Co. offered loan facilities to enable their men to buy local houses. However, there was never any difficulty in recruiting local men for training, from either Alsager or the surrounding neighbourhood, since a job on the railway was considered more desirable and certainly more secure than being a gardener's boy at one of the big houses or working down the pits. The shedmaster and foreman were in charge of the considerable staff required for operations. In its hey-day the sheds employed 101 footplate staff; a further seventy-six men, including thirty-six guards, were under the jurisdiction of the station master and worked in various capacities around the stations and marshalling yards. There a variety of goods would be dealt with including livestock, such as day-old calves in bags tied up around their necks, boxes of pigeons to be released at a given time; and grain for Finney's mill at Audley. As there was no telephone connection at the turn of the century, Sally Finney used to cycle over to check on its arrival before the mill cart set out to collect it.[19] Wicker baskets containing china samples used by commercial travellers, of whom quite a number lived in Alsager, spent the night on the platform. There was much rivalry among the station staff in producing the finest show of flowers. The top stations, in the best kept garden competition, were Trentham, Alsager and Radway Green, the latter most often the winner. Perhaps this was because it had fewer passengers and also that Waterhouses, the local nursery, who dispatched their ware from that station, supplied rose bushes free.

The hours worked by the enginemen were often unsociable. Shift work with twelve different turns was the rule six days a week, plus extra Sunday work. A knocker-up was employed to wake those who had to 'book on after midnight'. He would hammer on the door until he received an answer, and shout through the letter box the number of the engine to be 'fired up'. The signal boxes were often in isolated places, which meant a lonely work environment for the signalman with only the 'ding-ding' of the code bell for company. Many spent the time in between trains cleaning, and polishing the floor and signal handles. This sometimes led to odd habits and over fussiness about cleanliness. When firemen entered one box to sign the book, to comply with safety regulations, they would be instructed to shuffle across the floor on two small pieces of blanket so as not to leave footmarks. Another would not even allow them to enter his box, but brought the book to the door to be signed. Some grew vegetables on a plot at the side of their boxes, as at Alsager station. At the shunting yard box one occupant was skilled at cutting hair, and gave his mates, including the station master, a short back and sides when not engaged in pulling signals. The railway continued to be a major employer in the village for seventy-one years.

At regrouping, in January 1923, the Alsager shed still had 15 engines out of the 'NSR' total of 200. Only the Stoke shed had a larger number, having more than half the company's stock. In the years after the First World War coal traffic declined as collieries closed when reserves were exhausted. One closed in 1928 and five more in 1930. Also energy requirements changed, gas and electricity came into wider use, both in the home and in industry.

The general strike of 1926 affected the loco staff. Not all the work-force came out on strike, and although it only lasted nine days, the bitterness towards those few men who carried on working remained for the rest of their

---

[19] As related by the late Mrs. S. Howle (née Finney).

working lives. Since the miners continued with their strike the engine staff were working a three day week, in rotation, for up to a year. There was a further notable strike when 'ASLEF' called the men out in 1955. It lasted for three weeks and all but three Alsager men came out.

During the Second World War the railways were taken over by the government and run as a national service. Although Alsager crews were not specifically used to transport ammunition, they were used extensively in moving freight which was coming into the country through the north-west ports. This was intensified when quantities of army equipment, such as tanks and lorries, were being stockpiled at an army camp near to Eggington junction in the run-up to the invasion of Europe. Some passenger trains were worked, but only to and from the Royal Ordnance factories; at Swynnerton, Coldmeece and Radway Green, Millway. Peacetime passenger work was undertaken during the Potteries wakes weeks, when special excursion trains were worked to North Wales and Skegness. By 1957 all the major collieries from Talke to Leycett had closed and steam traffic on the railways was to be phased out in favour of diesel operation or electrification on the major routes. Under the Beeching re-organisation Alsager shed closed on June 18th 1962. Staff wishing to stay with British Rail could choose to be transferred and were split between the Crewe and Stoke sheds in roughly even numbers, with one man choosing to go to Northwich.

There were two fatalities among the railway staff. One of the first station masters at Alsager, Donald Macbeth, was knocked down by a goods train on the station's level crossing in May 1865. He was 47 years old and his widow and five children were asked to leave the station house immediately. The second accident happened during the second world war. Driver Owen Wilding, who was over retirement age, was concerned about a faulty injector on the engine. When inside Harecastle tunnel he leaned out of the cab to listen. His head was caught by a projection in the tunnel and he was killed instantly. His young fireman, Hinks, brought the train to an emergency stop at Chatterley station.

Chapter 10

From a Sleepy Village to a Thriving Town.

Queen Victoria's accession to the throne in 1837 marked the beginning of change not only for the nation as a whole but for Alsager itself. The recent Enclosures had redistributed land and altered its use in parts from common to managed farmland. The social structure following from this, however, revealed few extremes. There were no powerful magnates exercising autocratic power from a stately home, no single authoritative family governing the life of the community. The direct line of the Alsager family had died out and there was no resident aristocrat or squire to hold sway over the inhabitants of the little township. Society, therefore, was held together by the middle classes.

Much of the land in 1840 was still owned by descendants of the Alsager family. Mrs Mary Alsager Tryon and Robert Carlisle Pollock, heirs of the Alsager estate, though absent, retained a substantial interest in the soil and the mere. Alsager School land, provided by the Alsager sisters in the eighteenth century, was owned by the trustees. James Stamford Caldwell owned the area around Linley below his home, including Swallowmoor Wood, Mere Lake and Oak Farm. John Galley Jackson owned a considerable amount of land. Other influential landowners were Lord Crewe, the Lawtons of Church Lawton and Randle Wilbraham but their holdings were quite modest. All of these properties were tenanted and farmed. The rest of the land was owned by several individual owner-occupiers like the Edwards family, Michael Ashmore and William Barker.[1]

In 1841 the census revealed that there were 445 people in Alsager. Of these, 22 were farmers, many more were agricultural labourers and a few were skilled tradesmen. No-one was described as a 'gentleman' and apart from two clergymen there were no professional people residing in the village. The information suggests that as yet the village derived its social and economic life from farming with little in the way of outside influences.

The Vestry minutes of this period reflect the social hierarchy of the time with names of farmers like Thomas Lowe of Lane End Farm, the Barkers and the Masseys recurring throughout, alongside the miller, Thomas Holland and

[1] Apportionment of the Rent Charge in lieu of Tithes in the Township of Alsager, 1840. SECSU. ref. D/A/Land/3/1.

John Fox, a publican. All these hard working men were involved in community life and the administration of village affairs.[2]

The building of the railway station in 1848 opened Alsager to the outside world in a way not seen in earlier times. The Staffordshire Advertiser of October 14th reported the opening of the North Staffordshire Railway's new line:

> *"We have this week the pleasurable duty of announcing the opening of the CREWE BRANCH, which will give the district an outlet to Liverpool, Chester and Holyhead as well as for the present to Manchester and the north; and also of the portion of the MAIN LINE which extends from Stoke to Congleton...the opening took place on Monday and although the weather was most unpropitious for out-of-door manifestations, the event was celebrated in various ways in Stoke-on-Trent, Burslem, Congleton and other places, and crowds of spectators thronged the bridges, the approaches and almost every point of view, to see the trains pass."*

Within a few years this accessibility was to attract an influx of population. Some of the affluent pottery manufacturers of Stoke-on-Trent were buying up land in desirable areas, away from the grime of the Potteries, and began to consider Alsager. There were good reasons for their interest. Firstly, it was a peaceful rural village providing a healthy environment to raise a family and secondly it had a direct railway line to parts of Stoke-on-Trent where the manufacturers had their factories. The two factors combined to give the commuting potters a perfect home-base.

The 1851 census again portrayed Alsager as an unsophisticated farming community. The population was about 470 living in 96 households. 265 of the inhabitants had been born within the parish; 217 in Alsager itself. Almost 80% of the population, 376 people, had been born within the county of Cheshire. The majority of those who came from outside were born in adjacent counties, particularly Staffordshire. Of the 82 born in these surrounding counties, 77 were from parts of Staffordshire. Less than 3% of the total population came from further afield. 7 residents had been born in counties not adjacent to Cheshire, 4 people came from Wales and 3 from Ireland. Those from Wales were Mary Webster, the schoolmistress who assisted the curate in the church school, and Harriet Miller, his cook, a blacksmith named Isaac Williams and Elizabeth Preston, the nine year old niece of George Preston. The 3 from Ireland were Patrick O'Garna, Thomas Riley and Austin Riley. Their age difference suggests the latter may have been Thomas Riley's son although this is not recorded in the census. All three were agricultural labourers.

---

[2] Alsager Vestry Minutes 1848-89; CRO. LUAs/3134/8

Most of the population in 1851 worked in agriculture. There were 28 farmers. 24 of these were recorded as being first and foremost farmers while the remaining 4 gave farming as their secondary occupation. 8 of the farms were over 100 acres in size. The largest was Alsager Hall with 200 acres. The property was owned by the trustees of the Alsager estate and farmed by 29 year old John Massey and his wife Sarah. The farm employed 6 men. 4 of these were farm servants, that is, they lived on the farm. The other 2 were agricultural labourers who worked there but resided in their own households. The Masseys' also employed Mary Riley and Fanny Hares as domestic servants. John Massey, with his relatively substantial farm, would have been an important member of the community at that time.

Hole House Farm worked by Thomas Timmis covered 159 acres. The land was owned by the trustee of the late John Ford's estate and tenantedby Timmis. This was a large household of 14 people. Only 4 of these were family members; the widowed Timmis, his 17 year old son Richard and 2 daughters; Jane, who was 15 and Marianne, who was 9. 3 female servants were employed in the house in addition to a dairymaid. 6 boys and young men were engaged as farm servants. Thomas Timmis also employed 2 agricultural labourers.

Lane End Farm, with 100 acres was one of the few farms to survive until the 1980's. Situated opposite the site of the later Royal Ordnance factory, it was farmed in 1851 by the 60 year old landowner Thomas Lowe, and his wife Mary. They were assisted by 3 men who lived on the farm, Charles Barnett, aged 22, George Hickson aged 19 and Charles Hall, who was only 13. Another unknown labourer was employed on the farm but lived somewhere else. In addition to the men, Elizabeth Taylor aged 18 and Margaret Farrington aged 22, helped as domestic servants.

Some of the farmers mentioned in the 1851 census had other, primary, occupations. 3 of these farmers had distinctly industrial jobs. One was a 34 year old mine labourer by the name of Thomas Birch. In addition to his work in the mines he farmed 9 acres. He was born in Audley and probably acquired his mining experience in that area. Another was a machine maker. He was Joseph Edwards. Born in Newchapel, Staffordshire, we find him at the age of 26 not only listed as a machine maker but as a small farmer with 16 acres of land. He employed 2 men but the census does not tell us whether they assisted him with his industrial work or as agricultural labourers. The third of these farmers was 54 year old Samuel Faram, a brick maker with 60 acres of land. He also employed 2 men. Along with these industrially occupied farmers we also find the landlord of The Plough Inn, James Holland. He was aged 50 and was described as a victualler and farmer. He had 23 acres of land.

In 1851 then, Alsager's residents were very dependant on farming. 64%

of Alsager's working population were employed in agriculture. Indeed, the coming of the railway was not detrimental to this state of affairs, bringing as it did, the facility to quickly transport milk away from farms and to bring in the concentrated feeding products developed during the latter half of the century. The noise of clanking milk churns was a feature of platform life as they were collected or returned. This trade demanded different forms of cattle management from those used in cheese-making. The dates of calving changed and the buying in of newly calved cows as others became dry. The trade in cattle increased auction sales and the building up of herds. Winter feeding was expanded, made much easier by the products of the new growth industry of animal feedstuffs from factories established on Merseyside. The greatest single factor influencing herd management was the decline of cheese-making and the rise of milk-selling. Railways made it possible and the ready money made it attractive. North West Farmers Ltd. was formed in 1871 to protect farmers against exploitation in this changing environment.[3]

Most of the other forms of employment, such as domestic service and trades like blacksmithing, were associated with farming or gave indirect support to it. Other traditional skills, important in this kind of community, included wheelwrighting, shoemaking and tailoring. There were also some bricklayers which might indicate the beginnings of growth in the village.[4] Certainly within a few years of this census new homes were built as Alsager began to attract a different kind of resident.

The early years of the railway line through Alsager coincided with the activities of the North Staffs Freehold Land Society whose members were looking for plots on which to build residences to an exacting standard. In 1854 it came to the attention of the Society that a Mr Ashmore of Alsager had seven and a half acres of land for sale. This land was in the area near to the railway station and was therefore highly desirable for those wishing to continue to earn their living in Stoke-on-Trent while living in a pleasant place. On August 3rd of that year the purchase was completed for £850.[5] The land was to be divided into half acre plots and strict stipulations were made. For example, the committee resolved that a clause be added to the conveyance of the land *"not to allow any Beer or Public Houses on the estate."*[6]

[3] W.B.Mercer, *"A Survey of the Agriculture of Cheshire"*; County Agricultural Surveys No.4 1963
[4] 1851 Census, H.O.107\2168, SECSU database ALS51. F. Maxfield, *"Alsager 1851: A Census Study"*; Cheshire History; Spring 1992, No.29
[5] Minutes of the Burslem & Tunstall Freehold Land Society, Horace Barks Library, Hanley, Ref. S810.333
[6] Minutes of the Burslem & Tunstall Freehold Land Society, Special Committee Meeting, August 31st 1854

It is not clear from the Freehold Land Society's minutes who ultimately purchased and built on the apportioned land. However names which occurred throughout the minutes, many of them associated with earthenware manufacture, such as Josiah Wood, John Maddock, Joseph Latham and Ambrose Wildblood, appear in Alsager in subsequent census returns. Other names linked with the Society, like Eardley, Hammersley and Pidduck, also established connections with Alsager. It seems that the movement towards Alsager was a concerted one, concerning several affluent individuals searching for a home to which they could move their families from the unhealthy air of the Potteries while being themselves within easy reach of their businesses. This resulted during the early years of settlement in a concentration of housing in the south-eastern part of the village, known as 'The Fields', close to the railway line.   Today Fields Road takes its name from this early urban development.

The Dudson family who still have factories in Stoke-on-Trent lived at Hope House. Although the exact location of this home is not known there is evidence in the census that James and Jane Dudson lived in Fields Road. In 1871 James Dudson gave a house to his son which had recently been built only yards from the railway station, opposite the present "13 Club". During the Dudsons' occupancy it was known as Ivy Cottage and later Ivy House. Audrey Dudson in her book, *"Dudson: A Family of Potters since 1800"*, mentions the proximity of Alsager's railway station from where they were able to easily reach the factory.[7]

The Goss family, whose pottery is highly prized among today's collectors, also commuted by train. During the 1880's, for example, Huntley Goss cycled to the station each day in order to travel to Stoke.[8]

The attraction of easy access to and from the Potteries was soon recognised as a feature of Alsager life. In 1874 Morris and Company's Directory stated:-

> *"This village has become a favourite place of residence for gentlemen connected with the Staffordshire Potteries, and during the last few years numerous villa residences have been erected and occupied by them - the Crewe and Kidsgrove Junction Railway affording convenient means of transit."*

Other plots of land were privately purchased from the Alsager estate, i.e. from land belonging to the descendants of the Alsager family. In 1865, for example, John Maddock bought land from the curate of Christ Church, the Reverend Charles Alsager Tryon, very close to the railway station and built

---

[7] Audrey M. Dudson, *Dudson: A Family of Potters Since 1800;* (privately printed 1985), p.67.
[8] Lynda & Nicholas Pine, *William Henry Goss;* 1987, p.101

'Brundrett House'. Again there were strict regulations imposed on the conveyance of the land. Although the deeds do not reveal the purchase price there was a condition that any dwelling erected upon it must not cost less than £300 for a single house or £500 for a pair of semi-detached residences. The house or houses were to be built within two years and there was to be no *"Tavern, Beerhouse, Refreshment or Victualling house"*, nor *"any noisome or offensive trade whatsoever"* on the premises. Neither was there to be any building constructed for the purpose of religious worship without the written consent of the Reverend Charles Alsager Tryon.

Maddock was an influential and successful man. His sons followed in his footsteps becoming earthenware manufacturers themselves. Two of them went to the United States of America and imported ware from Stoke-on-Trent. James was influential in politics. He was the mayor of Burslem in 1880 and served on the newly formed Alsager Urban District Council in the later years of the century. Two of John Maddock's daughters were generous benefactors in their later life. Margaret left £2,000 when she died for the upkeep of the Congregational Church in Brookhouse Road. Jane built a pleasant almshouse in Crewe Road which provided homes for destitute spinsters. The building is still in use for elderly single or widowed women.

Like the other upwardly-mobile manufacturers John Maddock and his family brought wealth and influence to Alsager but did not introduce the dirt and commotion of industry. This meant that the nature of the village altered very little but gained from the prosperity of the migrants.[9]

Many of these migrants produced several generations who lived in Alsager for a long time. The Dudsons, for example. Of the family's purchase of Hope House in 1866, Audrey Dudson said: *"This began the family's association with Alsager which was to last for a hundred years"*.[10] Although the Dudsons have gone other potting families remain today. The Weatherbys, for example, came to Alsager in 1906 because they considered the climate to be preferable to the dampness of Trentham. The family continues to live here.

Although the rural charm of the village remained until the middle of the twentieth century the effects of expansion became evident during the late Victorian period in the changing nature of the occupations of Alsager's inhabitants. The 1891 census revealed some interesting differences from the record made in 1851. The intervening decades saw an influx of professional people. The clergyman and a governess were perhaps the only residents in

[9] F. Maxfield, *"Migration from the Potteries to Alsager 1850-1900";-.* Transactions of the Historic Society for Lancashire & Cheshire, Vol.144, 1994.
[10] Audrey M. Dudson, *Dudson: A Family of Potters Since 1800*, p.67

1851 who could be described as following a profession. There was no doctor recorded or other highly or specially educated person. By 1871 Alsager had its own doctor; 32 year old Henry Crutchley. He must have arrived during the decade between the 1861 and 1871 censuses. But the 1891 census included not only the doctor but a dentist, chemist, solicitor and a photographer in addition to engineers, teachers and other professional people. The expanding population provided an attractive environment for professional services. There were now sufficient people, some of whom were very affluent, to make setting up in practice worthwhile.

In 1890 William Burgess, the son of a potter who had moved to Baltimore in the 1850's, became the U.S. Consul for Stoke-on-Trent. He brought his family over on a White Star steamer and they lived at a house in Alsager known as "The Woodlands". The house no longer exists but it stood on the corner of Cranberry Lane where Cranford Park is today.

During William Burgess's time in Alsager (about four years) Colonel William Cody, known as Buffalo Bill, was at the height of his fame and came to Britain to present his exciting Wild West show. According to memoirs left by Burgess's son John, Buffalo Bill visited the family at 'The Woodlands'; an event which naturally thrilled the children and formed a lasting memory in John's mind. William had Indian clothes made for the children and wanted them to spring out of the shrubbery in a mock attack as Buffalo Bill came up the drive but when the time came they were too shy and overawed to act the part. The family visited the show and watched the shooting skills of Ann Oakley. Afterwards they were introduced to Chief Sitting Bull who deeply impressed the children.[11]

The 1891 census reflects not only the growth of the population, which had risen to 1,912, but a new diversity of occupations. Alsager was no longer a self-contained agricultural community. Some of the residents became commuters who travelled to work each day, bringing money and ideas back to the village and using newly provided or expanded services. The imported earnings of Alsager's commuting workers, especially the wealthier manufacturers, helped to support shopkeepers and artisans, whose numbers had significantly increased. For example, while in 1851 there were only 3 grocers, by 1891 the community was served by 13. Some other traditional crafts flourished with the influx of wealth. The 3 tailors and 2 dressmakers of 1851 had been replaced by 18 tailors and drapers with 8 assistants, in addition to 25 dressmakers.[12] Of course, some of these may have worked

---

[11] Extracts from the Memoirs of William Burgess, (Princeton University, U.S.A.), SECSU documentary archive.
[12] 1891 Census, SECSU database Ref. ALS91, H.O.12/2847

elsewhere but it seems reasonable to conclude that this also represents a significant increase of service within Alsager itself.

Growth is also evident in the building of churches during the latter decades of the nineteenth century. These were not only important to the religious behaviour of the community but also provided a social life. Choirs, committees, fund-raising events and so on were all organised by the churches and brought people together. Such activities were also related to the political life of the town as it gave people the opportunity to take responsibility for themselves. Without the patronage of traditional authority which shaped the life of a village like Barthomley, for instance, Alsager's residents were able to channel their social activities into more serious affairs.

In 1894 the Local Government Act provided Alsager with an Urban District Council. Its first meeting was held in the Primitive Methodist Schoolroom on Wednesday 28th March 1894. Present were James Maddock, Henry Crutchley, Robert Sudlow, Samuel Parton, Charles Percy Ford, Frank Rigby, James Barker, Alfred Morris and George Cotton. These represented a cross-section of Alsager's society from pottery manufacturing to farming. Henry Crutchley was the town's medical practitioner and the following month was appointed by the council as Medical Officer at a salary of £15. His place on the Urban District Council was taken over by Dennis Richmond.

One of the council's first duties was to resolve to appoint certain officers who would ensure the well-being of the town. These were to be advertised for in the Staffordshire Sentinel. A Collector for the local rates was to be paid £25 but would have to pay a security of £200. A Surveyor was required and an Inspector of Nuisances at £15 each. Until the surveyor was found Mr Sudlow was charged with the responsibility of engaging and paying men employed on the roads, sewerage and water supply. The rate was to be one shilling in the pound for houses and threepence in the pound for land.[13]

Much of the councillors' business in the ensuing years was concerned with water supply. During the 1890's 12,000 gallons of water were supplied daily to 330 connected houses. Sewerage was also a matter of importance which took up a lot of council time. On the 14th August 1895, for example, members resolved *"That the Wilderspool Brewery Co. be required to provide proper closets and cesspools to their Cottages in Cross Street and that pails be not allowed."*[14]

That year a voluntary fire brigade was formed and £18 was allocated to be spent on equipment. According to the minutes an appliance was already

[13] Alsager District Council Minutes 1894-96, CRO. LUAs/1/1
[14] Ibidem

owned by the council and would be made available for the brigade's use. However, this had to be hauled manually until some time later when a horse-drawn engine was acquired. Later, in the 1930's, the firemen had not yet been provided with a motorised engine and were still wearing the impressive brass helmets with an elaborate curl at the front. Stories are told of the difficulty of first catching the frisky horse from the paddock near the station before a blaze could be tackled!

In earlier times insurance was required before the services of the fire fighters would be employed, otherwise the fire had to be tackled by the occupants of a household and anyone who would help. A very haphazard business. To prove that insurance had been taken out a plaque bearing the policy number was fixed to the front of a building. Many Alsager residents will have seen such a plaque on the wall of Town House in Audley road. This was placed there in the late eighteenth century to show that the occupant Mr John Twiss had paid his insurance premium with the Sun Insurance Company. His policy for 1792-3 detailed buildings, including some in Stafford, contents and sundry items valued to a total of £1300. The premium was £2. 1s. 6d.[15]

There was much discussion about lighting the streets. The District Surveyor was charged with the task of ascertaining the cost of lighting *"with Gas and Electric Light."* On May 20th 1896 a report was put before the council which explained the merits and disadvantages of available systems. Electricity supplied by overhead cables was cheaper than an underground system but was thought to be somewhat dangerous and unsightly. Improvements had been made to gas lighting with the incandescent system and it was decided that the gas company should be requested *"to erect 3 columns at convenient distances apart (namely about 100 yards) and to fit them up with suitable lanterns and incandescent burners specially constructed for street lighting."* Once this pilot project had been accomplished it was felt that 70 such lamps would be required with a capital outlay of about £300. The Local Government Board was to be applied to for the necessary loan to cover costs and a committee established to deal with all matters concerning this issue.[16]

In 1897 Queen Victoria had reigned for sixty years. The Diamond Jubilee was celebrated throughout the country and Alsager made its own contribution. The school children were assembled by the headmaster Mr Peacock and at 2 o'clock, carrying flags and banners, they began a procession

---

[15] Copy of Sun Insurance Company policy transcript, SECSU documentary archive
[16] Alsager District Council Minutes 1894-96, CRO. LUAs/1/1

around the decorated streets. Headed by the St. Barnabas Band from Crewe, they stopped at intervals along the way to sing. The well-to-do ladies of Alsager - the Wilbrahams, the Pooles, Miss Candland, Mrs Godwin and the ministers' wives - provided a tea on the Parsonage Field in a large marquee. The gentlemen in their turn organised themselves into a sports committee and supervised games such as sack races and tug of war for the men and boys with egg and spoon races or needle and thread races for the "fair sex". Mr T. Paxton-Barratt officiated as judge while a large crowd of spectators added to the excitement. Prizes were awarded to the winners. According to the Parish Magazine: *"Everything passed off perfectly in the glorious Queen's weather, and Alsager will long remember with deepest pleasure its Jubilee Day."* Photographs of the procession produced by Adolphus Goss were later offered for sale for the benefit of the Church Building Fund.[17]

The last decade of the nineteenth century was a busy time for Alsager. By 1891 the population was 1,912.[18] With so many more people the town required a strengthening of its law enforcement facilities. Police business had been operating from the cottage at the Sandbach Road junction with Pikemere Road. The police constable resided there and though the cottage provided a lockable cell for those detained in custody it was felt necessary to build alternative premises. Consequently, in 1894, a new County Police Station was erected in Crewe Road at a cost of £650 which provided offices, cells and a house for the chief officer. By 1902 Sergeant Henry Thompson was assisted in keeping the peace by no less than 5 constables.[19]

Around the turn of the century an enterprising man named Joel Settle came to live at a lovely house called 'The Hill' (later renamed by his daughter as The Hall). The house was built in 1863 on land which had belonged to Hole House Farm and was sold to Joel Settle in 1903 by the Mellor family.

Settle was a mining engineer with several business interests. In the early years of the century he was the manager of Birchenwood and Madeley Collieries, owned 70 railway wagons and had a small wagon repair shop at Alsager. He was also a partner in the Liverpool firm of Philip Speakman & Sons. In 1911 he converted this business into a private company known as Settle, Speakman & Company, Limited which brought together his interests in London, Liverpool and Hull. He bought collieries and had a flourishing coal-washing business in several places. Much of the administration was conducted from the office at his home in Alsager.[20]

---

[17] *Parish Magazine,* June 1897

[18] 1891 Census, SECSU database Ref.ALS91, H.O. 12/2847

[19] *Kelly's Directory* 1902.

[20] *Settle Speakman & Co. Ltd. 1860-1960*; published by the company

Having begun his working life at 8 years, old weighing coal in his father's firm,[21] Settle no doubt appreciated the qualities of Francis Joseph, a company employee who was very much a 'self-made man'. Born in Liverpool in 1870 Francis, or as he was later to become, Sir Francis, married Joel Settle's second daughter Violet and became Chairman and Managing Director of Settle Speakman in 1927.

Joel Settle died in 1926. The Alsager Observer and Chronicle in its obituary drew attention to Mr Settle's interest in agricultural matters. He kept a pedigree herd of dairy Shorthorn cows at Home Farm along with pigs and some shire horses. He installed an up to date sterilising plant for the grade 'A' milk produced and was a member of the Dairy Shorthorn Association. Obviously, a man of many talents!

Settle left The Hill to his wife. On her death in 1930 the house was put up for auction but was not sold. Sir Francis Joseph and his wife Violet, the Settles' daughter, bought out the other beneficiaries of the will and made it their home, renaming it The Hall in 1932.[22]

The Settle Speakman Company continued for many years and expanded its operations. The initial wagon repair works at Linley was very modest. Timber used in the workshops had to be taken down the road by handcart to be sawn by a local wheelwright. However, business expanded between 1924 and 1939, resulting in the reorganisation and rebuilding of the entire wagon works.[23] The company continued as a motor body-building works until the last quarter of the century.

However, retracing our steps, before these industrious times much social development took place. Alsager continued to steadily grow as the new century began. It was perhaps the most idyllic period of time for those fortunate to live here. The town retained its rural pleasantness but had much to offer in facilities, transport and religious life. All this was in contrast to Barthomley which had for so long been the administrative heart of the parish but was now in decline. Alsager had developed an independent life with its own administrative and religious structure.

In addition to the political life of the town a great deal of social activity took place which gave people further opportunities to hold positions of influence and authority. Before the First World War several organisations were formed for recreational or charitable purposes. In 1911, for example, a group of men who met regularly decided to formalise their activities into a club. The idea was first suggested by Mr Frank Dutton on the 22nd July

---

[21] *"Memoirs of Joel Settle";* in the possession of Mr & Mrs Croydon of the Hall, Alsager.

[22] Documents in the possession of Mr & Mrs Croydon of The Hall.

[23] *Settle Speakman & Co. Ltd. 1860-1960*

1911. The body, calling itself the B'hoys, was duly formed and had its inaugural dinner on Tuesday August 15th of that year with Adolphus Goss, of the pottery manufacturing family, as the first President. This was to be a socially exclusive club with a charitable purpose.[24] At about this time Alsager Golf Club and the Alsager Club and Reading Room were also established. Again pottery manufacturers featured prominently in the affairs of these organisations. The Postal Directory of 1913 for instance, cites A.H. Maddock as honorary secretary for the Alsager Golf Club. The Reverend G.W. Skene, Rector of Barthomley started the Cricket Club. The town also had clubs for bowling and lawn tennis in addition to the Village Institute which could be used for many community activities.

The area around Lawton Road and Crewe Road developed into the heart of the trading part of the town, particularly around Betley Place, nowadays known as Bank Corner. Along this main highway everything could be bought: fresh eggs and milk, meat and fish, stationery, a full suit of clothes, boots and shoes. The services of a photographer were available, a dentist or a painter and decorator, to name but a few examples.

Even Ernest Craig, Member of Parliament for the Crewe constituency lived in Crewe Road, at Milton House. He was the constituency M.P. from 1912-18 and from 1924-29.[25] He became Sir Ernest in 1927 when he was made a baronet 'for distinguished services rendered'. Born in Houghton le Springs, County Durham, he came to this area as a child when his father, William Young Craig, was appointed general manager of the Lawton and Harecastle Collieries. The family acquired Milton House and after his mother's death in 1907 Ernest Craig took it over and lived there until his death in 1933.[26]

In the intervening years the impact of the First World War was to affect this closely knit community. Seventy-four recruits from Alsager joined the fight, some of whom were among the millions who died. At that time Alsager was a town so pleasantly rural that it still regarded itself as a village and consequently maintained its social bonds. Families from all classes lost sons in the conflict, wealth was no protection. The Settles lost their sons; Reginald in 1916 and Mellord in 1918. Hubert and Raymond, the sons of Adolphus and Sarah Ellen Goss also died fighting at the front. Their mother never recovered from her loss and died in 1919. Adolphus presented a stained

[24] S. Edwards, *History of the B'hoys of Alsager;* (unpublished)
[25] W. H. Chaloner, *The Social and Economic Development of Crewe 1780-1923.*
[26] Unattributed newspaper cutting

glass window to St. Mary's church to commemorate all three and became Chairman of the local British Legion.[27] In 1920 the town erected a monument at the junction of Ashmores Lane and Sandbach Road South inscribed with the names of all those who died in the conflict.

The First World War saw an end to Edwardian life in Britain. Alsager also experienced these subtle changes and continued to steadily grow. Further significant change was not to come, however, until the middle years of the twentieth century when the next international conflict would bring new industry and expansion.

Those intervening years saw the developments which the nation as a whole experienced. Improvements in transport, for example, particularly the use of the motor car and public conveyances, came to Alsager as elsewhere. Band's taxi service which in the later years of the nineteenth century had consisted of horses and carriages, was updated by the internal combustion engine. John Witter, the coal and coke merchant, intermittently used his coal wagon as a 'charabanc' by converting it with a canvas top and seats. On Thursdays it was used to take passengers to Sandbach market. It was also used for day trips further afield by organisations like the Guides.

In the 1920's, Frederick Holland who had a bicycle shop in Ashmores Lane teamed up with his brother Bernard and their friend Walter Hollinshead to establish a garage and car dealership in the old Coop premises at the corner of Wesley Avenue and Lawton road. All had previously worked for the Goss family as chauffeurs and were therefore experienced motorists. Ernest Dean, who was married to Frederick and Bernard Holland's sister, became a 'sleeping partner'. They sold new and used cars, claiming to always have 52 in stock (this was also their telephone number).

However, despite the increasing use of motorised transport, cattle and sheep were still walked from Crewe to the premises of Alsager butchers where the meat was prepared for sale. This practice was maintained until the Second World War. The bicycle also became a popular form of transport for young and old alike. South Cheshire's relatively even landscape made this a favourite means of getting about.

Services were plentiful and local shops prospered as many goods were still bought within the town itself. These flourishing businesses were assisted by transport and the increasing ease of communication as telephones were installed in homes and shops.

Most of Alsager's shops were placed along the roads either side of Betley

---

[27] ***Dolly 1894-1972***, biography of Dolly Harper (nee Goss) by her daughter Doreen, SECSU archive

Place, Bank Corner. Hancock's on the corner itself, now the site of Kwik-Save, became famous for its gingerbread made on the premises. Two flour-covered bakers worked through the night to produce the bread and pastries. At the end of the 1920's a maroon leather-covered cart delivered Hancock's goods around the town. This was replaced by a van driven by Billy McMahon, a local man known for his talent as a comedian. There was also a tea-room over the shop and a garden at the rear.

Other shops in Betley Place during the 1930's were a stationers, an ironmongers, a haberdashery and a greengrocery.

When Holland and Hollinshead established their motor car business in the old Cooperative Society premises, the Coop moved from the corner of Wesley Avenue to where Lawton Road joins Ashmores Lane. The store entrance was in Lawton Road and a laundry operated at the rear. In these early days the shop had sawdust on the floor and sold clothing in addition to groceries.

The telephone exchange was situated where Barclays Bank is today. This was the home of James Clowes who was badly gassed in the First World War. He was a stalwart of the Labour Party and was the keyholder for Alsager Library which at that time was housed in a cupboard in the Institute, just off Sandbach Road North.

Further down Crewe Road was Eddie Ryecroft's cake shop (now Shaffir's Indian Restaurant). Opposite was a wine seller's which later became a wool shop (now the chip shop). The Post Office was housed in what is now Maria's, the florist's, although this had had several venues.(During the early years of the century it had occupied 'The Poplars', the house opposite the garage in Sandbach Road South). A grocery by the name of Boyce Adams was next door to the Post Office and a butcher's shop was on the corner of Cross Street.

Across the road was a sweet shop (now the pet shop) kept by a lady called Nattie Walker. Next door was Wilson's newsagent's and Mr Steele's hairdressing and tobacconist's shop - these properties are now combined in Fryer's newsagent's.

Continuing down the road, the Allman brothers kept a cobbler's shop and Joe Burgess's greengrocery was next door. An entry alongside Joe Burgess's shop led to Alsager Printing Works. At the end of this row, where Kelvin's barber's is today, was a ladies' hairdressing business kept by Amy Durber.

Dorothy Barnett's shop was at that time three separate premises - Mr Dodd's greengrocery, Clough-Kinsman's gentlemen's outfitters and Mrs Smith's sweet shop. These three were opposite Bickerton's which was a high class grocery specialising in teas, spices and condiments.

On the other side of the Lodge Inn was Joe Wildblood's cycle shop, now the Chinese Restaurant. A little further along was Wood's general grocery store. This shop is remembered for its wonderful aromas. Scents of soaps, candles, turpentine, turnips and other commodities filled the atmosphere. Mrs Holland's draper's shop was a few doors further on. After 1930 this became a cobbler's owned by Mr Jones. The next shop was Baddeley's chip shop at the end of the Hall drive and finally, further along Crewe Road where the off-licence and video shop are today was Beswick's milk business.

Despite the economic difficulties besetting the nation during these years, the 1930's were remembered with great affection by Alsager's older residents. Many nostalgic stories are told of ice-skating on the mere in the winter; cricket on the Parsonage Field in the summer. These were also the years of the summer Carnival. This annual event raised much needed funds for local hospitals and was therefore often referred to as 'Hospital Saturday'. In 1931 for instance, under the presidency of Sir Francis Joseph, £435. 2s. 7d. was collected and added to the £19. 17s. 5d. remaining from the previous year's allocation. The money was shared among several good causes; £400 went to the North Staffordshire Royal Infirmary; £30 to the local Sick Nursing Fund; £20 to the Orthopaedic Hospital at Hartshill and £5 to the St. John's Ambulance Brigade. Between 1923 when the Carnival began and 1931 £4,055 was raised.[28] Arthur J. Leadbeater, who was President in 1932 reflected the mood of the age in his foreword to the Carnival programme:

> "*Although at the present moment times are still hard and the road to prosperity seems a long one, recent events lead one to believe that we are at last about to turn the corner, and we cannot better show our gratitude than by doing our utmost towards attaining the £5,000 mark on which our hearts are set.*"

The Carnival was not only an important charity event but was also regarded as a great social occasion. The streets were decorated with bunting. Flags were displayed outside homes. During the afternoon a parade was held which processed through the town from Church Road to the Station, down Fields Road, returning along Crewe Road and on to the Parsonage Field (now the Comprehensive School grounds) accompanied by bands. 'Floats' were drawn by huge dray horses decorated with horse brasses from local farms. Prizes were given for the best costumes of 'Walking and Mounted Characters' and 'Comic Characters'. Jazz bands from other areas and Morris dancers provided entertainment and a Rose Queen was crowned as part of the annual pageant. Stalls and side-shows offered games like hoop-la, a coco-nut shy or

---

[28] 1932 Carnival Programme, SECSU Ref. D\A\Rec\1\1

the wheel of fortune, and sold sweets and ice-cream. It was a special day enjoyed by the whole community.

In 1939 the threat of war once again disturbed life in Europe. In Alsager, significant change was to take place with the building of the Royal Ordnance Factory at Radway Green. This was the most crucial factor in the development of the little town and marked a turning point in its history.

Chapter 11

Alsager in World War Two

Alsager shared many of the experiences of war common to small town communities throughout Britain; the arrival of evacuees, the blackouts and sirens, the presence of the A.R.P. and the Home Guard, rationing and shortages, the absence of many men and women doing war work or in the forces. But the decision to build a new Ordnance Factory on a green field site at Radway Green exposed this small community to massive social pressures and permanent large scale changes. Those who lived in Alsager at the time testify unanimously to the great impact these war years had on the community as a whole and on the lives of individuals within it. Mr. Gilbert Band has described the war as *"nothing less than a watershed in the history of Alsager."*

During the first World War there had been up to 250 armaments factories in production, but these had been closed down in the 1920's, leaving open only those at Woolwich, Enfield and Waltham. Little was then done to restore capacity until 1936, when following the decision of the government to begin rearming, plans were approved for the construction of new factories, the majority of which were to be in areas out of range of German bombers. Strategically placed in an unobtrusive rural location between the railway junction at Crewe and the industrial conurbation of Stoke on Trent, Radway Green R.O.F. was the first and largest of the group of factories, designed for the production of small arms ammunition.

The site chosen consisted of 150 acres of agricultural land requisitioned from local farmers and the Duchy of Lancaster. 40 acres came from Alsager Hall Farm, 60 acres from Lane End Farm and 50 acres from the Duchy of Lancaster. One important consideration in selecting this site was the low range of hills at the back of the site, beyond the railway line, which provided camouflage for the larger buildings and chimneys. But the decision was resented and contested locally. The local Council expressed concern at the potential destruction of the village if an explosion were to occur due to bombing or accident, and at the danger to Alsager from German bombers trying to disrupt the Stoke-Crewe railway line on which the factory would depend.[1]

---

[1] Minutes Alsager Urban District Council meeting 1939.

After the area was surveyed and plans prepared by Mr. Lynam, Surveyor to Alsager U.D.C., the contractors Messrs Trollope and Colls set up their offices on site in October 1939, while layout plans from Woolwich were prepared and revised. The site presented a series of difficulties. The stream running across it had to be put into a culvert, there were several ponds which had to be drained and filled and the ground was sandy, with areas of mixed clay and fine sand, christened "cow-belly" because of its soft, yet springy nature when under load. Special reinforced foundations had to be put in throughout the site.

Another difficulty was access to the site before the 'new road' was built. The scale of building required rapid improvements. A local resident recalls that;-

> "vast diggers and machinery went trundling through the village. We had never seen anything like it." [2]

At first access to the site was possible at the old west gate, over Parton's bridge and by a second bridge adjacent to the sewage works. The present road from the Radway lights under the M6 to Oakhanger was referred to as the 'new road'. It was constructed during the war and replaced the old winding route from Alsager in the Crewe direction.

> "This went down past Lane End farm, past Siddall's farm, over a bridge and brook, then over the railway crossing. Then round and over another crossing and up a lane, to Speed's Corner at Oakhanger." [3]

Building Radway was a race against time, carried out initially during the terrible weather of the winter of 1939-1940 and involving vast numbers of workers, earth-moving and construction equipment. A wet early January added to the difficulties of putting in foundations and was followed by heavy frost and snow falls. A short extract from a report of the construction gives some indication of the scale of the problems faced:-

> "Boilers were installed to inject steam into the sand and aggregate for concrete making, and men and mechanical excavators were working on the main road to Alsager which was blocked by snow drifts for the whole length, in many places 4ft. to 5ft. deep. No snow ploughs were possessed by the local Council or the County Council and men were diverted from construction to enable materials to reach the site.
>
> During this period the excavation for the B. Block site was being started, but the hardness of the ground caused such heavy breakages to mechanical excavators that it was decided to break the top crust with explosives. These shots had to be put in at 6ft. spacing to be any use and it was found that the ground was frozen over 2'6" deep."

---

[2] M. Bebbington, oral testimony, 1999.
[3] Mr. Park, interview transcript, SECSU, 1990.

Subcontractors for the steelwork supply and erection were Messrs. Dorman Long. Hasphaltic were given the contract for roadworks and culverts. Additions and extensions to the buildings on the site went on throughout the war as production expanded to meet increasing demand. Further blocks were built, prosaically each block labelled after the next letter in the alphabet. Drainage and access were continually being altered and improved.[4]

Along with the machinery and building supplies came construction workers from all over Britain, craftsmen and labourers bringing tools and equipment. They found Alsager provided very inadequate accommodation; some slept in peoples' homes and others in haystacks or other makeshift shelters. The navvies were accustomed to living rough but for some it proved too hard.

> *"We were young men in our teens, walked all the way from London to join the team of workers. There was not food or accommodation to be had in the village. We slept in a haystack by pulling out the middle. It was very warm but uncomfortable. The landlord gave us pies when he had some. This was all we had to eat. The last straw came when I drove a tractor into the ditch and was soaked. It took three days for me to dry out so I went home to my mum. Good food, warm bed. War was hard."*[5]

It was essential to the war effort to get the factory into production as soon as possible: by May 1940 a pilot plant employing locally recruited labour was in production.

> *Directed by A.T. Barnard, a leading authority on the production of small arms ammunition, supervised by foremen from Woolwich Arsenal and using machinery left over from World War 1, the workers, by virtue of serving their machines for twelve hours a day for seven days a week were able to begin the manufacture of .303 Mk. V11 ammunition in time to make a contribution to the Battle of Britain.*[6]

Initially the factory was designed to manufacture the components to be loaded, filled and assembled at Swynnerton R.O.F., but after the Royal Arsenal filling factory at Woolwich was destroyed by bombs in September, 1940, loading and filling capacity was added to Radway Green to be followed by a foundry and rolling mill. By the end of 1941, after a supply of press tools was made available from Fenton, the factory became self-sufficient except for raw materials and explosives. The addition of railway sidings linking the packing sheds to Crewe enabled the ammunition to be dispatched to Royal Army Ordnance Storage depots. Peak production eventually reached

---

[4] The Development of the Royal Ordnance Factory, Radway Green, 1939-48. *(R.O.F. Development)*
[5] J.Skinner; Oral testimoney Mr. F.E. Shaw, in *"The Impact of World War Two on Alsager"*, (student dissertation, Crewe +Alsager College of Higher Education, donated to S.E.C.S.U.)
[6] *R.O.F. Development* 1939-48, op.cit. p.8.

a weekly output of 15 million rounds of .303 rifle ammunition and 1 million 20 mm. aircraft cannon shells. The workforce reached 15,000 at its peak.

Alsager U.D.C. concerns about the potential devastation of an explosion were not misplaced. The quantity of explosive used in the factory in the course of a week if detonated *"would have been sufficient to have destroyed the greater part of nearby Alsager."*[7] Strict safety regulations were enforced. Smoking was a sackable offence and safety clothing had to be worn by employees handling explosives. But there was more generalised resentment in Alsager at the coming of the factory.

> *"An ammunition factory was thought to be a dreadful thing. They thought of all the horrors that could happen."*[8]

> *"They took a dim view of R.O.F. being built. Sir Francis and Lady Joseph at the Hall were not too keen."*[9]

Labour recruitment and training were of the highest priority. The nucleus of staff from Woolwich Arsenal, transferred under the direction of Mr. A.T. Barnard, to supervise the layout and installation of the machinery and to train unskilled and semi-skilled recruits to take on the work, had to be found accommodation. Finding living quarters for these men and their families was at first the responsibility of the local billeting officers. But available accommodation in Alsager was limited and after the arrival of the women and children evacuated from Liverpool, it was necessary for the Ministry of Supply to requisition land for housing. 400 prefabricated 'flat topped' houses and flats were built on the Longview Estate to be rented to the London families and later to N.C.O.s from H.M.S. Excalibur.

This represented a very major addition to Alsager's housing stock and to the diversity of the community, given that the prewar population of the village was around 3000 inhabitants. For both the incomers and the residents the situation was not an easy one and relationships were initially not very cordial. One Alsager resident remembers first impressions:-

> *"The village filled up with these southerners. We didn't like them very much. They took control, they took over. They established themselves in the '13 Club'. They played hockey on the Parsonage Field. Young people resented this. The older people resented it."*

On the other hand, the wives of the Woolwich Arsenal workers, used to London life, thought Alsager was rural and primitive.[10]

Alsager Council was more concerned with the practical aspects of

---

[7] *R.O.F. Development*, p.10, op. cit.
[8] Ivy Bailey, oral testimony, 1991.
[9] Nan Barnard, oral testimony, 1991.
[10] Oral tetimony Mrs. S., in Skinner ob. cit.

providing services and working out the consequent rateable value of the properties. It was agreed in 1942 that the rates on a three-bedroom house on the Longview estate would be £ 20 p.a. and on a small first floor flat £10 p.a.

High unemployment in the Potteries, nearly 22,000 unemployed in December 1939, provided a large pool of labour for Radway, the majority of it female. Many of the women had previously worked in the pottery industry but had no experience of engineering.

> *"It was a potentially dangerous job for the women who risked their lives daily filling bomb and shell cases with explosives. Inevitably there were deaths and serious injuries. At Radway they worked twelve hour shifts seven days a week when the factory opened in 1940. They had to be trained from scratch to do precise engineering jobs."* [11]

In order to overcome the skills shortage, complex tasks were broken down into separate operations, which could be learned and carried out by the unskilled workforce. Training sessions were provided for those who needed to know how to use lathes and grinders. But serious skills shortages persisted especially in the tool making section and remained a threat to the maintenance of expanding production, with the introduction of three shift working for the men in June 1941. [12] The factory authorities pleaded with the War Office for the release of toolmakers from other R.O.F.s for a period of six months to train others.

Keeping up morale was very important in the face of long monotonous hours of work in artificial light, little free time and often long periods of travel to and from the factory. Absenteeism and sickness were a constant problem. Wartime indiscipline of the civilian workforce such as absenteeism was dealt with through the courts. Loudspeakers were installed so that workers could listen to Workers Playtime and I.T.M.A. and concerts on the radio. There was distribution of stockings, cosmetics, chocolate and cigarettes. E.N.S.A. shows were put on, at which villagers were welcomed. Notable individuals such as Mrs. Churchill and Duncan Sandys and a stream of officers, wounded war heroes and others came to tour the factory and give pep talks. [13] The women's 12 hour shifts were reduced to 8 in the summer of 1941 and their weekly hours to 48. It was this change which triggered a fresh demand for women workers and the building of the R.O.F. hostels. The men continued to work very long hours (66 hours per week in most cases) but union pressure eventually succeeded in getting reductions to an average of 60 hours per week and Saturday mornings off. [14]

---

[11] *Sentinel publication, The Way We Were,* June 1st 1993.
[12] Superintendent's weekly meetings file, *R.O.F. Development,* op. cit.
[13] Nan Barnard, oral testimoney, 1991.
[14] Superintendent's weekly meetings file; *R.O.F. Development,* op. cit.

Access to Radway remained a problem for Alsager throughout the war. Many of the workers from the Potteries arrived by train at the new station built for them by the factory. But there was a great increase in the volume of traffic through the village generated by the great stream of buses bringing workers in from outlying areas at the change of each shift. The extra volume of traffic necessitated road improvements, the provision of additional pavements and curbing, pedestrian crossings and decisions on where to site bus stops, and road widening in Hassall Road. Complaints were made to the Council about vehicles speeding through the village to the factory and the Council duly complained to R.O.F. The Radway authorities were more concerned about buses being late and not delivering workers punctually, and with the development of adequate bus feeder services to railway stations throughout North Staffs and South Cheshire. Concern was also registered about the shortage of space on the buses and long queues of people wanting to go to Crewe, Newcastle and Stoke, due to the increasing population.

The demands on Potteries labour by the neighbouring R.O.F. at Swynnerton and the build up of three shift working at Radway to meet increasing demand, together with increasing problems of absenteeism and unfilled vacancies reflected the shrinkage in available local employees.[15] Supplying a workforce of directed labour from different parts of Britain, made possible by Ernest Bevin's conscription policies issued in May 1940 and July 1941, was seen as an essential component in the expansion of work in the Radway Green factory. Alsager became the chosen setting for this development. Many possible hostel sites in the area were considered: after much debate, it was decided that the land where Coronation Avenue now stands was unsuitable for the proposed buildings because of the peaty nature of the ground. Finally it was decided that the sites at Fields Road and Hassall Road were the best since each was conveniently situated in relation to electricity, water and drainage services.

Part of Brunds Farm, off Fields Road, was requisitioned by the government as the site of one of the R.O.F. hostels from 1942 to 1943, but it was never filled to capacity. The camp was built using as access the entrance to Barker's sand quarry. The land adjoining Hassall Road (then known as Chapel Lane) was compulsorily purchased from the Bennion family after Ministry of Supply representatives inspected it in August 1940. It had been known as Heath Farm and the entrance to the University campus today is still where the original entrance to the farm had been. A tied cottage stood

---

[15] Superintendent's weekly meetings file, September-December 1942, *R.O.F. Development*, p.10, op. cit.

on the site of the Alsager Campus Library.[16] The farm house was situated to the right of the main gates.

Compulsory purchase could be a brutal business in that time of crisis. Mr. Charles Bennion remembers the government surveyors arriving.

> *"They came in on Thursday at 4.00 p.m. in the afternoon. They were back on Friday morning, a car and van came. They got their theodolite and measuring equipment out on our land, without any agreement. The Ministry of Supply told my father he would have to sell the farm within three weeks. My father pleaded with them to choose another site. But nowhere else was suitable. We had to sell the crops growing. My grandfather was asked to keep an eye on it for them. But there was a nine month delay before they started."*

Work was started on the hostel at Fields Road, which became known as 'The Brunds', in December 1940 by Messrs Hall and Robinson. It was originally designed to accommodate 1152 women while the second, Heathside hostel, in Hassall Road, started a month or two later[17] with J.S. Seddon as contractors, was designed for 768 men. Supervision of the layout and construction was carried out by a Mr. Cole of Trollope and Colls, a London firm, though Royal Ordnance staff had been responsible in the early stages.

The design and layout of both the Fields Road hostel and the one in Hassall Road were inspired by the pre-war Butlin's Holiday Camps, and with advice from the Y.M.C.A.[18] They were described by Mrs. Reuben Wesley as;-

> *"very substantial in terms of air-raid shelters and very flimsy in terms of dormitory hutments."* [19]

Both hostels were of similar construction: a central brick-built communal block, and sleeping quarters of 'Laing' huts with brick built bathrooms attached. Additionally, each bedroom designed to hold two persons had its own wash basin with hot and cold water supply. These rooms were furnished with two single beds, two chests and two wardrobes. Each site was supplied with a waiting room, sitting room, library, sick bay and a small shop with post office facilities. A week's board and lodging, which included three meals a day, and laundry, would cost twenty six shillings and sixpence. The young women (aged between 19 and 30) who lived in these hostels came from all parts of Britain and a wide variety of occupations, many of them from agricultural work in Ireland and Scotland.

During construction the distribution of male and female factory labour

---

[16] Mr. Charles Bennion, oral testimoney, 1991.

[17] *R.O.F. Development* op. cit.

[18] Skinner p.29. op. cit.

[19] S. Wilson, *The History of Excalibur C.P. School, Alsager*, unpublished dissertation, S.E.C.S.U.

requiring hostel accommodation varied, and the allocation use of the two hostels was changed three times, with consequent alteration of the washrooms. Variations in A.R.P. construction also proved a difficulty in completing the work speedily. Heathside Hostel was opened for female use early in 1942 and the Brunds in May 1942. The latter was only in use for a short time as a ministry hostel; demand for accommodation had been over-estimated. All needing this type of accommodation were housed at Heathside and the Brunds was handed over to the Admiralty.

Alsager Council shouldered the responsibility of providing water and sewerage services and refuse collection which provided a major additional demand on the local infrastructure. The building of a new waterworks and the laying of new pipes for water supplies was a major concern of the U.D.C. during the war years. Remarkably the Council was able to provide all the additional water supply demanded at Radway Green, at the hostels and to the Longview Estate and to negotiate a contract to supply Congleton Rural District. Since this was so vital to sustain the growing population and the munitions industry, it is unsurprising that guarding the waterworks became a vital necessity. The Alsager Home Guard was approached to defend it but eventually Western Command arranged for the Lawton Home Guard to undertake the responsibility as the Alsager H.G. was stretched and short of men to cover all its existing responsibilities.[20]

Heathside hostel provided the village of Alsager with wartime entertainment. The need to keep up morale and to provide relaxation for an overtaxed workforce was imperative. Popular celebrities like Violet Carson performed and dances were frequently held there which were attended by those living in the hostel, villagers and marines from H.M.S. Excalibur. The Workers Educational Association initiated a series of well-attended lectures on political and international relations. After the war the tradition continued with folk-dancing events put on by the residents of the D.P. camp at the Brunds.

Shortage of accommodation in Alsager led to further requisition of existing properties and their conversion into flats. The Gables, a large Victorian house with extensive grounds, on Church Road, along with a separate plot on the opposite side of Church Road with access to the Mere, was purchased by the Ministry of Supply early in 1942. Two flats were created, the upper one being taken over by the Food and Agriculture Office in 1945.

Another spacious property, Milton House, was offered to the Council at the beginning of the war in December 1939. The estate comprised the house

---

[20] Alsager U.D.C. minutes, 6.1.42.

and outbuildings set in 8 acres and was offered to the Council for £4,000. The Council Surveyor suggested that if purchased, it could be converted into much-needed new council offices and also provide a site for the new fire station and depot. But it was put to different use. In 1940 the Radway contractors, Trollope and Colls inspected and carried out internal partitioning of Milton House, adding an Annexe and adjacent Games Room to provide accommodation for R.O.F. personnel.

Defence of the munitions factory itself in the aftermath of the fall of France during the summer of 1940 was a priority. By June a platoon of Local Defence Volunteers was formed from among the workers. Within a year this group had been transformed into a factory based company of the Home Guard, the men being given one hour's production time per week for training. Its role was to defend the perimeter and the approaches through the fields and woods in the event of invasion. The internal defence of Radway fell to the War Office Constabulary. [21]

A more pressing and realistic need throughout the war was defence from aerial attack and bombardment: although Radway Green was never the object of an attack by the Luftwaffe, other R.O.F.s near the larger cities were frequent targets. The buildings themselves were reinforced with wire netting over the windows, brick internal partitions and the dispersal of machinery through the plant to keep production going in the case of attack. Civil Defence was organised by A.R.P. wardens raised amongst the workers and they became responsible for spotting aircraft, sounding the alert, and supervising the air raid shelters. In the event Radway Green got away lightly.

The factory records that the longest period in which production at the factory was halted as a result of the alarm being sounded was on the night of 20 December 1940 when the workers sheltered for 7 hours. During this time incendiary bombs and high explosives fell over a wide area of Staffordshire. The Shelton steel works and the Etruria area were damaged and people were killed and injured. One night Swynnerton had a narrow escape when incendiary bombs fell on the factory's railway line, but apart from a single stray bomb falling in a nearby field Radway Green remained unscathed.

Alsager residents have their own tales to tell about the air raid warnings and the bomb that fell in Alsager:-

> *"Nearly every night towards the tail end of 1941 during the intensive bombing of Liverpool and Manchester, we heard the droning of planes, and it was a great toll on the A.R.P. staff because all of them held jobs down...or were at school, because they had to report when they heard the siren. I remember going out at night and studying for School Certificate*

---

[21] Much of the material for this section is from *R.O.F. Development*, op. cit p.12 ff.

down the shelters at Crewe in 1941."[22]

Two days before Christmas 1940, on a bitterly cold evening, Audrey Cartwright and her mother were setting the table at Brookhouse Farm for the two R.O.F. workers living with them, who were expected home from the factory. The sirens were wailing. Suddenly there was a terrific explosion outside, the sound of rushing water and the light of flares dropping all round.

> *"There was a lovely white tablecloth all set out for the R.O.F. workers coming home. My mother and I had a roast in the oven for them and in the centre of the table was a table lamp. We had cleaned up and scrubbed the farm for Christmas and everything was looking beautifully polished. There was a beautiful fire roaring away in the chimney. It was a bitterly cold night outside when all of a sudden there was a terrific bang.. and the beautiful tablecloth was covered in soot which blew down the chimney. The blast toppled the mantle lamp. It scorched the side of my face but I saved the lamp, which would have set the place on fire. The bomb blew the windows out of the farmhouse and the shippon, and killed two cows. It made a huge crater, big enough to have buried a house in. It burst the banks of the big brook which flooded the land, but saved us, it saved lives. People came from miles round, for months and months to see it, from Hanley, Stoke and Burslem. And my father received mail for months afterwards addressed to 'Bomb Farm'."*

Mr. Charles Bennion remembers the occasion when an incendiary bomb and land mine dropped in the fields behind Close Lane leaving a large hole.

> *"We had some shrapnel and a piece of parachute in the house for years from it."[23]*

The organisation of Civil Defence in Alsager itself paralleled that in the factory. Throughout 1938 the Council was considering reports on the development of the A.R.P. Committee by the Air Raid Precautions Officer, Mr. Lynam. He followed guidelines in appointing four representatives from the British Legion to serve on the A.R.P. Committee, arranging for the enrolling of Volunteers and training Council employees. Lectures and instruction on first aid and anti-gas measures were given by a police sergeant and a gas-proof room was prepared in the council offices to contain a steel cupboard for the protection of valuable Council documents. The Town Clerk reported that he had received a communication from the Chief Constable that the telephone number of the Council had been included in the 'Special' and 'Action' lists and asking for an undertaking to be given that in the event of a national emergency, the Council telephone would be manned continuously day and night. The Committee reported progress on the trenches being built on the recreation ground, Home Nursing, and available or needed equipment.

---

[22] M. Bebbington, oral testimony, 1999.
[23] Mrs. Ivy Bailey, oral testimoney, 1991.

It is clear that by the end of 1938, expenses were mounting significantly as people were sent on training programmes, with remuneration for services, car expenses and the cost of purchasing boots, caps, badges and other items. The Council's aim in all of this was to ensure that all grants, loans, and defraying of expenses were met by the appropriate authorities and did not fall on the hapless ratepayers of Alsager, whilst retaining as much local autonomy as possible in the face of mounting demands. The A.R.P. wardens were told in March 1939 that they could use the Council Offices to assemble gas cartons *"subject to payment of heating, lighting and cleaning."* [24]

By July 1939 the A.R.P. Committee was arranging to appoint local people to special posts of responsibility. These Volunteers were key personnel in the expanding preparations for Civil Defence and provided valuable support to Mr. Lynam, the Council Surveyor: Mrs. H. Dudson, First Aid Point; Miss M. Walker, Storekeeper First Aid Appliances; Capt. J. Swindells, i\c Despatch Carriers and Messengers; and Mrs. M.J. Palfreyman, Ambulance and other First Aid Drivers. They in turn organised their own teams of volunteers. Their duties expanded and became more numerous and complex as war approached, engaging in communications exercises, providing respirators for small children, emergency petrol supplies and earmarking of vehicles, supporting the Fire Emergency services and a host of other tasks.

One of the priorities, since the Fire Brigade Act of 1938, was setting up adequate emergency fire services and the Council wanted to purchase No. 61 Crewe Road because it was adjacent to the Mere. Alsager was receiving fire appliances issued on loan by the Home Office, including a trailer pump and hose, which was stored in the Council's Highway Depot. This became the subject of a long running dispute with the Home Office, which flatly refused the Council request for a loan to purchase No. 61 Crewe Road and to hire additional auxiliary firemen. The Home Office thought the expenditure unjustified. In 1939 the contract for fire cover with Stoke on Trent was due to expire and Alsager, after protracted negotiations, entered into an agreement with Sandbach for provision of fire protection on an annual fee basis. The emergency fire officers were organised as the Auxiliary Fire Service. They had to hasten to Fairview by the Council offices when the sirens went. Mr. Norman Fisher was the C.O. assisted by Mr. P. Band who was second in command.

The Council busied itself complying with orders to construct public, surface air raid shelters, which were provided in Linley and Lawton Road, in the centre of town. Alsager citizens were only expected to make use of these if they were out in the streets and not near home when the sirens sounded.

---

[24] Minutes of Alsager U.D. Council, 1938-39.

Eventually there was an issue of Morrison shelters to people in Crewe Road West to erect on their own land as there was no public shelter available.[25] Black out regulations were issued and air raid exercises were held. The Council had to stock sandbags and ensure telephone communications were established between key personnel on the various Council Committees and the Council offices. Much war work was unpaid or conscripted labour! There are local memories of schoolboys filling sandbags.

> *"At the commencement of the war, the youngsters of Alsager were mobilised to go to Barker's sand quarries and fill the bags which were transported to the Council offices and stacked on the outside for protection."*[26]

The volume of work and responsibility shouldered by the Council involved a search for additional accommodation and they were very anxious to acquire Prospect House in the centre of town. The Council was also concerned with camouflage regulations. One of their concerns was the perceived need to camouflage the newly opened wagon sheds belonging to Settle Speakman at Linley. At first Sir Francis Joseph replied that he would put the work in hand, but in fact there were long delays and the Council was clearly concerned that as nothing was done, the sheds might attract German attention with dire consequences for the safety of Alsager itself.

Alsager was littered, as the war went on, with blockhouses (there was one right outside the police station which was cited as obstructing traffic) and command posts (the A.R.P. had a command H.Q. on what is now Alsager School playing field at the intersection of Church Road and Chancery Lane). It had its own Home Guard which used to meet at Wood Corner in Sandbach Road. The Home Guard headquarters were at Grove House in Lawton. It was a very well-run unit under Mr. Gradwell. Rifle practice took place at Brownlow under instruction from Mr. Bill Hollinshead, who had practised target shooting as a hobby before the war. Ivy Bailey remembers them being chased through a field by a bull at Barthomley when they were out on an exercise.

The war affected all aspects of village life. Many women remember having to go out at night in the dark at this time and finding it a rather frightening and novel experience. It was made worse by the blackout conditions and the lack of lights on vehicles moving through the village. One woman fell off the platform at the railway station and had to be taken away in the local ambulance. It was widely believed locally that an ambulance, with its lights *on*, crossing the bridge near Siddall's Farm to pick her up, drew the

[25] Alsager U.D.C. minutes 1st December, 1941.
[26] Mr. G. Band, oral testimony.

attention of the German bombers to the presence of Radway, on the night of the incident described above.

The war undoubtedly transformed the appearance and extent of Alsager in significant ways, but the arrival of so many different groups also changed the social and cultural texture of Alsager life. The streets were congested with traffic and frequent complaints were made to the Radway authorities about vehicles speeding up Audley Road or buses travelling with interior lights lit. In one way the war produced a disciplined and very efficient level of local co-operation but it also unleashed a wilder element which could disturb and challenge local patterns and assumptions.

The pubs in Alsager did a thriving trade in the war, providing for the needs of an expanded clientele. The publican's son at The Plough remembers that the business boomed after the opening of the Radway Green factory.

> *"The workers were on a three shift basis, you know, round the clock. They use to come in before, when they were on nights, they used to call in. And when they were coming off at two o'clock, in the afternoon, they used to call in to get topped up."*[27]

The Railway Inn catered for the   sailors from H.M.S. Excalibur   and Radway workers coming off the trains. Many of these people were on their way to and from the Potteries and when there was any disturbance the publican had to get help from the Radway authorities. Other forms of behaviour provoked dismay.

> *"The chap come from the cottage next door and he said ' Mrs. D.', he says, ' I don't like to complain but my Missus says I've got to complain to you. There's, er, people, er, couples coming off the Radway train and out round to our back door and having sexual intercourse.... it was terrible at The Plough."*[28]

Food rationing was one of the first ways in which the coming of war had its impact on Alsager. At the end of September 1939 the Town Clerk received instructions from the Board of Trade to choose a Food Executive Officer and a Food Control Committee. Local tradesmen were appointed: Mr. George Hancock, grocer and baker, Mr. R. Beswick, milk dealer, Mr. A.J. Dodd, greengrocer and Mr. G. W. Mitchell , the manager of the Alsager branch of the Butt Lane Industrial Co-operative Society. By the following January the National Register proposed to include Alsager with Sandbach for Food Control administration. There were certain areas of autonomy which Alsager did not want to relinquish, and the the authorities agreed to Alsager's proposal to keep a separate Food and Control Committee, and to control the slaughter and distribution of meat. The system seems to have run efficiently

---

[27] Mr. P.1. 90A, p.4., interview transcript held in S.E.C.S.U.
[28] Mrs. D. 1. 90A, interview transcript held in S.E.C.S.U.

at local level without any notable complaints being received by the Council. Alsager was still semi-rural and the farms round about could supply some items on the black market at first.

> *"I think people coped with the rationing very well indeed. Well, I mean, all right there was a little bit of a black market, ... home cured bacon and farm butter and things at the beginning of the war, but even that dried up later on."*[29]

It is not clear how widespread in Alsager was the practice of keeping pigs and poultry to enhance domestic food supplies but in 1940 the Council received and agreed a memorandum from the Ministry of Health suspending the restrictions of pig keeping on housing estates and the next year were asked to enforce the Domestic Poultry Keeping regulations.

The development of allotments for food production had a big impact in Alsager. Local authorities were empowered at the beginning of the war to take possession of unoccupied land or to enter into agreements with owners to make such land available where it was suitable. In 1939 Mr. Rogerson offered the U.D.C. part of his tenancy of Parsonage Field, held from the Trustees of the Alsager Free School Charity, to be used free of rent as allotments. The ground was situated at the rear of the Marl Pits and was considered unsuitable. Mr. W. McClurg offered to let to the Council free of charge, 4.5 acres of land and the Council resolved to take up the land if more was required.

The Council was under pressure from Ministry of Agriculture, Fisheries and Food to increase and satisfy demand for allotments and intensive land use. In 1940 it agreed to turn over the football playing area of the recreation ground for cultivation. The secretary of the Alsager Football Club enquired whether the Club should proceed with the arrangements for the second half of 1940-41. He got the green light to go ahead, but in vain. In February 1941 a notice was received from the Cheshire War Agricultural Committee requiring the Council to plough up the football playing portion of the recreation ground by March 31st next and to prepare the ground for the cultivation of a 1941 crop of oats. The Council resolved to inform them that such action had already been taken![30]

It proved difficult to match supply and demand for allotments. By the end of 1941 there was a shortage of land and an inundation of applications, but by August 1942 demand was running out. The succession of Dig for Victory campaigns in 1941-42 had encouraged more people to grow vegetables in private gardens.

---

[29] Mrs. B. 1. 88A, interview transcript, S.E.C.S.U.
[30] Minutes, Alsager U.D.C. 1940-42.

Much farmland in Alsager was requisitioned for building purposes or for the installation of amenities. The growing, incoming population and the expansion of industry tipped the balance towards urban and away from agricultural use, at a time when agriculture generally was so vital to the war effort. Labour shortages were met in a variety of ways, but round Alsager most notably, by Italian prisoners of war who were housed in a purpose-built camp at Snape Farm, Weston, on land requisitioned from the farmer Mr. Reg Williamson. Frank Coles, the camp commander, had previous experience of managing P.O.W.s, including British fascists at Huyton in Liverpool. Farmers were allowed one Italian each to work on their land. Many of the Italians went off in buses each day to work in Crewe: those on the local farms received varying treatment.

> *"Farmers would ring up and say 'what sort of bloody chap have you sent me' or even sometimes make them eat in their shippons. There was always some complaint. Some of the farmers were awkward and wouldn't give them a drink. They each had their timesheets from the Agricultural people in Crewe. A lot were from Turin and the North but also from the South. The ones from the North couldn't understand the ones from Sicily."[31]*

However, many of the Italians dated local girls, married and stayed on in Crewe after the war. Mr. Bennion at Heath Farm had not only Italian prisoners of war working for him, but also German P.O.W.s from Crewe Hall, including one who was a trained vet. One stayed on after the war, before returning to Berlin.

A great deal of work was undertaken during the war to provide an adequate water supply to the growing population by expanding waterworks capacity, sinking boreholes and putting in pipes. The night soil cart was marginalised progressively as the houses in the village were sewered up in the wake of the massive sewerage schemes required for the factory and hostels.

Alsager certainly emerged from the war with a greatly improved utilities infrastructure, thanks to the dedicated work of the Council Surveyor, the backing of the relevant Council Committees and fruitful co-operation with Radway and the ministries.

Many groups of military and civil workers were stationed temporarily in Alsager during the war; for instance, detachments of the South Staffordshire Regiment were billeted for a year in the large Victorian houses, commandeered for them in Station Road. But the evacuees from Liverpool, for whom meticulous and dedicated preparations were made over a considerable period of time, caused more concern and stayed for a much shorter time than anticipated. The Council was asked by the Ministry of

---

[31] Oral testimony, Mr. John Williamson, Snape Farm.

Health to begin making preparations in January and February of 1939 for house inspections by lady volunteers known as 'visitors'. 400 houses were inspected. Evacuation procedures were being drawn up in Chester at the time. A window card was prepared by the Ministry of Health for display in the windows of those householders who had undertaken to accommodate unaccompanied schoolchildren in their homes if war broke out. In August 1939 Mr. J.B. Harwood was appointed Evacuation Officer and Mrs. Harpur, Chairman of the Council was appointed with Councillor Barber to the Evacuation Tribunal. Oak Villa in Station Road was to be rented as a reception centre. Wright's Shop in Lawton Road was to be in temporary use as a medical examination centre, and the local Medical Officer of Health announced the takeover of St. Mary's schools as a fully equipped first aid post. Vast numbers of blankets were bought or borrowed along with mackintosh overlays for young children. The Ministry of Health said it would be supplying beds later. In the event, the evacuees only stayed eight weeks and then returned home when no bombing occurred during the phoney war. We have a graphic eye-witness account from a wartime diary kept by an Alsager schoolgirl of fifteen;-

> *"On the 1st September we were told that the evacuees were coming and we spent the day filling palliasses with straw, and on the 2nd September, that was the day before war broke out, the evacuees came and we marshalled them into St. Mary's Church, and in my diary it said, Whoo.. they were horrid. You saw them to their billets and I was on duty at Oak Villa.. and I remember we rocked a baby to sleep on a handcart as we took the bedding round. War was declared on the 3rd September and we spent the day unpacking rations after our return from the Hall, where I was when war was declared and we took bedding out and dealt with evacuee complaints and there were many complaints. And a lot of the evacuees took off and went to Winsford, they refused to stay here. And all through my diary I have got about stamping ration cards; reporting for duty; taking blankets out on the handcart and all this ..up to 25th November. But I remember the bedding was so filthy off the evacuees who'd gone back, that there were bugs, I'd never seen a bug in my life and my mother was horrified when I went home and told her we'd been killing bugs. And we had to burn all the bedding in the yard at the back of the Council Offices."[32]*

American G.I. officers were billeted at The Rectory in Barthomley from 1944 and the troops were out at Weston. Some of them used to walk up to The Plough past local children who sat on the fences in the lane past Radway, calling *"Give us some gum, chum!"*[33] Alsager locals were amazed to see coloured Americans as there were no black people in Alsager in those days. Some of them went out with Audley girls and after the G.I.s vanished from

---

[32] Mrs. B. 1. 88 A, interview transcript held in S.E.C.S.U.
[33] Oral reminiscence, Mrs. I. Johnson.

the area before the D-Day landings, a number of coloured children were added to the population of the area.

The Admiralty acquired the R.O.F. hostel site off Fields Road in 1942 when it became surplus to requirements, and used it as a naval 'dry land' training ship for young officers. The local story goes that when the officers sent down by the Admiralty to inspect the site they had to name the new 'ship'. Walking by Alsager Mere its appearance put them in mind of the Arthurian legend about the hand rising mystically out of the water to receive the king's sword, so they dubbed it H.M.S. Excalibur. They put six cutters on Alsager Mere for rowing practice, which on Alsager Council's request, in December 1942, they accessed by Sandbach Road, through a garden belonging to Mrs. Holland which had just been planted up at some expense by Waterhouse's Nurseries. The N.A.A.F.I. was at the back of The Cedars and was run by the W.V.S.

> *"The trainees were very conscious of being watched all the time because wherever they went they used to chant OLQ which was 'Officer like quality'. And they were hopping up and down on the right side of the road so that if you went out with any of them you know, they always stood on the outside."*[34]

From 1944 the base was run by the Fleet Air Arm as a training ship for young marines, 17 year olds, who completed six weeks training in Alsager before moving on elsewhere in the United Kingdom. Local residents remember watching lorries full of marines going from Bank Corner down to H.M.S. Excalibur.

The young sailors from H.M.S. Excalibur contributed to the youthful social life of the village, going out with the local Alsager girls to tea dances, to talent contests and the cinema in the Heathside Hostel. They were very welcome in the village as so many of the local young men were away on war service. Inevitably, some married local women and stayed on in Alsager when most had left. They put on P.E. displays and demonstrations on the Parsonage Field which local people enjoyed watching.

After the end of the War, when the navy no longer needed the site, Excalibur became a camp for Displaced Persons, and Alsager became a temporary home, though in some cases a permanent home, for Baltic refugees. The Baltic states had been invaded by the Russians in 1940, were then occupied by Nazi Germany until 1944 and then returned in 1944 to Russian influence. Many of the refugees fled in small boats to Finland or Sweden, or even to Germany, anywhere to escape the Russians. Those who came to

---

[34] Mrs. B. 1. 88A, p.28, interview transcript S.E.C.S.U.

Alsager had arrived in Hull during 1947 and 1948, after being displaced in Germany. The men were being found work in different parts of Britain. Until they were earning enough to be able to afford accommodation for their families, their families were housed in temporary camps like Alsager Excalibur. Latvians, Lithuanians and Estonians were housed in Excalibur. The Estonians spoke a language related to Finnish, whereas the Letts and Lithuanians spoke Slavonic. Such differences were sometimes overlooked by the bemused population of Alsager. One Estonian D.P. Mrs. Richard Tulp, remembers when questioned that:-

> *"It was very nice in Alsager.. they were very friendly... but they thought we were all Polish."*

Many of the Balts had German as a second language, and conversed with one another in it, but some had studied English as well. On arrival in Britain they had no money.

> *"When we came here we didn't have a penny. We all got a pound from a charity like the Red Cross in Hull".*

The British Red Cross had played a significant part in bringing them over to Britain. Once in Excalibur the women held a little exhibition of knitting and embroideries, to which they invited local people, and they began to make some money out of sales. In one part of the barracks wooden toys were being produced.[35]

Meals were eaten in the old navy canteen and the families had small rooms of their own. The barracks were near the entrance, 24 rooms in each long building. There were twelve or more of these on each side. 300 to 400 people were housed here and the camp was for a while very full. There was a separate building painted white which housed the laundry and sick bay. Only women and children lived in the camp, the husbands only coming at weekends.

Complaints and queries were dealt with by Miss Hughes who lived in Alsager, and for 8-9 months Mrs. Tulp assisted as interpreter and translator. There was an office on site placing displaced persons and Alsager women into cleaning and canteen work, but many of the displaced persons found it difficult to get work.

A school was opened in the camp for their children where they had English lessons from Mr. Fielding and Mr. Armstrong who spoke fluent German. During the 1950's there were still children of Baltic parentage attending schools in Alsager.[36] Later the site housed the primary school (see chapter 7 for details) which adopted the name of the naval base. The school

---

[35] Notes from interview with Mrs. Tulp, 18.10.91.
[36] M. Bebbington, oral testimoney.

moved to its present location in Ivy Lane in 1965 where it used to display the Excalibur Plaque presented to it by the Council some years ago.

Some of the refugees from Excalibur used to go to Alsager Training College to sing national songs, for dancing and entertainment. It is clear that the wartime practice of using the Heathside Hostel as an entertainment centre for Radway workers, Alsager residents and Excalibur personnel was still alive down to 1948. One Estonian, Mr. Racid, played an accordion there to accompany the national folk dances performed in national costume.[37]

Eventually most of the inhabitants of the D.P. Camp moved away to the places where their husbands worked and the government closed the camp down after all had been permanently relocated. One Alsager resident remembers speaking with them in German and recalls that;-

> *"they were all requesting to be sent on to Canada or Australia".*[38]

The site became the property of Alsager U.D.C. who turned it over to industrial use. It was purchased from the Council by Freshpack Ltd who have since redeveloped large areas of it. Some of the old wartime buildings can still be seen having been converted to a variety of uses on the industrial estate. Others have been totally or partially demolished to make way for their successors.

It was certainly a great relief to all who had lived through it when the war ended and some of the strains and stresses were over.

Victory in Europe was celebrated in Alsager as elsewhere in the United Kingdom with public displays of relief and rejoicing. Appropriate rituals were observed. The Council played a leading role in planning what was to happen. Residents were asked to put out flags and bunting to decorate the streets, and the Alsager Times states that there was *"a ready response"*. The Council Minutes of May1 stae the decision to request helpfrom the Royal Ordnance Factory at Radway Green and H.M.S. Excalibur in finding suitable flags. The Council offices were clearly the focus and meeting point for the diverse activities arranged. On the evening of V.E. Day floodlights lit the offices and a crowd gathered to hear the King's broadcast to the nation. A procession led by the Alsager Army Cadet Force, made its way along Hassall Road to the Marl Pit, sited on land now belonging to the Alsager Campus of the Manchester Metropolitan University. There a 'huge bonfire was lit' by two schoolchildren and an address given by representatives of the three major organisations dominating village life during the War, the Chairman of the District Council, James Edwards, Mr. L.S. Flatman of Radway Green and Lt-Col. Webber, R.M. The text of the speech was printed in full in the Alsager

---

[37] Notes from interview with Mr. Richard Tulp, 18.10.91.
[38] Mr. B.1.88 A, p.22. interview transcript held in S.E.C.S.U.

Times. It must have been a moving if brief address, playing to local as well as national patriotism, in stating:

> *"The war in Europe has ended, and nowhere more than here, in this beloved village of ours, amongst the beautiful architecture of nature, could we realise to the full the blessings and freedom with which we are endowed."*

The Council minutes tell of the use of broadcasting equipment from the Royal Ordnance Factory so the King's message could be heard be everyone. It was recorded on 12 June 1945 that grateful thanks were extended to Kidsgrove Gas Company who provided floodlighting for the occasion, free of charge.

The churches also engaged in acts of celebration, thanksgiving and fundraising.. There is record of services held at Wesley Place Methodist Church. At St. Mary's a collection was held for the restoration of war damaged churches throughout England. The following Tuesday in St. Mary's Church Hall a Victory dance was held. Even as these events were taking place, however, thoughts were turning to reconstruction including future needs and policies. The Chairman of the District Council referred in his V.E. Day speech to the Council's continuing responsibilities for: salvage collection, fostering the savings movement as well as the local administration of Food and Fuel Control. In addition he spoke of the Council's decision to help the pressing post war housing shortage by the purchase of land for building 100 houses.

Chapter 12

Village Miscellany,
People, Places and Things.

This chapter includes a number of subjects and items, details of which have been found by the authors during their research for material included in the more thematic chapters of the book. Whilst it has proved difficult to incorporate this material elsewhere it is felt that it adds colour and interest to the book as a whole and forms part of the story of Alsager and Its People. Accordingly gathered together here are items regarding people, organisations and events which have contributed to village life over many years.

People

Thomas Sidway

According to the parish registers the Sidway family were only living in Alsager for three generations, but as the registers only begin in 1562 and the first reference to the family is the marriage of Thomas senior in 1581 it is uncertain whether the family were here earlier or whether they arrived as servants of Lord Brereton about this time. However, the records contain details of three generations and it is with Thomas junior that this section is principally concerned. The record begins with the marriage of Thomas Sidway to Elizabeth Alsager at Barthomley church on the 9th December 1581. Shortly thereafter baptisms are recorded, John in 1583, Anne in 1584, Ellena in 1586, Margaret, *'daughter of Thomas Sidwaye of Awger'*, in 1596; this is the first positive indication that Thomas was living in Alsager. Infuriatingly, there is no record of the baptism of Thomas junior, but as Thomas and Elizabeth were still producing children in 1596 they were almost certainly his parents; although it is just possible that John, born 1583, might have been his father. Thomas junior later called his own eldest son John and his second son Thomas. Nor is there any reference in the registers at Barthomley to the marriage of Thomas, but this may result from him marrying outside the parish.

The family appear to have exercised some influence in the township. In 1590 Thomas sen. was witness and overseer to the will of Randle Hilditch, and an appraiser of the inventory of Randle Brereton in 1595, both tenants of Lord Brereton. Thomas died in 1628, unfortunately his will and inventory do not survive. After this date Thomas jun. appears as an appraiser to the inventories of Thomas Hilditch in 1631 and his wife Amie in 1635, who are both likely to have been from the Bank or Bank House tenement, and those of Richard Alsager of Brook House in 1647, and Thomas Hilditch of The Hole in 1657. All the above were tenants at one or other of Lord Brereton's Alsager holdings; our Thomas was his bailiff and one wonders if his father had been so before him.

Thomas's real claim to fame comes in the aftermath of the civil war, see pages 44-45. The earliest document relating to his conduct in this period is dated March 1645 and includes the following passage-;

> *"his delinquency that he assisted the Lord Brereton in raising forces against the Parliament."* [1]

This is followed in the next document with more details;-

> *"The Humble Petition of Tho Sidway in ye county*
> *of Chester yeoman.*
>
> *Humbly showeth that your petitioner being Bailiffe and tenant to the Lord Brereton was by his ingagements and the commands of his Lord and Master (through ignorance at the beginning of these unhappy warrs) so farr deluded as to warne the Tenants to appeare, and doe as he was appoynted and in some particulars so to demeane himself as that he was brought under the notion of a Delinquent . . . ."*

Had Thomas mustered Lord Brereton's Alsager tenants when his lord was raising troops for the crown? It has been noted that several of the Brereton tenants had arms and military equipment included in their inventories, and their leases contained clauses requiring them to provide some form of military service in time of war.

The summary of Thomas's assets, also included in this collection of documents, clearly states that he was the tenant of two Brereton holdings in Alsager but to date these have not been identified. In addition to these holdings in Alsager Thomas appears to have had an interest of sorts in land at Harecastle. A somewhat cryptic entry in 'The Order Book' of the Stafford Committee,[2] that is the Parliamentary ruling body in the county, for 8th November 1644 reads;-

> *"Burnes.*
> *Whereas Mr. John Burne receyves of Mr. Willm. Bourne his sonn 20li. yearly forth of his estate at Ewtree It is ordered that the said Mr. John Burne shall pay forth of his said annuytie the weekely pay that shall be payable for the same.*
> *Sidway.*
> *Whereas Thomas Sidway of Alsager receyves of Mr. John Burne of*

---

[1] Refs PRO. SP. 25/177. fols. 807 and 808.

[2] SHC. 4th Series Vol. I. p. 204.

Harecastle for a certain tearme by way of mart 20li. yearly for payment of
which part of the said Mr. Burnes estate is engaged for It is therefore
ordered that the said Thomas Sidway shall pay the weekely pay
proporionate for the same duringe the contynuance of the said terme."

It will be recalled that Thomas had to borrow £60 in order to pay his
fines in 1645, *"that so he might be inabled to maintain his aged wife and 8*
children". The age of his wife is not recorded but details of the baptism of
seven children do appear in the parish registers which suggest that his eldest,
John, would have been 23 years old in 1645 and the youngest, Richard, 12
years old. His wife would not be quite the toothless crone that the documents
suggest!

Thomas died in February 1662 and his will and inventory survive. His
will makes reference to the following leasehold, additional to his Alsager
holdings;-

". . . that parcell of ground I have in Foxley Sprink beinge in quantitie
about twelve Statute Acres . . . which I tooke from William Boughy of the
great oake in Erdley end . . .duringe . . . the terme of the original Lease
thereof. . . . "

It also refers to the possibility of his 'aged' wife, Ann, marrying again! The
will bears his signature rather than his mark.

His inventory totals £309.10.6., a considerable sum for the time. The
Foxley Sprink lease is valued at £70; his livestock, comprising eight cows,
four twinters and four calves, two mares, a nag, ten sheep and two swine, at
£71.17.4; household effects £82.12.6; implements and husbandryware £19.2.4;
crops and produce £44.18.4; money and apparel £10.0.0., and debts owed to
him £11.0.0.

His eldest son John probably succeeded him in the Alsager holdings, at
any rate later that year, 1662, he is shown in the Hearth Tax Assessments as
occupying a house with four hearths; as big as any house in Alsager.

Ann, Thomas's wife, appears to have died in 1666, his son John in 1684,
and thereafter the few remaining references to the name in the parish registers
all relate to Barthomley. One final detail remains to be told. In 1733 Richard
Parrott of Bignall End, Audley, produced his *"An accountt off the parish of*
Audley in the county off Stafford. And a particular off most of the estates
shewing who has enjoyed them for about 200 years last past."[3] In this he
describes his wife's descent in a somewhat odd way;-

". . . 6 generations ago one Gabriel Smith enjoyed it. He had one son and
one doughter. His son dyed parson of Aulem. . . . . The parson off Aulem
marryed Elizabeth the doughter of John Sydway of Alsager in Cheshire. He
had issue 4 sons named Gabriel, Abraham, Isaac and Jacob. They are al

[3] Parrott 1733. SHC. 1944

dead. He had two doughters, Dorothy and Anne; Dorothy is dead, Anne (Mrs Richard Parrott) is living . . ."

The Twiss Family

In a manner not dissimilar to that of the Sidway family, members of the Twiss family also appear in the records of the Township, and elsewhere, holding positions of some influence, and then depart with little trace.

They are of interest for two specific reasons. The first is that the family has left a prominent physical mark on Alsager, in the shape of 'Town House' in Audley Road, which they built around the year 1790, and for which an insurance policy exists, dated 1st October 1792,[4] referring to Mr. Twiss's new dwellinghouse and to various older stables, barns, outbuildings and contents. The policy can be linked to the house which still carries the insurance badge, bearing the policy number, clearly visible, high on the front wall.

The second mark the family made is that from a very early date they were connected with commercial activity, being in business as carriers. Unlike other local tradesmen and craftsmen they appear to have looked outwards from Alsager in order to develop and extend a business activity conducted successfully here for a number of generations. This resulted in an expansion of their commercial activity in the closing years of the 18c., when they were competing with such firms as Pickfords on a regional basis.

The first reference to the family comes in the Barthomley parish registers. As early as 1604 these record the birth of *"Jacobus Twisse, son of Oliver Twisse of Crue"*. After a further reference to Minshull Vernon the family became domiciled in Barthomley parish, with the first reference to Alsager being in 1635 when a Thomas Twisse is described as *"servant or apprentice of Thomas Hancocke of Alsager"*. In 1695 the birth of Joseph, son of James Twiss of Alsager, is recorded. From the Audley parish registers it appears that this James Twiss married a Sarah Boughy of Audley in March 1684 and some of their children were baptised in that parish, as well as at Barthomley, during the period 1685 to 1705. At this time no distinguishing trade or social description is added to the register entry.

Writing in 1733 Richard Parrott[5] refers to 'Thomas Twist' of Alsager, a carrier having married the daughter of John Henshall of Miles Green, Audley, and at the time of writing Thomas was in possession of the former Henshall holding. There is no record of this Thomas in either the Barthomley or Audley parish registers but the name Thomas does recur in the Twiss family. About the same time John Twisse of Alsager was variously described in the

---

[4] *Sun Insurance Office, Policy No. 605393.* Copy of typescript at SECSU.

[5] Parrott 1733. SHC. 1944

registers as 'husbandman' in 1722, 1728, 1729, 1731 and 1733; 'farmer' in 1723 and 1724; and 'carrier' in 1722, 1725 and 1726. This same John Twisse appears as a witness to the will of Robert Proudlove in 1715 and an assessor of the inventory of Joseph Alsager in 1729. Ormerod, in his pedigree of the Alsager family, reproduced in his History of Cheshire, makes reference to a Margaret Twiss or Twist, wife of Raphe Alsager of the late 17c. and in respect of whom there was a post nuptial settlement made in 1729, but to date no evidence of the relationship, nor the identity of Margaret, has been discovered.

By the second half of the 18c. it is clear the family was well established as a local firm of carriers. All male members of the family were described as such in either the parish registers or their probate documents, with the exception of poor Samuel, who died in 1771 described as a lunatic! In the same year there is evidence that the Twiss' business consisted of rather more than a man and a cart; John Hall is described in the parish registers as *"Outrider for Mr. Twiss"*, and in 1790 the same documents record a Robert Hamblett of Alsager *"waggoner"*.

It was John, son of the poor demented Samuel, who appears to have expanded the family business and fortune. He was born in 1740 and died in 1804. It was he who built the front section of Town House and whose policy for 1792-3 detailed buildings, including some stables in Stafford, contents and sundry items valued to a total of £1,300. The premium was £2-1-6. By 1771, the date of his father's death, John was a township officer acting as Overseer in 1771 and 1798; Surveyor in 1773, 1778 and 1788; and Constable in 1775, 1785, and 1792.[6] In 1778 he undertook the taking down and rebuilding of the bridge at Crappilow at a cost of £3-7-2. This is the bridge where Sandbach Road crosses the stream by the Wilbraham Arms, presumably the reference is to a foot-bridge, the road would cross the stream by means of a ford. In 1788 he drew heavily on his own commercial resources when acting as surveyor and paid significant amounts to himself for this contracting. During this period he was appointed trustee of the estate at Ravens Lane, Bignall End, held by Barthomley parish as educational charity land. In August 1802, John Crewe, later first Lord Crewe, writing to the Rector of Barthomley on this matter wrote;-

> *"There can be not the smallest doubt but Mr. Twiss as Trustee has the sole power of letting the estate and I do not think it could be placed in better hands . . ."*[7]

During this period the business was expanding. There is a reference to

---

[6] Alsager Town Book, 1771 - 1863. ref. CRO. P.278/11

[7] Barthomley Charity Papers, Barthomley Church.

a 'John Twist', in Elizabeth Raffald's Manchester Directory of 1772, operating a weekly waggon to Birmingham from the 'White Lion', in Deansgate, each Friday. By 1773 he was operating from premises in Dolefield, clearly shared with other carriers travelling other routes. The fullest entry occurs in 1794 and reads;-

> *"Birmingham through Congleton, Newcastle-under-Lyme, Stone, Stafford, Litchfield, Walsall. NB goods are forwarded to Oxford, Bristol and all parts of the West of England. John Twiss comes in and goes out Tuesdays and Fridays, 69 Bridge Street"*[8]

In January 1795 an advertisement appeared in the Manchester Mercury offering a reward of £5-5 following the theft of cloth, in Manchester, from John Twiss carrier; and in 1796 there was reference in the same paper to Twiss's warehouse in Dolefield, Manchester. In Aston's Manchester and Salford Directory of 1804 Higginson, Twiss and Co. are shown to be operating out of Star Yard, Deansgate and running waggons to London each day other than Sundays. One of their principal competitors was Thomas and James Pickford and Co. But it was not only on the roads that the Twiss business transported goods, they had canal boats also as is shown by an advertisement in the Staffordshire Advertiser, dated 11th August 1804, notifying the public of the formation of the 'Inland Navigation Association for Apprehending and Prosecuting Felons'; there were thirteen names attached to the notice including those of John Twiss and Co., and of T. and J. Pickford and Co.

John's son, also John, succeeded him as his heir in 1804, although he had moved his home to the Boarded Barns in Odd Rode on his marriage in 1798.[9] Copies of the Court Roll of the Manor Court of Audley testify that he was admitted as the heir of his father to the copyhold estate held by Barthomley parish for which he also was the trustee. The Barthomley charity papers read like the draft of one of Trollope's Barchester novels from this time until John's death in 1817, their story would make a book in itself. Unfortunately the correspondence is incomplete but it is clear there was no love lost between the Rector, Edward Hinchliffe, and Twiss. Reading between the lines it seems that Hinchliffe considered himself the most important man in the parish by far, after Lord Crewe, and resented Twiss's authority as trustee. Twiss was far from being a perfect trustee, the parish had persistent difficulty with him in getting him to give account of his stewardship. It also seems that there were doubts as to his financial soundness. The general tone of the correspondence can be seen from one sample letter written by Twiss to Hinchliffe, like many of his letters, undated.

---

[8] Scholes Manchester Directory 1794; Manchester Central Reference Library.

[9] CRO. DBW/L/-7,8, 13, 14, 24, 27, 28, and 29.

> *"Mr Twiss has things of more importance to himself to attend to (on leaving home) than such an Account that concerns the <u>Parish</u> of Barthomley, he will enter the Account in the Book on his return when Mr. Hinchliffe will have an opportunity of <u>Scrutinizing</u> it.*
>
> *Rode Thursday Morning."*

Perhaps the concern of the Rector was justified. Although the Baker-Wilbraham papers make reference to John Twiss, carrier at Odd Rode, erecting buildings at Boarded Barns to use as warehouses, wheelwrights' and blacksmiths' shops, and stables for his carriers business, he seems ultimately to have been unsuccessful commercially. Enties, unaltered from 1794, continue to appear in successive Manchester Directories until 1814 but by 1818 the entry reads, *"J.& W. Ashmore, Late Twiss."* Perhaps the Pickford brothers proved too much for him! In a letter dated 3rd May 1828 from London solicitors to Randle Wilbraham[10] we are told:-

> *"Mr. Twiss died in 1818 leaving a widow and 6 children, John, Thomas Tegg, Henry, Harriet, Ann, and Julia, the youngest now being 18 years of age . . . . Mr. Twiss died in insolvent circumstances the residue of the property devised in his will being very insufficient for the Payment of His debts. His widow has since intermarried with a person by the name of Broadbent . . . "*

What happened to the Twiss family thereafter is unrecorded. John's will reveals that his eldest son John was articled in Barbados and his inheritance of £25 was made conditional upon him satisfactorily completing his articles.[11] Was he in disgrace? Did he survive that white man's grave? Of the remainder nothing is known. It seems probable that Boarded Barns was sold to the Wilbraham estate in 1828 for the sum of £3,150, it extended to 34 acres, 3 roods, 3 perches.

Extracts from the autobiographical notes of James Holland Lunt 1852-1923[12]

Reminiscences of an Alsager Farmer's Boy

For the greater part of two years after leaving school at ten years old I was employed in the Summertime on a Brick Bank in Close Lane and in Winter in driving a plough on a farm in Barthomley. On the Brick Bank I earned from 3 to 6 shillings a week, working from 6 o'clock in the morning until 6 or 7 o'clock at night. For my farm work I obtained my food and one shilling per week working from 5 or 6 o'clock until 7 or 8 o'clock at night.

---

[10] ibid.

[11] ibid.

[12] In the possession of Mrs. Beryl Fox of Alsager.

I next became hired for twelve months at a time. For the first two years I lived with Mrs Julia Barker at the Oak Farm. For the first year I received £3 and my food and lodging. I went to Oak Farm before I was twelve and left before I was fourteen.

The work on farms was heavy and the hours long; the food was of a plain and very often coarse character. Brown flour made from an inferior quality of corn which sometimes had been badly weathered produced very brown, sometimes black bread. This bread with cheese constituted one of the principal items of food. Butter was only allowed on Sundays for tea and then was limited in quantity.

A basin of milk and water thickened with meal (porridge) was provided for breakfast and supper, with bread and cheese and sometimes the old-fashioned raised pies filled some times with potatoes and meat (mostly the former) and at other times with apples or plums.

At dinner we generally fared better. Family and servants usually dined together and flesh meat with potatoes, and sometimes boiled or baked pudding, was provided.

At Oakhanger Hall where I next worked we had to wash at the pump in the kitchen yard with soap, even in the middle of winter. As it was impossible to wash them clean and my hands were hard in nature, they used to get badly chapped, open wounds extending right across them. When washed they would burn like fire. During the night they would close up and reopen when the sun shone next day.

During 1863-5 a terrible disease among cattle was raging and went by the name of cattle disease with very few cattle recovering. Multitudes of stock up and down the country were swept away completely. The government at last undertook to deal with it, slaughtering infected stock and paying compensation. The churches looked upon the scourge as a visitation and called for a fast. Mr. Dale's cattle were unaffected but those at Oak Farm were destroyed.

Sir Ernest Craig

Sir Ernest was one of Alsager's most eminent residents during the last years of the 19c. and the first thirty years or so of the 20c. He lived at Milton House and by profession he was a mining engineer but later turned to public affairs. He was prominent in the local community, there are frequent references to him in this book, and he represented the Crewe constituency in the House of Commons from 1912-1918 and again from 1924-1929. Following his death in 1933 a lengthy obituary appeared, a copy of which remains,[13] but unfortunately there is no record as to the original publication in which it appeared. The following extracts are taken from it.

"Philanthropist and Friend of the Poor.

We deeply regret to announce the death of Sir Ernest Craig, Bart., ... at . . . . Milton House, Alsager . . . . Sir Ernest who was 74, was created a Baronet in 1927 for distinguished services rendered, particularly during the war, was the eldest son of the late Mr. W.Y. Craig who died in 1924 on the eve of completing his 97th year. Sir Ernest was born at Houghton-le-Spring, Durham, in 1859. and on the appointment of his father as general manager of the Lawton and Harecastle Collieries, ... in 1861, came to live at Floodgates, Lawton. In 1864 his father went to live for a short time at Coppenhall near Crewe, while Milton House, Alsager was being built.[14] The family took up their residence at Alsager two years later . . . . Sir Ernest acquiring the property in 1907 on the death of his mother.

EARLY MINING EXPERIENCE

Sir Ernest Craig received his education . . . . principally at Sandbach Grammar School, and at the age of 14 went to Zurich, where he took the scientific course at the Canton School . . . . In 1877, at the age of 17 he was apprenticed to John Daglish, one of the leading mining engineers in the North of England. . . . . In 1880 he went to assist his father in the Podmore Hall Collieries in Staffordshire, of which he was then owner . . . .

In 1883, he took a step which proved to have an important influence upon his subsequent career. He went to the United States, and entered the services of W.P. Rend, owner of several collieries, and while there he was invited to advise on the putting out of serious fires that had broken out in pits owned by Messrs Gray and Bell. He undertook to subdue the flame and resuscitate the colliery, and succeeded after a long and dangerous fight. . . . . He than turned his attention to precious metal mining in the Western States . . . . In 1888 he returned to England . . . . In 1893, his late father, his brother and himself became owners of the Brynkinalt Collieries, Chirk, which they resuscitated.

The father and two sons acquired a reputation as model employers, and were popular with the work people. In 1896 Sir Ernest Craig again went to the United States. . . . After engaging in general practice as a mining engineer, he finally settled in New Mexico . . . . at that time greatly depressed owing to the fall in prices of silver. . . . Here, his grit in the conquest of difficulties stood him in good stead. He devoted some years to the perfection of a process for the treatment of the ores, during which he developed the mines, and the result was the establishment by him of a process, a combination of concentration and cyanidation. . . .

ENTRY INTO POLITICS.

in 1907, on the death of his mother, Sir Ernest Craig purchased Milton House, Alsager, belonging to his father, and had lived there ever since. His first

---

[13] SECSU.

[14] Some doubt attaches to the date of Milton House. The eastern gable bears a date stone *1866*, which fits with the information given here, but the census of 1861 records that it was occupied by John Maddock Jnr., a pottery manufacturer. Perhaps the Craigs extended, modernised and refurbished it between 1864 and 1866.

experience of politics was in 1880, when his father successfully contested North Staffordshire as a Liberal, a constituency which has since been split up into the Leek and Newcastle Divisions. At the General Election in December 1910. Sir Ernest contested Crewe for the first time, in the Conservative interest. His opponent was the late Mr. W.S.B. McLaren. On that occasion he was defeated by 1704 votes, a reduction however of the previous majorities. The figures were W.S.B. McLaren (L) 7,629; E.Y. Craig (L.U.) 5,925. In July 1912, a by-election was caused by the death of Mr. McLaren, and this time Sir Ernest was victorious in a three-cornered fight, his majority being 966. His opponents on this occasion were Mr. Harold Murphy (Lib.) and Mr. J. Holmes (Labour). The figures were ; E.Y. Craig (U.) 6,260; H. Murphy (L.) 5,294; J.H. Holmes (Lab.) 2,485.

HIS WAR SERVICE.

As member for Crewe during the war, Sir Ernest Craig was most assiduous in his attention. He addressed a number of public meetings in the division on behalf of the Parliamentary Savings Committee, and at Crewe Works gave inspiring addresses to the men who were engaged on the production of munitions. He gave up his salary of £400 a year as a Member of Parliament during the war. He was in charge of labour questions in the Ministry of Munitions, ... and was in charge of the supply department. . . . . During the war, Sir Ernest Craig served his country's interests in many ways, necessitating his absence abroad frequently. For this reason he retired from Parliament in 1918, and handed over the seat to the care of Sir Joseph Davies (Liberal), ... At the 1924 General election Sir Ernest was prevailed upon by the Conservative Association to re-enter the political arena. At the time his health was giving cause for anxiety, but he consented to contest the seat, and he won it back from labour. . . . .

Sir Ernest was noted for his generosity throughout the division. He never refused to assist any worthy cause. By his death charitable and philanthropic societies have lost a true friend. The poor people of the district have also lost a warm hearted and generous friend. For many years he gave fifty tons of coal to the poor people of Crewe, and cheques for fifty guineas frequently came from him for distribution among the distressed. He was also a liberal supporter to the funds of the local Conservative Association. . . . ."

The obituary continues further at some length giving details of the history of the Craig family, in particular an account of the life of his father, William Young Craig. He was a remarkable character in his own right. As a young man he assisted Robert Stephenson in the building of the Royal Border Railway Bridge at Berwick-on-Tweed before being engaged in the building department of the royal palace at Osborne on the Isle of Wight. Later he returned to the North of England as a mining surveyor before being transferred to North Staffordshire as colliery manager at Harecastle. He retained his interests in the mining industry throughout his life. In 1913, at the age of 86 he directed the sinking of the Gertrude Pit at Ifton. In addition to being MP for North Staffordshire he was also a magistrate in both Staffordshire and Cheshire. He had thirteen children, nine of whom survived him.

In addition to the obituary a detailed account remains of Sir Ernest's funeral. This appears under the heading *"Alsager in Mourning"*. This records not only the principal mourners who attended the service held at St. Mary's church, but also the fact that;- *"As a token of respect a quarter peal (1260 changes) of Grandsire Triples was rung on the bells of Christ Church, in 45 minutes. The bells were heavily muffled"*. Sir Ernest had at one time been an honorary member of the Crewe Branch of the Chester Diocesan Guild of Bellringers, and took a great interest in the Alsager bells. The ringers are all named.

Sir Francis Joseph[15]

Sir Francis Joseph was almost certainly the most prominent, most popular and most influential figure connected with Alsager during the 20c. Not only was he heavily involved in the commercial life of the township and committed to its social life as well as being a resident but he also played an influential part in the affairs of the nation as a whole. When he died in 1951 obituaries were published in many papers including the Times and the Evening Sentinel which gave over almost the entire editorial page, and that was when the paper was printed as a 'broadsheet', to an editorial and obituary acknowledging Sir Francis's achievements. The editorial read as follows:-

> *"Sir Francis Joseph*
>
> *Sir Francis Joseph whose death is mourned by the country as a whole but particularly by his native Merseyside and most of all by North Staffordshire, was one of the outstanding figures in the industry and Commerce of Great Britain through the first 50 years of the present century.*
>
> *From a start in life considerably less promising than the vast majority of boys enjoy today, he advanced to a commanding position in the business world and in national affairs by the exercise of a courage, strength of character, driving force, faith in his own future and in that of his country, and a business brain which functioned with wonderful speed, acuteness and perception.*
>
> *He was a North Staffordshire man by adoption, not by birth, but he touched the life of the local community at every point and became in many important fields its acknowledged leader, both inside and outside its physical boundaries.*
>
> *Nobody did more in the inter-war years to make Stoke-on-Trent and its staple industry known*

---

[15] The information relating to Sir Francis Joseph has largely been taken from biographical details held in the library of the Staffordshire Sentinel Newspaper. The editor is obliged to the Sentinel for permission to make use of this material and for the help and assistance the newspaper has given in this connection..

*all over the world. A notably successful man him-
self, he was determined that the Potteries as a
whole should prosper, both materially and in the
prestige earned by its craftsmen, its artists and
its athletes. To this end he devoted in season and
out, his shining gifts as public speaker and writer
and a kind of unofficial ambassador-at-large for
the district.*

*His ability and character, and the influential
contacts which these made for him all over the
world, brought him success in this aim, as in so
many others.*

*The North Staffordshire scene will not be the
same without the genial, brisk, alert figure of Sir
Francis Joseph to grace it. He was 80 years of age
last July, but it was quite impossible for any who
knew him to think of him as an old man. It was
only in the last year or two of his life that he
began to shed some of his great business interests
-- and then only those that entailed constant long-
distance travelling. In all other directions the
mental and physical activity, the devotion to affairs
in general, which had marked his life in the prime
of his powers, was sustained right up to his last
illness. And that, one is certain, is how he would
have wished it to be.*

*The community has lost one who made a
return, many times over, for the rewards and the
success life had brought him. Individuals of high
state and low, in North Staffordshire and far
beyond will feel they have lost a real friend."*

This tells us a great deal about the esteem in which Sir Francis Joseph
was held but very little of his life story and what he did. Many of his local
interests and activities, and evidence of the affection with which he was
regarded locally, are recorded elsewhere in this volume. But there is still
room for an outline of his life's story.

Francis L'Estrange Joseph was born in Liverpool on 31st July 1870 of
Irish parentage. He attended the Caledonian School in Liverpool until he was
twelve when he left to become a railway messenger boy, before being a clerk,
commercial traveller, printer, advertising agent and stock-broker. By 1903 he
was elected to Liverpool City Council and remained a member for ten years.
In the general election of 1910 he was the unsuccessful Liberal candidate in
the Walton Division, opposing F.E. Smith, later the famous first Earl of
Birkenhead and Lord Chancellor in 1919. He was again an unsuccessful
candidate in the election of 1918.

During the First World War, in 1916 and 1917, he worked on the
administrative staff at the War Office, holding the rank of captain, before he

reorganised the work of the Ministry of National Service in Wales. By the end of the war he was Director-General of National Labour Supply.

In 1917 he had married Miss Violet Settle, second daughter of Joel Settle of The Hill, Alsager. From that time Sir Francis's interests were permanently identified with those of North Staffordshire and South Cheshire and he embarked upon the most successful phase of his career as an industrialist and public figure. He had been awarded the C.B.E. in 1918 and this was followed by a knighthood in 1922. In 1923 he became President of the North Staffordshire Chamber of Commerce, an office he held until 1932. 'Say it with pottery' was the watchword he carried with him around the world on his many foreign travels.

His business interests expanded at a national as well as local level. He was, as has been mentioned elsewhere, chairman of Settle Speakman and heavily involved in the mining industry locally. He became a director of Settle Speakman in 1919 and was chairman from 1927 until his death in 1951. During this period he maintained very good relations with the miners and labour leaders. He was reasonable yet firm, recognising their views and arguments and conducting negotiations with fairness and honesty. Whilst he was chairman no 'local' strike ever took place in any of the firm's collieries and this was at a time when labour relations in the coal industry were very strained, following the events of the General Strike of 1926.[16] The Company's Centenary Book illustrates his character with the following anecdote.

> *"He had a horror of untidiness, either of mind or of plant. A full and straight answer to a question gained a quick smile of approval; his wrath descended quickly on any who sought to evade an issue. An incident related by Kenneth Yates, then the manager at Park Hall Colliery, aptly illustrates this side of his character. On one of the tours which he loved making, he was poking about and found a beautiful tarmac yard behind some buildings where before there had been a large dump of rubble and scrap. As this was a time when expenditure had perforce to be kept to a minimum, he enquired the cost, which turned out to be not inconsiderable. "On what authority?" he next enquired. "On mine", replied Yates. As the sum involved exceeded that beyond which managers were empowered to spend without Board authority, down came the ire of Sir Francis on Yates' defenceless head! When the inspection was over, Sir Francis drew Yates aside: "That new yard is a big improvement; you were right to clean up that mess, but next time . . . !"*

In addition to his local interests Sir Francis was also a director of the L.M.S. Railway, Midland Bank, Rio Tinto, B.S.A., the Birmingham Wagon Co., Birmingham Canal Navigations, and Imperial Airways. He was awarded a K.B.E. in 1935 when President of the Federation of British Industries.

His interests were not restricted to his commercial activities. He was a

[16] *The History of Settle Speakman & Co. Ltd.,* Published by the Company. SECSU.

vice-president of Lancashire Cricket Club, President of Stoke City Football Club when he donated Coronation loving cups to all the clubs of the First Division to mark the Coronation in 1937. Later in 1947, he did the same for the Scottish F.A. In 1932 he served as High Sheriff of Staffordshire and was a Deputy Lieutenant for the county. Other honours and interests included, Honorary Colonel of the 71st H.A.A. Searchlight Regt., Royal Artillery, Freeman of the City of London, Justice of the Peace for both Cheshire and Staffordshire. The list is almost endless.

In 1942 his knighthood became a baronetcy, due largely to the significant contribution he was making to the country's war effort, both through his many private business interests and as Chairman of the United Kingdom Commercial Corporation. The Corporation had been formed in 1940, primarily to resist German pressure on the Balkans, from then until the end of the war its turnover was massive, between £400 and £500 million. The value of supplies sent to Russia through its agency was in excess of £100 million.

A man with such a distinguished career might be forgiven for the odd human weakness, particularly having so much to be proud of in having overcome the disadvantages of his early life. He wrote regularly to the Chief Executive of the Sentinel Newspapers ensuring that the paper's list of his appointments, interests and honours was maintained up to date. On one occasion he included an extract from the proposed autobiography of his friend Lord Swinton which purported to be Lloyd George's opinion of Sir Francis;-

> *"If I want to know what people are thinking between the Trent and the Tweed, I think I would rather have Joseph's opinion than that of anyone else"*

In a further extract Lord Swinton says, of his joining the board of the United Kingdom Commercial Corporation;-

> *". . . my colleagues on the board welcomed this appointment. Some were old friends; all knew him well by repute. Joseph had all the qualities and qualifications for the post. Coalowner, manufacturer, merchant and banker he was rich in business experience, and he was hardly less at home in Government service. But I think that perhaps Joseph's most valuable quality was his human sympathy. To understand men you must love them."*

Not a bad epitaph for any man!

Because he loved his fellow men it did not mean he must suffer fools gladly. In a speech at Liverpool in November 1948 it is reported that he said of the new generation of local politicians holding mayoral office:-

> *"Strip some of them of the trappings of office and they would find it difficult to enter the Town Hall even by the tradesmen's entrance".*

The Odd Bods.

This is not intended to be a derogatory term, but rather one which includes the names of individuals who have played some part of the history of Alsager but whose stories have not been researched and they have not been introduced as characters in any of the preceding chapters. Their names have largely been chanced upon in documents researched for other purposes but reference to them helps to give a touch of colour to the narrative. These men and women come to us largely through the pages of the Alsager Town Book,[17] the Barthomley Parish Registers and the presentments made to Nantwich Hundred Court in the 17c.[18] In the early years of local government two presenters were chosen by the township twice a year and they reported to the court on a variety of township matters; such as the state of its highways, its stocks, its pinfold and its butts; all of which Alsager had. They informed who was keeping greyhounds and had guns, and most of all who was brewing ale. This last item features prominently in the returns and consistently refers to one named person only, this suggests that he was an alehouse keeper, brewing for profit. Following a hearing in the court the names of those presented were entered on a roll, an estreat or copy, with the appropriate fine against the name which was to be collected by the bailiff.[19] It seems that the fine was a form of licence payment.

The Nantwich Hundred Court estreats for the period 1594-1699 consist of short rolls of parchment containing a list of the hundred townships and the names of those fined. Regrettably only a few remain and Alsager does not appear on the earliest, 1594. By 1619, 1620 and 1621 John Sherrat is fined variously 6d. and 12d. for breaking the assize of bread and ale; and in 1620 Hugh Lowndes, Constable was fined for *'not appearing to doe his stint and serve there'*. There is then a long gap up to the last two decades of the century when John Beckett seems to be the ale-house keeper between 1681 and 1687 to be replaced by 1693 by Daniel Boulton whose name appears regularly, to be followed in 1701 by Thomas Symson. The fine remained at 6d. every six months. The names of Richard Knight, Randle Hilditch, John Brereton, Daniell Poole, Ralph Merrill and William Darwell occur with great frequency for keeping a gun and a greyhound and being fined, usually 6d. A note from the presenters of October 1696 reads, *"We present John Brereton and Richard Knight for keepinge greyhounds and doe order them to make them a way in a mounth or to forfeit 10s. a piece"*. As these names continued to occur with great frequency it would appear the threat was not carried out.

---

[17] Ref. CRO. P278/11 (mf.235/3).

[18] Ref. CRO. DCH/Y/5.

[19] Ref. CRO. DCH/Y/6.

Some were keeping a greyhound for their landlord as an obligation under the terms of their lease.

Women's names appear to be entirely absent from these early records and it seems unlikely that they had any role in local government at this time. They do appear however in the town book in the later years of the 18c. when it seems that the Overseers made use of women in receipt of parish relief to undertake services in respect of making provision for other paupers. This is evidenced by the record of a payment of 5s. to Ann Robinson in October 1771 for *"Taking care of J. Keeling's girl with small-pox"*. It is also possible that Mary Taylor, Sarah Corve and Dolly Broad whose names appear in the Overseers' accounts at this time for carrying out services to paupers were also themselves in receipt of relief.[20] By 1852 the town book records that Mrs. Beresford was taking her turn to act as an overseer.

Places

Alsagers Bank

Alsagers Bank lies outside the township of Alsager, about five miles away to the south, on the far side of Audley but its name intrigues. Why *Alsagers* bank, does the name have any significance to the township or to the family bearing the name Alsager? It seems as though it does. Richard Parrott, in his account of Audley in 1733 has this to say in describing the properties at the top of Halmerend.

> The next tenement stands at the side of the lane cawled Augers Green. That house was built by one Randle Auger who was a naler. He had two sons, Thomas and Richard. Thomas was a naler [and] enjoyed the tenement after his father's death soe long as he lived. He left one son when he dyed named Edward. He enjoyed the tenement soe long as he lived. He left a widdow but noe issue. She held it some years then dyed. It is now tenented by one Randle Shaw under the heirs of Apedale."

This was written in 1733 and if a period of between twenty and thirty years is allowed for each intervening generation it would seem reasonable to suppose that the Randle Auger, or Alsager, who built the house might have lived some 60 to 100 years earlier, that is between 1630 and 1670. Richard Alsager of Brookhouse died in 1647 leaving a widow Amy and two sons, Ralph and John. When Amy died in 1661 one of those who valued the contents of her inventory was Ralph(Randle) Alsager of Alsager, naylor. This Ralph was almost certainly the son of Richard and Amy and he should have

---

[20] Mrs P.E. Ormerod; *A Glimpse into Alsager's Past 1770 to 1810;* published privately 1990.

inherited the Brookhouse estate under the terms of his father's will but it seems instead to have gone to his brother John who occupied it when he in turn died in 1688. However there is an implication in the will of John that his brother Ralph had predeceased him in 1670 although why Ralph's widow Margaret should not have inherited is not told. It is quite possible therefore that this Ralph Alsager, nailer of 1661 may have been the Randle Auger, builder of Auger's Green referred to by Parrott.

A further possibility also exists. The parish registers of Barthomley record that a Ralph Alsager of Alsager, nailer, baptised his daughter at Barthomley on the 9th October 1631. He also might have been the person who gave his name to the place.

Whatever the true facts it seems very likely, based on the available evidence, that Alsagers Bank takes its name from a member of the Alsager family who moved there in connection with his skill as a nailer sometime in the 17c.

The Mere

Probably the most distinctive feature of Alsager and yet there is surprisingly little recorded of its past history or significance. The Mere was situated on the heath, enclosed in 1834 and it is quite possible that the commoners, those with rights and privileges over the heath, may have enjoyed special rights on the Mere also. These may have included a right to take fish and perhaps cut reeds and water grazing cattle.

The first recorded mention of the Mere comes in a deed of about 1280,[21] when John son of Nicholas, son of Adam of Allesacher grants a piece of land to William, son of Ranulph, son of Adam, which is described in part as *"extending from the mill lade to the highway to le witemere."* This is almost certainly a reference to Crewe Road on the section between the Lodge and the Plough inns today. The name 'witemere' is of interest. In 'The Place-Names of Cheshire', Vol. III, Dr Dodgson suggests that the name comes from the Old English *wīte* a place of punishment rather than colour being implied by the name. In subsequent correspondence, when it was suggested that the name might have been mis-spelt for 'wiht', which means curving and could reflect the shape of the Mere he saw no reason to change his mind saying *"Remember right back into the Darkest Ages there's been a habit of ducking and drowning whores and cowards and witches . . ."* Does this have any relevance to the old superstition that beneath the finger post that used to stand at the junction of Lodge Road with Sandbach Road North witches were buried!

[21] PRO. C146 4929.

After this early reference there is no further mention of the Mere until the Enclosure Award of the early 19c. Section 30 of the Alsager Inclosure Act of 1821 reads as follows:-

> *"That the Mere or Pool of Water called Alsager Mere with a Border or Margin round the same of the width of nine yards from the High-Water mark, together with all convenient roads or ways to the said Pool of Water shall remain vested in the Ladies or Lady Lords or Lord of the said Manor and shall not be taken by the said Commissioners to be any part of the Land or Ground to be allotted divided or inclosed by this Act."*

This ensured that the Mere and the immediately surrounding land remained in the possession of the Alsager family and their heirs. Subsequently, when the Alsager Estate was sold in 1876 the Mere was conveyed to Edward Fox Leake, Arthur Tomkinson, George Plant and Robert Beswick. Later, in 1877, it is recorded in a deed dated 9th March between Messrs Leake, Tomkinson, Plant and Beswick of the first part, John Rigby of the second part and E.F. Leake of the third part, that the 11 acres 1 rood 27 perches of the Mere, together with an adjoining area of 20 acres and 13 perches were conveyed on Trust to E.F. Leake. He was to lay out the same in lots to form streets and roads and generally adapt the land for building purposes and sell it.[22]

By the 24th March 1882 this had evidently been done and the area of the Mere reduced to between 8 and 9 acres. The lands around the Mere had been partitioned into plots together with the first 20 feet of adjoining Mere water. Later the same year the Mere, apart from the first 20 feet around its perimeter, was granted to W.H. Dutton to hold on Trust for Leake, Tomkinson, Plant and Beswick as tenants in common.[23] The four legal owners agreed by covenant, for themselves and their heirs:-

i.   The Mere shall be used by the four and such of their friends to whom they grant permission, for the purpose of boating, fishing or skating.

ii.   It shall be unlawful for any of the owners to receive or take any payment from any person using the Mere as in i. above, or to make any profit from this.

iii.   The four would not permit any sewer or drain to run or open into the Mere.

iv.   All expenses for controlling the level of the Mere would be paid for by the four.

When the partitioned lands bordering the Mere were sold off by the heirs

---

[22] The information included here on the history of the Mere has been taken from papers prepared to brief Alsager Urban District Council when counsel's opinion was sought as to the question of public access in 1945.

[23] A state of ownership by two or more persons each having a distinct but undivided share in the property, each being entitled to occupy the whole in common with the others.

and successors of the four the purchasers of these plots and houses have been granted rights to use and enjoy the Mere subject to the four conditions set out above.

Sometime between 1882 and 1920 the old drain serving the Mere must have become stopped up or damaged, as in 1920 several of the frontage owners approached the Urban District Council seeking assistance in lowering the water level. The Council's minutes show that it was ultimately agreed that the Council should consent for the surplus water from the Mere to be used to sluice the sewers and that a manhole and sluice should be constructed, under the control of the Council, at the expense of the frontagers.

With the passage of time the Council acquired a number of plots of land giving access to the water, today these are represented by Northolme and Coronation Gardens. Inevitably the question arose; 'If the Council own land giving access to the Mere does that not give ratepayers the same rights on the Mere as enjoyed by other frontage owners?' The Council sought counsel's opinion which decreed;-

1.   *"The Council as owners of the land have, in my opinion, a right of access to exercise such rights over the Mere as they may possess. The ratepayers have no right of access except by the permission of the Council and subject of course to the limited rights of the Council."*

As a result of counsel's opinion the Council deemed that there was nothing to prevent them giving the public access to the Mere, subject to adequate control and precautionary arrangements being made and accordingly the public gardens were created which remain today.

In addition to these legal facts there are a number of stories told of how the Mere has played a part in village life over a long period of time. Older residents can remember being told in their youth, by even older residents, that horses were raced around the edge of the water; the Tithe Award map certainly suggests that there was a trackway of some sort following the water line. It is probable that if such races took place they were no more formal events than have been the motor cycle races which have taken place on the Fairview car-park on summer evenings in recent years! Slides can still be seen of skating parties on the frozen surface with heaps of snow piled up alongside the skaters. The pictures suggest more participants than the frontages could have provided, and it must be considered that when Alsager was a more intimate community than it is today, and the surrounds of the Mere were not completely developed, access to special events was relaxed somewhat.

All villages have their fund of stories relating to events long past, beyond the recall of the memory of those living today. Some of these tales are undoubtedly true but cannot be authenticated, others, alas, owe more to the inventive genius of their authors than to the accuracy of their memories. The difficulty lies in distinguishing between the two when there is no corroborative evidence. Alsager is no exception to this tradition and the following tales concerning the Mere and its surroundings can be believed or not as the reader chooses. They were told many years ago by an old man, long since dead, they are his stories and only he would perhaps know how much they reflected his knowledge and how much his inventive genius. Occasionally a comment has been added to clarify a point of fact.

The racing of horses referred to above is supposed to have been organised in The Lodge Inn, where better! When this stood on the site of the present West Mere Lodge the local worthies would have been able to sit and watch such an event, pint in hand and pipe in mouth. Indeed in recent years when giving a talk on Alsager and referring to this story Mrs M. Bebbington was interrupted by the then owner of West Mere Lodge who said they were always finding broken clay pipes in their garden and wondering how they had got there.

It was further suggested by the story teller that there had been a bull-ring and a wheat market in that area of the Mere but there is no known evidence to support this. What is almost certain is that at one time Lodge Road ran much closer to the water than it does today[24] and this, together with traces of old farm buildings may have given rise to this belief.

At one time there were two very old thatched, timber framed cottages standing on the site occupied today be Coniston Lodge in The Avenue. A man named James Hollerhead is said to have lived in one and a quaint character called Machin lived in the other. Machin killed two pigs and owing to the unstable condition of both cottages he wisely decided to hang these outside on the branch of a pear tree in the garden. They became a source of interest to the village boys who began to throw stones at them causing Machin to take them inside and hang them from the cottage beams. This proved to be too much for the walls and both cottages collapsed thereby destroying another link with the past. Regrettably the name of the occupier of the cottage on the site of Coniston Lodge does not coincide with the name in the story, its T.A. ref. is 308 and in 1840 it was occupied, together with the adjoining croft, by Frances Warburton. The only person recorded in 1840 with the name of Machin was Thomas Machin who occupied a cottage, ref. 332, in Crewe Road opposite to where the Police Station is now situated.

In addition to the story of the burial of witches beneath the finger post at the junction of Lodge Road and Sandbach Road, referred to as 'Gallows Corner' by the story teller, is the tale of the poor unfortunate who hanged himself on a tree on the shore of the Mere. As was the custom of the time

---

[24] See the Map accompanying the Inclosure Award.

he was cut down and buried beneath the sign post with an ash stake driven through his heart.

Over the years Alsager people believed that a right of way existed around the Mere claiming that such a path was shown on old maps before the Inclosure Award of 1834. Prior to the Alsager estate being sold a path did run from the boundary with Church Lawton, at the bottom of the present football field, along the Donkey Path by the cricket ground, out into Sandbach Road; from there it was claimed that it continued into what is today The Avenue, down to the shore of the Mere emerging onto Crewe Road opposite Cross Street before continuing on into Well Lane.

The story continues that when the Alsager estate was sold in 1877 the new owners erected fences across the path and the public were denied access. A man called Wildblood gathered together a party of men and one night they broke down the fences and once more established the right of way they believed to be theirs. The fences were again erected and again removed until the matter was taken to court at Sandbach, but as neither party turned up the case was never resolved. Had the Wildblood faction succeeded in their claim the village would certainly have developed in a very different way.

The earliest known plan of Alsager to show the Mere is the one which accompanies the Inclosure Award and has been used as the cover for this book. This must have been prepared between 1821 and 1834. It shows the first section of this footpath and a track running from Sandbach Road about where the Avenue entrance now lies. This track led into the fields which formed part of the Lodge Inn Farm and receives no mention in the Inclosure Award as being a public footway. It is quite possible that in the days before enclosure, when the heath was open to general access there was no impediment to casual usage of such a path as a short cut to the far side of the water but it seems never to have had formal status. Interestingly this apparent trackway around the water is ref. 306 in the T.A. and is described as being in the possession of John Fox of Alsager Lodge Inn, consisting of Alsager Mere and border. A further point of interest lies in the fact that in the census of 1841 a William Wildblood is recorded as being aged 15 and resident in the household of the Lodge Inn employed as an agricultural labourer; might he be one and the same who threw down the fences forty years later?

In 1877 when the sale of the estate took place it is said that one of the underbidders for the Mere and surrounding land was the company who owned the Belle Vue botanical gardens and zoo in Manchester. Had they bought it Alsager would certainly not have been as we know it and there would certainly have been no footpath around the water.

Mere Lake and Swallow Moor.

Mere Lake has been referred to on a number of occasions in this book. It is the small hamlet of cottages situated at map reference 812537, where the old railway line to Audley crosses the lane leading up to Talke. It lies right on the boundary of Cheshire and Staffordshire and takes its name from this old boundary which is almost certain to be older than the county division it represents today. The reason for saying this is that the county boundary cannot be any older than the date when the county was created, sometime between 900 and 950 A.D. and yet the origin of the name attributed by Professor Dodgson in The Place-Names of Cheshire, Vol. III is older than this and means 'boundary watercourse'. There are no references found to the name in any of the old deeds of Alsager although the neighbouring 'Swallowmoor' is mentioned in three documents, two dated 1384 and one 1399.[25]

Here two field or farm names are referred to, 'le Hersichecluff', the cliff at the higher watercourse, and 'Swalomore', marsh frequented by swallows, Dodgson Vol.III. p.4. Dodgson also refers to *'swille'* as meaning to wash, a swill of water, a messy place; which might describe the early topography of Swallow Moor where both the Mere Lake Brook and the stream that runs down to Creswellshaw rise. To 'swale' or to 'sweal' is to burn grass or heather under control, a modern dialect term. This might indicate that the area of Swallow Moor had been assarted by burning. The fact that the document describes the land and holding as being *"in quodam campe"*, in a certain field, suggests that the names may have applied to one or more furlongs of arable land. Swallow Moor Wood, Flat Swallow Moor and Bankey Swallow Moor are references 647, 657 and 658 on the Tithe Map of 1840. The map gives no indication as to the whereabouts of 'le Hersichecluff'.

Prison Bars Field

A name to conjure with, but no, not the local lock-up! There was a field of this name lying on Crewe Road, through which ran the later Hall Drive, identified as ref. 408 on the Tithe Map. It got its name from a popular team game played in the 18c. which had originated as a street game, 'aux barres,' in medieval France   The rules of the game are complex and are best quoted from the *'Oxford Companion to Sports and Games,"* page 798.

> *"Two bases or camps are . . . . marked in a field with sticks or cricket stumps . . . . At the other end of the ground, or about twenty yards away, two prisons are marked out. Two captains pick sides (it is best if there are some twenty players), and each side takes possession of a base, but the prison in which they hope to place their captives is the one diagonally opposite, not the one nearest to them. The captain of one side sends one of*

[25] Refs. Brit. Lib. Add. Charters 53538, 53539 and 53540.

his players into the middle to taunt the others and start the game. The captain of the other side sends one of his players to catch him, and the first player has to try and get back to his own base. He is helped by the fact that as soon as someone has been sent to catch him, his own captain will send someone in pursuit of his pursuer, whereon the other captain will send someone to pursue that pursuer, and the first captain will send someone after him. Thus each player, other than the first, will be both chasing and being chased, and as soon as a player gets back to his base, he can be sent in pursuit of someone else. But a player may only chase the one person he has been sent after."

Further to confound the confusion, the game allowed for players to be sent to rescue any of their number who had been captured or imprisoned. Not infrequently the game ends when the players are in such confusion that few know who is chasing , or rescuing whom. Played, as it had to be once, in narrow streets, the confusion and the violence made the 'childish amusement' attractive to boisterous young men and for many years matches were arranged between carefully selected teams in north Shropshire, Derbyshire, and Cheshire. In the 1790's a team of Cheshire men challenged a team of Middlesex men to a match at Lords cricket ground.

Alsager Landscape.

There are of course no early pictures or maps of Alsager to tell what the landscape looked like before the middle of the 19c. The earliest known map is one of the Brookhouse estate drawn in 1761 for its then owner Peter Somerfield.[26] This is very sketchy and tells us little of the appearance of the place but does provide useful information concerning field names and the names of adjacent land owners. An undated plan of similar age exists for the Creswellshaw Estate[27] and whilst a better prepared document than its Brookhouse equivalent it provides rather less information. Not until the Tithe Award and its accompanying map of 1840 is there really reliable information on the townships physical appearance.

On the information available though it is likely that the appearance of the Alsager countryside changed little for many hundreds of years before the coming of the railway. Evidence suggests that there was some open field agriculture practised here in the early medieval period but as demonstrated in chapter 4 this was probably phased out during the 14c. and 15c. as was the case in many pastoral townships. The biggest difference noticed today by someone returning from the 18c. would perhaps be the reduction of tree cover in the open countryside. This is borne out by the evidence of an advertisement appearing in the Staffordshire Advertiser in January 1796

[26] ref. CRO. P.278/10/1

[27] ref. CRO.DBW./A/packet J.

This was in respect of an auction sale to be held by a Mr. J. Twemlow, to take place at the Lion and Swan Congleton, of standing timber in Alsager. The advertisement claims that the timber was suitable for ship building or mill-wrights' work. There were many such sales advertised at this time; demand may have been influenced by a wartime naval building programme or other types of war effort. The Alsager sale was on the land of the Alsager family estate and included the holdings of William Wallworth, Alsager Hall Farm; Jonathan Thorley, Dunnocksfold Farm; Widow Thorley, probably Heath End Farm; John Twiss, Town House; and Michael Ashmore and Acton Taylor, the former occupying Brookhouse and the latter the Plough. All these formed part of the Alsager estate. The timber sold on the Twiss holding amounted to 236 oaks, 33 ashes, 25 alders, 1 fir, 1 poplar, 1 birch, 34 cyphers. In total the number of oaks amounted to 1,817 and ashes 440 together with a lesser number of smaller trees. The area must have appeared denuded of tree cover after this event and other local landowners may also have taken advantage of the demands of the time to part with their timber.

Societies

The Alsager Association for the Prosecution of Felons.

Like many towns and villages in Cheshire and Staffordshire during the late C.18 and early C.19 Alsager had its own Association for the Prosecution of Felons. The evidence for this comes from a newspaper advertisement appearing in the Staffordshire Advertiser on the 10th June 1815. This reads as follows;-

County of Chester
Alsager Association
For the Prosecution of Felons, &c.

We whose names are hereunto subscribed, having formed ourselves into a Society, to pursue and prosecute any person or persons who shall commit, or attempt to commit any felony or robbery against or upon our persons or property, particularly house-breakers, horse stealers, or stealers of cattle, sheep, pigs, poultry, fish, coals, hay, straw, iron, timber, leather, hedge-wood, &c. do offer the following Rewards:- that is to say--

	£.	s.	d.
For every person convicted of any capital offence, the sum of	5.	5.	0.
For every person that shall be cast for transportation, the sum of	2.	2.	0.

For every person convicted of a less crime,
the sum of . . . . 0. 10. 6.
For every Toll-Gate Keeper who shall give information of any horse stealer, highway rob-
ber, or any person who shall have stolen any
cattle or sheep, or any house breaker, so that
he, she or they may be apprehended, the
sum of . . . . *One Guinea*

Alsager.	John Dale
John Twiss,(*Trustee.*)	William Barker
Samp. Holland,(*Treasurer*)	George Edwards,
Rev. J. Richardson,	John Cork,
Thomas Twemlow, sen.	Peter Moors,
Thomas Twemlow, jun.	George Morris,
James Morris (Cresw.)	James Smith,
Charles Edwards, jun.	James Morris,
William Thorley,	*Hassall.*
William Ball,	Walter Daniel Esq.,
James Moreton,	Jonathan Thorley,
Samuel Jackson,	*Lawton.*
Humphrey Lowe,	John Morris,
Edmund Gould,	Michael Peake,
Thomas Edwards,	*Betchton.*
John Edwards,	Thomas Beech.

The purpose of these associations was to provide a degree of protection to the property of their members and to assist in the cost of prosecution in the days before there was an established police force or any form of public prosecution service. Members paid an annual subscription to cover the expenses of the association and agreed to abide by the rules which would usually include a requirement to prosecute in the event of a felon being caught and to follow in pursuit when a crime had been committed against a member. In return the association would pay or contribute to prosecution costs and advertise the names of members to warn the criminal fraternity that they stood a greater chance of conviction if they committed a crime against a member than would be the case when a crime was committed against a non-member. A glance at the rewards offered shows that the principal desire of members was to rid themselves of undesirable elements, the greater the chance of a hanging or transportation the greater the reward offered.

What of the members? A little is known of these and generally they were rock solid pillars of society,[28] usually living in a degree of isolation without any protection from the law. Horses were very vulnerable to theft, as is the case with fast cars today, and they were frequently stolen to order and moved with great speed, hence the payment of rewards to turnpike keepers. In the

[28] CRO. ref. QDV 2/11. Land Tax Assessments 1781-1831.

case of Alsager, John Twiss is already well known to us, it is hoped that he fulfilled his duties as trustee to the Association more effectively than he did to the Barthomley parish Educational Charity! Sampson Holland was the licensee of The Plough and a tenant of the Alsager estate; the Rev. J. Richardson was the incumbent of Christ Church. Thomas Twemlow jun. on the other hand was a land-owner, being the freeholder of Galley's Tenement or Manor Farm; whilst Thomas Twemlow sen. appears to have been the tenant of Richard Jackson at Town End Farm (now the Manor Hotel) farming around 200 acres. James Morris or Morrey farmed 150 acres at Creswellshaw as a Wilbraham tenant, as Charles Edwards jun. did on 114 acres at Lane End. William Thorley was the probable Alsager estate tenant at Heath End Farm, with 75 acres; and Samuel Jackson an estate tenant at Town House Farm with 112 acres. Humphrey Lowe was the tenant of Dr. Latham at Day Green Farm, 104 acres. Thomas Edwards, possibly brother of Charles, appears to have farmed Dunnocksfold, only a minor portion of which lay within the Alsager boundary. John Edwards may have been the father of Charles and Thomas, he cannot be identified as holding land in 1815, but in 1820 he is shown to be tenant of Alsager Hall Farm extending to 200 acres. He was succeeded there by Thomas Edwards who in turn was succeeded at Dunnocksfold by another Charles Edwards, perhaps his son. John Dale was John Ford's tenant at Hole House Farm, occupying 123 acres; William Barker at that time was at Bank Farm, the tenant of Agget, Hagett or Halchett, the name appears in a variety of forms. George Edwards cannot be identified in 1815 but the Lawton Estate subsequently had a tenant of that name at Longstile. John Cork was the licensee of the old Lodge Inn, in Lodge Road, with 45 acres; and Peter Moore farmed 47 acres at Heath House Farm, as tenant of Daniel Hawthorne, this was on the site of St. Gabriel's school in Well Lane. Finally James Morris was the tenant of Thomas Lowe at Bank House Farm, 53 acres. William Ball is not identified in the land-tax records, nor are James Moreton, Edmund Gould, George Morris or James Smith.

It can be demonstrated from this data that membership of the Association was generally restricted to those having recognised social status in the community, as might be expected, as they had most to lose from thieving and violence.

Other associations were active at this time at Barthomley, Betchton, Odd Rode and Audley.

The Alsager Bowling and Recreation Club.

Approximately one acre of land lying between Fields Road and Ashmores Lane was purchased in 1904 in order to establish and maintain a club in Alsager and to lay out a bowling green and tennis courts.

The original subscribers to this enterprise were:-

James Edwards,	Greenway Cottage, Alsager.	Gentleman.
Robert Sudlow,	Hampton House, Alsager.	Earthenware M'ftr.
William Halliday,	Woodlea, Alsager.	Tailor.
Thomas Baxter Barrett,	Rosedale, Alsager.	Gentleman.
Adolphus W.H. Goss,	Lyndhurst, Alsager.	Commercial Traveller.
Alfred Ecclestone	Station Road, Alsager.	Coal Agent.
Charles Hill Bailey,	Heath Cottage, Alsager.	Timber Merchant.

The Club has been in continuous existence since its formation and has a large bowling membership who play friendly matches with other clubs in North Staffordshire and South Cheshire. The tennis section fields three teams in the City and Suburban League.

The B'hoys

The B'hoys is a village organisation which has survived to the present time; it was founded around 1911 and continues to thrive. Its constitution requires that membership is restricted to 50 residents of Alsager. At first, membership was open to any male living in Alsager or the surrounding district, but, surprisingly, by December 1920, the Minutes were recording *".... owing to our membership now being about full, that nobody living outside the Village shall be nominated for membership."* The Village was later defined as, *".... within the boundaries of the Alsager Urban District."* The Society continues to meet as a supper club during the winter months, holding meetings on the second Thursday of each month from October to March.

A little over three weeks after the first meeting the following is recorded:-

> *"Mr. Adolphus Goss was chosen to be chairman at the first dinner which was held at The Arms Hotel, Alsager, on Tuesday, August 15th 1911. A first class repast was served up by Mr. A. Parkes, and was thoroughly enjoyed by those B'hoys and friends whose signatures follow."*

The name of the Society has always been a cause for comment and there are various stories told as to where this came from. A history of the early years of the Society was compiled a few years ago by Sydney Edwards[29] who was its secretary for many years and he tells us that;-

> *"We have it on good authority from Roy Palfreyman that his father, listed above as a founder member, explained to him that the name "The B'hoys" came from a song. In the early part of this century a famous and popular music hall artiste to be seen from time to time at the old Grand Theatre in Hanley, was song and dance comedian Mark Sheridan. One of his songs had the line "I'm one of the b'hoys," and our Founders, being familiar with this comedian, adopted the word to form the name of their new organisation."*

---

[29] The Editor is indebted to Mr. Edwards for almost all the information recorded here relating to the B'hoys.

During the First World War years of 1914-1918 the Society barely continued to function. Through 1918 practically no meetings were held and the years 1919 and 1920 saw only 15 members being listed. Three members, Bert Mayer, Harry Davies, and Freddy Leek, were killed in action in the course of the war, their memory being perpetuated by the Society's 10 o'clock Remembrance to Fallen Comrades, which was instituted for the first time on 24th November, 1922.

It was in 1912 that the office of Recorder was created, and Mr. H.V. Lynam was the first member to be elected to fill this position which he held for a remarkable 47 years until 1959. Mr. Lynam was Surveyor to the Urban District Council for very many years and in his Recorder's report at the Annual Dinner in 1925 he referred to the possibility of the Village being provided with an electrical supply, though this did not materialise, and then only partially, until 1928. He went on to say he had been trying to persuade the Council for ten years to settle the matter of improving the water supply. He was now sorry to have to tell the assembly that he believed they would be "deprived of free coffee for breakfast, soup for dinner, and mud baths before retiring, because it had now been definitely decided to fix the long hoped for filters and they should be in operation before the year was out."

An interesting short extract from the Committee Minutes of 5th January, 1924, records that the menu for the Annual Dinner;-

> "....was discussed in conjunction with Mrs. Brooksbank and approved; Soup, Fish, Boiled Mutton, Roast Beef and Veg., Sweets, and Cheese, at 4/-. (20p)."

On 24th November, 1922, a resolution was passed which established "The B'hoys of Alsager Benevolent Fund", all members subscribing individually *"with enthusiasm"* to create the first fund. For some years this fund was devoted mainly to providing parcels of food to needy families in Alsager. It is worthy of special mention that during all the years from the mid 1920's to the late 1930's the B'hoys Society raised considerable sums of money in support of the Alsager Hospital Saturday Committee, with many donations going from that Committee to the North Staffordshire Royal Infirmary. The contribution made by The B'hoys of Alsager was recognised in 1924 by the appointment of the Recorder, Mr. H.V. Lynam, as a Governor of the North Staffordshire Royal Infirmary, a position he held for many years.

An Extraordinary Meeting was called for 6th March, 1928, to discuss;-

> "....a letter from Mr. Lucas in which he suggested the Society should consider presenting a Standard to the Alsager Branch of the British Legion, and Captain Maddox, who was also Chairman of the Legion Branch was asked to give the meeting details regarding the proposition. The possession of a Standard would enable the Branch to compete for the Haig Trophy, and would help to cement the already existing friendship between the two Societies."

The proposal was strongly supported by all present. The local papers later reported that a very large congregation assembled at St. Mary's Church on 6th May, 1928, where a Service of Dedication for the new Standard was held. After a parade from the church to the War Memorial a Drumhead Service was held and the Standard presented by the President, Mr. F.G. Edwards, to the President of the Alsager Branch of the British Legion, Mr. Adolphus W.H. Goss. The 'Last Post' and 'Reveille' were impressively sounded by R. Crinean of the Alsager Boy Scouts.(later to become a member and a President of the Society.) The Standard was placed in front of the Memorial, where it remained until sundown, with a formal guard mounted by members of the British Legion.

On 18th December, 1930, a proposal was made by Mr. H.V. Lynam that the B'hoys Society should give their support to a Committee which had been formed in the Village to take steps towards the formation of a cricket club for Alsager.[30] Mr. S. Elsby spoke enthusiastically for the proposal, and members agreed to assist in the formation of a club.

Throughout its history the Society has had the welfare of Alsager and its people at its heart. It has made many valuable contributions to the town, donating our first ambulance, and presenting the gates and railings at Northolme Gardens on the Mere, on the occasion of the Coronation of Queen Elizabeth II; supporting countless village projects, participating in village functions and offering help, both financial and practical when needed. The authors of this book have been given a generous loan of £1000 by the Society to assist in the cost of publication.

The Boy Scout Movement

In 1907 Major-General Robert Baden-Powell, after seeing the social conditions that many children had to face, decided to form a youth movement based upon the life-style of the messenger boys used during the Boer War. Since it was a requirement of these young boys to carry messages over considerable distances without being observed by hostile Boers they were referred to as Scouts.

The youth movement that Robert Baden-Powell founded was therefore called 'The Boy Scouts' and the aim and method was to encourage the Physical, Intellectual and Spiritual development of boys by the use of a structured training programme supervised by adult leaders. This type of training was quite innovative in its day since it encouraged self-determination and the development of leadership skills by forming the boys into patrols of

---

[30] This record of the Society is at variance with records confirming that a cricket club had existed in the village since it was started by the Rev. Skene in 1881-2. The precise circumstances of the B'hoys financial support are not clear.

six to eight boys. Each patrol was led by a Patrol Leader, who would be one of the older boys, with a Second (Assistant Patrol Leader).

It was with the above thinking in mind that the first Boy Scout Group was formed in Alsager in February 1908 when the South West Cheshire Local Association was founded. The original national structure was somewhat overwhelmed by the growth of the movement nationwide and it was on 12th May 1923 that the formal registration under number 845 as 6th South West Cheshire at Imperial Headquarters in Buckingham Palace Road was made.

Records of this early group have been lost over the years but we do know that the earliest remembered meeting place was in the Old Pumping Station in Well Lane. This building was situated where the drive to Saint Gabriel's School now runs. During the nineteen-fifties the group, under the patronage of Mr Douglas Frayling prospered and needed to find a larger headquarters and eventually leased a building on the HMS Excalibur estate, this needed to be refurbished before they were able to meet there.

At this time the group comprised two Wolf Cub Packs and one Scout Troop. The group continued to flourish under the leadership of the Group Scout Leader Mr R. Barratt and in September 1964 a small committee was formed to raise the funds to provide a new and purpose-built Scout Hall.

On 1st January 1967 the movement changed their name to 'The Scout Association' and with this came the change in uniform to generally what is seen today.

The New Headquarters Committee worked tirelessly and the group was able to embark upon a building programme such that on 7th December 1968 the new headquarters was opened by Mr C. Marshall Amor, the Secretary of the Stoke-on-Trent and Newcastle Divisional Scout Council, in the presence of local dignitaries.

The hall, situated in Cedar Avenue, was named The Frayling Scout Hall in acknowledgment of the assistance given by Mr Douglas Frayling both physical and financial. On 31st March 1970 the group transferred from the South Cheshire District to become the 13th Stoke-on-Trent and Newcastle Group in Tunstall District of Staffordshire Scout County.

The Group continued to prosper under the leadership of Mr Peter Coleman and in 1975 was designated a Super Group owing to its size of:

4 Cub Scout Packs (Including an outlying pack at Smallwood)

3 Scout Troops, and

1 Venture Scout Unit

The group membership at this time totalled in excess of 200 members.

The Alsager group continues to do well and is still one of the jewels in the Tunstall District Scout District.

The Girl Guide Movement

In 1910 a group of girls went to the Crystal Palace Boy Scout Rally calling themselves "Girl Scouts" and as a result of this surge of interest the Guide Movement, as we know it today, came into being and was officially recognised by 1914.

In 1924, under the leadership of Mrs R. Stevenson, the 1st Alsager Guide Company was formed, in its early days it is believed to have met in the Congregational Church hall. Throughout the country interest in the movement was growing and younger girls, below the age of eleven, were demanding to join. The 1st Alsager Brownie Pack gathered for their first meeting in 1926. Among their first leaders were Miss Lucas, Miss Forshaw, and later Win Holmes, who was associated with the work of the movement for over sixty years. Support grew steadily and the 2nd Alsager, meeting at Wesley Place Church, was formed with sisters Marion and Pamela Rigby in charge.

Mrs Steventon, who had handed over the reins of the 1st Alsager Company to Nell Chamberlain, became District Commissioner. Mrs Steventon was a strict disciplinarian and was always addressed as 'Madam'. Freda Thompson was Lieutenant to Nell Chamberlain, who later married and changed her name to Murray. In the Guide Headquarters, in Cedar Avenue, are two clocks in memory of Nell who gave devoted service to the movement for fifty years.

The older girls of the district were catered for when a Ranger Unit was formed under the leadership of Lilian Thompson.

In 1939 the 3rd Alsager Company was registered with Rosamund and Cynthia Joseph in charge. Their meetings were held up at the Hall and the members were able to have the use of the extensive grounds and swimming pool. When the Joseph sisters went into the W.R.N.S. during the war, the company was run by Margaret Bebbington assisted by Phil Edwards and Joan Shaw. The Ranger Unit reformed as a Sea Ranger Company on the return of Rosamund Joseph from her war service in the Navy. Amongst former Rangers who went on to give valuable time to the movement were:- Isa Price, who became Captain of the 1st Alsager; Ruth Harrison, her Lieutenant; Margaret Kennerly, who, with the help of Barbara Price and Sheila Edwards restarted the 2nd Alsager Company.

Anyone who has been enrolled as a Guide or Guider is encouraged to become a member of the Trefoil Guild, a branch of which was formed in Alsager in 1948 by Nell Murray. The Trefoil Guild members work behind the scenes, not only to help the Guide movement to prosper, but to help other local and worldwide charities.

In the early days of Guiding the Alsager and District Girl Guides Local Association was formed to advise and assist with outside administrative work and responsibilities in a variety of fields, such as dealing with local authorities, educational matters, parents and the general public, and to provide financial and other support. The L.A. members were drawn from a wide range of people who were interested in the movement.

Two of the early Presidents were Lady Joseph and Lady Baker-Wilbraham, the latter having already served over twenty years at the time of the Golden Jubilee in 1974.

The L.A. worked tirelessly to bring about the dream of a guide headquarters. Meetings had to be held in various church halls etc. and one venue especially was very cramped indeed; it was the old Rates Office, which in its heyday was the cottage home of the Band family and was situated where the Library stands today.

Eventually, in 1960, the dream came true and the new headquarters was opened, but its building had encountered many problems on the way. The guides had purchased an unwanted timber-framed shop from a Co-operative Society in Derbyshire and it was at first erected on a site, at the entrance to the 'donkey path' in Sandbach Road, North. Sadly, the residents of the area objected, fearing noise. Further expense was incurred when the structure had to be taken down and re-erected in Lawton Road where it still stands today. Having been used as a Library it is now part of a Christian Centre.

In 1974 the Girl Guide Movement in Alsager celebrated its Golden Jubilee and Dr. Ruth Hickson, District Commissioner at that time wrote in the magazine which recorded the events of that year stating that 320 girls in Alsager were members of the Guide Movement. She then went on to say;-

> "At present we all enjoy the help of the New Hall Project Committee, formed in May 1973 and committed to fund-raising to enable a permanent brick building, somewhat similar to the Frayling Scout Hall, to be erected on the adjacent site in Cedar Avenue. This project depends on local fund-raising, supplemented by a grant from the Cheshire Education Committee. Our application for such help was unsuccessful in 1973 but we hope for good news in 1974 or 1975."

The good news did arrive and on Saturday, October 30th 1974, Mrs W. M. Robinson, J.P., County President of Cheshire Border Girl Guides, officially opened the new Guide Headquarters in Cedar Avenue. It had taken a great deal of hard work and effort, coupled with determination, to achieve but was well worth the striving as Guiding still forges ahead today.

Public Health[31]

At a council meeting in 1875 Dr. Crutchley urged the council members that;-

> "*in consequence of the great increase in population of the District of Alsager and the general want of sanitary arrangements, it is desirable that the Public Health Act of 1875 should be adopted for the benefit of the district and immediate steps taken*";

but the members were reluctant and at future meetings Dr. Crutchley continued to show concern in this area.

At the December meeting a proposal that Alsager should be deemed a Local Government Board was defeated 50 to 42, so it was decided to put it to the ratepayers. 450 ballot papers were ordered and a 'poll was proceeded with.' A total of 361 votes were cast and the counting took place in the Lodge Inn, the result being 233 in favour and 128 against. However, it was not until twenty years later in March 1894 that Alsager became a Local District Board to be known as the Urban District Council.

Dr. Crutchley was appointed Medical Officer and his main concern was a pure water supply and improved sanitation. It was recognised that the water supply was inadequate for the needs of the growing town. It was obtained from one borehole at the pumping station in Well Lane and stored in an uncovered reservoir at the top of the hill. The pumping attendant reported that the engine was in good order considering its age and was serving 330 houses, but an average of 24 new houses were being connected every three months. Many houses had their own wells or pumps at this time as did Milton House and Mr. John Maddock at The Laurels. There was no piped water at Sunnyside, and the well was not satisfactory. The council were told of the poor state of the sewers and the meeting resolved to "*carry out the Medical Officer's recommendations where it could be done WITHOUT SPECIAL EXPENSE.*" The additional water rates for business premises were:-

Bakehouses	10s an oven
Cows	3s
Hosepipe	10s
Horses (trade)	3s
Blacksmith	3s
Carriage (trade, 4 - wheels)	4s
Carriage (trade, 2 - wheels)	2s
Slaughterhouses (Parkes)	15s
Other slaughterhouses	11s

[31] Taken from the Alsager Vestry minutes, ref. CRO. LUA's 3134/8 and Alsager UDC. minutes 1894/96, ref. CRO. LUA's /1/1

An embryonic rubbish collection was started that year. Tenders were put out for 'scavenging' and George Moore of Moorhouse Farm was given the job at £35. The newly appointed nuisance inspector had received complaints about pigs kept at the back of the Post Office in Alsager Road (Sandbach Road South) and of a cow shed at Daniel Hancock's grocer's shop on Bank Corner. Some houses had no ashpits and were tipping their ashes on to the pavement. Shop keepers were causing a nuisance by brushing their rubbish into the gutter.

Night soil was a problem, since water closets were a rarity, and night soil had to be disposed of. It was generally taken down Hassall Road and tipped on to the marl pits where the university campus is today and it was stipulated that *"potatoes should not be grown on sewage land."* The nuisance inspector reported that night soil carts were passing through the village at all hours despite being restricted to night and early morning - James Ashmore was a regular offender and when challenged by the inspector at 1.45pm, *"he said he should come at any time he liked, and I saw him again next day at 2.15pm."*

On the plus side free disinfectant was supplied *"to the poor"* and was still available in the 1930's for 2d. It was dispensed from a barrel which was kept near to the old pump house in Well Lane.

Fire Service

The council owned some fire-fighting equipment comprising a hand cart with a fire hose and probably a water tank attached. There were fixed hydrants at the end of the water mains to attach to the hoses, but there were no regular firemen. At its meeting in March 1895, the council resolved to form a voluntary fire brigade. At a later meeting the question of clothing was discussed, and £18 was granted to the brigade for equipment.

A map of Alsager, dated 1909, marks the Fire Station as being on a site in Crewe Road, opposite to the Mere Inn. A former owner of that property recalls demolishing a building in the 1950's, which had stabling for two horses, and which he was told had been the old Fire Station. Later the appliance was kept on the opposite side of the road, by the side of Mrs. Heath's Post Office. By 1930 it was stored on Fair View land at Bank Corner. The chief fireman at that time was Tommy Cartwright of Brookhouse Farm and his working horses were used. It is said that they got to recognise the bell rung to summon the firemen. At the beginning of the war the local fire chief was Mr. Fisher the dentist.

Activities reported in the Parish Magazine

The annual parish Tithe Audit dinner had been held at the White Lion in Barthomley from time immemorial. No doubt the prominent Alsager landholders had participated in it but the township had never held its own celebration until Rector Skene introduced the first in January 1885. It was held at the Alsager Arms with the Rector in the chair and with Mr. James Barker of Town House on his right. *"Much gratification was expressed with regard to the new arrangements in which the convenience of the residents at this end of the parish was so evidently consulted . . . and great cordiality was manifested throughout."*

* * * * *

On December 17th 1889 a dancing class was formed and admission was by personal invitation only. Rector Skene made a point of being there and reported that *"nothing could have been done better or in better taste and it will afford a healthful and refining recreation . . . and a counter attraction to the evils and temptations outside."*

* * * * *

High on the social calendar for September 1885 was the marriage of the Rector, George Skene and Mrs. Lawton of Lawton Hall, widow of Squire Lawton. The ceremony was performed by the Bishop of Ripon at Lawton Church. The Rev. the Earl of Mulgrave was the best man and Lord Erskine, the bride's brother gave her away. Among the wedding guests were Lord Crewe and Mr. Skene's aunt Mrs. Thompson, who was wife of the Archbishop of York. A six-week honeymoon was spent on the Continent. Alsager parishioners gave them a tea and coffee service for a wedding present.

In January the following year the Rector and Mrs Skene, who were temporarily living at Lawton Hall while the Rectory was being renovated, gave a ball for ninety of their Alsager parishioners with *"carriages at 2am."* The following day the cottagers were invited to a party, and to view the presents at Lawton Hall. Tragically, in 1892 Mrs. Skene caught influenza and died a few weeks later leaving a three year-old daughter.

* * * * *

Rector Skene started the Horticultural Society in 1882, stressing that it was not just a church activity, but for the benefit of all the township. The second annual show, held on the Brunds, opened with a luncheon for about thirty of the prominent members, and the exhibits were judged by the gardeners from Crewe Hall and Moreton Hall. Besides the competitions, other attractions were laid on such as a display of bee manipulations, roundabouts and swings, with tea and dancing to round off the day. In later years it merged with the Shepherds Gala.

* * * * *

The Chrysanthemum Show held its first exhibition in November 1891 and grew to be a very popular annual event. In its heyday the rivalry among the wealthier competitors became so intense that they would employ their gardeners on the merits of their chrysanthemum growing. A very substantial sterling silver cup was presented each year inscribed with both the name of the gardener and his employer. William Huntley Goss and his gardener Henry Holland, for example, were the victors in one of the early years of this century.

* * * * *

May was the month in which the Nonconformists held their special Sunday School festivals known as the Anniversary or Sermons, when the children dressed in their best clothes stood on a 'stage' made up of several benches on rising tiers and sang their hearts out.

Each chapel had its fixed Sunday, Chapel Lane's being first. Next came the 'Prims' followed by the 'Congos' on the third Sunday, with Wesley Place's service on the fourth. The hymns with choruses were practised for weeks beforehand, and it was deemed a great honour to be given a solo; but woe betide anyone who did not turn up to the twice weekly practices. Choir masters who could not muster enough children to fill the stage cast around for good singers to borrow from other denominations, offering a reward of an extra Sunday School treat and tea. A girl or boy with a good voice would go round them all.

The dressmakers of the village were also frantically busy making up white dresses for the girls, and frilly blouses for the boys. Wise mothers took their material to Miss Wood, Mrs Horrocks, or Janet Tyrer well in advance to avoid disappointment. The girls also had new straw hats trimmed with flowers and there was much rivalry. The three services of each day would be packed to the doors for as well as the regulars, members of the other chapels would attend to lend support and to see how the opposition sang. It was customary for adults who had left the village to work and teenage children in service to come home for the Anniversary and enjoy special teas laid on by their relatives.

* * * * *

Amateur Dramatic Societies

They seem to have been a source of entertainment for over a century. In 1884 there was a flourishing society and it displayed its histrionic talent at the

National School, the little school opposite to Christ Church. The selection of plays does not seem particularly memorable. Two farces made up the programme; 'Make your Wills' and 'D'ye know me by now?'

Between the wars the production of plays seemed to be in the hands of the wealthier class. The venue was St. Mary's School and as it was considered a social occasion the best seats in the front rows were for patrons in evening dress. Also in St. Mary's School in the 1940's, a successful concert party was run with Alsager's own comedian, Billy MacMahon, Hancock's bread delivery man.

The present drama group, known as Alsager Community Theatre, or 'ACT', has been running for twenty-six years and replaced an earlier 'Alsager Players'. Its choice of plays is eclectic, from outdoor productions of Shakespeare at Little Moreton Hall to Aykbourn comedies.

The Cricket Club

It was started in 1881-2 by George Skene, the Rector. Aged thirty-six when he came to Barthomley, he had been wicket keeper in the first eleven at Eton and it is significant that he associated himself with forming a club in Alsager rather than Barthomley. Here, there were a number of like-minded young men among the growing middle class families who had played cricket when away at school. Ernest Craig recalled helping him to arrange matches when he was home from school. In 1884 the Alsager Amateur Dramatic Society gave their services for the purpose of *"clearing the cricket club from an adverse balance in their accounts."* It was reported in the parish magazine that they ended the season with a supper which was held at the Plough Inn.

The original cricket field was on land attached to Woodside Farm opposite to the Plough Inn. It was farmed by the Timmis family who were cricket enthusiasts and produced some outstanding players. Later the club played on glebe land called the Parsonage Field where they had a small wooden pavilion. It became known as 'the cricket field' although both hockey and football were played there also. It is now part of the Comprehensive School ground.

Football in Alsager

Over the years there have been many teams playing football locally, some of these have represented schools, churches, chapels, youth clubs, public houses, places of employment and the village itself. Sadly there are no remaining records of the game before 1924. That it was played by a village team before that date is not in doubt. In her booklet 'Alsager 1798 - 1906', published privately, Mrs McEwen states, when describing the pronunciation of Alsager as 'Aucher';-

> *"This latter pronunciation of the name is still a common one, and a favourite on the football field, as one may hear any Saturday during the season, in the Parsonage Field. 'Play up Auger' is the rallying cry."*

A photograph taken in 1924 shows Mr. Les Cowden sitting proudly in front of his team holding a football inscribed 'A.J.F.C. 1924'. Mr. Cowden says that this team played on land farmed by a Mr. Jones in the area of Shady Grove - Moorhouse Avenue; there were two teams representing Alsager, a junior and a senior side.

In the same season there was an account in the parish magazine stating that Alsager Red Rovers played a match which was refereed in a *'wonderful fashion'* by a Mr. Jesse Grocott.

Sometime before 1940 Alsager Football Club played on a ground situated behind what is now the town centre Fairview carpark. In 1941 the club had to find another ground as the land was turned into allotments for the wartime 'Dig for Victory' campaign. Highfields Primary School now stands on this site. To compensate, a temporary ground was found alongside Talke Road, now built upon and forming part of the 'Tree Estate'. This ground was shared with H.M.S. Excalibur during the war years, and an occasional visiting circus.

In 1947 the beautiful setting of the Parsonage Field was home to the team but eventually this land was needed by the Educational Authority for school playing fields and with the help of the local Council a more permanent ground was established off Cedar Avenue, fondly called 'Mole Hill Park'. This ground had excellent parking facilities and proved to be very popular with all age groups for both training and matches. Today it is still used by various local teams.

Alsager United Football Club entered many competitions, including the 'Sentinel Cup', which the team dearly wanted to win but sadly it was not to be. Their finest hour, in 1950/51, season came when they reached the 4th round of the Cheshire Amateur Cup and were to play Dukinfield. The whole village was engulfed by football fever and a number of coach loads went north to support the team. Alsager won and drew a Middlewich team - Seddons Ramblers in the 5th round. Alas, disaster struck, the goal keeper withdrew from the match and a replacement had to be borrowed from Kidsgrove. The match was a very even game and went to extra time but Middlewich won on a penalty. The two outstanding players of that match were Fred Hancock and Mick Barratt.

During the 1950's Peter Barratt was captain and living in houses on either side of him were Joe Bebbington, Ron Smith and Ken Hodgkinson, all holding positions in the club and members of the committee. Ken

Hodgkinson went on to reach international fame as a referee when he officiated in Athens, Turin and Leipzig, and of course at Wembley, after which he named his house at Englesea Brook.

In 1967 the Club moved to its present home at Wood Park. This move was mainly due to the pioneering work of Rennie Steele whose enthusiasm spurred members on to seek a permanent ground with better prospects. Sadly Rennie died at a rather early age.

The club secretary at this time was Councillor Tom Smith and due to his efforts the club acquired a pre-fab building for changing facilities. Further buildings appeared at the ground and the foundations of todays Alsager Football Club came into being.

Today the ground has been approved and the team is allowed to play in the North West Trains League (Higher Standard Division II).

Epilogue

In our preface we said that we hoped this book would fulfill a purpose by creating a better knowledge of the past which in turn would lead to a better understanding of the present. We hope that after reading it a better understanding has been reached of how today's society in Alsager has evolved over past centuries, and why our community is as it is today.

In some chapters the authors have been able to put forward tentative conclusions of their findings, based upon the evidence of their research; in other cases the known facts have been recited and the reader has to consider what conclusions, if any, can be drawn from them. Wherever possible references have been given for sources used, these may be followed up by future researchers who we have no doubt will be able to add significant detail and create a fuller picture to the stories outlined here. Indeed we believe that sufficient evidence exists for a complete volume to be written in respect of each of the foregoing chapters.

Inevitably a book of this nature has omissions which we hope will be made good elsewhere in the future as further research is undertaken. There may also be errors, of both fact and conclusion, which will require rectification at some future time but notwithstanding these doubts we believe that we have achieved our objective in producing a well researched volume which will both inform and entertain.

Index

Chapter headings and sub-headings are shown in bold type.

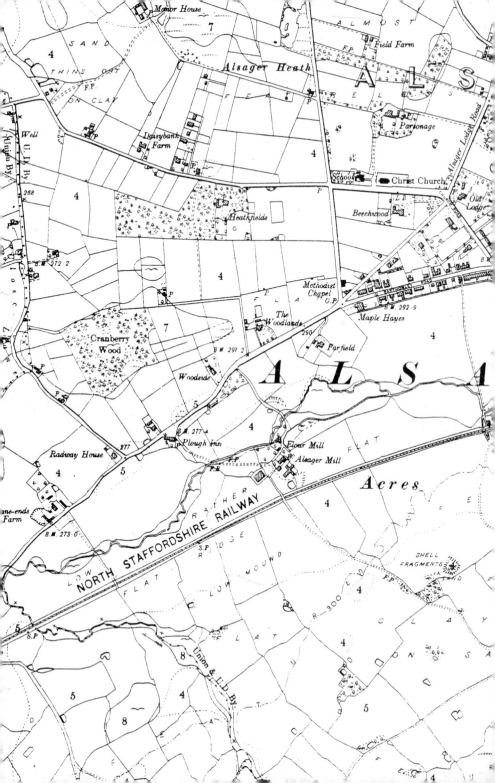